On Language and Linguistics

Collected Works of M. A. K. Halliday

Volume 3 in the Collected Works of M. A. K. Halliday

On Language and Linguistics

M. A. K. Halliday

Edited by Jonathan Webster

continuum
LONDON • NEW YORK

Continuum
The Tower Building, 11 York Road, London, SE1 7NX
15 East 26 Street, New York, NY 10010

First published 2003

British Library Cataloguing-in-Publication Data
A catalogue record for this book is available from the British Library.

ISBN 0–8264–5869–6 (hardback)
ISBN 0–8264–8824–2 (paperback)

Typeset by BookEns Ltd, Royston, Herts.
Printed and bound in Great Britain by MPG Books Ltd, Bodmin, Cornwall

CONTENTS

PART THREE: LANGUAGE AS SOCIAL SEMIOTIC

PREFACE

This volume has three parts: the place of linguistics as a discipline; linguistics and language; and language as social semiotic. From the papers in this volume we find a compelling presentation of Professor M. A. K. Halliday's perspective on linguistics as the scientific study of natural language. What struck me in reading these papers was his integrity as a scientist engaged in the study of this most human of all phenomena, namely, language; his humility in the face of its potential and power; and his humanistic vision of a socially accountable linguistics, which is wholly compatible with his appreciation of the role of language in our lives as social beings.

Unlike some who in the name of science subtract out the very humanness from natural language, Professor Halliday instead provides a sound systemic basis for interpreting language as an essential part of the human experience. He sees in every act of meaning the potential for discovering the true nature of language, even and especially in the speech of children – for it is out of the mouths of babes, so to speak, that language develops and humanity evolves. Every act of meaning is an opportunity for change in language and society.

The papers in this volume also reflect Professor Halliday's sense of social responsibility for himself personally, as well as for a discipline engaged in the study of language as social semiotic. What comes across in his writings is a man with a great social conscience and strong convictions. While he makes no exaggerated claims about being able to radically transform language and society, he nevertheless sees the contribution linguists can make through achieving a better under-standing of the power and potential of language for doing both good and bad.

Understanding language for all that it is rather than for how little we can make it out to be comes down to asking the right questions and having the necessary framework in place to search for answers.

Professor Halliday asks the crucial questions about language and develops the theoretical framework within which the search for answers may proceed. A highlight of this volume is a new piece from Professor Halliday, entitled "The architecture of language", in which he focuses on the assumptions or working hypotheses that enabled him to explore – as he has in the chapters presented in this volume – important questions about how language works. Describing the underlying theme of this volume, Professor Halliday writes that it is "the exploration – and perhaps celebration! – of the awe-inspiring power of language".

ACKNOWLEDGEMENTS

We are grateful to the original publishers for permission to reprint the articles and chapters in this volume. Original publication details are provided below, and also at the beginning of each chapter.

'Syntax and the Consumer' from the *Report of the Fifteenth Annual (First International) Round Table Meeting on Linguistics and Language Study*, edited by C. I. J. M. Stuart (*Monograph Series in Languages and Linguistics* 17), published by Georgetown University Press, 1964, pages 11–24. Reprinted by permission of Georgetown University Press.

Grammar, Society and the Noun (lecture given at University College London on 24 November 1966), published by H. K. Lewis & Co. Ltd for University College London, 1967. Reprinted by permission of the HMV Media Group.

'The Context of Linguistics' from the *Report of the Twenty-fifth Annual Round Table Meeting on Linguistics and Language Study*, edited by Francis P. Dinneen (*Monograph Series in Languages and Linguistics* 17), published by Georgetown University Press, 1975. Reprinted by permission of Georgetown University Press.

'Ideas about Language', from *Occasional Papers* I, 1977, pages 32–55. Reprinted by permission of Applied Linguistics Association of Australia.

'Language and the Order of Nature' from *The Linguistics of Writing: Arguments between Language and Literature*, edited by N. Fabb *et al.*, published by Manchester University Press, 1987, pages 135–54. Reprinted by permission of Manchester University Press.

'New Ways of Meaning: The Challenge to Applied Linguistics' from *Journal of Applied Linguistics* 6 (*Ninth World Congress of Applied Linguistics Special Issue*), published by the Greek Applied Linguistics Association

(GALA), Thessaloniki, Greece, 1990, pages 7–36. Reprinted by permission of the Greek Applied Linguistics Association.

'A Brief Sketch of Systemic Grammar' from *La Grammatica; La Lessicologia*, published by Bulzoni Editore, 1969. Reprinted by permission of Bulzoni Editore.

'Systemic Background' from *Systemic Perspectives on Discourse,* Vol. 1: *Selected Theoretical Papers from the Ninth International Systemic Workshop*, edited by James D. Benson and William S. Greaves *(Advances in Discourse Processes 15)*, published by Ablex Publishing, 1985, pages 1–15. Reprinted by permission of Greenwood Publishing Group, Inc.

'Systemic Grammar and the Concept of a "Science of Language"' from *Waiguoyu (Journal of Foreign Languages)*, No. 2 (General Serial No. 78), 1992, pages 1–9. Reprinted by permission of *Waiguoyu.*

'Language in a Changing World' from *Occasional Papers* 13, 1993. Reprinted by permission of Applied Linguistics Association of Australia.

'A Recent View of "Missteps" in Linguistic Theory' from *Functions of Language* 2.2, published by John Benjamins Publishing Co., Amsterdam and Philadelphia, 1995, pages 249–67. Reprinted by permission of John Benjamins Publishing Co.

'Linguistics as Metaphor' from *Reconnecting Language: Morphology and Syntax in Functional Perspectives*, edited by Anne-Marie Simon-Vandenbergen, Kristin Davidse and Dirk Noel, published by John Benjamins Publishing Co., Amsterdam and Philadelphia, 1997, pages 3–27. Reprinted by permission of John Benjamins Publishing Co.

'Is the Grammar Neutral? Is the Grammarian Neutral?' from *Communication in Linguistics,* Vol. 1: *Papers in Honour of Michael Gregory*, edited by Jessica de Villiers and Robert J. Stainton *(Theoria Series No. 10, 2001)*, published by Editions du Gref, Toronto, 2001. Reprinted by permission of Editions du Gref.

'The Functional Basis of Language' from *Applied Studies towards a Sociology of Language*, Vol. 2, *Class, Codes and Control*, edited by Basil Bernstein, published by Routledge and Kegan Paul, 1973, pages 343–66. Reprinted by permission of Routledge.

'Towards a Sociological Semantics' from the series of working papers and prepublications (14/C, 1972), edited by Centro Internazionale di

Semiotica e Linguistica of the University of Urbino, 1972. Reprinted by permission of Professor Pino Paioni, Director of the Centro Internazionale di Semiotica e Linguistica of the University of Urbino.

'The History of a Sentence' from *Bologna: la Cultura Italiana e le Letterature Straniere Moderne*, Vol. 30, edited by Vita Fortunati, published by A. Longo Editore, Ravenna, 1992, pages 29–45. Reprinted by permission of A. Longo Editore.

'The Act of Meaning' from *Georgetown University Round Table on Languages and Linguistics: Language, Communication and Social Meaning*, edited by James E. Alatis, published by Georgetown University Press, 1992, pages 7–21. Reprinted by permission of Georgetown University Press.

'On Language in Relation to the Evolution of Human Consciousness' from *Of Thoughts and Words (Proceedings of Nobel Symposium 92: The Relation between Language and Mind)*, edited by Sture Allen, published by Imperial College Press, 1994. Reprinted by permission of World Scientific Publishing Co.

'Systemic Theory' from *Encyclopedia of Language and Linguistics*, Vol. 8, edited by R. E. Asher, Pergamon Press, 1994, pages 4505–8. © 1994 Reprinted by permission of Pergamon Press, a division of Elsevier Science Publishing Co.

INTRODUCTION: ON THE "ARCHITECTURE" OF HUMAN LANGUAGE

The chapters which follow will inevitably contain various assumptions about language. In some cases it will be clear how these assumptions were arrived at; this is the advantage of being able to present in a single volume papers that were written at different moments in my career, and to arrange them, by and large, in the order in which they were written. But not all the basic concepts will be made explicit in this way: partly because I never fully foregrounded them – and partly because, even when I wanted to do so, I used to think that an academic article should be like a finished garment, with all the tacking removed before it was put on display. That was a big mistake! In any case, simply by being presented in the context of a published text the organizing concepts are bound to appear as ready-made, as if they had been in place from the start and were at the controls directing my engagements with language. But they weren't; rather, they emerged as the by-product of those engagements as I struggled with particular problems – problems that arose in my own work, in literary analysis or language teaching or translation, human and mechanical; but also, increasingly, problems that were faced by other people in other disciplines and professions. The "assumptions" were more like working hypotheses that enabled me to formulate, and to begin to explore, a broad variety of questions concerning language.

But since these chapters were all written on different occasions, in response to different demands, they do not show any very consistent line of pursuit. So it seemed sensible to begin with a few observations outlining my sense of (as I used to put it) "how language works". Not because the ideas contained are original, still less revolutionary (or "challenging", in today's academic parlance); but because anyone coming to read these chapters is entitled to ask what sorts of things about language are being taken for granted – and even more, perhaps,

1

what things are **not** being taken for granted. Thus the presentation here is a compromise: I have not tried to rethink how I might have formulated the various points at other times during the four decades over which these chapters were first written, but nor have I set them out systematically in the way that I would do (and in fact have done elsewhere) if presenting them in a different context today.

1 Systems of meaning

A language is a system of meaning – a *semiotic* system. Here, as in all my writing, "semiotic" means 'having to do with meaning (*semiosis*)'; so a system of meaning is one by which meaning is created and meanings are exchanged. Human beings use numerous semiotic systems, some simple and others very complex, some rather clearly defined and others notably fuzzy. A language is almost certainly the most complicated semiotic system we have; it is also a very fuzzy one, both in the sense that its own limits are unclear and in the sense that its internal organization is full of indeterminacy.

What other kinds of system are there? I shall assume there are three: physical, biological and social. One way to think of these is as forming an ascending order of complexity. A physical system is just that: a physical system. A biological system, on the other hand, is not just that; it is a physical system (or an assembly of physical systems) having an additional feature, let us say "life". A social system, in turn, is an assembly of biological systems (life forms) having a further additional feature – which we might call "value": it is what defines membership; so, an assembly of life forms with a membership hierarchy. So a social system is a system of a third order of complexity, because it is social and biological and physical. We could then think of a semiotic system as being of a fourth order of complexity, being semiotic and social and biological and physical: meaning is socially constructed, biologically activated and exchanged through physical channels.

But this picture has to be reconciled with another: that of the two orders of phenomena which make up the world which we inhabit. Here "semiotic" contrasts with "material": phenomena of matter, and phenomena of meaning. George Williams puts it like this:

> Evolutionary biologists ... work with two more or less incommensurable domains: that of information and that of matter ... These two domains will never be brought together in any kind of the sense usually implied by the term "reductionism". You can speak of galaxies and

particles of dust in the same terms, because they both have mass and charge and length and width. You can't do that with information and matter. Information doesn't have mass or charge or length in millimetres. Likewise, matter doesn't have bytes. You can't measure so much gold in so many bytes. It doesn't have redundancy, or fidelity, or any of the other descriptors we apply to information. This dearth of shared descriptors makes matter and information two separate domains of existence, which have to be discussed separately, in their own terms.

(Williams 1995: 43)

But "information" is, I think, a special kind of meaning – the kind that can be measured (in bytes, as Williams says). Most higher-order meaning, it seems to me, cannot be measured, or at least cannot be quantified; it can sometimes be graded in terms of value. So I will prefer the opposition of "matter" and "meaning", the realm of the material and the realm of the semiotic.

The four types of system then appear as different mixes of the semiotic and the material, ranging from physical systems, which are organizations of material phenomena, to semiotic systems, which are organizations of meaning. (I am using "semiotic" in both these taxonomic contexts, but not, I think, with any danger of ambiguity.) Biological systems are largely material – except that they are organized by genes, and at a certain point in evolution by neurons, which are semiotic phenomena; and with social systems the meaning component comes to predominate. But even semiotic systems are grounded in material processes; and on the other hand in post-Newtonian physics quantum systems are interpreted as systems of meaning. Meaning needs matter to realize it; at the same time, matter needs meaning to organize it.

Human history is a continuing interplay of the material and the semiotic, as modes of action – ways of doing and of being. The balance between the two is constantly shifting (presumably the "information society" is one in which the semiotic mode of exchange predominates over the material). This is the context in which language needs to be understood.

Of all human semiotic systems, language is the greatest source of power. Its potential is indefinitely large. We might characterize it as matching in scope all our material systems – always able to keep up with the changes in the material conditions of our existence. But putting it like that overprivileges the material: it spells a technology-driven view of the human condition. Language is not a passive reflex

3

of material reality; it is an active partner in the constitution of reality, and all human processes however they are manifested, whether in our consciousness, our material frames, or in the physical world around us, are the outcome of forces which are both material and semiotic at the same time. Semiotic energy is a necessary concomitant, or complement, of material energy in bringing about changes in the world.

Whether or not language matches the scope of all other human **semiotic** systems must be left open to question. Some people claim that it does; they would say that anything that can be meant in any way at all can also be meant in language. In this view, the scope of **semantics** (the meaning potential of language) is equivalent to the whole of human semiosis. I am not so sure. Some semiotic systems may be incommensurable with language; witness the sometimes far-fetched attempts to represent the meaning of a work of art in language (but, again, cf. O'Toole 1994). But while the question is important, and deserves to be tackled much more subtly and fundamentally than this rather simplistic formulation suggests, it is not necessary for me to try and resolve it here. All that needs to be said in the present context is that other human semiotics are dependent on the premise that their users **also** have language. Language is a prerequisite; but there is no need to insist that language can mean it all.

The crucial question is: how does language achieve what it does? What must language be like such that we are able to do with it all the things that we do?

2 Types of complexity in language

The simplest account of a semiotic system is as a set of **signs**, a "sign" being defined as a content/expression pair, like "red means 'stop!'" A set of such signs is turned into a system by means of closure:

$$
\longrightarrow \left[\begin{array}{l} \text{'stop!'} \searrow \underline{\text{red}} \\ \text{'go!'} \searrow \underline{\text{green}} \end{array} \right.
$$

When we represent it like that we can see that it is not complete: we do not know how we get into the system. There must be a condition of entry: let us say "control point":

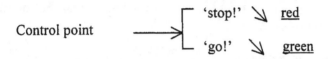

This states the domain of the system. At control point, the system is entered: one or the other option must be chosen. Other than at control point, the system cannot be entered. Note that 'control point' is itself a semiotic feature, though no doubt realized materially, like 'stop!' and 'go!'

Some semiotic systems are minimal, like this one (as presented here). A language, obviously, is not; it is vastly more complicated. The question is: how? In what ways is a language more complex than a minimal system of signs? We need to spell out the kinds of additional complexity which could transform a simple sign system into a language. The system is "thickened" along a number of different dimensions. If we posed the question in these terms, with the thought that language could be built up by expansion from a simple system of signs, we might recognize four dimensions along which such expansion would be taking place:

1. Signs may be combined, to form larger signs [syntagmatic complexity].
2. Signs may be uncoupled, to create new pairings [realizational complexity].
3. Signs may be layered, one cycling into another [stratificational complexity].
4. Signs may be networked, in relations of dependence [paradigmatic complexity].

We shall not remain within this schema – it is a builder's perspective, rather than an architect's; but it will serve to provide a way in.

2.1 Signs may be combined

We do not usually make just one meaning and stop there, like a traffic light. Meanings follow quickly one after another, each setting up a new context for the next. In this way, larger meanings are built up out of combinations of smaller ones: minimal signs – words, or even parts of words, like *I/you* realizing the contrasting roles of 'speaker' and 'addressee' in a dialogue – combine to make up larger signs, realized as a clause, or a paragraph, or an entire text like a public speech, a novel or a scientific treatise. These are all "signs", in the sense that they are units, or unities, of meaning.

2.2 Signs may be uncoupled

We are not bound by a fixed one-to-one mapping between a content and an expression. A given content may come to be realized by a different expression, or a given expression may realize a new content; and in this way new signs are being created, since variation of this kind tends to open up new meanings – new pairings are unlikely to take on if they are not in some way expanding the total resource. Then, putting this feature together with the last means that the domain of the content is not limited by the form of the expression: thus, in English, the content 'POLARITY: positive/negative' is typically realized as a small fragment attached to a word, the *n't* in *did/didn't*; but its domain is an entire clause.

2.3 Signs may be layered

We are not restricted to a single semiotic cycle. The expression of one content comes to be, at the same time, the content of another expression. So, for example, in English the content 'RESPONSE POLARITY: negative' is realized by the expression *no*; the content *no* is realized by the expression /alveolar nasal consonant + half-close back rounded vowel/(or some other vowel, according to the dialect). How many cycles of content + expression we need to recognize is in the last resort a theoretical decision; but there must be at least these two: (i) meaning to wording, (ii) wording to sound.

2.4 Signs may be networked

We do not construct meaning out of sign systems that are unrelated to each other. Systems are organized together in the form of networks, in such a way that some are dependent on others for their condition of entry. To come back to the traffic lights: there may be a set of options 'keep straight'/'turn left'/'turn right': but if so, this is obviously dependent on selecting the option 'go!' at 'control point'; the feature 'go!' becomes the entry condition to this further option. Some sets of options, on the other hand, may share the same entry condition but be independent of each other. It is this organization in system networks that makes it possible for a language to expand its meaning potential more or less indefinitely.

6

When we observe the way very small children develop their powers of meaning, we can see all these different kinds of complexity emerging. Children's first language-like semiotic system, which I labelled "protolanguage" when I observed and described it thirty years ago, begins as a collection of simple signs. These signs soon come to be organized into minimal systems, like 'I want'/'I don't want'; and these show the beginning of further organization in clusters, on a functional basis; but they are not yet combined, nor are they yet layered or uncoupled. All these types of complexity, including the network, develop together as the necessary condition for the move from protolanguage to mother tongue. Not that they have somehow to be put in place in advance, as this formulation might imply; rather, they are essential features of our evolved human semiotic, and children take them up as they come to construe language in its new, post-infancy form.

It is through this "thickening" of its meaning-making resources that human language has evolved. What has been called the "architecture" of language is the organization of these resources within a space defined by a small number of interrelated vectors, those of stratification, metafunction, and the two compositional axes (syntagmatic and paradigmatic); all, in turn, predicated on the vector of instantiation (the relation between an instance and the system that lies behind it) which is based on memory and is a feature of all systematic behaviour. In some ways "architecture" is a misleading metaphor, because it is too static; if we want a spatial metaphor of this kind we might perhaps think more in terms of town planning, with its conception of a spatial layout defined by the movement of people, or "traffic flow". The organization of language is likewise defined by the movement of meanings, or **discourse flow** (I use this term in preference to "information flow" for various reasons, one of which was mentioned in Section 1 above). In the remainder of this chapter I shall try to sketch in this organizational framework, especially those aspects of it which are most relevant to the discussion in the chapters that follow.

3   Paradigmatic composition: how big is a language?

This is a question that seems to be seldom asked. I first asked myself this question when I became a language teacher, teaching Chinese to members of the British armed services; I wanted to have some idea of the scale of the task that is faced by someone learning a foreign language

7

– a task which seemed to me remarkably ill-defined. Then the same question arose for me some years later, when I started working in computational linguistics (which at that time, in the mid-1950s, was conceptualized solely as machine translation). It seemed to me that the computer had to become a meaning machine, and so needed to model a language in the form of a meaning potential; yet we still had no informed idea of the size of the job.

The nearest anyone came to spelling this out was by counting the number of words listed in a dictionary. But meaning was not made of words; it was construed in grammar as much as in vocabulary, and even if we could assess the quantity of words the learners knew it would give little indication of what they could do in the language. By the same token, the idea that a machine translation program consisted largely of a bi- or multi-lingual dictionary was not going to take us very far.

Typically in linguistics the paradigmatic dimension has been reduced to the syntagmatic: that is to say, sets of items (usually words) have been assigned to classes on the grounds that they occur at the same place in the syntagm – represented as a linear string or, more abstractly, as a structural configuration. This is, of course, an essential component in the overall organization of the system. But meaning is choice: selecting among options that arise in the environment of other options; and the power of a language resides in its organization as a huge network of interrelated choices. These can be represented in the form of **system networks** (from which "systemic theory" gets its name). In a system network, what is being modelled is the **meaning potential** of the overall system of a language, irrespective of how or where in the syntagm the meanings happen to be located.

Represented graphically, the system network has a horizontal and a vertical dimension. For example:

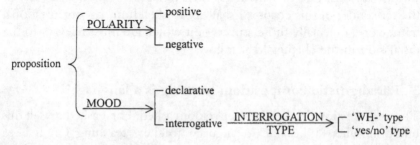

Figure 1

8

The vertical dimension represents combinatorial possibility: if you choose "proposition", you select simultaneously for POLARITY and for MOOD. There is no ordering on this vertical axis; systems related along this dimension are freely associated and it does not matter in which order the systems themselves, or their terms (features) are set out. The horizontal dimension, on the other hand, is ordered in *delicacy*, whereby entry into one choice depends on another, or on more than one other. Interpreted procedurally (as in a text generation program), the output feature of one system becomes the input feature to another: 'if you select "interrogative", then choose either " 'WH-' type" or " 'yes/no' type".' A *selection expression* is the set of all the features chosen in one pass through the network; this is the *systemic description* of the type – clause type, group type etc. – in question.

The most general options, at this level (the stratum of *lexicogrammar*), are those that we recognize readily as grammatical systems: small, closed sets of contrasting features which are implicated in very large numbers of instances, like POLARITY (positive/negative), MOOD (indicative/impera-tive), TRANSITIVITY (types of process: material/semiotic/relational), TENSE (time relative to some reference point: past/present/future) and so on. Systems of this kind, exemplified here from English, are central to the organization of meaning in every language.

By contrast, we think of lexical items as occurring in ill-defined, open sets with highly specific discursive domains; and so, in fact, they do. But they are not different in kind. They simply occupy the more delicate regions of one continuous lexicogrammatical space; and they can be networked in the same way as grammatical systems. But the systemic organization of the vocabulary is in terms not of lexical **items** (words) but of lexical **features** (see for example Hasan's (1985) study of the field of lending and borrowing in English). In other words, those regions of the meaning potential that are crafted lexically are organized in networks of more or less domain-specific features; certain of the combinatorial possibilities are taken up – that is, are represented by words, or *lexicalized* – while others are not. We become aware of such disjunctions when we find ourselves asking 'why isn't there a word for . . .?' (for instance, why isn't there a word for 'wheeled vehicle' in English?).

The power of language comes from its paradigmatic complexity. This is its "meaning potential". So to explore the question 'how big is a language?', we model it paradigmatically: not as an inventory of structures but as a network of systems (this follows Firth's theoretical distinction between system and structure). A *system network* is a means of theorizing the meaning potential of a semiotic system and displaying where any part of it is located within the total semiotic space. It is designed to offer an overview – a comprehensive picture covering a language as a whole.

Comprehensive in coverage; but not exhaustive in depth of detail (delicacy). There is in fact no objective criterion for how far in delicacy the description should be pursued, because that would require a determinate answer to be given every time the question is asked 'Are these two instances the same (i.e. tokens of a single type) or not?' In practice, of course, we know that there are different occurrences of 'the same thing' – of a word, a phrase and so on, and we know when they arise; the best evidence for this is the evolution of writing systems, which require such decisions to be made: if two instances are written the same way, then they are (being said to be) tokens of the same type. But this also shows up the anomalies: for example, the English writing system does not mark intonation (despite the fact that it is highly grammaticalized), so clause types which are widely different in meaning when combined with different tones are treated as if they were identical. However, our networks are still some way off from reaching the degree of delicacy where such indeterminacy becomes problematic. A language will always be bigger than we are able to make it appear.

So how big **is** a language? Consider the example of a single English verb, say *take*. (We will leave aside the question whether *take* in *take medicine, take time, take a shower* etc. are or are not 'the same word'!) This may be either finite or non-finite; let's just consider the finite forms to start with. If the verb is finite, it selects either temporality ("primary tense") or modality; but there are three primary tenses, past (*took*), present (*takes*) or future (*will take*) and a large number of possible modalities. To simplify the illustration we will recognize just 24 of these, organized in four systems: value: low/median/high (e.g. *may will must*); orientation: away from/to speaker (e.g. *may can*); direction: neutral/oblique (e.g. *may might*); type: probability/obligation (e.g. *that may take time/you may go*). This gives us 27 possible forms. But each of these may be either positive or negative (e.g. *took/didn't take*); and each of these polarities may be either unmarked (e.g. *took, didn't take*) or marked (e.g. *did take, did not take*); $4 \times 27 = 108$. Each of these may be active or passive in voice, and there are two kinds of passive, neutral/mutative (e.g. *took, was taken, got taken*); $3 \times 108 = 324$. Then, each of these may select any of twelve secondary tenses, built up serially by shifting the point in time taken as reference (e.g. *took, had taken, had been going to take, had been going to be taking*); $12 \times 324 = 3,888$.

10

Picking up now on the non-finite options: there are two aspects, imperfective (*taking*) or perfective (*to take*); each may be positive or negative, active or either type of passive, and with any of the 12 secondary tenses: $2 \times 2 \times 3 \times 12 = 144$. Adding these to the 3,888 finite variants we arrive at 4,032. But this is without taking account of any of the prosodic options, the presence or absence of contrastive focus, and, if the option 'focal' is selected, the different locations, degrees and kinds of contrast that may be chosen. These options depend on other selections (for example, the number of possible locations of contrastive focus depends on the selections of tense and voice); at a conservative estimate, they increase the potential by an order of magnitude, yielding about 40,000 possibilities in all.

There are all kinds of further wrinkles, such as the choice between two variants of the secondary future (*is going to take*/*is about to take*), that between formal and informal finite forms, and different informal variants (e.g. *he is not taking*/*he isn't taking*/*he's not taking*), or that between different locations of the non-finite negative (e.g. *not to have taken*/*to have not taken*). But this account will suffice to illustrate the point – to suggest that the meaning potential of a language is extremely large. These are all variations on one lexical verb. If there are 10,000 transitive verbs in the English language (intransitives have no voice system, so their paradigm is reduced by about two-thirds), this would give 4×10^8 possibilities in choosing a particular variant of a particular verb.

To make this a little more real, let us fabricate an example and then toy with it. Here is a possible clause with the verb *take*:

You might have been getting taken for a **ride**

The verbal group *might have been getting taken* is finite; the voice is passive, mutative; the contrast is non-focal; the modality is low value, oblique direction, orientation away from speaker, probability; and the secondary tense is present in past. Any one of these features could be varied by itself, leaving all the others constant:

you might be going to get taken [tense]
they might have been taking you [voice]
you might not/needn't have been getting taken [polarity]
you **might** have been getting taken [contrast]
you must have been getting taken [modality]

... and so on. These are all real-life alternatives; they are not picked out of the grammar book – in fact it is hard to find a grammar book which takes note of more than a small subset, because grammarians have traditionally assumed that their paradigms must be listable. They appear in the rich and ever-creative grammar of daily life.

If we extrapolate from this one illustration, we can expect the system network of clause types in a language to run into the hundreds of millions. Such a figure might seem beyond the capacity of the human brain – or might have seemed so, until recent research came to demonstrate its extraordinary power. But this is where the concept of the system network is important (cf. the discussion in Butt 2000). There is no suggestion that the speaker selecting one out of 40,000 variants of a verb is running through and rejecting the other 39,999 (any more than in choosing a word our brains are flipping through a dictionary). The network diagram shows that in arriving at any one of these selections the speaker has traversed at the most about two dozen choice points. As Wimsatt (1986) has shown, the amount of neuro-semiotic energy that is involved in such a task is not at all forbidding; and it becomes less with each exact or approximate repetition.

I will have more to say about systemic representation of language in the final section of this chapter. First, though, I need to discuss the other aspects of the organization of language – other vectors contributing to the "thickening" process whereby language evolved to its present complex state.

4 Stratification: the layering of meaning

As I remarked earlier (Section 2), an infant's protolanguage – the "child tongue" that children typically construe for themselves towards the end of their first year of life – consists of an inventory of simple signs. We can see how these are beginning to be "networked" along functional lines if we look at the meaning potential of Nigel or Hal or Anna at around 12 months old (Halliday 1975a; Painter 1984; Torr 1997).

All these children exchange meanings all the time with their immediate meaning groups. But whereas their parents and elder siblings talk to them in adult language – it may be modified in the form of "baby talk", but that still has the organization of language – their own contribution is qualitatively different. Each element of their proto-language – each sign – consists of a meaning paired with an expression (which may be sound or gesture), with no further organization – no *wording* – in between. It resembles the signs that domestic pets use in communicating with their human families (I hope it will be clear that this is not to be read as derogatory!).

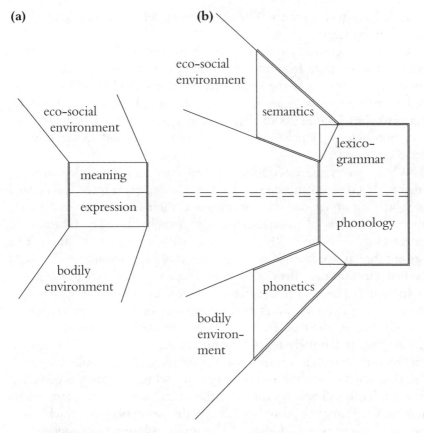

Figure 2 Protolanguage **(a)** and language **(b)**, in relation to their eco-social and bodily environments

If we look back on this phase using the concepts from adult language, we will say that the protolanguage has a semantics and a phonology, but no level of grammar between the two. In other words, it is not yet **stratified**. The grammar emerges later, as the child moves from child tongue to mother tongue during the course of the second year of life. This process has been observed and described in some detail in the books referred to earlier (and cf. Halliday 1978a, 1979b, 1983; Painter 1989; Phillips 1986; Qiu 1985); my own papers on child language development will appear in Volume 4 in this series, and I will not attempt to track it any further here. Essentially, children are following the route by which human language evolved – except that as they come to walk upright they leap over hundreds of generations of evolutionary time in reconstruing their language as a

13

stratified semiotic system. The question is, what do they achieve by this forward leap?

If I may borrow an expression from Gerald Edelman, what is achieved is a release from the "tyranny of the extended present". The move into grammar is the step from primary consciousness to higher order consciousness – again, as conceptualized by Edelman (1992; Edelman and Tononi 2000). Higher-order consciousness is the form of consciousness in which semiosis is organized around the stratum of lexicogrammar.

When our primary semiotic evolved into a higher-order semiotic (that is, when protolanguage evolved into language), a space was created in which meanings could be organized in their own terms, as a purely abstract network of interrelations. By "purely abstract" I mean not interfacing directly with the ecosocial environment. It is this organizational space that we refer to as *lexicogrammar*. We could perhaps sum up the effect of this stratification under four headings.

In the first place, since the grammar served as a kind of interlanguage, it meant that the two facets of the (original) sign need bear no iconic resemblance to each other; the relationship could be purely conventional, thus indefinitely extending the range of "meanable" things. In the second place, it meant that the sign could be pulled apart – deconstructed – into meaning components which could then be varied independently of one another: so, the articulatory shape (consonants and vowels) might mean one thing, the sequence in which signs occurred might mean another, the prosodic colouring yet another.

In the third place, following from the first two it meant that meanings could be organized into functional orders (see next section), in such a way that every utterance included selections from all; this makes it possible for an act of meaning to be both 'doing' and 'thinking' at the same time (to incorporate both reflection and action). In the fourth place, it meant that meaning could be created on the hoof, in the course of (in fact by means of) dialogue (and later also monologue). Taken together, the effect of this evolutionary leap was to turn a closed, meaning-bearing system into an open, meaning-creating one (not just semiotic but *semogenic*).

What I have been talking about here is the stratification of the "content" facet of the original sign. Simultaneously, an analogous stratification took place in the "expression" facet. Sound displaced gesture as the primary modality, and this likewise split into two: an abstract organizational space (*phonology*) where sound is systemized to

14

meet up with the lexicogrammar, and speech sound as articulatory and auditory processes taking place in the human body (***phonetics***).

There is thus, across the stratal dimension as a whole, a balance between the natural and the conventional as the essential form of the relationship at each interface. Within the (original) "content" facet, the relationship between the semantics and the lexicogrammar is **typically** natural: in general, what is construed systemically in the grammar (think of primary systems like polarity, number, person, tense/aspect, mood and so on) will resonate with some feature of our experience of the ecosocial environment. Likewise in the "expression": phonological systems usually "make sense" in terms of the way sounds are produced and heard (b : p : : d : t : : g : k : : . . .). There are arbitrary elements, on both sides – as there are bound to be, because there are too many variables to allow everything to "fit", and anyway languages change in all sorts of ways over time; but the predominance of the natural will always be preserved; otherwise the system as a whole couldn't function.

By contrast, the frontier between the grammar and the phonology – the two facets of the original sign – is **typically** crossed in an arbitrary fashion: things which sound alike don't mean alike, and vice versa – relatedness in sound does not match relatedness in meaning. There is no way in which *bill pill dill till gill kill* . . . make up a semantically reasonable set. Again there is a minor motif the other way (various forms of sound symbolism); but the principle of conventionality is preserved. And again, it has to be, for the overall system to work.

Stratification opened up the potential for another vector in the "content" region, that of metafunction.

5 Metafunction: the grammar at work

When children learn their first language, they are doing two things at once: learning language, and learning **through** language. As they learn their mother tongue, they are at the same time using it as a tool for learning everything else. In this way language comes to define the nature of learning.

Most obviously, perhaps, when we watch small children interacting with the objects around them we can see that they are using language to construe a theoretical model of their experience. This is language in its *experiential* function; the patterns of meaning are installed in the brain and continue to expand on a vast scale as each child, in cahoots with all those around, builds up, renovates and keeps in good repair the

15

semiotic "reality" that provides the framework of day-to-day existence and is manifested in every moment of discourse, spoken or listened to. We should stress, I think, that the grammar is not merely **annotating** experience; it is *construing* experience – theorizing it, in the form that we call "understanding". By the time the human child reaches adolescence, the grammar has not only put in place and managed a huge array of categories and relations, from the most specific to the most general, but it has also created analogies, whereby everything is both like and unlike everything else, from the most concrete to the most abstract realms of being; and whatever it has first construed in one way it has then gone on to deconstrue, and then reconstrue metaphorically in a different semiotic guise. All this takes up an enormous amount of semantic space.

But from the start, in the evolution of language out of protolanguage, this "construing" function has been combined with another mode of meaning, that of *enacting*: acting out the interpersonal encounters that are essential to our survival. These range all the way from the rapidly changing microencounters of daily life – most centrally, **semiotic** encounters, where we set up and maintain complex patterns of dialogue – to the more permanent institutionalized relationships that collectively constitute the social bond. This is language in its *interpersonal* function, which includes those meanings that are more onesidedly personal: expressions of attitude and appraisal, pleasure and displeasure, and other emotional states. Note that, while language can of course **talk about** these personal and interactional states and processes, its essential function in this area is to act them out.

This functional complementarity is built in to the basic architecture of human language. It appears in the view "from above", as distinct modes of meaning – construing experience, and enacting interpersonal relationships. It appears in the view "from below", since these two modes of meaning are typically expressed through different kinds of structure: experiential meanings as organic configurations of parts (like the Actor + Process + Goal structure of a clause); interpersonal meanings as prosodic patterns spread over variable domains (like the distinction between falling and rising intonation). Most clearly, however, it appears in the view "from round about" – that is, in the internal organization of the lexicogrammar itself. When the grammar is represented paradigmatically, as networks of interlocking systems, the networks show up like different regions of space: instead of being evenly spread across the whole, the networks form clusters, such that within one cluster there are lots of interconnections but there is rather little association between one cluster and another.

This effect was apparent when the "Nigel grammar" (the systemic grammar of the English clause used in the Penman text generation project) was first represented in graphic form. When it had reached a little under one thousand systems, it was printed out in network format in about thirty large "tiles", which when assembled covered one entire wall of the office. The most obvious feature was that the systems bunched into a small number of large dense patches. One such patch was made up of experiential systems; another was made up of interpersonal systems. What this meant was that the meaning potential through which we construe our experience of the world (the world around us, and also the world inside ourselves) is very highly organized; and likewise, the meaning potential through which we enact our personal and social existence is very highly organized; but between the two there is comparatively little constraint. By and large, you can put any interactional "spin" on any representational content. It is this freedom, in fact, which makes both kinds of meaning possible – but only via the intercession of a third.

There was in fact a third systemic cluster: those systems concerned with organizing the clause as a message. This is an aspect of what subsequently came to be called "information flow"; but that term suggests that all meaning can be reduced to "information", so I prefer the more inclusive term "discourse flow". These are the systems which create coherent text – text that coheres within itself and with the context of situation; some of them, the thematic systems, are realized in English by the syntagmatic ordering of elements in the clause. Others are realized by a variety of non-structural devices described by Hasan and myself (1976) under the general heading of "cohesion". I labelled this third component of meaning simply the *textual*.

It turned out that one needed to recognize a fourth functional component, the *logical*; this embodies those systems which set up logical-semantic relationships between one clausal unit and another. Grammatically, they create *clause complexes*; sequences of clauses bonded together tactically (by parataxis and/or hypotaxis) into a single complex unit, the origin of what in written language became the sentence. These systems extend the experiential power of the grammar by theorizing the connection between one quantum of experience and another (note that their "logic" is grammatical logic, not formal logic, though it is the source from which formal logic is derived). Seen "from

17

below", they are very different from experiential systems, because their realization is iterative rather than configurational: they form sequences of (most typically) clauses into a dynamic progression; but seen "from above" they are closest in meaning to the experiential, and there is a lot of give-and-take between the two. It was important, therefore, to be able to bring together the logical and the experiential under a single heading; this was what I referred to as the ***ideational*** function.

The overall meaning potential of a language, therefore, is organized by the grammar on functional lines. Not in the sense that particular instances of language use have different functions (no doubt they have, but that is a separate point), but in the sense that language evolved in these functional contexts as one aspect of the evolution of the human species; and this has determined the way the grammar is organized – it has yielded one dimension in the overall architecture of language. Since "function" here is being used in a more abstract, theoretical reading, I have found it helpful to give the term the seal of technicality, calling it by the more weighty (if etymologically suspect) term ***metafunction***. This principle – the metafunctional principle – has shaped the organization of meaning in language; and (with trivial exceptions) every act of meaning embodies all three metafunctional components.

In Part 3 of Volume 1, the chapter on "Language structure and language function" described how structures deriving from experiential, interpersonal and textual metafunctions are mapped on to each other in the clause of modern English. Another chapter made the general suggestion that the metafunctions are also distinct in the types of structure by which they are typically construed. Thus while the metafunctional principle is a semogenic one, concerned with the making of meaning, it has repercussions "below", in the form by which meaning is constructed in the grammar. It also has repercussions "above", resonating as it does with the semiotic parameters of the context in which the discourse is located – the features characterized as ***field***, ***tenor*** and ***mode***; this is referred to at a number of points in the present chapters, and will be treated more systematically in a later volume.

6 Syntagmatic composition: parts into wholes

There is one further dimension in the organization of language to be taken account of here, and that is that of syntagmatic composition: constructing larger units out of smaller ones. This is the simplest and

18

most accessible form of organization for any system whether material or semiotic. The principle guiding this form of organization in language is again a functional one, that of *rank*. Units of different sizes – different ranks – have different functions within the system of a language as a whole.

The principle of rank is fundamental to the two "inner" strata, that of lexicogrammar and that of phonology. In grammar, it seems to be true of all languages that there is one rank which carries the main burden of integrating the various kinds of meaning – that is, selections in the various metafunctions – into a single frame. This is what we call the *clause*. The clause, in turn, consists of a number of elements of lower rank that present structural configurations of their own. In evolutionary terms, we can think of these smaller elements as *words*: the origin of constituency in grammar was a hierarchy of just two ranks, clause and word, with a clause consisting of one or more than one word. Again this can be observed in the language of infants as they move into the mother tongue: for example, from my observations, *man clean car* 'a man was cleaning his car'. As languages evolved this basic pattern was elaborated in a variety of different ways. English displays a variant which is fairly typical; we can model its evolution in outline, in a theoretical reconstruction, as follows.

1. Words expand to form *groups*: e.g. nominal group *a man, that tall middle-aged man*; verbal group *was cleaning, must have been going to clean*.
2. Clauses combine to form clause complexes, e.g. *he used a hosepipe and cleaned/to clean his car.*
3. Clauses contract to form prepositional *phrases*, e.g. [*he cleaned his car*] *with a hosepipe.*
4. Clauses and phrases get embedded inside (nominal) groups, e.g. *the middle-aged man who had a hosepipe/with the hosepipe.*
5. Words get compounded out of smaller units (*morphemes*), e.g. *cleaning, hosepipe.*
6. Units other than clauses combine to form their own complexes, e.g. nominal group complex *the middle-aged man and his son*, verbal group complex *was preparing to start cleaning.*
7. Groups and phrases "meet in the middle", in such a way that each can be embedded inside the other, e.g. *the car outside the gate of the house with the green roof* . . . .

We thus arrive at a typical "rank scale" for the grammar of a language, something like the following:

19

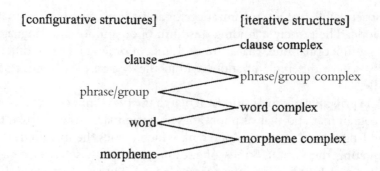

[configurative structures]   [iterative structures]

Figure 3

This enables us to model syntagmatic composition in theoretical terms. Every text consists exhaustively of (i) configurations and (ii) iterations, at each rank, with the limiting case of one element at each structural node. We can then express the "output" of any systemic feature in terms of the contribution it makes to the functional organization of the syntagm – to the **structure**.

It is helpful to distinguish terminologically between a syntagm and a structure, making a distinction that is analogous to that between a paradigm and a system. A syntagm is a linear string of classes, like "nominal group + verbal group + prepositional phrase", "free clause + dependent clause". A structure is an ordered (non-linear) set of functions, like "Process · Medium · Manner" or "Outcome · Cause". There is, of course, no bi-unique relation between syntagms and structures – if there was, we should not need to recognize the two as different orders of abstraction.

But, equally clearly, the relationship between them is not random. A functional element "Process" is likely to appear in the syntagm as a verbal group. What there is, is a relation of **congruence**.

7   Congruent and metaphorical modes of meaning

The principle of congruence depends on the association among the three dimensions of rank, metafunction and stratification. It is important because of the potential for departing from it, which is a way of adding to the overall meaning potential.

Departing from the congruent is what we refer to as **metaphor**. Metaphor is an inherent property of higher-order semiotic systems, and a powerful meaning-making resource.

Let us set up a familiar example of a realizational chain as we find it operating in English. Come back once again to the child's observation *man clean car*. Semantically, in its experiential mode, this is a **figure**; more specifically, it is a figure of "doing" with a process 'clean', a doer 'man' and a done-to 'car'. This construes one particular instance in the child's experience in such a way as to relate it to a large variety of other instances. Grammatically, the figure is realized by a clause; we can describe it as a selection expression having a number of systemic features including material, effective, doing, dispositive, . . . ; this particular combination of features is realized by the structural configuration Actor · Process · Goal; the Process is realized in the syntagm as a verbal group; the two participants, Actor and Goal, by nominal groups; and the relationship among them by their arrangement in this particular linear sequence. The groups, in turn, have their own distinct sets of features, also with their chains of realization which could be followed through in analogous ways.

Each link in this realizational chain exemplifies the way the grammar is first developed by children learning English as their mother tongue. The child who produced this particular utterance, at twenty-one months of age, was heading rapidly along the path of transition from protolanguage to post-infancy, adult-like language. By the same token, this is also the pattern in which the language itself first evolved. It is this primary pattern of realization that is being referred to as "congruent". Congruent relations are those that are evolutionarily and development-ally prior, both in the construal of experience (as illustrated here) and in the enacting of interpersonal relationships.

This pattern is a powerful resource with which children make sense of their experience, theorizing it in terms of categories and their relations. The grammar sets up proportionalities which create multiple analogies – numerous and varied dimensions along which different phenomena can be construed as being alike. But its semogenic power is vastly increased when any of these links can be severed and a different chain of realization can be constructed. In time the child will learn wordings such a *give the car a good clean, a well-cleaned car, the cleaning of the car, car-cleaning materials, a carclean* (or at least a *carwash*), and so on.

All these depart in some way from the congruent pattern; they are all to a certain degree metaphorical. The process of metaphor is one of **reconstruing** the patterns of realization in a language – particularly at the interface between the grammar and the semantics. A meaning that was originally construed by one kind of wording comes instead to be construed by another. So, for example, processes are congruently

21

construed as verbs; in *a carwash*, however, a process is realized instead in the form of a noun. But nouns congruently construe entities, not processes; so something that started off as a 'doing', namely *wash*, is being reconstrued as if it was a 'thing'.

In calling this "metaphor" I am not indulging in any fancy neologism. I am simply extending the scope of the term from the lexis into the grammar, so that what is being "shifted" is not a specific word – a lexical item – but a word **class**; and I am looking at it from the perspective opposite to that which is traditionally adopted in the discussion of metaphor: instead of saying "this wording has been shifted to express a different meaning" (i.e. same expression, different content), I am saying "this meaning has been expressed by a different wording" (same content, different expression). We can represent this as in Figures 4 and 5.

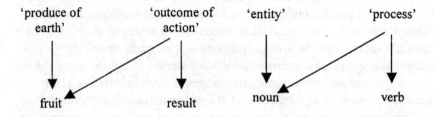

Figure 4   Lexical metaphor   **Figure 5**   Grammatical metaphor

The point is, however, that it is no longer the same meaning. If a process (congruently realized by a verb) is reconstrued in the grammar as a noun (which congruently realizes an entity), the result is a semantic hybrid, which combines the features of 'process' and of 'thing'. In an isolated instance, such as *taking the car in for a wash*, this is of no great significance. But when large areas of human experience are reconstrued wholesale, through a wide range of different metaphoric processes in the grammar, as has happened in the evolution of the languages of science, the result is dramatic. It is no exaggeration to say that grammatical metaphor is at the foundation of all scientific thought. You cannot construct a theory – that is, a designed theory, as distinct from the evolved, commonsense theory incorporated in the grammar of everyday discourse – without exploiting the power of the grammar to create new, "virtual" phenomena by using metaphoric strategies of this kind.

This domain will be explored in more detail in Volume 5 of this series.

8 Probability

Let me come back for a moment to the question of size: how big is a language? We had reached a figure of the order of half a billion different verbs. It is quite likely, of course, that any one we might generate at random, say *couldn't have been going to go ŏn cringing*, or *ought nòt to have been getting telephoned*, has never before been either spoken or written; but it is still part of the meaning potential of the language. To put this in perspective: adults conversing steadily in English would be likely to use between 1,000 and 2,000 verbs in an hour; taking the lower figure, that would mean that half a billion occurrences (instances) would need about half a million hours of conversation. Now, if we collected half a billion clauses of natural speech (not inconceivable today), and processed it (still a little way off!), we would probably find that about half of them had one of the verbs *be*, *have* or *do*. We already know a good deal about the relative frequencies of lexical items, and something about those of the most general grammatical systems: for example, the negative will account for about 10 per cent of the total, the rest being positive; about 90 per cent of finite verbs will have primary tense or modality only, with no secondary tense, and within those having primary tense the past and present will account for over 45 per cent each, the future about 5–10 per cent. So if we combine the relative frequency of the verb *cringe* with the relative frequency of the grammatical features selected in that example above, we could work out how much natural conversation we would have to process before it became more likely than not that such a form would occur. And it would be a very large amount.

These issues will be brought up in Volume 6 of this series. The point here is, that these quantitative features are not empty curiosities. They are an inherent part of the meaning potential of a language. An important aspect of the meaning of negative is that it is significantly less likely than positive; it takes up considerably more grammatical energy, so to speak. The frequencies that we observe in a large corpus represent the systemic probabilities of the language; and the full representation of a system network ought to include the probability attached to each option in each of the principal systems (the figure becomes less

23

meaningful as we move into systems of greater delicacy, because the entry condition of the choice becomes too restrictive). We have not yet got the evidence to do this; but until it can be done, grammars will not have come of age.

What this is saying is that, to give a realistic estimate of the meaning potential of a language – of its semiotic power – we need to include not only the options in meaning that are available but also the relative contribution that each of these options makes. We take a step in this direction when we locate the options in system networks, according to their entry conditions: a system way down in the delicacy scale will have a relatively small domain of operation (for example, clausal substitute polarity transfer in English, as in *I think not/I don't think so*, which figures only in a certain type of projected clause nexus). But the relative contribution to the meaning potential also depends on these quantitative factors: a system whose options are very skew makes less contribution than one whose options are more or less equiprobable; and a system that is accessed only via a chain of low probability options makes less contribution than one that is accessed in a majority of selectional environments. Thus semiotic power is not simply a product of the number of choices in meaning that are available; their different quantitative profiles affect their semogenic potential – and therefore affect the meaning potential of the linguistic system as a whole.

Finally, we do not yet know how many systems it takes, on the average, to generate a given number of selection expressions. In other words, we do not know what is a typical degree of association among systems having a common point of origin – say, the systems of the English clause. The estimate given earlier of the total number of possible verbal groups did take account of the interdependence among the various systems; as already remarked, that network is unusual in the degree of freedom the various systems have to combine one with another – it took less than thirty systems to specify all the options available to any one verb. We can of course define the outer limits of possible association among systems. Stipulating that all systems are to be binary (they are not, of course; but it makes it easier), then given a network of n systems, (a) if all are dependent on each other (i.e. they form a strict taxonomy), there will be $n + 1$ possible selection expressions; whereas (b) if all are independent, the number of possible selection expressions will be 2^n. Compare four systems associated as in (a) and as in (b) in Figure 6.

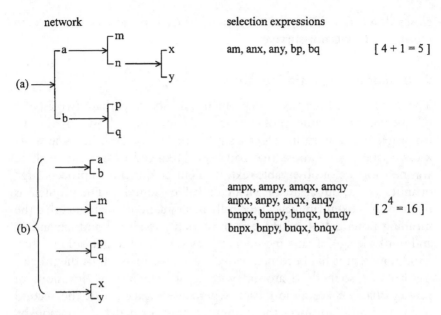

network   selection expressions

                                           am, anx, any, bp, bq   [4 + 1 = 5]

(a)

                                           ampx, ampy, amqx, amqy
                                           anpx, anpy, anqx, anqy
                                           bmpx, bmpy, bmqx, bmqy $[2^4 = 16]$
(b)   bnpx, bnpy, bnqx, bnqy

Figure 6

The networks written for the two major text generation projects in English that have used systemic grammar – the NIGEL grammar developed by Christian Matthiessen for William Mann's PENMAN project at the University of Southern California, and Robin Fawcett's GENESYS grammar used in his COMMUNAL project at Cardiff University – each had of the order of a thousand systems. Clearly they did not specify anything like two to the thousandth different selection expressions! The more systems there are in a network, the more densely they will be associated. When I wrote the prototype NIGEL grammar, consisting of 81 systems of the clause, Mann's off-the-cuff estimate was that it defined between half a billion and a billion selection expressions. This seems reasonable.

But such figures don't really matter, because we are far from being able to measure the size of a language in any meaningful way. All we can say is that a language is a vast, open-ended system of meaning potential, constantly renewing itself in interaction with its ecosocial environment. The phenomenon of "language death", so familiar in our contemporary world where the extinction of semiotic species matches the extinction of biological species as a by-product of our relentless population growth, is one where the community of speakers is no longer able to sustain this kind of metastable adaptation, and their language as it were closes down (see Hagège 2000). If a language no longer creates new meanings, it will not survive.

9 Instantiation, variation, fuzz

The problem for linguists (two problems, in fact; or perhaps two aspects of one and the same problem) has always been: how to observe language, and how to interpret what has been observed. In some well-known languages – those that had been "reduced to writing" – there was no shortage of observable text; it might be difficult to process large quantities of it, but at least it yielded reliable examples. The problem is that it is in spoken language, especially in spontaneous dialogue, that the meaning potential of language is most richly explored and expanded; and until the age of tape recorders it was very hard to get hold of that. (And now that it has become relatively easy, for many of us the process has become so hedged around with legal restraints on invasions of privacy that we are almost back where we started!) But the second major technical advance, the computer, transformed the situation by making it possible to process large quantities of data; and meanwhile parsing programs are slowly being developed which enable us to recognize mechanically some of the principal grammatical patterns for large-scale quantitative analysis.

The second part of the problem is no less intractable: this concerns the relationship between what is observed and the systemic principles that lie behind. Another way of formulating this is to say that it concerns the nature of a semiotic fact. In fact the two parts of the problem probably have to be solved together, as they were in physics by the efforts of Galileo and Newton (and of the age in which they were both able to flourish). Before their time, when technology had not yet evolved to permit accurate observation and experiment, even advanced thinkers such as Roger Bacon, who were aware of the need to experiment and observe, could still not formulate adequately the relationship between observation and theory. This relationship is complex enough with phenomena of matter; it is much more complex with phenomena of meaning; in that respect, twentieth-century linguistics was more or less where physics had been back in the sixteenth century.

Physical processes could be measured, and that gave rise to a rather clear conception of a physical theory: it was one formulated in terms of mathematics. Mathematics made it possible to predict physical outcomes; it became an essential component of physics, but at the same time continued to have a life of its own, eventually reconstituting our entire view of the nature of the physical universe. Semiotic processes cannot be measured (or only a small subset of them can); and they cannot be observed to make predictions, at least not in the Newtonian sense. (This is the inherent contradiction in the idea of a "human science", as long as science is defined in that limiting way.) What we observe in semiotic processes are instantiations of an underlying potential. This formulation could also apply to physical systems: we observe instances of "weather", and these instantiate an underlying potential we call "climate". But the predictions that follow from our observations are not about tomorrow's meanings. They are about statistical effects; and they tell us, for example, that in English the most common fifty verbs will account for 90 per cent of all verb occurrences, that active verbs will be about ten times more frequent than passive verbs, and so on. The larger the sample of texts, the more closely the actual frequencies will approximate to these predictions – provided the scale of the observations has been adequate in the first place; and the predictions may be able to take account of functional variation, showing how the proportions may vary around the overall (unconditioned) values if they relate specifically to one or another particular register.

These statistical properties of language are critical to the way language is learnt and the way language is used. When children learn their mother tongue, they are sensitive to relative frequencies: they learn the more common options before the rarer ones, and gradually approximate to the frequency patterns of the discourse they hear around them. As mature speakers, listening and reading, we are all the time expecting what might be to come; and we use quantitative evidence when switching in to the appropriate functional variety. In learning a foreign language we tend to transfer the probabilities from some language we know already – not always with the right result. So when as grammarians we try to explain how a language functions as a semogenic resource, we want to find out how it manages its quantitative effects.

At the same time (and unlike physical systems), instances in a semiotic system carry differential value. Poets, scientists, statesmen often produce instances of text that turn out to be significant events in their own right, not only perturbing the evolving system of the language but sometimes even affecting the course of history. These contrast notably with the "innumerable small momenta" of run-of-the-mill instances in daily life, which are what bring about the typical processes of gradual linguistic change. The particular impact between such a highly valued semiotic instance and the events surrounding it, both semiotic and material, is something we still need to understand, in terms of the overall architecture of the linguistic system. In some way or other resonances are set up, moments of harmony and tension, within the networks of the language itself and with other meanings that are being enacted somewhere in the environment.

It helps, I think, to bear in mind that in theorizing any higher-order semiotic system we are always involved in compromise. This is partly because the categories we set up to explain how a language works are almost all inherently fuzzy. Some contrasts in meaning are continuous (for example, in English, the systemic differences between different angles of falling pitch movement); but even apparently discrete categories like the grammatical classes of verb, noun, and so on, are highly indeterminate: there are core members, with close to 100 per cent probability of membership, and there are stragglers at the outer fringes, whose membership is at a much lower degree of likelihood and may be dependent on contextual variables. Whether we are considering highly abstract features, such as the degree of association among grammatical systems (modelled in our networks as either/or – either dependent or independent – but in fact needing to be graded once we have the data from the corpus), or the meanings of individual lexical items, such indeterminacy is a positive and essential characteristic: it is this which gives a semiotic system the necessary "play" without which it would freeze up and collapse in on itself.

But the need for compromise also arises as a consequence of stratification, because the stratal organization of the system opens up several different prespectives. Suppose we are focusing on the lexicogrammar, as the powerhouse of language where meaning is construed – sorted out along the continuum from the grammatical (very general meanings associated with almost any domain) to the lexical (very specific meanings associated with particular domains). We may view any phenomenon along this continuum – any aspect of the *wording* –"from above", asking what meanings are being construed by this wording; or we may look at it "from below", asking how this wording is realized as a syntagm. The analogies that appear in these two contrasting perspectives typically do not match: what goes together when seen from above is not the same as what goes together when seen from below. And there is also the view "from around about": what goes with what inside the grammar itself, the patterns of agnation as revealed in the system network. Any of these perspectives may be given prominence. What is called "functional linguistics" means privileging the view from above; but whatever perspective is favoured the resulting account involves compromise – most of all, of course, if one tries to give equal weight to all three. This "metacompromise" by the grammarian is both model and metaphor for the compromise that is a central feature of the grammar itself, whose theorizing of the human condition is nothing more than a massive reconciliation of conflicting principles of order – this being the only way of "semioticizing" our complex ecosocial environment in a way that is favourable to our survival.

In other words, the all-round thickening of language, its multi-dimensional "architecture", reflects the multidimensional nature of human experience and interpersonal relationships. If the processes whereby we interact with the ecosocial environment are now so exceedingly complex, then any system which transforms these processes into meaning – which *semioticizes* them – is bound to evolve analogous degrees and kinds of complexity. Language is as it is because of what it has evolved to do. The underlying theme of the chapters which follow is the exploration – and perhaps celebration! – of the awe-inspiring power of language. Different languages differ, of course, as regards what, and how much, is demanded of them; this is a manifestation of the variety of human culture. But all languages have the **potential** to meet any demands that their speakers may contrive to make of them.

PART ONE

THE PLACE OF LINGUISTICS
AS A DISCIPLINE

EDITOR'S INTRODUCTION

In the first paper in this section, "Syntax and the consumer", originally presented in April 1964 at the Fifteenth Annual Round Table Meeting on Linguistics and Language Studies, Professor Halliday makes the point that "the features of a description, and therefore of the model that lies behind it, are relatable to the aims of the model and through these to particular applications of linguistics". Halliday characterizes his own work as aiming "to show the patterns inherent in the linguistic performance of the native speaker". One of the requirements for such exploration into 'how the language works' is "a general description of those patterns which the linguist considers to be primary in language, a description which is then variably extendable, on the 'scale of delicacy', in depth of detail". The concept of delicacy "proves useful in providing a means whereby the linguist analysing a text can select a point beyond which he takes account of no further distinctions and can specify the type of relation between the different systems in which he is interested". The expectation being that textually oriented studies – involving "a characterization of the special features, including statistical properties, of varieties of the language used for different purposes ('registers'), and the comparison of individual texts, spoken and written, including literary texts" – should contribute to "literary scholarship, native and foreign language teaching, educational research, sociological and anthropological studies and medical applications".

The next three papers in this section were originally delivered as open lectures, spanning the decade from 1967–77. They were later published together by the Applied Linguistics Association of Australia (1977). "Grammar, Society and the Noun" was first presented in 1967 on the occasion of the inauguration of the Department of Linguistics at University College London; "The Context of Linguistics" was given at a Georgetown University Round Table Meeting (1975); and "Ideas about Language" celebrated the foundation of the Linguistics

33

Department at the University of Sydney. The three papers are intended to "contribute towards some kind of a picture of the place of linguistics in contemporary scholarship, and of the relevance it has – or could have – to the life of the community". The linguist's ability to relate language, mind and society, to understand the role of language as both mediator and metaphor, rests on "a sound interpretation of language as a system", which can only be achieved "when we set out to answer questions that have arisen in an attempt to interpret language in the broadest context of its place in human society". Halliday argues for greater 'social accountability' in linguistics, not simply in terms of "satisfying our own individual consciences", but rather "in eliminating some of the artificial disciplinary boundaries ... which hamper intellectual development, and induce both overspecialization and underapplication". To say that one is discussing ideas about language, "should not be thought to suggest that these ideas are isolated from ideas about everything else", nor should it be just about language as we choose to define it, ignoring everyone else's idea of language. Arguing against keeping the discussion as a private conversation within a single discipline, Halliday urges linguists "not to absent themselves from the dialogue of disciplines", warning that "if they do, the study of language will simply go on without them".

Natural language is a dynamic open system, "an evolved system, not a designed system: not something separate from humanity, but an essential part of the condition of being human". It is the means by which "we construct the microcosmos in which each one of us lives, our little universes of doing and happening, and the people and the things that are involved therein". When language came to be written down, there entered an element of design into the 'distinctively human semiotic', creating a new theory of experience, a new 'grammar'. This complementarity between speech and writing and its impact on our ways of knowing and learning is explored in "Language and the order of nature", which appeared in an edited volume entitled *The Linguistics of Writing* (1987).

The problems facing humankind, such as classism, growthism, destruction of the species, pollution, are not just problems for biologists and physicists, argues Professor Halliday, "They are problems for the applied linguistic community as well. I do not suggest for one moment that we hold the key. But we ought to be able to write the instructions for its use." This challenge comes from a paper first read to the Ninth World Congress of Applied Linguistics, Thessaloniki, Greece, and subsequently published in *Journal of Applied Linguistics* (1990), "New ways of meaning: the challenge to applied linguistics". Ways of meaning are a significant component in historical upheavals. The introduction of writing, for example, and its corresponding grammatical construction of reality, marked the shift from hunting and gathering to pastoral and agricultural practices. Language likewise participated in the shaping of other such major upheavals as the 'iron age' of classical Greece, India and China; the 'renaissance' leading up to the industrial revolution; and the present age of information. This comes about because "language is at the same time a part of reality, a shaper of reality, and a metaphor for reality". Interpreting the grammatical construction of reality is the task for applied linguistics. As Professor Halliday explains, "We cannot transform language; it is the people's acts of meaning that do that. But we can observe these acts of meaning as they happen around us and try to chart the currents and patterns of change."

Chapter One

SYNTAX AND THE CONSUMER
(1964)

At the Seventh Annual Round Table Meeting, held at the Institute of Languages and Linguistics in 1956, Professor Archibald Hill read a paper entitled 'Who needs linguistics?' In it he referred to "the kinds of people who can now be shown to be in need of linguistic knowledge for practical reasons", including among them teachers of foreign languages and of the native language, literary scholars and those concerned with the study of mental disorders. His concluding paragraph contained the words "It is the linguists who need linguistics. ... It is we who have the task of making linguistics sufficiently adult, and its results sufficiently available so that all people of good will, who work within the field of language, language art, and language usage, can realize that there are techniques and results which are of value to them."

Professor Hill could, if he had wished, have added others to the list; what he was emphasizing, as I understand it, was that any benefits which those other than the linguists themselves may derive from linguistic work depends on the linguists' own pursuit and presentation of their subject. Within those areas of activity, often referred to as "applied linguistics", in which languages are described for other than purely explanatory purposes, the linguist's task is that of describing language; and he will not, for example, attempt to tell the language teacher what to teach or how to teach it, nor claim to be a pediatrician because his work may contribute to studies of language development in children.

While recognizing the limitations on their own role, however, linguists are not unaware of the needs of the consumer. Language may be described for a wide range of purposes; or, if that is begging the question I want to

First published in *Report of the Fifteenth Annual (First International) Round Table Meeting on Linguistics and Language Studies*, edited by C. I. J. M. Stuart (*Monograph Series on Languages and Linguistics* 17). Georgetown University Press, 1964, pp. 11–24.

ask, there is a wide range of purposes for which a description of language may be used. The question is: do these various aims presuppose different ways of using the same description, or are they best served by descriptions of different kinds? Is there one single 'best description' of a language, or are there various possible 'best descriptions' according to the purpose in view?

One of the many important contributions made by Chomsky has been his insistence that linguists should define the goals of a linguistic theory. According to his own well-known formulation, the grammar should provide a complete specification of an infinite set of grammatical sentences of the language, enumerating all sentences and no non-sentences, and automatically assign to them structural descriptions. The theory should include a function for the evaluation of grammars, so that a choice can be made among different grammars all of which fulfill these requirements. The grammar can then be validated for compatibility with the given data and evaluated for relative simplicity (Chomsky 1961, 1962).

Associated with this is the underlying aim that "the formalized grammar is intended to be a characterization of certain of the abilities of a mature speaker"; "we should like the structural description to be the basis for explaining a great deal of what the speaker knows to be true of speech events, beyond their degree of well-formedness" (Chomsky 1962: 531–2). Compare also Katz and Fodor's formulation: "Grammars answer the question: What does the speaker know about the phonological and syntactic structure of his language that enables him to use and understand any of its sentences, including those he has not previously heard?" (1963: 172), and Chomsky's summing-up: "As I emphasized earlier, the central problem in developing such a theory is to specify precisely the form of grammars – the schema for grammatical description that constitutes, in effect, a theory of linguistic universals and a hypothesis concerning the specific nature of the innate intellectual equipment of the child" (1962: 550).

The evaluation of a linguistic description means, naturally, its evaluation in the light of the goals recognized for the theory. A formalized grammar is evaluated for its success in achieving the aims of a formalized grammar, or of that particular formalized grammar; the relevance of this evaluation to any other aims will depend in part on the extent to which a formalized model yields the kind of description that is most appropriate to them. That there are other possible aims is not, I think, in question; to quote Chomsky (1962: 530) again, "I do not, by any means, intend to imply that these are the only aspects of linguistic competence that deserve serious study", to which I would like to add that linguistic competence is not the only aspect of language that deserves serious study: the explanation of linguistic performance can also perhaps be regarded as a reasonable goal and one that is still, as it were, internal to linguistics. But I would also wish to include, among the possible goals of linguistic theory, the description of language for the purpose of various specific applications; goals which may be thought of as external to linguistics but for which linguistics is part of the essential equipment.

This is not of course to question the validity and importance of the goals defined by Chomsky; nor is it to suggest that, given these specific goals, the model that provides the 'best description' will not be of the type he specifies. But we should not perhaps take it for granted that a description in terms of a formalized model, which has certain properties lacking in those derived from models of other kinds, will necessarily be the best description for all of the very diverse purposes for which descriptions of languages are needed.[1] In assessing the value of a description, it is reasonable to ask whether it has proved useful for the purposes for which it is intended; and such purposes may be external as well as internal to linguistics.

There tends no doubt to be some correlation between the model a particular linguist adopts for his own work and the place where he grew up, linguistically speaking. Nevertheless I would defend the view that different coexisting models in linguistics may best be regarded as appropriate to different aims, rather than as competing contenders for the same goal. One may have one's own private opinions about the relative worth and interest of these various aims, but rather in the same way as most of us probably like the sound of some of the languages we study better than we like that of others. Estimates of the relative attainability of different goals may be more objective, although even here the criteria for the assessment of one goal as more difficult of attainment than another can probably be made explicit only where the two are basically different stages in the pursuit of a single more general aim. It is difficult to measure the relative demands made on a theory by requirements such as, on the one hand, that "the structural description of a sentence must provide an account of all grammatical information in principle available to the native speaker" (Postal, 1964: 3) and on the other hand that the grammar should be of help to the student learning a foreign language or to the pediatrician in his diagnosis and treatment of retarded speech development; nor is it any easier to measure the degree of success of a description in meeting these demands.

Yet in spite of the difficulty of measuring attainment linguists "intuitively" – that is, by their experience as linguists – recognize a good description, and most of them seem to agree in their judgements. This is not in any way surprising, but it illustrates an important point: that linguistic theory is no substitute for descriptive insight. Naturally different descriptions of a language will follow when different models are used to describe it; but the differences imposed by the model tend to obscure the similarities, and also the differences, in the linguists' interpretation of the facts. It is true, in the first place, that two descriptions will differ precisely and directly because different models are being used and these impose different kinds of statement. In the second place, however, the descriptions may differ because the linguists disagree at certain points in their interpretations. And in the third place, the models themselves may impose different interpretations, either because one solution is simpler in one model and another in the other or because they have different terms of reference and different aims.

For example, transformational grammars of English recognize a passive transformation relating such pairs of sentences as *the man eats cake* and *cake is eaten by the man*. The analogue in a "scale-and-category" grammar (to use a name by which the version of a system-structure grammar that my colleagues and I have been working with has come to be known) would be a system at clause rank whose terms are active and passive: as for example the question transformation is paralleled by a clause system whose terms are affirmative (transformational grammar's "declarative") and interrogative. In fact no system of voice at clause rank is introduced into our present description of English. We could say that this is because it does not represent our interpretation of the facts. But the question is: what "facts" are being interpreted? The **system** implies proportionality: given a system whose terms are a, b, c, then the set of their exponents $a_1 a_2 a_3 \ldots$, $b_1 b_2 b_3 \ldots$, $c_1 c_2 c_3 \ldots$ are proportionally related: $a_1 : b_1 : c_1 :: a_2 : b_2 : c_2$ and so on. This holds good, it seems to us, to a reasonable extent (such that the simplicity of the general statement is not outweighed by the complexity of further statements that are required to qualify it) of affirmative and interrogative in the clause, and of active and passive in the verbal group where the description does recognize a system of voice; but not of active and passive in the clause. In other words, *John was invited by Mary, this house was built by my grandfather, the driver was injured by flying glass, John's been dismissed from his job* and *it was announced that the committee had resigned* are not explained as all standing in the same relation to a set of their active counterparts. Such a relationship is shown, but indirectly (as the product of a number of systemic relations) and not always by the same route.

39

But this does not necessarily imply different notions about English; it may simply mean a difference in what is being required of the description. While there may be some similarity between the system in a scale-and-category grammar and the transformation in a transformational grammar, in the sense that instances of the two often correspond, they are not and cannot be saying the same thing, because these are different kinds of model.[2] The nature of a grammatical description, in fact, is determined as a whole by the properties of the model in which it has status, as well as being conditioned by the goals that lie behind the model.[3]

If I were asked to characterize the work in which I have been engaged together with some of my colleagues, I would say that our aim is to show the patterns inherent in the linguistic performance of the native speaker: this is what we mean by "how the language works". This presupposes a general description of those patterns which the linguist considers to be primary in the language, a description which is then variably extendable, on the "scale of delicacy", in depth of detail. It involves a characterization of the special features, including statistical properties, of varieties of the language used for different purposes ("registers"), and the comparison of individual texts, spoken and written, including literary texts. This in turn is seen as a linguistic contribution towards certain further aims, such as literary scholarship, native and foreign language teaching, educational research, sociological and anthropological studies and medical applications. The interest is focused not on what the native speaker knows of his language but rather on what he does with it; one might perhaps say that the orientation is primarily textual and, in the widest sense, sociological.

The study of written and spoken texts for such purposes requires an analysis of at least sentence, clause and group structures and systems, with extension where possible above the rank of sentence. The analysis needs to be simple in use and in notation, variable in delicacy and easily processed for statistical studies; it needs to provide a basis for semantic statements, and to handle with the minimum complexity grammatical contrasts such as those in English expounded by intonation and rhythm; and it should idealize as little as possible, in the sense of excluding the minimum as "deviant". Idealization of course there is; as Putnam (1961: 26) has said, "I shall assume here that some degree of idealization is inevitable in linguistic work, and I shall also assume that the question of how much idealization is legitimate is one that has no general answer ... Anyone who writes a grammar of any natural language is ... automatically classifying certain sentences as non-deviant, and by implication, certain others as deviant." For our purposes it is important that as much as possible of ordinary speech should be shown to be – that is, described as – non-deviant; in this analysis spoken English is much less formless, repetitious and elliptical than it might appear in another kind of description. But there are deviant utterances, and it is important to specify in what ways they are deviant.

For a brief, and necessarily oversimplified, illustration of one feature of the sort of description that we are attempting I shall refer to the *scale of delicacy* which, besides being of theoretical interest in providing a measure of the status of a given contrast in the language, and of the degree and kind of deviation of deviant utterances,[4] has proved of value in textual analysis because it provides a variable cut-off point for description: the analyst can go as far as he wishes for his own purpose in depth of detail and then stop. Delicacy can be illustrated with reference either to structure or to system; the present example relates it to the category of system.

Delicacy is in effect a means of having things both ways; that is, of saying that two utterances are both like and unlike each other at the same time. Any two utterance tokens, of any extent, may be alike in one of two ways: they may be occurrences of the same formal item (tokens of the same type), or they may be different formal item exponents of the same grammatical categories (tokens of different types with the same grammatical description).

Both types of likeness are properties of the description: that is, it is the linguist who decides what are occurrences of the same item and what are different items with the same grammatical description. One possible decision of course is always to aim at maximal differentiation of tokens into types: this seems to be the point of view taken by Katz and Fodor when they write "almost every sentence uttered is uttered for the first time" (1963: 171), since this can presumably only mean that the criteria adopted for token-to-type assignment should be such that almost every sentence uttered will be **described** as being uttered for the first time.[5] This would no doubt reflect a desire that the description should be capable of making all distinctions that the native speaker recognizes; this does not provide criteria, though it may be used to test their adequacy.[6] But token-to-type assignment is one point where the native speaker's intuitions tend to be most uncertain,[7] and this uncertainty reflects the multiple nature of the type-token relation in language: two utterances may be tokens of the same orthographic type but not of the same phonological type (the same "expression"), or vice versa, and neither determines whether or not they are tokens of the same formal type

41

(grammatical or grammatico-lexical, according to the model).[8]

Whatever the criteria adopted for token-to-type assignment, the question whether these items (types) are or are not assigned the same grammatical description is one to which it may be useful to be able to answer 'both yes and no'. What this means, however, depends on the ordering in delicacy of the systems by which they are related and differentiated. Suppose for example that, of a set of clauses (items of clause rank) in English, it is required to describe each of those in set (1) as distinct from all the others, but without taking into account any further related distinctions such as that represented in set (2).

(1) 1 *the Smiths are having a party this evening*
    2 *it's the Smiths that are having a party this evening*
    3 *a party the Smiths are having this evening*
    4 *it's a party that the Smiths are having this evening*
(2) 1 *the Smiths are having a party this evening*
    5 *they're having a party this evening the Smiths.*

Out of the total set of systems operating in the system-complex of **theme**, in which selection is made by the clauses in English, it would be possible to isolate the systems shown in Figure 1.

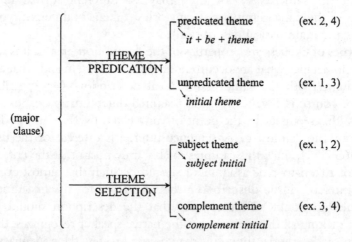

Figure 1 The right-facing brace indicates simultaneous selection; the right-facing square bracket indicates the terms in a system. Names of systems are shown in upper case, names of terms in systems in lower case. The horizontal arrow means "is related by delicacy to"; the diagonal arrow "is related by exponence to (is expounded by)". For simplicity, generalized statement of exponents (shown in italic), relating only to affirmative clauses, has been substituted for the structural notation.[9]

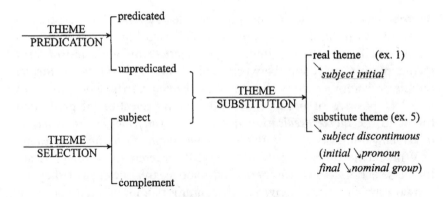

Figure 2 The left-facing brace indicates multiple (conjunct) derivation; the other conventions are as in Figure 1.

With the cut-off at this point, the clauses in set (2) have the same grammatical description. In order to discriminate between them, the further distinction shown in (4) may be introduced; the members of set (2) will then have different grammatical descriptions.

Substitution as such is not of course restricted to the **thematic element**: compare *a party they're having this evening the Smiths, we've invited them the Smiths, I call it a good idea to do that*; but the thematic element can be "substitute" only if it is both subject and unpredicated, and this would justify the treatment of **theme substitution** as a separate system. Theme substitution is required, incidentally, to explain a number of ambiguities, as for example *they're leaving the others* (as ex.1, or as ex. 5) and *it's the truth that we don't know* (as ex. 4 'what we don't know is the truth', or as ex. 5 'that we don't know is the truth').

Each system represents a dimension of potential discrimination in the grammatical description of items. Thus where one system is shown as derived by delicacy from a term in another – that is, as hierarchically ordered in respect of another – this represents a point at which the analysis may either proceed further or stop short. At this point a pair of items distinguished only in the higher-order system have not yet been differentiated: they have the same description. When the lower-order system is taken into account, however, they have different descriptions, and are thus shown to be distinct. Here therefore the answer 'both yes and no', to the question whether such items have or have not the same grammatical description, means as it were 'first yes, then no'.

The ordering of two systems in this way, by derivation in delicacy, means that freedom to select in the lower-order system is conditional on the selection made in the higher-order system. The illustration above shows multiple derivation, in which two higher-order systems are involved: only the conjunction of **subject theme** with **unpredicated theme** permits selection between **real theme** and **substitute theme**. Simple derivation could be illustrated by **theme polarity**, where freedom to select positive or negative depends on the selection of predicated theme in the **theme predication system**: *it's a party the Smiths are having this evening* contrasts with *it isn't a party the Smiths are having this evening*.

Where two systems are simultaneously ordered in delicacy, as are theme selection and theme predication above, this means that they are shown as being related (derived from a common point of origin) but with no restriction on the combination of their terms. Each item that selects in the one system thus selects also unconditionally in the other. If two items are differentiated in the one system but not in the other, the question whether such items have or have not the same grammatical description might still be answered 'both yes and no', but here this would mean 'partly yes, partly no', or 'in this respect yes, in that respect no'.

These two kinds of ordering in delicacy, the hierarchical and the simultaneous, may be used to represent the simple relations of dependence and independence between systems: fully dependent systems are ordered hierarchically, fully independent systems simultaneously. More often than not, however, the linguist is faced with systems displaying one or another of various kinds of partial dependence, where selection in one system is partly conditional on selection in another: the relation of theme substitution to the other two systems above is in fact one of partial dependence.[9] Such systems may be shown either as hierarchical or as simultaneous in delicacy; nor are they necessarily all to be treated in the same way, since they fall into different types.[10]

Perhaps I might conclude with an illustration from familiar material in English of a grammatical feature which is connected with one kind of partial dependence between systems: this is the apparent "neutralization" (in one of the many senses of this word) of systemic distinctions. Such "neutralizations" are related to, though not exactly coterminous with, Bolinger's category of "syntactic blends" (1961: 21).

Clauses in English containing, as predicator, a verbal group in the passive and, as adjunct, a prepositional group initiated by *by* yield examples such as *he was deceived by a trick* where it does not seem to matter whether the prepositional group is considered as agentive or as instrumental: whether, in other words, the voice/theme contrast is with *a trick deceived him* or with *they deceived him by a trick*. Other examples are *he was comforted by their reception of him, this is proved by Gödel's theorem* and *he was killed by a blow on the head*.

These are of course quite distinct from the ambiguities, involving agentive or instrumental on the one hand and locative on the other hand, such as *he was knocked down by the wall* or *she was comforted by the warm fire*. Each of these represents two discrete items and two grammatical descriptions are required, any occurrence being assigned to one only. This ambiguity arises also with active verbal group: *I'll toast it by the fire* may mean 'I'll use the fire to toast it' or 'I'll go near the fire while I toast it'; compare *hold it there by the handle* and *he came out by the back gate*.

The point at which neutralization occurs may be regarded as the intersection of two unrelated systems in partial dependence: voice in the verbal group and what we may call **agency** (agentive and instrumental) in the prepositional group, agency combining only with passive. Exponents of active and passive are of course monovalent (unambiguously identifiable), but both terms in the agency system may be expounded by the prepositional group with *by*.[11]

There are restrictions, in one direction, on the classes of verb and noun: some verbs and some nouns cannot occur with the instrumental, so that *suggest* and *colleague* in *this is suggested by Gödel's theorem* and *this is proved by my colleagues* seem to make these uniquely agentive. Of the two, the noun class seems the more obvious one; but animate and even human nouns can occur with the active verbal group and therefore, on this criterion, instrumentally: *they make their money by their travelling salesmen, he does his correspondence by a secretary.* Moreover, in many instances it is difficult to specify what marks a particular item as clearly agentive: this often seems to result from the collocation of noun and verb together.

Since the word-class restriction is both indeterminate and one-way, it seems useful to consider agentive and instrumental as systemically contrasting classes of the prepositional group operating at the same place in clause structure. Since further the contrast between agentive and instrumental is one which can be neutralized, unlike that between these two on the one hand and locative on the other, the former is best treated as more delicate than the latter: that is, agentive is shown as distinct from instrumental only after the two together have been separated from the locative and other classes of the prepositional group. In other words, combining these two requirements, the description may show a system of

45

agency in the prepositional group, with terms agentive and instrumental, which is in partial dependence with the system of voice in the verbal group, instrumental combining with active and passive but agency only with passive;[12] agency is in turn fully dependent on a higher-order system contrasting agentive/instrumental with locative (and others), which is fully independent of voice and where multivalent exponents are in fact ambiguous. In an analysis which stopped short of the system of agency, the ambiguities would have different grammatical descriptions but the "neutralizations" would not.

Instances of this kind, where a systemic contrast appears to be "neutralized", may perhaps be thought of as those where the answer 'both yes and no' to the question whether or not two items have the same grammatical description means 'both yes and no at the same time'. In other words, *by his colleagues* and *by his efforts* are both alike and different in respect of the same variable. Here possibly one single token might be said to be at the same time a token of two grammatical types: the clause occurrence *this is proved by Gödel's theorem* would represent two items with different grammatical descriptions. Be that as it may, it seems appropriate perhaps that systems which yield "neutralizations" of this sort should appear at a lower order of delicacy than those which yield ambiguities.

This brief discussion of the scale of delicacy has been meant to serve a twofold purpose. I have hoped both to illustrate an aspect of the current work of a small group of linguists with whom I am associated, bearing in mind here the title of the present panel; and to exemplify my earlier point that the features of a description, and therefore of the model that lies behind it, are relatable to the aims of the model and through these to particular applications of linguistics. In this instance the concept of delicacy proves useful in providing a means whereby the linguist analysing a text can select a point beyond which he takes account of no further distinctions and can specify the type of relation between the different systems in which he is interested.

In speaking about one possible approach to a particular type of pattern in language, I am not implying that we handle it more effectively than other linguists working with different models, but intending to show how its treatment links up with other features of a model conceived with the specific aims we have in view. Other models will handle such patterns differently in light of their own goals. But while accepting, and indeed applauding, the fact that linguists today are working with models of different kinds, I would at the same time underline one point of which no teacher of linguistics needs to be reminded: that there exists a vast store of knowledge which is just linguistics, and common ground to all linguists whatever model they happen to be using.

Notes

1. This is, of course, a different question from that of the relative evaluation of different formalized grammars.
2. The issue is **not** whether, as Katz and Fodor say (1963: 206) "sentences that are related to each other by the passive transformation ... have the same meaning, except perhaps in instances where quantities are involved". The system does have implications for the grammatical semantics, but not this one; it implies that exponents differing only in respect of the selection in question (i) differ in meaning but (ii) differ in a regular way. Thus exponents of different terms in a system by definition have not the same meaning; but this merely illustrates the fact that the line between 'have' and 'have not the same meaning', like that between grammar(/lexis) and semantics, is drawn by the theory (or rather, by the description and in the light of the theory).
3. Compare Chomsky, on the procedures by which different structural descriptions are assigned (1962: 534), "These specifications must involve no appeal to the intelligence or linguistic intuition of the reader because it is just this that we are attempting to characterize". I use here the term "grammatical description" in preference to Chomsky's "structural description" since in this model the description of an item is (by definition) structural-systemic.
4. This is analogous to the procedure suggested by Chomsky (1961: 236–7).
5. Katz and Fodor (1963: 171). Such an assertion cannot be 'substantiated': it is true or false by definition, as is shown by the suggested procedure for its substantiation, "checking texts for the number of times a sentence is repeated". On any reasonable interpretation of the grammatical type-token relation the repetition rate for sentences would obviously be low, although it might be predictably rather than indefinitely low. (Extrapolation from the repetition rate for morphemes, words and groups in English in a manageable sample of texts would permit the prediction of at least the order of magnitude of the average repetition rate of clauses and sentences; there is no reason to assume that the sentence is unique in this respect – the group already admits recursive structures, for example.) Cf. Dwight L. Bolinger (1961: 381): "At present we have no way of telling the extent to which a sentence like *I went home* is the result of innovation, and the extent to which it is a result of repetition, countless speakers before us having already said it and transmitted it to us in toto." To say this is of course in

no way to deny or minimize the ability of the fluent speaker "to produce and understand sentences never before encountered" – and, one might add, clauses, groups and words.

6. The point is made by Chomsky with regard to grammaticalness (1962: 533).

7. That is, his intuition as to what are tokens of the same type and what are grammatically similar types; cf. Putnam (1962: 36–37). Putnam concludes his discussion of this point by remarking "here we are reminded that linguistics is after all a social science and that its fundamental concepts have the same kind of dispositional and human character as do the fundamental concepts of any other social science".

8. One could perhaps specify that where two utterance tokens have potentially (with maximal delicacy) different formal descriptions they are shown ipso facto be tokens of different types; but if we go no further than this it is at least questionable whether almost every sentence uttered will be described as being uttered for the first time. The native speaker may not always go as far. He might well consider *he helped me do it* and *he helped me to do it* as 'different sentences', though their distinction can be ignored at least until a very late stage in delicacy, but //1 ∧ he / helped me to / do it // and //4 ∧ he / helped me to / do it //, or the former and //1 he / *helped* me to / do it //, or all three (notation as in Halliday 1963), as 'the same sentence', although these contrasts are of a high order of generality and should, in my opinion, be reflected in the assignment of tokens distinguished in this way to different types. Here the observer is likely to be in the familiar position where his intervention modifies the observation, since an inquiry will call attention to the distinction.

9. Only nominal themes have been considered here; in fact the theme selection system covers also the selection of non-nominal elements as thematic. Other related systems have been omitted, for example that of *information focus* expounded by tonicity, which distinguishes // ∧ the / Smiths are / having a / party this / *evening* // from // ∧ the / Smiths are / having a /*party* this / evening // and so on.

10. Partial dependence of this kind is indicated as hierarchical derivation with the derived system having an "unmarked term", here **real theme**. The difference between the selection of an unmarked term in a system and non-selection in the system in question is that the former implies choice: thus while *the Smiths have invited us* contrasts with *they've invited us the Smiths*, there is no parallel clause-item corresponding to *the Smiths we've invited*. A similar example would be the restriction of thematic selection in "WH-clauses": *who did he ask, where did he go* in contrast with *he asked who, he went where*, but there is no corresponding item in contrast with *who did it*.

11. Systems in partial dependence are well described by the use of matrices as developed by Pike (1962); from the point of view of ordering in the scale of delicacy this represents a form of simultaneity. Partial dependence may

also be manifested statistically, where the selection in one system affects the relative probabilities of selection of the terms in another system.

12. It might be considered that the agentive always has *by*, and that items such as *he was overcome with sleep* and *he was misled through his own stupidity* are "blends" in Bolinger's sense (the latter, for example, being perhaps a crossing of *he was misled by his own stupidity* with *they were able to mislead him through his own stupidity*).

13. Where, as in this instance, the systems concerned are shown as unrelated, their partial dependence appears in the description as a feature of exponence.

Chapter Two

GRAMMAR, SOCIETY AND THE NOUN
(1966)

The central concern of linguistics is the systematic study and interpretation of language. But in the course of this study there are times when we need a broader framework than that which is provided by linguistics itself, at least in its narrower academic sense. My aim here is to look into certain questions of language from the outside, with the focus on language in its social environment. The questions I have chosen fall within an area that might be called "sociogrammar" – or perhaps "sociosemantics", since grammar is a mode of entry to the study of meaning. In the study of human behaviour, and not only linguistic behaviour, there are some questions that can, it seems to me, be posed only in sociolinguistic terms; and for our purposes the definition of sociolinguistics as 'the study of the relations between linguistic structure and social structure' can be allowed to stand, provided that "structure" is taken in its broadest sense, to include the underlying semantic patterns of language on the one hand and systems of cultural behaviour and of knowledge on the other. For while some sociolinguistic questions arise from an examination of co-variation between linguistic and social phenomena, others face the linguist in the course of his own work.

There are many questions which a linguist may think of asking for himself for which he has to go outside linguistics to begin looking for an answer: for example, concerning the function of language in establishing and maintaining value systems and systems of social control, and in defining the roles which for the individual, child or adult, make up the role set that constitutes his identity – not only his identity from the point of view of society but also the identity he

First published as *Grammar, Society and the Noun* (lecture given at University College London on 24 November 1966). H. K. Lewis & Co Ltd for University College London, 1967.

regards as his "self" (note in passing that in English 'you' and 'I' possess our 'selves', while 'he' and 'they' are merely qualified by theirs – we say *myself*, *yourself* but *himself*, *themselves*). The late J. R. Firth, Professor of General Linguistics in the University of London, wrote in 1950:

> The meaning of *person* in the sense of a man or woman represented in fictitious dialogue, or as a character in a play, is relevant if we take a sociological view of the *personae* or parts we are called upon to play in the routine of life. Every social person is a bundle of *personae*, a bundle of parts, each part having its lines. If you do not know your lines, you are no use in the play ... [Linguistics] is mainly interested in persons and personalities as active participators in the creation and maintenance of cultural values, among which languages are its main concern.

As an example of the sort of enquiry Firth envisages, involving both a precise formulation of certain questions and an experimental approach to their solution, might be cited the work of Basil Bernstein, of the University of London Institute of Education. Bernstein's starting point is the differential response of children of different types of social background to educational opportunity. Asking "The behavioural implications of the physical and social environment are transmitted in some way to the child. What is the major channel for such transmissions?", Bernstein suggests that the answer must be sought in a sociolinguistic study of "the interrelationships between social structure, forms of speech and the regulation of behaviour" (1964). In other words, he finds it necessary to confront linguistic and sociological findings in order to be able to understand the social processes involved.

Bernstein's questions arise out of a sociological enquiry; but the linguist seeking to understand the nature and functioning of the linguistic system will find himself asking questions that are not unrelated or dissimilar to these. It has sometimes been said that linguists have shown too little interest in the social background of language, although it might be argued that, if they had not concentrated, almost exclusively for a time, on the internal workings of the linguistic system in its specific manifestations in different languages and dialects, such further questions could never have been broached. Be that as it may, it seems likely now that in the coming decades some of the most fundamental work on language will take the form of sociolinguistic enquiry. This may be taken to include both the comprehensive, qualitative approach envisaged by Hymes in his programme for a "comparative ethnography of communication" (1964), which implies the "structural analysis of the cultural behaviour of a community", and the microscopic, quantitative methods of Labov in which "hypotheses are established by observing the co-variation of objectively defined variables" (1964), for example hypotheses about the status of individual phonemes in the New York dialects. From the linguist's point of view, the focus must be allowed to shift.

In this connexion we might note Fishman's apparently fairly confident hope that "the linguist aware of the social context of language will lose his naïve sociological outlook" (1967):

> The linguist might realize that categories represented by "natural" human groups (whether these be generational, religious, ethnic, educational, occupational, etc.) ... merely represent the palest reflection of folk sociology. The sociologist's categories and strata are no more than handy ways of getting at recognizably different rates of various social behaviours: values, attitudes, socialization patterns, leisure activities, political behaviours, interactions across group boundaries, etc.

Fishman also expresses the hope that sociologists will lose their naïve linguistic outlook; and while applauding both these sentiments I should wish to add that the ethnographic study of folk linguistics, such as can be observed for example in the 'Eng. Lit.' classes in our schools, is itself a valuable area of sociolinguistic research, just as the study of folk sociology is an important branch of the sociology of knowledge. Professor Randolph Quirk, in describing the aims and scope of the Survey of English Usage which he is directing at University College London, wrote: "One should aim at seeing educated usage as far as possible against the background of educated reaction to usage" (1960). The study of any culturally determined behaviour involves the study of its description and evaluation by the culture.

One of the lessons of sociology is that all knowledge is folk knowledge, and all science folk science; there are merely different folk, and any one of us may include among our roles different levels of folk membership. Ever since Schliemann discovered Troy we have been being encouraged to believe in our own mythology; and the danger nowadays, at least in linguistics, is not so much one of a false dichotomizing between myth and truth as one of failing to keep different mythologies apart. Now I want to take, on this occasion, a folk linguistic standpoint; to start from a statement of a kind often made about language, and to ask what questions and assumptions lie behind it. This particular example is of something that is said not only about English; and that is usually couched in general linguistic terms with at least typological and perhaps universal implications. But the discussion will relate to English, since that presumably is our common language here if we have one – we may not in fact understand each other but we have to keep up the pretence, since it is a faith in communication, rather perhaps than communication itself, that marks our claim to social interaction.

In his well-known *ABC of Plain Words*, under the entry headed "Abstract words", Sir Ernest Gowers writes (ascribing the sentiment to Mr. G. M. Young): "an excessive reliance on the noun at the expense of the verb will, in the end, detach the mind of the writer from the realities of here and now, from when and how and in what mood the thing was done, and insensibly induce a habit of abstraction, general-ization and vagueness" (1951). This is an example of the formulation of a very general attitude to what Rulon Wells, in his summary of such attitudes, calls "nominal style" or "nominality" (1960). (One might also add that it is a good example of what it is criticizing, containing as it does, aside from linguistic technical terms, eight abstract nouns.) Two questions may be asked: first, what is this "nominality", or "nominal style", and second, what are the reasons for it? It is not something unnoticed by linguists; but it is also, unlike many features of English, something of which there is a general cultural awareness, and which is widely subjected to popular linguistic criticism, an activity at which the English excel. It is thus not only part of our cultural knowledge but also a determinant of cultural behaviour.

Nominality, we may assume, has something to do with nouns. At the simplest, it might be merely a matter of the number of nouns per running words of text; but in fact it is easy to show that it is not, and it is likely therefore to involve either, and probably both, of two other factors; some entities other than simple nouns, and some aspect of the functioning of nouns (and of the other entities if these can be specified) rather than merely their density of occurrence. It is often suggested, moreover, that the features referred to in this way are such as to distinguish Modern English, or at least some varieties of it, from any or all of: earlier stages of the English language, other styles of contemporary English, or other languages.

In one sense, rather superficial but perhaps not totally irrelevant, it may be true that the noun is very much in the air, so to speak. Among other things, nouns are used to name classes of objects; and with every advance in technology there are likely to be more classes of object to be named. A few may disappear, like trams, although even some of these are still talked about; but many more come into existence, and the language has to make provision for them. Not that every time a new machine part is designed a new word of the class "common noun" is added to the vocabulary. There are various ways of meeting this need, as described in studies of industrial lexicology; an existing lexical item, for example, may be transferred through formal or functional analogy, like the word *goose-neb* (goose's beak) introduced for a part of the loom by early immigrants to the towns and preserving for them a linguistic shadow of their cultural past. In modern English the preference is rather for recursively structured nominal compounds: we keep up with the technological times by devising forms such as those described by Joan Maw (1963) in her study of the instructions issued to fitters of gas appliances: *flue pipe support strap, gas pressure test nipple* and (an invented one on the same model) *main burner oil feed adjustment cover retaining screw*. This tendency is then reinforced by the use of similar structures in headlines, as an example of which we could construct *tourist holiday coach death crash enquiry verdict appeal decision sensation*. Such inventions may be monstrous, but we have no difficulty in knowing how to pronounce them.

Compounds of this kind are built up structurally by a linear process of regressive bracketing (bracketing associating to the left), in which the addition of each new item puts a bracket round all those that have preceded it. The rightmost item is the head of the structure; when a further item is added to it this has the effect of making it a modifier. Such a pattern yields a taxonomy, going from most specific, on the left, to most general on the right; a form like *flue pipe support strap* implies that we can ask 'what kind of strap?' (there will be other kinds), 'what kind of support strap?', and so on. There may be some internal bracketing, but if so this merely inserts either a co-ordination or a sub-structure of the same type.

This form of the structural organization of lexical items is reminiscent of the systematic taxonomic organization of the lexicon itself. The lexicon of a language can be viewed at least partly as a set of taxonomies, or even perhaps as a single taxonomy. Roget's *Thesaurus*, for example, could be interpreted as a ten-level taxonomic arrangement of the lexicon of English, though the nodes are in fact not named (they are labelled where referred to at all); and sociolinguistic studies of folk taxonomies suggest that some taxonomic naming is a universal feature of the organization of lexis. It seems moreover that this form of organization is very early learnt by the child; as he masters the class-naming principle he also quickly understands that some classes include other classes: the class of *spoons* includes that of *teaspoons*, that of *men* includes that of *uncles* and so on. But the manifestations of this organization, and its relation to syntactic patterns, vary considerably among different languages. It is noticeable that nominal compounds such as those cited above do not reflect any arrangement of their own constituent items in a lexical taxonomy, since almost any of these can be more or less specific than any other: beside *gas pressure test nipple* we could have *gas nipple test pressure, nipple pressure gas test* and so on, with no added linguistic discomfort to the layman.

Some languages seem to reveal the taxonomic organization of the lexis more systematically and more explicitly than others; and sometimes in curious ways. Robert Dixon's (1970) work on Dyirbal, an Australian language, shows that the taxonomic structure of the vocabulary of the daily language is partially, but quite unambiguously, retrievable from correspondences with the mother-in-law language: in talking to one's mother-in-law one must preserve a decent level of generality. In Chinese, the taxonomic organization of the nominal section of the lexicon is more apparent than is that of English, since the greater part of it is organised into sets of compound items having a specific followed by a general component, with the latter also occurring alone as the corresponding generic term: most nouns, in other words, fall into sets like English *dessert spoon, teaspoon, . . . spoon*. This provides the model for most new coinings, as observed already by Samuel Kidd, Professor of Chinese at University College London from 1837 to 1843. In his *Lecture on the Nature and Structure of the Chinese Language* (1838) Professor Kidd wrote:

> All languages require new terms, or new combinations of words, to express new ideas ... [In Chinese, this] object might ... be attained by periphrasis; as 'a watch' is designated *she shin peaou*, 'time indicator'; steam vessels *ho ke chuen*, 'fire breath ships'; and a steam carriage would be understood by *tsze tung chay*, 'self-impelling vehicle'. [This] mode of conveying new ideas is the only one accessible to foreigners, unless they should attempt to spell their own names of things by native characters, which would be very barbarous and unsatisfactory.[1]

"Spelling one's own names of things by native characters" is perhaps rather an unusual way of referring to linguistic borrowing, viewed as it is from the standpoint of the lender; but Professor Kidd is quite right in observing that Chinese does not extend its vocabulary significantly in this way. The history of technology in China (and the Chinese were at the forefront of technological progress throughout most of human history up to the sixteenth century) is at the same time a history of a part of the Chinese language; new terms were created by the formation of nominal compounds from native Chinese elements in a way which both exploited and reinforced the explicit taxonomic structuring that has been mentioned as characteristic of nouns – though absent from other word classes – in the Chinese lexicon. Joseph Needham has referred to problems caused by certain gaps and skewnesses in technical nomenclature; what Malinowski called the "gaps, gluts and vagaries" of terminology. Needham (1958) mentions

> a memorial made by Su Sung to the Emperor towards the end of the 11th century when he was presenting his astronomical clock-tower to the throne. He [Su Sung] ends by saying: ". . . in any case, if we use only one name all the marvellous uses of these three instruments cannot be included in its meanings; yet since our new instrument has three uses, it ought to have a more general name ...". In other words, with its mechanized armillary sphere, celestial globe, and jackwork, it should not be called just a *hun hsiang* or a *hun i*; it ought to have more general name such as *hun thien (chi)* which we might translate as 'cosmic engine': ". . . and we are humbly awaiting your Imperial Majesty's opinion and bestowal of a suitable name upon it." That was in 1092, but the Emperor had no ideas whatever. As a matter of fact, he was only about seventeen at the time, but in any case he did not produce a name, and nobody else did, so the mechanical clock did not get one, and the arrival of a new term six centuries later gave rise to the idea that there had arrived a new thing.

It is interesting that both these sinologists have used their understanding of the principles of naming in Chinese to create new Chinese words; and one wonders whether there is any evidence to suggest that it is easier for a Chinese child to predict new names, and to construct hierarchies of classes of objects, than it is for a European child. English, with its relative lack of explicit taxonomic ordering, could seem to a Chinese rather inadequate as a medium of technological research and communication; and the irrelevance of this observation is perhaps a useful comment on the views sometimes put forward about the languages of under-developed countries, often by native speakers of these languages, as being unfit for use in science, education, law, or government.

It is sometimes suggested that the complex bracketing of English and Chinese nominal compounds leads to excessive structural ambiguity; but this is merely one of many forms of the structural ambiguity that is found in all languages. Headlines are often cited in this connexion, like *nude murder detectives* and *police drink test tables review*; these are more noticeable, because they tend to strike us without context – the owner of the newspaper leaves the train before we can read the smaller type. But there are many other sources of structural ambiguity in English besides these complex nominals. The texts from which I cited some of the earlier examples also contained *to replace, insert the lip on the top of the front panel behind the return flanges at the top edge of the opening in the main casing* and *remove battery holding down bolts or hook bolts at both ends of the battery*, each of which may represent any of about a hundred possible structures. This sort of ambiguity is normal in language, and nominal compounds are no exception; there is usually only one possible interpretation in the context (provided one includes here the social context: in this case the reader must have been trained as a gas fitter), although it is true that headlines and other display languages have to a certain extent their own 'economy grammar' dictated by the simultaneous requirement of communicative effect and extreme brevity.

Among other English naming devices is the brand name, which has a rather special linguistic status. Etymologically, a brand name may be more or less anything: proper noun (*Morris, Ajax*), possessive proper noun (*Kellogg's*), common noun, count or mass (*Embassy, Surf*), modified common noun (*Double Diamond, Gold Leaf*), or not a noun at all (*Digestive, Startrite*); it may be an existing item of the language, like the foregoing, with or without orthographic innovation, or an invention within the limitations of the phonological system, or anything in between. Syntactically, as pointed out by Geoffrey Leech (1966), "there are signs that brand-names have an unstable syntactic function". The brand name has some of the features of a proper noun – its modifiers are usually descriptive, not defining, for example – but more of those of a common noun: it is assigned count or mass status (*a Morris, some Ajax*; this assignment is independent of the status of the model where this is an existing common noun, cf. *some Tide*), and selects for specific or non-specific determiners *a, the*, etc. The brand name may play a significant role in the search for names for new objects, although there is wide variation here between different language communities. English is particularly prone to accepting brand names into the language; this may in the long term have its effect on the nature and functioning of the English noun, by contributing to a blurring of the distinction between common and proper, the extension of countability to all nouns, and a still greater tendency for interchange of membership between the noun and other word classes. It is possible to construct whole sentences in English in which every lexical item is a brand name, like *the dripolator needs brilloing; let's just have some nescafé in the denby.*

So the simple common noun is certainly outnumbered, in modern English, as a device for naming classes of concrete objects. Proper nouns, as in brand names, nominal compounds and modified forms of various kinds (as in *vitreous enamel, locking nut, tin opener, spirit of salt*) are all widely exploited. What all such forms have in common is that, with minor exceptions, they take on all the syntactic potentialities of their parent class the common noun. This means not only the potentiality of entering into further compound forms and susceptibility to the various choices that are open to the English nominal group – all forms of determination and numeration – but also the set of functions which the nominal group may take on in the clause: subject, direct object, and a number of others. When function in the clause is taken into account, however, there turn out to be still further elements that behave in a noun-like way.

It is for this latter reason that grammarians group together nouns, nominal groups (noun phrases), and nominalizations. The noun is the class of words (including compounds) that name classes of things; centrally, concrete objects and persons, but also abstractions, processes, relations, states, and attributes: whatever can stand for a pronoun, as Quine (1948) suggests ("Pronouns are the basic media of reference; nouns might better have been named propronouns"). Nominal groups are nouns plus their determiners and any other modifiers; while in nominalizations some element other than a noun, a verb perhaps, or a whole clause, has nominal status assigned to it. There is no sharp line, in English, dividing compound nouns from nouns plus modifiers, or the latter from nominalizations. So if scientists or others are said to write in a "nominal style" (and nominals are no less relevant to poetry), this refers to the use of nominals of all kinds; and criticism of such a style does not necessarily mean that the critic has found more nouns per sentence than he likes. Rather otherwise, perhaps; what is objected to is more likely to be the use of nominalizations, since it is the nominalization for which alternative devices could be found, whereas there is ordinarily no alternative to the use of a simple common noun like *cat* or *carburettor*, except not to talk about cats and carburettors at all.

What are these alternatives, and what is the nature of the choice among them? There are certainly many ritual features associated with stylistic variation in language: features whose function is merely to signal a particular mode of linguistic behaviour. But it seems strange that nominalized structures, which are very often longer than the non-nominalized alternatives, should be so consistently preferred in uses of language in at least some of which brevity might be thought to be a virtue. The question that might be asked is whether there are any significant corollaries, within the language, of the phenomenon of being or behaving like a noun.

Other than in certain minor sentence functions, appellative, exclamatory, and responsive, the speaker of English structures his message around a verb. If we use the term "process" as a general term for that which is designated by the verb, then two broad types of process are distinguished: action, including perception, as in *he threw the ball, he heard a noise*, and what we may perhaps call "ascription", the assigning of attributes, as in *he is clever*. In many, though not all, respects action and ascription are alike: both must be located in time, with the same range of tense choices; both are subject to modality; and these and other similarities are what justify the introduction of a general term such as "process" by which to refer to them both together.

If the process is of the "action" type a distinction is made, at least in terms of potentiality, according to whether or not the action implies a goal. Hence the familiar distinction into transitive (goal-directed) and intransitive verbs. However, a cursory glance at a dictionary shows a large number of verbs assigned to both classes ("vb. trans & intrans."); and this is because the potential distinction, between implying and not implying a goal, is largely overlaid in modern English by an actual distinction according to whether or not a goal, or more accurately a goal feature, is present in the clause. Since with many, probably most, verbs this feature may be either present or absent, the potential distinction has relatively little significance, in the sense that it has very few 'consequences' (co-variants) elsewhere in the grammar of English. It is thus the clause rather than the verb that is transitive or intransitive. So although, for example, *ride* is transitive and *walk* intransitive, English does not show a grammatical difference according to type of action between the two halves of a sentence like *you ride and I'll walk*.

We could put this positively: the two clauses are treated alike in important respects. In particular, taking "directed" action (action on a goal) is equated, in English, with enforcing non-directed action: *she's walking the horse* and *he's riding the bicycle* are structurally parallel, as shown by the fact that *he's opening the door* can be said to be like either of them ('he's doing something to the door' or 'he's making the door do something') and it makes no difference: *he's opening the door* is not an ambiguous sentence. So making someone do something is the same as doing something to someone, and there is a proportionality such that *we're selling cosmetics* is to *cosmetics are selling* as *we're running Jones for chairman* is to *Jones is running for chairman*. Reflexives, too, enter into this pattern: *she washed the baby* is to *she washed herself* as *she sat the baby on the settee* is to *she sat herself on the settee*, with *herself* optional in both cases.

In English, therefore, rather than two kinds of action, corresponding to transitive and intransitive verbs, we have really only one kind of action with which may be associated two different combinations of participants. Either one participant only is involved with the action, in which case his or its role is that of the person or thing 'affected', or two participants are involved, one 'affected' and one 'causer'. To express this in terms of actor and goal: the 'affected' is the goal of a directed action (object of a transitive verb) or the actor in a non-directed action (subject of an intransitive verb); the 'causer' is the actor in a directed action (subject of a transitive verb). But the 'causer' is also the initiator of a non-directed action (subject of an intransitive verb used causatively), so that in an action of this type the 'affected' may be an enforced actor (object of an intransitive verb used causatively).

Every action, therefore, can be said to imply an obligatory 'affected' participant and an optional 'causer'; but it needs to be made clear in what senses the causer is optional. In grammar, as in sociology, a participant is to be thought of not as an individual but as an occupant of a role. In one type of clause, exemplified by *he stood up, he washed* (meaning 'he washed himself'), there is only one participant, occupying the role of 'affected'; there may be 'causation' involved, in the sense that the action is intentional, but in that case the two roles of affected and causer are combined in the one occupant (contrast these examples with *he fell down*, where there is no causer and thus *he fell himself down* is impossible). In other clause types the roles are discrete; the causer may then be specified, as in *she stood him up, she washed him*, or it may not be, as in *he was stood up, he was washed*. Here the distinction is that between active and passive clauses, the desire not to specify a causer being one of the principal reasons for choosing a passive: the great majority of passives in texts in modern English have no agent (Svartvik 1966).

The basic pattern of organization in the English clause seems thus to be more readily describable not primarily in terms of action and goal but rather in terms of cause and effect. The variable is not 'is the action goal-directed or not?' but rather 'is the cause external to the action or not?' These two patterns may be called respectively the "transitive" and the "ergative". In English, transitive and ergative co-exist: a distinction is found between verbs which tend to have actor and goal, the "transitive" verbs, and those which tend to have only actor, the "intransitive"; but the predominant pattern is the ergative one, since with very many verbs we have both the active-passive construction, with two participants, and the 'middle' construction with only one participant. This pattern cannot be generalized in terms of actor and goal, since the obligatory role, the affected, may be either goal or actor, and the optional one, the causer, may be either actor or initiator. So the roles of participants are defined primarily by causation: x is engaged in a process – is it caused by x or not? This contrasts with a transitive form of organization where the roles are defined by extension: x is engaged in a process – is it directed outside x or not? The ergative pattern appears clearly from the proportionality in pairs such as the following:

the clothes were washed	:	*the clothes washed*
the door was opened	:	*the door opened*
her hair's being grown long	:	*her hair's growing long*
the horse shouldn't be jumped	:	*the horse shouldn't jump*

where the distinction represents the speaker's choice whether to suggest external causation or not: those on the left imply that the role of causer is discrete from that of affected.

I have discussed this aspect of English more fully elsewhere (1967/ 68); here what is of interest is its significance for the understanding of nominality. If I may use "transitivity" as a general name for this aspect of the organization of the clause, whether the basic pattern is transitive or ergative, then the significance of transitivity in this connexion is that it defines some of the roles which nominal elements may occupy. The notion of a role in grammar is not limited to persons; the occupant may be a person, an object, a concept, or – and this should be stressed here – anything else that is nominalized. In specifying these roles, therefore, we are making generalizations about the function of nominals in English. In addition to the two roles just mentioned, the affected and the causer, I shall refer briefly to some others, including certain roles defined not by transitivity but by another dimension of clause patterning known as "theme". First, however, it may be useful to ask how far this cause and effect pattern which I have referred to as the "ergative" form of organization may be thought of as a significant characteristic of English in its own right, in the sense of whether it has

61

any bearing on the speaker's awareness of processes and of the status of participants therein.

In his discussion of noun and verb as universals of language, Robins wrote (1952):

> No longer can it be argued that since we all inhabit a world with a common metaphysical structure, our languages must exhibit a common structure of grammar. Rather we must say that since certain basic grammatical terms, with certain semantic implications, are found to be generally applicable over the ever-growing field of known languages, we are justified in inferring that the experience of human societies is similarly ordered.

One might ask, bearing in mind the work of Whorf, whether if certain other grammatical terms are found to be variably applicable, to some languages but not, or not so centrally, to others, we are justified in inferring that the experience of human societies is differently ordered. The question might be paraphrased, in another terminological framework, as: is there a language-specific "deep" grammar?

Underlying either of these is the prior question whether we are justified in inferring anything about the experience of human societies from the applicability or otherwise of grammatical terms to the description of their languages. If we give anything but a wholly negative answer, which is perhaps somewhat unconvincing, it is difficult to see why we should dismiss as irrelevant to human experience just those features in a language which are not found in all languages. In one of the most important discussions of linguistic theory in recent years, Hymes wrote (1964):

> In structural ethnography, as in any discipline with the anthropological vocation to interpret both human differences and similarities [and here I should certainly want to include linguistics] ... a dialectic is mandatory in which neither facts nor categories speak for themselves, and in which the search for structure is never divorced from the search for the concrete.

Pointing out that "the comparative, or universal level, depends on the identificational as well as the contrastive properties of structural features within a system", Hymes thus argues for what he calls "the concreteness of universals". The point is well brought out by Lyons (1966) where, claiming that "the noun is the one substantive universal of syntactic theory", Lyons goes on to say that "nouns are primary, in the sense that they are linked referentially with 'things' (in the 'nuclear' instances)";

and later, in reference to an imagined language in which all nouns were derived from verbs: "What is not conceivable is that the language in question could function, outside a rather limited range of situations, without the association between "things" and the nouns used to denote them becoming, not merely motivated, but CONVENTIONAL."

The relevance to our underlying question seems clear, and indeed is stated clearly by Lyons:

> ... neither extreme nominalism nor extreme realism is an acceptable approach to this question [of linguistic relativity ("Whorfianism")]. If there were no correspondence at all between the structure of language and the structure of the perceptual world, there would be no sense in the suggestion that language imposes a particular categorization upon the world ... [although] this fact ... does not imply that they are necessarily in correspondence in any particular instance.

In the particular instance of transitivity in English, and granted the noun as a constant (though it should be noted at the same time that Whorf did not grant it; he wrote of Nitinat (1945) that "the terms verb and noun in such a language are meaningless"), we are asking in fact whether the systematic patterning of nouns in the clause allows us to infer anything about the speaker's categorization of the perceptual world. If we think it does, this is significant whether such patterning is universal or not; as Hymes (1964) says, it would be absurd to claim that "there could not have been one human culture until there were two". But, equally, only if we think it does, does the question whether it is universal or not become of any interest.

In his discussion of the relevance of Whorf's views to the notion of synonymy, Quine remarked (1953): "It is not clear even in principle that it makes sense to think of words and syntax as varying from language to language while the content stays fixed", although "there are many basic features of men's ways of conceptualizing their environment, of breaking the world down into things, which are common to all cultures". Whorf himself wrote (1941): "It is in its constant ways of arranging data and its most ordinary everyday analysis of phenomena that we need to recognize the influence [language] has on other activities, cultural and personal". He made it clear that such recognition could be sought only through a perspicuous and highly sensitive grammar ("a deep analysis into relations"); and he cautioned: "I should be the last to pretend that there is anything so definite as a "correlation" between culture and language, and especially between ethnological rubrics such as "agricultural", "hunting", etc., and linguistic ones like "inflected", "synthetic" or "isolating" " (1941). Whorf perhaps had in mind here notions such as the "stadial" theory advanced by Marr and his followers in the USSR, according to which language developed by stages corresponding to postulated stages of socioeconomic development, with, for example, parts of speech arising in conjunction with the social division of labour. The ergative construction, as it happens, played a prominent part in discussions of stadial theory, being associated, in one account, with a primitive level of technology in which man was powerless in the face of action by external, natural (including supernatural) forces; in which he saw himself as an agency rather than an actor, as an intermediary rather than an initiator of processes and changes.

The term "ergative" was first introduced by Dirr (1928) in reference to certain Caucasian languages, although the feature which it referred to had been recognized much earlier. Its use has been extended to a fairly wide range of phenomena in different languages (Meščaninov, 1949); but according to Matthews (1953): "In nearly all cases the ergative construction demands the presence of three elements: 1) a transitive verb, 2) an expressed object figuring as the grammatical subject, and 3) the logical subject denoted differently from the way it is when paired with an intransitive verb." To paraphrase very roughly, in an ergative construction the subject of an intransitive verb is in some way or other, such as case, resembled by the object and not by the subject of a transitive verb. In many languages the ergative does not occur unrestrictedly but co-exists with a transitive construction and is itself limited to a certain aspect of the verb or to certain verb or noun classes (Allen, 1964).[2] In using "ergative" in the present discussion of English I am referring not to a construction but to a system: a system, however, characterized by the fact that within it the actor in an intransitive clause type resembles in its potentialities the goal rather than the actor of a transitive one, so that there are identificational grounds for suggesting an ergative-type distribution of roles into 'affected' and 'causer' rather than, or (at least) as well as, a transitive-type one into 'actor' and 'goal'.

One might here attempt to replace the Marrist formulation referred to above by one more along Whorfian lines, asking, for example, whether this form of clause organization tends to direct the attention of a speaker towards an explanation of processes rather than towards a classification of them in terms of their extension. If the ergative implies a notion of causation, by contrast with the transitive notion of action, does this supply as it were a magical-scientific component of clause meaning where the transitive supplies a technological? But whereas the Marrist hypothesis is at least partially verifiable (and can in fact be shown by counterexamples to be untenable), it is difficult to see how one would even set about verifying a hypothesis couched in this more Whorfian form.

Such a hypothesis might be expected to be verifiable in terms of some culturally determined non-linguistic behaviour, on the lines of Firth's view of "situational meaning": as Robins (1963) expresses it,

> the situational level of analysis and situational meaning are distinct from other levels of analysis and meaning in that they involve relations with extra-linguistic features of the world at large and non-linguistic parts of the speakers' and hearers' culture.

But, as Firth himself pointed out, any linguistically significant concept of "situation" can only be sought in the most abstract terms, even when one is considering the context of situation of single utterances or units of discourse; much the more is this so if one is considering the "situational meaning" of the underlying grammatical patterns of a language. We are concerned here with the language system; and the relevant "non-linguistic parts of the speakers' and hearers' culture" will be embodied in systems of cultural knowledge, even if we might hope to find their reflexes in particular patterns and modes of behaviour.

In his concern with language typology, therefore, Whorf was surely right to switch the beam away from social structure on to the structure of knowledge; and if his suggestion of a link between Standard Average European grammatical concepts and the Newtonian model of the universe is not easy to evaluate (would the ergative perhaps supply an Einsteinian component?), it remains an interesting suggestion which, taken in the context of Whorf's work as a whole, is not without some hint of a direction in which evaluation might be sought. It has long been recognized in ethnolinguistic work that, while neither the structure of the universe nor that of society can be deduced from the study of a language, kinship and other terminologies are interpretable as cultural knowledge and are thus behaviourally relevant; there is nothing implausible in the search for a sociolinguistics of knowledge on a more macroscopic scale. Only, we do not yet know enough about the underlying typology of language systems; so that the questions of immediate concern are likely to be questions internal to language. In other words, the line of investigation leads in the direction of Whorf's language-specific "deep" grammars, towards semantically significant generalizations about the grammars of languages which may serve, more adequately than do present descriptions, as linguistic evidence for any enquiry into language and cultural knowledge.

So it is time to get back to English, in the expectation that it will be the internal corollaries of a grammatical feature, its consequences within the language, that most directly reflect its significance and its validity. It seems in the present context, for example, that the ergative pattern differs from the transitive in more readily admitting other participant roles into a direct relation with the process; where the relation of nouns to the verb is one of involvement rather than one of extension there may be many different ways of being involved. In English we find as it were a clustering, around the verb, of variously related nominals, rather than a quasi-linear arrangement of one 'on either side'. In a sentence like *shall I play Mary some Bach?* it is not very clear how the participant roles would be distributed into an actor and goal pattern; one is tempted to suggest that not only the record player but even the electricity company would have some claim to be represented. In fact, and more seriously, in clauses like this one, or like *this book won't teach you much French*, or even *he left the house*, a number of fairly distinct participant roles are associated with the process, and the appropriate generalizations that can be made about them are by no means immediately obvious; but the occupants are all nominals (they can, for example, all be subjects) and all have, like the affected and the causer, a sort of direct line to the verb which represents their direct involvement with the process.

We have considered only processes of the "action" type; but when the process is what I referred to earlier as "ascription" the general picture is still one of cause and effect: *she kept quiet, he kept her quiet* is very like *she sat down, he sat her down*. In other words, even an attribute is subject to a form of causation; and the attribute can thus enter into a clause of any kind as a by-product of the process: *he knocked him flat, run the water hot*. Interestingly – this is an aspect of the ergative patterning – only the central participant, the affected, can acquire attributes in this way; none of the others. The effect of this extension is that the attribute becomes itself almost another participant role in the process; it can be a nominal, as in *this will set you up a new man*, although at this level of abstraction the adjective in English is itself a kind of noun – the traditional classification into "noun substantive" and "noun adjective" reflects one level of structural organization.[3]

Of the numerous verbs which can assign attributes, there is one verb which can have this as its sole meaning: the verb *be*. At the same time there is a second verb *to be* which has a different function, that of equating or identifying, as in *John is the leader*. Here *be* identifies one nominal with another, so that the two roles are those of 'identifier' and 'thing to be identified'; and since these roles are reversible in sequence (we can have **John** *is the leader* or *the leader is* **John**, the relation being one of equivalence and not of inclusion as with attributive *be* clauses), the identifying process is syntactically one of action rather than one of ascription; it is as if this *be* was a transitive verb. The identifying structure is one of the favourite clause types in many varieties of modern English. In a sample of two hundred clauses of contemporary scientific writing, taken from the texts analysed in the course of an investigation by Huddleston and others (1968), thirty-two are of this identifying type. An example is:

> The conversion of hydrogen to helium in the interiors of stars is the source of energy for their immense output of light and heat.

This represents perhaps the most nominalized form of communication; and the prevalence of clauses of this type is I think one of the diagnostic features of what is referred to as a "nominal style". The clause is structured into two nominalized segments, containing between them all the lexical items, and the one is then equated with the other. The "process" is thus reduced to one of simple equation. But this clause type is no more than an extreme form of the very general pattern whereby a cluster of assorted nominals is linked each to the other by a verb whose function is little more than that of glue: it holds them together. What we have been calling the "process" is then merely a relation among objects, the elements that designate processes being, along with everything else, nominalized. In Whorf's terminology, such processes are "objectified": that is, patterned on (some aspect of) the outer world rather than on our subjective experience of them as processes. In this case the model is the outer world of concrete objects (including, as I shall suggest below, persons, so that this 'objectifying' includes 'personifying').

Such objectification may be achieved simply through the use of process nouns, of which there are many, like *dawn* and *song*. So instead of *they danced* we prefer to say *they did a dance*; instead of *they dined, they had dinner*; instead of *they erred, they made a mistake*; instead of *he contended that they had conspired, his contention was that there had been a conspiracy*. It is no wonder that Basic English is able to operate with only eighteen verbs. Or it may be achieved through nominalizations; and here there is no limit to the range of concepts that can be brought within the nominal compass, since a whole clause, or any part of it, can be nominalized.

We may here take a very brief glance at what is perhaps the most important concomitant of nominality in English: its relation to the structure of the English clause considered as a message, as a piece of communication. In his study of the language of Dickens (1959), Quirk pointed out the timelessness, the "oppressive simultaneity" as he expressed it, of a narrative in which "entirely verbless sentences ... are placed in a network of sentences whose verbs are participles"; one of the features of nominalized structures is that within them marking for tense and person is, or may be, avoided, and Wells (1960) noted that this is sometimes advanced in defence of a nominal style. But there is also a more positive side to the picture: nominality opens up other realms of choice which are not accessible without it.

We have seen that the effect of nominalizing something is to bring it into structurally immediate relation with the verb; and, to the extent that the verb is itself only a relator, thereby with other nominals. Now the English clause is structured not only in terms of participant roles but also, and independently, along a different dimension in which roles, or functions, are assigned as components of a message. There is a 'theme' – what is being talked about; a 'focus' – what is being presented as the main item of information; and so on. These roles are freely combinable with those of affected, causer and the like, so that any nominal element can take on any one of them; but they are not all freely combinable with the functions of non-nominal elements in the clause. There are thus more different ways of structuring the information in a clause like *the announcement of his resignation put an end to the discussion* than there are in, for example, *because it was announced that he had resigned they stopped discussing*. The distribution into identifier and identified is itself a powerful device for the structuring of information: it is no accident that the slogan *what we want is Watney's* lasted very much longer – no doubt it turned out to be more effective in promoting the sale of beer – than the *we want Watney's* which it superseded.

The English nominal style, whatever one's feelings about it, may thus perhaps be seen in the light of its associations with the grammatical organization of the English clause; with the functions that are open to nominal elements on the two principal dimensions of clause structure: the cause and effect dimension, that of "transitivity", and the communicative dimension which I have elsewhere (1967/68) referred

68

to as "theme". On both these dimensions, nominality means freedom of movement. When processes, qualities, states, relations, or attributes are "objectified" they take on the potentialities otherwise reserved to persons and objects. I should like as a final note to look briefly from a different angle at one particular instance of this "objectifying", considering here the noun in the language of social relations.

The use of nouns to express relations is regular in the functional terminology of mathematics and the sciences, including linguistics where, for example, the noun "subject" expresses a relation 'is subject of'. This phenomenon is not restricted to technical discourse, and it is the basis of the language of social relationships. One instance is that of kinship terminology. We take it for granted that terms like *father* and *parent* should be nouns, although as Lamb (1965) has shown, a linguistic analysis of kinship terminology suggests that all semantic components of kin terms, except those of sex, are in fact relational: not 'parent' but 'is parent to'. The meaning of *father* is defined by the relationship 'is parent to' plus the non-relational component 'male'.

The nominalization of social relationships by the naming of the occupants of the roles they define is not confined to kinship systems; it appears in relationships derived from social systems of all kinds, as in *boss, pupil, friend*. Some such nouns are deverbals, like *teacher, employee* – note the distinction between *he taught me* 'was a teacher to me' and *he taught me* 'involved me in the teaching process, caused me to learn' – although such nouns tend to have a collocational life of their own distinct from that of their base verbs. That such relationships assign status is seen in the derivation of verbs such as *he bosses (people around)* 'behaves in the manner of one having the status defined by "is boss to" ', showing that there is an expected behaviour pattern characteristic of the status in question, itself referred to by a noun *bossiness*. Sets like *father, fatherhood* or *paternity*, and *paternalism* give us nouns for the occupant of the role defined by the relationship, the status that role confers (including the status as institutionalized in the legal system) and the characteristic behaviour pattern.

The use of a noun to name the occupant of a social role is quite general and makes no distinction between roles defined primarily in terms of social relationships, like *father, friend*, or *tenant*, and those which are primarily occupational like *milkman* and *lawyer* and the numerous terms for roles in games, such as *goalkeeper*; a word like *teacher*, which may be either, shows the same sort of ambiguity that we found with *teach*. All these exemplify a general pattern whereby the language refers

69

to a function by naming its occupant. In the case of social functions such nouns are characteristically accompanied, in English, by a possessive modifier; this refers to the other term in the relationship, as in *my father, my friend*, but is also commonly used when the roles are relationally defined as in *my lawyer, my milkman*, thus giving such roles the linguistic status of social relationships.

The study of kinship terminologies, and of folk taxonomies in general, lends itself very readily to the drawing of rather naïve conclusions about the individual's experience of society, or other aspects of his environment, from the organization of the vocabulary. Nevertheless, the linguistic patterns are not wholly irrelevant. To use an over-simple illustration, a child may know very well that his father's brother and his mother's brother are differently related to him, while at the same time the word *uncle* does confer for him a common status on both, as well as on others that he knows are not related to him at all – just as when I find tigers labelled *cats* in the zoo I cannot help wanting to stroke them. One's experience is organized on many levels at once; the language has played a part in structuring it for us, not the less important because largely at a time in our lives that is now beyond the reach of recall.

Within language, nouns probably play the central part in building up the child's view of his environment. They name concrete objects, definable at one stage perhaps, experientially, as the class of 'droppables', things which fall to the ground when released in the course of his experiments with gravity at the age of about one year, like *teddybear* and *sandwich*. Concrete objects and personal relationships are both central to the child's experience; and some, though not all, of the terms used to name the human beings in his environment fit in to the class of 'droppables', the concrete count nouns; an uncle can be singular or plural, possessed and numerated like a sandwich or a pencil, and therefore would presumably fall to the ground if some means could be found of dropping him. Of course uncles are grammatically distinct from pencils; they have different pronominal reference. Moreover we say *this pencil isn't mine* but not normally *this uncle isn't mine*; and whereas one *has* a pencil and also *owns* it one *has* an uncle but does not *own* one. But some of these refinements are probably learnt later; and one might cite here the sentence, from Elizabeth Bowen's novel *The Little Girls*: "There were three or four popular fathers, and one uncle, vouched for by his owner as being funny."

This is all lighthearted enough. But we should not perhaps ignore the linguistics of social roles, the grammar of the processes through which the child comes to define his own identity at the intersection of a network of social relationships. To understand the socialization process we need not merely to observe the ways in which parents talk to their children, answer their questions and so on, but also to consider how the forms of the language predetermine the framework within which this interaction takes place; to understand the linguistic system as the range of possible choices within which the speakers are operating. In the process of learning, for example, the distinction in English between common nouns and proper nouns, the child also learns that *mummy* is a common noun (*my mummy, hasn't Jane got a mummy?*), while *Johnny* is not, so that there is a grammatical distinction between elder kin and others – peers, including coeval kin, and strangers. Any significance this may have in his conceptual development is irrespective of whether or not all other languages make the same distinction. All the various distinctions that the child learns to associate with nouns, such as common or proper, general or specific, count or mass, concrete or abstract, definite or indefinite, as well as the various roles occupied by nouns in clause structure, provide a part of the conceptual framework for his mental development, and thus for the formation of his ideas about himself and about society.

When Gulliver visited Lagado, on his voyage to Laputa, he found three professors engaged in a project for improving the language of their country. Phase I of the project was "to shorten Discourse by cutting Polysyllables into one, and leaving out Verbs and Participles; because in Reality all things imaginable are but Nouns". (Phase II was "a scheme for entirely abolishing all Words whatsoever".) We are not told whether the professors had their grants renewed – or how they managed to apply for them. But we do, as Swift implied, grow up in a highly nominalized environment; and while recognizing, and striving to avoid, a sort of vulgarized Whorfianism (for which Whorf himself would not be to blame) whereby language is held to imprison the whole of one's thinking, we may nevertheless need to enquire into the relation between language and man's view of society – not forgetting here his view of language, of words and things, since linguistically as well as culturally man is both the creation and the creator of his environment.

Linguistics, as Hymes reminds us, is the least independent of disciplines. The declaration of independence of linguists of a generation ago was a prelude to significant advances; its aims were achieved, and times are different. But it is nonetheless a unified field, with its own range of tasks and objectives; and we should perhaps be wary of any cleavage between, for example, a linguistics that looks to psychology as its nearest relative and one which looks to sociology and social anthropology. The psychologist, concerned primarily with human constants, or at least not culturally determined variables, may seek to make all languages look alike; the sociologist, concerned with the diversity of human cultures, is predisposed for languages to look different. Neither is wrong; all languages are alike and all languages are different. But this is not a simple dichotomy. We cannot simply say that all languages are alike underneath and different on the surface, and the work of Whorf is a useful reminder here. A grammar is not thereby less perspicuous because it embodies an empirical attitude towards the concrete universals of description. It is possible to conceive of a language in which uncles are verbs.[4]

It is possible, that is, provided one is aware of language; and in our own culture, from force of necessity, this awareness is increasing. The philosopher's concern with the relation between natural and logical languages becomes crucial when one has to talk to a computer; and in fields of knowledge from sociology to theoretical physics problems arise of the limitations and preconceptions inherent in the form of a language. Such problems may be new ones for the scientist and the programmer; but for the poet they have always existed, as so well brought out by McIntosh (1966) in the discussion of Gerard Manley Hopkins and his "continuous struggle to come to terms with a medium which he felt was fundamentally unsuited in certain ways to the expression of some of his deepest perceptions". Once again the noun is in the front of the picture, just as it so often is, not surprisingly perhaps, in discussions at a more everyday level of linguistic awareness.

But it was perhaps misleading of me to start on this occasion from a folk linguistic observation (it will be clear, I hope, that "folk linguistics" is not being used as a derogatory term). The generalizations I have been suggesting about English, in interpretation of the awareness many speakers of English have of the prevalence of nominal patterns, did not in fact result from an attempt to explain this awareness. They arose quite naturally out of the study of English grammar, within a framework based on the underlying notion of choice, in which the question being asked was a linguistic 'why?': 'why?' in its usual sense, in the social sciences, of 'what goes with what?'. What I was trying to explain was a set of internal features, at first sight unrelated to each other, that are found in the semantics of Modern English.

The questions of sociolinguistics, to return to the point from which I began, involve correlations of some kind between language and society. I have suggested that these may need to be approached through a consideration of correlations that are found within language itself. It is important therefore to keep both aims in focus. We cannot hope to relate language and society except on the basis of a sound interpretation of language as a system. But this in turn will be achieved only when we set out to answer questions that have arisen in an attempt to interpret language in the broader context of its place in human society.

Notes

1. The full quotation reads: "All languages require new terms, or new combinations of words, to express new ideas. Perhaps the union of two or three existing symbols in one would be most agreeable to the genius of the Chinese. The same object might, however, be attained by periphrasis." Kidd's first alternative reveals his misunderstanding of the nature of the Chinese script; cf. his (1841) criticisms of Du Ponceau (1838), and discussion in Halliday (1959b: 32 and n. 4). Du Ponceau was, as it happens, right; Kidd was representing the current folk linguistic view (as held by westerners), although the fact that the Chinese never did adopt his first alternative might have been seen as convincing evidence against it.

2. Lyons (1966) argues that "since ... the 'ergative', in certain languages at least, is aspectually restricted ..., it is by no means certain that there is a 'deep' structure difference between transitive and 'ergative' constructions" (p. 228 n. 7). I would agree that it is by no means certain; but the fact that transitive and ergative constructions may co-exist in one language is no evidence against it.

3. There is considerable overlap of structural function between noun and adjective: for example, both enter with, in the main, the same set of functions into nominal compounds and, as modifiers, into nominal groups. Lyons' rejection of the identification of adjective and noun (1966: 226) is valid at one level; but at another level, representable in dependency terms, or in terms of structural functions, the traditional view that the two are sub-classes of the same class embodies important generalizations.

4. I am indebted to Dr J. E. Buse, of the School of Oriental and African Studies, University of London, for the information (personal communication) that this is in fact the case in Rarotongan (Cook Island Maori).

73

Chapter Three

THE CONTEXT OF LINGUISTICS
(1975)

There is a feeling abroad in some quarters that linguists are on the endangered species list. The reasoning seems to be that, when the climate changes, the ones who are most exposed are those who have become so specialized as to live off just one particular kind of tree.

Most subjects have their periods of specialization: moments when the focus is narrowed, the perspective sharpened, and the rest of the world shut out. It is often said that this has to be so, that such specializing is a necessary condition for a great leap forward; and this may well be true, if we are talking about specialization as a posture for research. It is less certain that it need determine the scope of operations of a university department, or of its offerings to its students.

To be highly specialized is in its way a kind of defence, a means of protecting one's identity. We are constantly being reminded of how many others feed on language: philosophers, psychologists, rhetoricians, speech pathologists, communications and media experts, and many more besides. Yet there are significant aspects of language that none of these groups takes account of; so linguists have tended to retreat and to consolidate the terrain that is out of others' reach. How often do we read statements like "Linguists concern themselves only with invariant forms", or "Linguists ignore the cognitive aspects of language", or "Rhetoric is not acknowledged to be a part of linguistics".

It must be said at the outset that there have always been linguists whom this image did not fit. But it is true that during the 1960s the majority, in the United States at least, did adopt a highly specialized work style. Faced with a choice between two ways of being unique, one

First published in *Report of the Twenty-fifth Annual Round Table Meeting on Linguistics and Language Study*, edited by Francis P. Dinneen (*Monograph Series in Languages and Linguistics 17*). Georgetown University Press, 1975.

that of seeing language in the round, from all angles (where disciplines for which language is an instrument, not an object, see only one or two angles), the second that of seeing what lies at the core of language (to which the other disciplines do not penetrate), linguists chose the second, in this way marking out their own area of specialization and using the discipline 'linguistics' rather than the object 'language' to characterize their domain. Linguistics became the study of linguistics rather than the study of language.

Associated with this specialization was a determination that linguistics should be useless, that it was a theory without applications. It was widely held, for example, that linguistics had no application in language teaching. Now it is true that harm has been done in the past by exaggerated claims about what can be achieved through linguistics – so much so that in some areas of the world students expecting to be taught a second language (which they needed) found themselves being taught linguistics instead (which they did not need). But the other extreme view, one denying that linguistics has any relevance in language teaching, is merely a reflection of the way the linguist conceives of his subject; it is not a considered appraisal of the language teaching process. The effect of this attitude has been to discourage linguists from working in applied linguistics, and to make it difficult for those who do to gain support.

Other instances could be cited; in my opinion machine translation is one of them. It is not unusual to be told now that all the funds spent on this were wasted; but I do not think so. Once it was established that machine translation was a problem in linguistics as well as in computer science, significant progress was made, only to be cut short when the community of linguists rejected the kinds of investigation on which it was based as being of no theoretical interest. So the work was abandoned, when it was just beginning to look realistic. Now there are many parts of the world in which people are not being educated in their mother tongue; and one of the reasons for this is the cost of translating textbooks and background materials. Some form of machine translation – and machine translation is not an "all-or-nothing" kind of activity – might eventually have made a critical difference.

In matters such as these, theoretical linguists refused to admit the social accountability of their subject, and withdrew their expertise from activities that could have been beneficial to large numbers of people. I am not saying that all linguists held aloof. Nor am I implying, in an excess of linguistic paternalism, that miraculous solutions lay around the corner. A massive accumulation of knowledge and experience was needed, and still is. But to interpret this knowledge and experience requires linguistic theory.

There seems to be a general consensus now that linguistics had tended to become overspecialized and underapplied; the point need not be laboured. I would like to suggest a third characteristic, which I think is related to these two, but whose validity is more likely to be challenged. This is the assumption that a human being is bounded by his skin.

J. B. Priestley, the writer and critic, wrote in 1949: "Art to me is not synonymous with introversion. I regard this as the great critical fallacy of our time." (He later developed this theme at length in his account of "the moderns" in *Literature and Western Man*.) Let me adapt this maxim and say: human science is not synonymous with introversion.

I am not referring to the point, repeatedly made, that the technique of introspection into one's own knowledge as a speaker has tended to be overvalued as a source of facts about language. I have in mind a much more general point: that in recent work in linguistics, all the emphasis has been placed on language as stored within the organism, as "what the speaker knows". A representative formulation is one from Postal (1968): "It cannot be too strongly emphasized that grammar is a description of part of what people **know**, not of what they **do**." What has happened here is that a real and important distinction, that between the potential and the actual – between what people **can** do and what they **do** do – has become conflated with another opposition that is distinct from and independent of it, that between knowledge and interaction – between what goes on 'within' the organism and what goes on 'between' organisms (or between the organism and its environment). And this second distinction is a rather more problematical one.

It is related to the question that has exercised philosophically minded linguists from Saussure onwards: 'where is' language – 'in here', or 'out there'? Pribram (1971) observes that "Language and culture appear to have unique characteristics which are hard to define as either mental or physical"; and he aptly illustrates this by reference to the legal problem of whether a computer program is subject to patent or to copyright. We can try to resolve this issue, as Saussure and Chomsky have done, by making the distinction between knowledge and behaviour and parcelling out language between the two (and likewise with culture). If we do this, we should recognize that behaviour is no more accessible to observation than knowledge is. Behaviour is a potential, and what we observe are instances of behaviour.

76

But the distinction between knowledge and behaviour is largely transcended in a context such as that of Pribram's "Biologist View". "Consciousness", he says elsewhere (1973), "describes a property by which organisms achieve a special relationship with their environment", and "the basic function of the brain is to generate the codes by which information becomes communicated". Many people now see the "language and culture" complex as an information system. If information is to be located somewhere, no doubt it will have to be at the interface where the organism joins with its environment; but why do we need to localize it by reference to the skin? Meaning inheres in the system: in the information system that constitutes the culture, and in the various semiotic modes (of which language is one) that serve to realize the culture. The system is more general than its representation either as knowledge or as behaviour:

	System	*Instance*
Interaction (*behaviour*)	behaviour potential ('can do')	instantial behaviour ('does') (= "performance")
Introaction (*knowledge*)	knowledge potential ('knows, i.e. can bring to consciousness') (= "competence")	instantial knowledge ('brings to consciousness')

In recent years theoretical linguistic studies have focused predominantly on introaction, to the exclusion of the interactive perspective. As a philosophical standpoint, this has a particular consequence for the description of linguistic systems: either the environment is left out of account, or, if it is taken into account, its role is conceived of as static and as passive. It figures as a decorative background to semantic interpretations, but not as a dynamic element in linguistic processes, or in the learning of language by a child. Riegel (1972) remarked that:

> Both Chomsky and Piaget . . . while [their] orientation has set them clearly apart from most American psychologists, . . . have failed to assign an appropriate role to the cultural-historical conditions into which an individual is born and within which he grows. . . . There is no place in these theories . . . for an active role of the environment and for a codetermination of an individual's development by other active organisms.

The child has been represented as learning language in isolation from his environment, instead of as constructing a social reality through interaction with it.

This situation arises when an equation is set up such that what is inside the skin is identified with the potential, and what is outside the skin is identified with the actual. "Competence" is defined as knowledge, and interaction is then characterized as "performance" – the concept of a "theory of performance" cannot, in these terms, be other than self-contradictory. Reality then becomes psychological; meaning is located entirely within the organism, and the social fact is reduced to a mere manifestation. In other words, to idealize is to psychologize.

Here is Lyons' (1968) statement: ". . . linguistic theory, at the present time at least, is not, and cannot be, concerned with the production and understanding of utterances in their actual situations of use . . ., but with the structure of sentences considered in abstraction from the situations in which actual utterances occur". This recalls Chomsky, in 1966: "It is only under exceptional and quite uninteresting circumstances that one can seriously consider how 'situational context' determines what is said, even in probabilistic terms". The impression is given that "situation" and "actual situation" are synonymous, and this being the case the linguist cannot concern himself with interaction and the environment – because interaction is 'what a particular speaker does' and the environment is 'on a particular occasion'. In this way linguistic theory idealizes out the social context, and with it social phenomena of any kind.

To exclude the social context from the study of language is, by implication, to exclude human interaction and the exchange of meanings from the scope of serious enquiry. But there is an alternative, which is to recognize that the "situation" is an idealized construct, as it was interpreted by Firth (1950) and developed by Hymes (1962). In Goffman's (1964) words, "It can be argued that social situations, at least in our society, constitute a reality *sui generis* . . ., and therefore need and warrant analysis in their own right, much like that accorded other basic forms of social organization". (I would leave out "at least in our society".) The situation, interpreted as situation type, or "social context", is a representation of the semiotic environment in which interaction takes place. Such concepts – social context, environment, interaction – are of the same theoretical order as "knowledge" and "mind". Interaction explains knowledge no less than being explained by it.

It has been said that an obsession with what goes on inside oneself is characteristic of the modes of thought of the end of an era, when intellectuals, not liking the reality that lies outside, the social upheavals and wholesale resymbolization, find a pleasanter or at least more ambiguous reality within. Behind this somewhat facile observation there lurks perhaps an element of truth – that for the linguist at least the reduction of human behaviour to mental operations does avoid the awkward consequence that (to adapt David Hays' formulation) between semantics and reality lies social structure. However that may be, the effect has been to turn attention away from social meaning, and from the social act as a source of explanation.

It is here that speech act theory – the work of Austin, Searle and Grice – has had such significance for linguistics. When the social context has been idealized out of the picture, a theory of speech acts provides a means of putting it back again. It celebrates the linguists' rediscovery that not only do people talk – they talk to each other.

The study of speech acts, which as Searle remarks is important in the philosophy of language, starts from the speaker as an isolate, performing a set of acts. These include, among others, illocutionary acts – questioning, asserting, predicting, promising and the like; and illocutionary acts can be expressed in rules. In Searle's (1965) words,

> The hypothesis . . . is that the semantics of a language can be regarded as a series of systems of constitutive rules [i.e. rules that constitute (and also regulate) an activity the existence of which is logically dependent on the rules] and that illocutionary acts are performed in accordance with these sets of constitutive rules.

The meaning of a linguistic act thus comes within the scope of philosophical enquiry. But a language is not a system of linguistic acts; it is a system of meanings that defines (among other things) the potential for linguistic acts. The choice of a linguistic act – the speaker's adoption, assignment, and acceptance (or rejection) of speech roles – is constrained by the context, and the meaning of the choice is determined by the context. Consider a typical middle-class mother and child exchange: *Are you going to put those away when you've finished with them? – Yes. – Promise? – Yes.* The second of these yesses is at one level of interpretation a promise, a concept which (in Searle's now classic demonstration) can be explained by reference to conditions of three types: preparatory conditions, the sincerity condition and the essential condition. But its significance as an event depends on the social context: on modes of interaction in the family, socially accepted patterns of parental control, and so forth – and hence on the social **system**, Malinowski's "context of culture". To describe the potential from which this utterance derives its meaning, we should need to specify such things as (sub-culture) professional middle class, (socializing agency) family, (role relationship) mother–child, (situation type) regulatory, (orientation) object-oriented; and to interpret it as, at one level, a move in a child's strategy for coping with a parent's strategy of control. (How this may be done can be seen from the work of Bernstein and Turner, from one viewpoint, and of Sacks and Schegloff from another.) We shall not want to say that the child's utterance is 'insincere'; but nor shall we want to interpret it as 'one speech act conveying another', which introduces an artificial distinction between a speech act and its use, as if to say "As an idealized structure, this is a promise; when it is instantiated, by being located in a social context, it functions as something else".

This is not to be construed as a rejection of speech act theory, which is concerned with the logic of individual classes of acts and not with the ongoing exchange of interpersonal meanings. It does not claim to account for interaction as a dynamic social process. But this does raise an important issue in the study of language as object, when one is trying to understand the nature of the linguistic system. It is one thing to idealize out the social process when one is accounting for the ideational part of semantics, where the relevant 'environment' is a second-order construct of objects and events (Malinowski's "context of reference"). It is quite another thing to do so in accounting for the interpersonal part, since this is, in effect, the semantics of interaction. If speech act theory is taken as a point of departure for describing the interpersonal component of meaning, the social context has to be added in afterwards; and this is somewhat like idealizing the nourishment out of a loaf of bread and then adding vitamins in order to enrich it.

Among the interpersonal meanings expressed in language are the sets of roles that the speaker can select for himself and for the hearer from the social relationships that make up the potential inherent in the speech situation. In the most general terms, the options are (i) either giving (offer, or response) or accepting (ii) either information or goods-and-services; derived from these is a rich network of more specific choices. But the meaning of any specific role-relationship that the speaker can assign depends on the social context. The notion of 'offering information', for example, means one thing in school and another thing in the family; and something else again in the young children's peer group. It is difficult to account for these patterns – or for how a child comes to learn them – in terms of a semantics in which the speech role has an idealized meaning abstracted from the social situation.

The speech role system is one which has a great deal of 'play', or variation, in it; it is highly sensitive to individual differences, and to differences among social groups, and so plays a significant part in the differentiation of meaning styles. Individuals differ widely in their meaning styles; this is how we recognize people by their meanings. Subcultural meaning styles – what Bernstein calls "sociolinguistic coding orientations" – show the same phenomenon at the subcultural level. Both individuals and social groups vary in the meanings they typically associate with given social contexts; and the selection of roles in the speech situation is a rich source of variation. If any general interpretation is to be given, such variation has to be treated as inherent in the system.

Of course, there will always be idealization; in any systematic account of language, certain phenomena will have to be dismissed as irrelevant. But the nature and extent of this idealization is a function of the purpose in view. In order to achieve a syntax that could be stated by rules, linguistic philosophy first idealized out natural language altogether. Chomsky then showed that natural language could be brought within the scope of rules, given a particular kind and degree of idealization (labelled "competence") which, among other things, excluded all but the ideational component of meaning. If the rules are to be extended to (that part of the syntax which expresses) meanings of an interpersonal kind, it is still necessary to let the indeterminacy in as late as possible, by idealizing out the social context – since it is this that is responsible, so to speak, for the variation within the system. This is not the only possible scheme of priorities; we can conceive of a sociological semantics which excluded all ideational meaning – and which would be equally one-sided. As it is, however, linguistics has been dominated by a perspective which, because of its emphasis on knowledge in contrast to interaction, has favoured a semantics without social structure, rather than one that characterizes the meaning potential inherent in the contexts that are defined by the social system.

Progress has then been achieved by further extending the scope of rules. From having been first used in the representation of isolated sentences having neither verbal context nor situational context, their scope has been extended in these two directions: towards text grammars, and towards the structure of interaction.

Text grammars have been described by van Dijk (1972) as grammars in which

> ... derivations do not terminate as simple or complex sentences, but as ordered *n*-tuples of sentences ($n \geq 1$), that is as *sequences*. The intuitive idea, then, is that the text grammar must formulate derivational constraints such that certain sequences are grammatical and others are not, viz. that the set of well-formed texts of a language is a subset of all possible sequences of sentences.

Here there is verbal but no situational context; hence the concept of a text grammar relates primarily to those registers in which the "situation" is contained within the text as a second-order field of discourse, typically various forms of narrative. Any descriptive ideal that proves to be unattainable with a sentence grammar will be doubly unattainable with a text grammar; for this reason text grammars in this sense are likely to remain purely formal exercises.

The structure of verbal interaction has been described by Sacks and Schegloff in the form of rules of sequencing, turn-taking and the like (Schegloff 1968; Sacks, Schegloff and Jefferson 1973). Such rules do not specify relations between the social context and the text, but they do take account of features of the non-verbal environment in specifying the sequence of verbal events. The question at this point is how far rules can take us in representing interactive sequences, and how much this in turn tells us about the exchange of meanings as a social process. Mohan (1974) suggests that a more appropriate model for interpreting utterance sequences may be found in social action theory:

> I shall view certain patterns of dialogue as the result of rational goal-oriented linguistic action by the participants. ... [The] rational order does not determine the specific sequences of utterances, but rather places constraints on the sequencing of utterances.

In Mohan's view the "means–ends" concept of the purposive, rational actor may be more relevant to human action and interaction than a system of rules.

If utterances are directed by rational action, what is the status of the system that has evolved to produce them? Without going into problems of the nature of functional explanations of human symbolic systems, or their relation to rational action as an explanation of the behaviour of the individual, I shall assume that it makes sense to say that language has evolved in conditions which relate it to the creation and maintenance of the social system. Given some form of "means–ends" interpretation of language (cf. Jakobson 1963), such as enables us to transcend the distinction between the system and its use, what are the "ends" to which the linguistic system provides the "means"? Essentially, language expresses the meanings that inhere in and define the culture – the information that constitutes the social system.

Language shares this function with other social semiotic systems: various forms of art, ritual decor and dress, and the like. Cultural meanings are realized through a great variety of symbolic modes, of which semantics is one; the semantic system is the linguistic mode of meaning. There is no need to insist that it is the "primary" one; I do not know what would be regarded as verifying such an assertion. But in important respects language is unique; particularly in its organization as a three-level coding system, with a lexicogrammar interposed between meaning and expression. It is this more than anything which enables language to serve both as a vehicle and as a metaphor, both maintaining and symbolizing the social system.

I do not mean by this that language provides a formal model for the representation of culture. As John Lyons pointed out in the context of a recent conference on communication studies (1973),

> ... the structuralist approach to non-linguistic material in terms of lower-level linguistic concepts would tend to support the view that there is a fundamental difference between linguistic and non-linguistic modes of communication. ... We cannot expect to be able to apply very much of the framework of concepts and categories established by linguists to non-linguistic material.

If we do find partial similarities between language and other symbolic systems having semiotic value in the culture, this may suggest that common functions determine common forms, but its significance lies in explaining how one symbolic system can serve as metaphor for another and is interpreted as such. For example, language has certain properties in common with games: it has tactic systems, or sets of rules; it requires the adoption and assignment of roles, based on turn-taking, and so on. Not surprisingly, the two can serve a similar social function; so we find verbal contexts alternating with contexts in other spheres. Compare also Mead's view of language and games as the two "social conditions under which the self arises as an object" (1934). But we are not projecting the form of language on to other semiotic systems; the link between them depends not on a common mathematics but on a common social function and social value.

83

In using language, we are both observing the environment and intruding on it. Nearly every utterance has both an ideational meaning, relating to the processes and things of the real world, and an interpersonal meaning, relating to the roles and attitudes adopted and assigned by the speaker. The semantic system is organized around this dual focus, of reflection and of action; and because it is so organized, it also stands as a metaphor for the culture, since culture is a construct of two environments, the natural and the social. Lévi-Strauss has stressed how the two are interlocked: the natural environment is a focus both of action and of reflection, and the social system is encoded in natural as well as in behavioural symbols. This interdependence is also both expressed and symbolized in language: to speak is to be both thinker and actor at the same time, and the two together define the act of meaning – which in turn has shaped the inner structure of the semantic system. Yet by the same token the act of meaning transcends this duality of thought and action. Let me quote here a passage from an article by Tambiah (1969), which makes the same point in quite another context, that of the study of animal classification systems. Discussing the problem of whether rules tend to accrue to animal species for symbolic or for pragmatic reasons – because they are 'thinkables' or because they are 'eatables', in Lévi-Strauss' mode of discourse – Tambiah concludes:

> Between Lévi-Strauss' sign-oriented intellectualism ... and Fortes' actor-oriented moralism ... lies scope for an imaginative reconstitution and reconciliation of the structural properties of symbolic systems quâ systems, and the effectiveness of symbols to bind individuals and groups to moral rules of conduct. Cultures and social systems are, after all, not only thought but also lived.

This I think provides a perspective for a humanistic interpretation of language. This is a very abstract conception; but it has practical consequences in explaining how language comes to symbolize the social structure, and thus social values come to be attached to linguistic forms. Let me cite a rather extreme example, that of Podgórecki's interpretation of the "second life" – the subculture, or anti-culture, of corrective and penal institutions which he has studied in Poland and in America. This "second life" takes the form of hierarchy which represents in symbolic form the social order of the world "outside"; it is ritualized through a "language" which appears to have as its primary function the maintenance of the social order of the second life, symbolically and through the regulation of behaviour. In Podgórecki's words (1973),

> The essence of the second life consists in a secular stratification which can be reduced to the division of the inmates into 'people' and 'suckers'. The 'people' are equal; they differ [only] in the degree of acceptance of the patterns of behaviour which are the second life rituals. ... The body of those rituals are called 'grypserka' (from 'grypa' – a slang word designating a letter smuggled secretly to or from a prison); Malkowski defined it as "the inmates' language and its grammar". In this language, certain ... words are insulting and noxious either to the speaker or to one to whom they are addressed.

It may be said that these are pathological phenomena, of no general interest. But only the most determined idealist would claim to distinguish clearly between the pathological and the normal; it is pointless to ignore the pathological aspects of the social system. The second life comes into existence in response to conditions created by the system; it also stands as a metaphor for the system, representing it as though projected into a closed shell. The anti-society is the society as it becomes when cut off from nature and openendedness and forced to close in on itself. A linguistic study of phenomena of this kind may shed new light on more familiar patterns of interaction and their relation to social structure.

In our concern with the rules of forms and the forms of rules, the social structure tends to be forgotten, and language is set apart from the linguistic community. But the linguistic community is an important component of a linguist's reality. In its traditional sense, as a linguistically homogeneous population linked together in a network of communication, it is an idealized construct to which probably no human group ever fully corresponds, and from which our modern urban social structure is very far removed. But whether we think in terms of the United States, or New York City, or the Lower East Side, we are still referring to what are in a real sense semiotic domains, entities throughout which meanings are exchanged in regular, socially defined contexts. A modern city is an elaborate cosmos of symbolic interaction in which language functions as a powerful and yet sensitive instrument for the fashioning of social life. The patterns of interaction recall in many ways the dialectic of society and anti-society, though without the sharp boundary which separates the two; between language and anti-language there is, rather, an uneasy continuum, in which the street gangs and criminal subcultures define one pole (Halliday 1976). In this sort of environment, the language of a social group that is under pressure, for example what Labov (1972) calls "BEV" (Black English

Vernacular), becomes a major factor in the definition and defence of that group's identity.

The linguistic "order" (to borrow the sense of "social order") in a complex society is closely bound up with variability in the linguistic system, our understanding of which is due first and foremost to the pioneering work of Labov. Wherever human behaviour is perceived as variable, social value tends to attach to the variants; and language is no exception. In many instances, the value assigned to a variant is simply the value assigned to the social group with which it is thought to be identified; this is the source of the "prestige form". From the point of view of language as system, the assignment is arbitrary: there is no intrinsic reason why $+/r/$ should be favoured over $-/r/$, or the other way round as the case may be. At other times, the value attaches to meanings, and here the effect is non-arbitrary. Semantic options, especially perhaps (though not only) those of an interpersonal kind, forms of address, politenesses and insults, modalities, and the like, mark not only individuals but also social groups: these too have their "meaning styles", as I expressed it earlier. Elements at other levels, syntactic, lexical, morphological and phonological, may become "foregrounded" through association with these semantic features, giving a sense of mutual reinforcement – what in the context of a literary work is called its "artistic unity", where in layman's terms 'the style (or the sound) suits the meaning'. An example is the social status of vocabulary derived from different sources: in English, Graeco-Romance words are associated with learning, and hence by a natural extension with pomposity and pretence (a "latinate" style). Either way, value-charged elements become available as coinage in verbal exchanges of all kinds; the speaker may "follow the rules", or he may play with them, bend them, and break them, as Sherzer has described. Gumperz' work brings this out strikingly in a number of different contexts (1971). Variation in language is a rich source of symbolism for the elaboration of the social structure.

Since in the main stream of linguistics language had been isolated from its social environment, work in this area came to be known by the somewhat self-conscious label of "sociolinguistics", the prefix suggesting that here, by contrast, language is studied in its natural environment. "Sociolinguistics" thus corresponds to what at other times and places has been called simply linguistics. It has led to some striking new linguistic insights, particularly in the interrelation of descriptive and historical theory. On the other hand, it has had little to

86

say about society; "nor", as Bickerton (1972) remarked, "has there been any stampede of sociologists into the linguistic corral, looking to see what there is for them there, as there has of educationists or philosophers".

It will not do, in the present context at any rate, to read too much into the "socio-". Most sociolinguistic studies still accept as given the linguist's own rather simple model of the social structure. They still concentrate on phonological and morphological indices; and they still assume a situational determinism based on a concept of style as something somehow separate from meaning. The next step is to see where language might suggest some new interpretations of the social structure; to work towards a social semantics which could explain patterns of social value in terms of more than the "prestige" of arbitrarily selected formal features; and to investigate the question of how the social system, as a whole, works through the linguistic system as a whole – which Hymes has referred to as the central problem for sociolinguistics in the immediate future.

Until this step is taken, the frame of reference for the discourse will continue to be the traditional subject-matter of linguistics. This is the basis of the definition of sociolinguistics as "the study of language in a social context", as distinct from "the study of language-and-society", perhaps again reflecting the prevailing "intra-organism" mode of thought in its reluctance to postulate a deeper social reality. Contrast in this respect the different and largely complementary conception of sociolinguistics to be found in the work of Bernstein (1971, 1973), directed towards a theory of society, but one in which language has a critical function as the effective channel of transmission of the social structure.

Bernstein's studies of socialization suggest how the semiotic patterns of culture and subculture perpetuate themselves in language, and how a child is drawn into the systems of social values in the course of, and as a concomitant of, learning his mother tongue. Among these value systems are those relating to language itself, and these carry with them a whole baggage of largely negative attitudes to which the child is exposed – it is over-simple to suggest that a child has no conception of linguistic inferiority other than that which he learns through school. These attitudes are prevalent in family and peer group. But they are sanctioned from beyond; and the authority that comes from the adult world is felt most strongly in the context of the third of the primary socializing agencies, the school.

Through the accumulation of debate and experiment in the education of non-standard speakers, it seems to emerge that it is no great burden on a child, or even an adult, to live with two (or more) dialects provided the conditions are not unfavourable. This is not surprising once one accepts that, in language, variation is the norm. Unfortunately, however, an environment of linguistic prejudice constitutes a very unfavourable condition; as Riegel expresses it (1973),

> Children raised under poor economic conditions ... are commonly also raised under the least favorable linguistic contingencies, those leading to confounded bilingualism. They are prevented from transferring knowledge in one language to the other because the two languages are not sufficiently separated. ... The first step to aid them has to consist in accepting the two languages, e.g. standard and non-standard English, as separated and equal.

Riegel's concept of separateness raises interesting questions of a different kind, that we cannot go into here; but on the equality issue there can be no hedging.

I think it is fair to claim as a positive achievement for linguistics its part in modifying the prevailing social attitudes to dialectal varieties. This is not to claim that the battle has been won. But those who have worked in an educational context over a period of time can testify to the increasing objectivity towards, and tolerance for, non-standard forms of speech; it seems to go hand in hand with a greater interest in and concern for the spoken language. There has been opposition, of course, both from within and from outside the academic community; there are those for whom the recognition of social value in non-standard speech is nothing but sentimental egalitarianism, as well as others who have seized on the idealizations of formal linguistics as a justification for worn-out perscriptivism – a move made easier for them by the prevailing but quite erroneous notion that casual speech is fragmentary and formless. It is fairly generally known, by now, that linguists have always insisted that the standard/non-standard distinction has to do not with language as a system but with language as an institution – it is a function solely of the relation between a language and its speakers – and that all forms of language are equally deserving of respect and attention. No other group than the linguists has consistently espoused and explained this position.

No one would wish to imply, therefore, that linguists everywhere have contracted out of the social system. But the participation of a group is not measured by the number of individuals in it who get their feet wet. We cannot divorce the social context of linguistics from its intellectual context; and it cannot be disputed that the profession as a whole has tended to dissociate itself from many questions of language that are of serious and understandable concern to laymen. We have disclaimed interest in questions of rhetoric; in socially weighted languages, such as those of politics and the law; in writing, journalism and the media; in technical languages and technical terminology; in translation and interpreting; and in the whole problem of evaluating and monitoring human communication. An example of what linguists are doing in these areas can be found in Ferguson's (1973) studies in the language of religion; but such studies are still rare. It is as if, far from struggling for social recognition, we have struggled to reject the recognition that society wants to thrust on to us, and the responsibility that goes with it. At an academic level we have wooed those disciplines which allowed us to maintain our own purity of thought; while the intellectual exchanges with other neighbouring disciplines, such as English, education, and rhetoric, have been minimal.

In short: linguistics has not yet faced up to the question of its social accountability. Social accountability is a complex notion which cannot be taken in from one angle alone. It is not defined as satisfying some abstract or symbolic entity such as a board of trustees, the business community or the taxpayer. Nor is it the same thing as satisfying our own individual consciences, which is a purely private luxury. There is an ideological component to it, which consists at least in part in eliminating some of the artificial disciplinary boundaries that we have inherited and continued to strengthen. At this level, many of the arguments lead back to this same point: that there are strong boundaries between academic disciplines, which hamper intellectual development, and induce both overspecialization and underapplication. Perhaps we need some "semi-revolutions" of the sort envisaged by Bennison Gray (1974), with his plea for unifying linguistics and rhetoric in a "semantic grammar". At any rate, in the human sciences, private conversations within one discipline seem to have outlived their usefulness; as Mary Douglas has said (1973),

> The specialists have had half a century to confer with their inner circle of initiates and to evolve rules of discourse appropriate to the fields they have hedged off. The time has come for a renewal of the original community and of the free-ranging conversation about the social basis of knowledge that it once enjoyed.

Nothing represents the unity and the social basis of knowledge better than language. Here "represents" is being used in both its senses: as I have tried to suggest all along, the linguistic system both realizes and symbolizes the social semiotic, of which academic knowledge is one part – to quote Mary Douglas again, "The time has come to treat everyday knowledge and scientific knowledge as a single field". The "truly comprehensive semiotic", which as envisaged by Maclean (1972) "must find its point of departure in a humanistic perspective upon social life", will have linguistics – or, at least, the study of language – as a vital component. In more concrete terms, if we are prepared to think of meaning as energy, and the exchange of meanings as the social creation of energy, linguistics can help to ensure that this energy is effectively released and that people come to achieve, much more than they are doing at present, their full potential as meaners.

But this role can be filled only by a linguistics "in the round", as I expressed it earlier, and unhampered by disputes over territoriality. Linguists cannot afford to absent themselves from the dialogue of disciplines; if they do, the study of language will simply go on without them. The public image of linguistics – one that unfortunately reflects the reality of some linguistics departments – is that it continues to be defined by a single interest and a single intellectual mould. Both the image and the reality are changing, especially as linguists reopen their contacts with teachers and educators. But there are many other avenues of public activity that have hardly begun to be explored.

This is partly, no doubt, because of our ignorance. How much do we yet know, for example, about linguistic interaction in the young children's peer group, and the part it plays in their construction of reality? Or about how a doctor or a politician or a poet makes language work for him? Or about why one example of speech or writing is judged more effective than another? But it is partly because we have not yet given up our right to put our chosen object, language, in its glass case and scrutinize it from just our own favourite angle. It has to be everyone else's idea of language that we look at, not just language as we choose to define it.

In this sense, the context for linguistics in the future is likely to be one in which linguistics in its present form as a social phenomenon ceases to exist. Society, language and mind are indissoluble: society creates mind, mind creates society, and language stands as mediator and metaphor for both these processes. That is the slogan. In terms of practicalities, provided there are still universities ten years from now, I am confident that there will still be students of language. I imagine they will have little patience with an academic distinction between language structure and language use; but they may be very much concerned with the concept of language and the social system – with the language of politics, education, religion, ideology; with language and poetry, cinema, theatre, music, dance; with the language of mathematics and science, and with how it differs from the language of literature or of everyday conversation. Also, I think, with the whole question of how people use language to learn, and to construct the various levels of reality by reference to which we define ourselves. These concerns, in turn, should enable theoretical linguists to see more deeply into the semantics of language, the systems of meaning with which we actually operate as a symbolic potential. In my opinion, this is an area which we have hardly yet begun to understand.

Chapter Four

IDEAS ABOUT LANGUAGE
(1977)

Linguistics may still be a fairly new name; but it is by no means a new phenomenon. The objective and systematic study of language (if we call this "scientific" linguistics, it will serve to distinguish it from the "folk" variety) was already under way in classical times – in Europe, in China, and above all in ancient India. One of the greatest of our predecessors is the Indian scholar Pāṇini, who lived, probably, in the fifth century B.C. Of Pāṇini's Sanskrit grammar, Robins remarked that it "manifestly came at the end and as the culmination of a long line of previous work of which we have no direct knowledge". And while the linguistic insights of ancient Greece do not perhaps attain the same high level of sophistication as those of India, there too there must lie behind them a long period of speculation about the nature and evolution of language.

In this perspective, of more than 2,000 years of linguistic enquiry (and there have been remarkably few gaps in the tradition), it is hardly surprising that all of us have rather explicit ideas about language. The folk linguistics of western man now contains various technical terms such as noun and verb; and even elaborated concepts like participle and preposition, active and passive, imperative and subjunctive find their way into everyday conversation. It must be admitted that they are not always elegantly used. A friend of mine in the public service once drafted a letter for his head of department to sign, only to have it returned for correction. In it, he had written "As soon as the contract is ready we will send you a copy of it"; this had been amended to "we will send you a copy of same". Incensed by this barbarism, my friend complained; to which the senior official replied, in tones of shocked reproof, "But you can't end a sentence with a proposition!"

First published in *Occasional Papers* I, 1977, pp. 32–55.

Much of our adult folk linguistics is no more than misremembered classroom grammar (or was, in the days when there still was classroom grammar); it may be wrong, but it is anything but naïve. If therefore we want to find out what it is that people know about language simply by virtue of the fact that they speak, we have to go back a little farther; and since we cannot go back in the history of the culture, at least not back to ultimate beginnings, we will go back for a brief excursion in the history of the individual. What does a child know about language before his insights are contaminated by theories of the parts of speech?

The earliest linguistic terms an English-speaking child learns to use are not terms like *noun* and *verb*, or even *word* and *sentence*; in fact they are not nouns at all – they are verbs, typically *say* and *mean*, and shortly afterwards *tell*. So for example Nigel, at 1 year 8 months, told the story of what happened on a visit to the children's zoo. He had been stroking a goat, while in his other hand clutching a plastic lid he had picked up somewhere; the goat worked its way round so that it could nibble at the lid, but the keeper took it away. Here is Nigel's account:

> goat try eat lìd ... man said nò ... goat shòuldn't eat lid ... (shaking head) gòodfor it.

'The goat tried to eat the lid. The man said "No. The goat shouldn't eat the lid – not good for it."' A child must understand a great deal about the nature of language to be able to report speech in this way. He must have internalised the concept of an act of meaning – of speech as symbolic action, distinct from but interdependent with acts of a non-symbolic kind. And when we look more closely, we find that he can already report acts of meaning before he has an explicit verb *say* with which to do so. Here is Nigel at 1 year 7 months. A kite had fallen and its string lay stretched along the ground; his father had warned him not to trip over it. Nigel recalled the incident later, saying

> qài ... "qài ... māiṇʰ tìŋ"

Translated into adult, Nigel's sentence meant, '(there was a) kite, (and Daddy said "there's a) kite, mind (the) string".' Already for Nigel at a year and a half, saying is a part of experience; like other actions and events, it can be observed, recalled and narrated.

By 1 year 9 months Nigel has distinguished 'saying' from 'meaning'. He is told to keep away from a friendly dog, and reports:

> lady said "don't touch Pènny; not feeling wèll"

This contrasts with:

"lailai ... lailai" ... Ì don' know lailai méan
"trȳget èvl" ... what that méan?

He also has a clear concept of 'naming', which is the converse of meaning. Once again, the concept is developed long before it gets a name, and Nigel progresses towards it through various stages: at 10 months, dɔ̀ 'let's look at this together' (togetherness through shared experience); at 13 months, æ̀ ::: dæ̀'let's look at this – you say its name!'; at 16 months, adʸdà 'tell me its name!'; at 20 months, *whát thàt*, and at 24 months, *what's that cálled?*

By the time he is two years old, a child has a considerable awareness of the nature and functions of language. When he starts to talk, he is not only using language; he is also beginning to talk **about** it. He is constructing a folk linguistics, in which (i) saying, and (ii) naming-meaning, denote different aspects of the same symbolic act. And language functions for him both in reflection and in action: as a way of thinking about the world (including about himself), structuring his experience and expressing his own personality, and as a way of acting on the world, organizing the behaviour of others and getting them to provide the goods-and-services he wants. The one thing he does not do with language at this stage is to impart information. In fact – and despite the predominance of this motif in adult **thinking about** language – the imparting of information never does become the unique primary **function** of language even among adults (except perhaps those who do it for a living).

Soon, however, the child will go to school; and once he is there, his ideas about language will be superseded by the folk linguistics of the classroom, with its categories and classes, its rules and regulations, its do's and, above all, its don'ts. Here a fundamental ideological change takes place in the child's image of language – and, through this, in his image of reality. Up till now, language has been seen as a resource, a potential for thinking and doing; he has talked about it in verbs, verbs like *call* and *mean, say* and *tell*, and *rhyme*. From now on, language will be not a set of resources but a set of rules. And the rules are categorical – they operate on things; so he must talk about language in nouns, like *word* and *sentence*, and *noun* and *verb*, and *letter*.

It would be wrong to suggest, however, that the image of language as resource is totally submerged and lost. Unlike the linguistics of the classroom, which is codified (organized as a cultural institution), and so conscious and explicit, the linguistics of the family and neighbourhood, though it is *coded* (organized semantically), is not codified; it is partly implicit ("covert", in Whorf's terminology), and so below the level of conscious awareness. For this reason it has considerable staying power; and the adult, however much he may traffic in categories and rules, and sentences ending in propositions, and all the niceties of verbal etiquette which show how well he was brought up, retains some insights of the earlier kind, and even adds to them in the course of his everyday informal discourse, a great deal of which is talk about talk. So when we say "I know what he means. But he could have worded it differently." we are showing an awareness of language as a multiple coding system, in which meanings are coded or expressed in wordings; we also know that the wordings are in turn expressed, or recoded, in speech (and, in some languages, in writing); and this is exactly what the linguist means when he says in more ponderous terms that language is a tristratal system consisting of a semantics, a lexicogrammar, and a phonology. The committee man who says about some resolution that we should "keep the meaning, but change the wording" is expressing the folk linguistic insight that the coding is not one-to-one; it is always possible to change how you say what you mean – though, in fact, as he would probably admit, the meaning that results is never **exactly** the same as it was before.

So we have enshrined in our folk linguistics these two views, one of language as resource, the other of language as rule. The two co-exist; but since one is a product of our primary socialization, and belongs to the reality that is learnt at our mother's knee, while the other is part of a secondary reality and belongs to the realm of organized knowledge, they impinge on each other scarcely at all. But in our prevailing ideology, the dominant model is that of language as rule (our schools teach the formal grammar of logic, not the functional grammar of rhetoric); and it is only when we come across the writings of those with a different vision of language, like Malinowski, Hjelmslev and Whorf, or alternatively when we make a deliberate effort to change the prevailing image, as some teachers and educators are trying to do, that the notion of language as resource surfaces from our unconscious and we begin to build on the insights that we possess by virtue of this simple fact, observed from the moment of birth (if not before), but so easily forgotten by the philosophers of language, that people talk to each other.

It is in this light that we should look for a moment at the earliest traditions of linguistics in the West. We do not know, of course, what went on before the development of writing; many non-literate cultures have extensive folk taxonomies for different types of speech event and the social values which accrue to them (see Bauman and Sherzer (1975), for descriptions of Tzeltal, Mayan, Maori, Iroquois, etc.) and it is not unlikely that language was a topic of systematic explorations in early pre-classical times, with what Peter Minkus calls "campfire grammars" as a forum of linguistic ideas. The amount of attention given to language by Plato (Plato often uses language as a source of his analogies; there are also systematic observations on it in the *Sophist* and elsewhere, and the *Cratylus* is wholly devoted to language – it is an elaborate etymological fantasy, which Socrates is made to offer with some embarrassment) suggests that a great deal of intellectual discussion of language went on in fifth-century Athens. We can only guess what forms it took. Far too little is known of the work of Protagoras and the sophists, and what is known comes largely from their detractors; but from these slender indications, it seems likely that it is they who were the originators of systematic linguistics in the West. According to Diogenes Laertius, Protagoras identified the basic speech functions of statement, question, command and wish; these were what formed the basis for the first steps in grammatical analysis.

The sophists were concerned with rhetoric; with the nature of argumentation, and hence with the structure of discourse. We know that they were familiar with elementary grammatical categories like number and gender. We do not know how far they took the analysis of sentence structure. But it seems likely that the insight recorded by Plato in the *Sophist*, that a piece of discourse consists of two parts, ὄνομα and ῥῆμα, was their achievement. This was an analysis of a unit of discourse considered as something that is **arguable**, something that can be maintained, denied, disputed, contradicted, doubted and urged. It was **not** an analysis in terms of logical structure, and it said nothing whatever about truth value. What then would be the meaning of ὄνομα and ῥῆμα in such a context? Here is how Plato introduces these terms, in the *Sophist*. Stranger: "There are two modes of the expression of existing things in sound ... That which is an expression for actions we call ῥῆμα. The vocal sign for those who do the things, is the ὄνομα." And later, "If we combine ῥήματα with ὀνόματα, we are not only naming; we are doing something (οὐκ ὀνομάζει μόνον, ἀλλά τι περáίνει)." And finally "Discourse (λόγος) must be about something; it cannot be not about anything (λόγον ἀναγκαῖον ... τινός εἶναι λόγον, μηδέ τινος ἀδύνατον) – otherwise it is not discourse (οὐκ ἐστι λόγος)". The Stranger gives an example: "I will say a piece of discourse to you, in which a thing and an action are combined, by means of ὄνομα and ῥῆμα; you tell me who the discourse is about ... *Theaetetus is sitting* ... Who does this discourse speak of?" And Theaetetus answers, "Of me. It is about me."

There are three distinct and important steps here. First, there is the identification of two grammatical classes based on meaning, on semantic function: verb, expressing (an) action, and noun, expressing (the) actor; the two combine to make up a piece of discourse. Here verb and noun are the names of **classes** (categories), but they are defined by their *functions*, functions in transitivity – in the linguistic representation of actions and events; and, naturally, the verb is identified first, the noun being then derived from it. Secondly, discourse must be **about** something; so the noun also functions as 'what the discourse is about'. Plato does not label this function; Jowett translates using the term "subject", but it is not subject in the later Aristotelian sense, from which we get subject-predicate analysis; it is rather what in modern linguistics is called "theme". A discourse must have a theme. Thirdly, once we form discourse, by combining words into structures, we are not just naming: we are accomplishing (ἀλλά τι περάινει). Discourse is a mode of doing: whoever says something, does something.

It is this last point in particular which makes it probable that the theory derives from the sophists. The immediate context is, of course, a refutation of sophist theory, especially sophistical relativism; the Stranger goes on to relate discourse to the question of truth. But the view of language is a rhetorical one. A sentence has a theme; this is what makes it arguable – gives it the potential for being stated, refuted, queried and so on. And stating, refuting, querying – all these are forms of action. The Platonic model of language, in this respect, seems to have remained very close to sophist thought.

The next steps we know of were taken by Aristotle, and with Aristotle the picture of language undergoes a drastic change. Aristotle was above all a logician. In the controversy about the arbitrariness of language – whether the relation of language to the real world of experience was natural or conventional – where Protagoras had emphasized language as natural symbol and Plato (in the mouth of Socrates) had allowed for both possibilities, Aristotle opted explicitly for the conventionalist viewpoint. Names arise solely by "contract" or convention: τό δέ κατά συνθήκην, ὅτι φύσει τῶν ὀνομάτων οὐδέν ἐστιν, ἀλλ' ὅταν γενήται σύμβολον (*On Interpretation* II, 16a.27); nothing is by its nature a name. Out of the earlier notion of λόγος as connected speech or discourse has evolved the concept of 'sentence', which likewise has meaning by convention: ἐστι δέ λόγος ἄπας μεν σημαντικός, οὐχ ὡς ὄργανον δέ, ἀλλ' ὡς προείρηται, κατά συνθήκην (*ibid.* IV, 17a.1). The sentence is made up of parts – the expression μέρος λόγου, 'part or component of the sentence' (the term which was later mistranslated into English via Latin, as **parts of speech**) although it is not I think found as a technical term in Aristotle, derives from his terminology; each of these parts has meaning by itself, but only when the parts are combined do they form a judgement such that one can say whether it is true or false. It is the sentence as bearer of truth value – the proposition – with which Aristotle is primarily concerned. Other types of sentence, such as prayers, he admits to be meaningful; but he considers that, since they lack truth value, they belong to the province of rhetoric or poetics (*ibid.* IV, 17a.5).

So ὄνομα and ῥῆμα become the components of a proposition; and the proposition is then redefined in terms of subject and predicate, as the functions in a premiss. But subject and predicate are **logical** concepts; they have to be clearly distinguished from the **linguistic** elements which enter into these logical relations. As a consequence, the linguistic element come to be reinterpreted purely as classes – as lists of linguistic items (τά λεγομένα). In other words, since linguistic *functions* are being treated as logical, the analysis of language itself (i.e. grammar) becomes purely *formal*, something to be stated in terms of classes not of functions. Hence the Aristotelian image of language is that it is a set of constituent structure rules. In the *Poetics* Aristotle enumerates the units of discourse, including letters (the ultimate constituents – in fact sound units, as in the English sense of letter in the sixteenth to eighteenth centuries), syllables, conjunctions, articles, nouns, verbs, affixes and sentences; and he defines these units in terms of rules for their combination (*Poetics* 1456^b – 1458^a].

This is a long way from the sophists' ideas about language, and even from Plato's. The sophists saw language as a resource; as a mode of action and a means of putting things across to others. They were concerned with meaning, but not with truth value; if language had any relation to truth this lay in its ability to demonstrate that truth was relative to the believer, and that there was another side to whatever question was at issue. Aristotle saw language as a set of rules; as a mode of judgement and a means of affirming and denying, without reference to other people. He was concerned with truth value, and hence subordinated language to the structure of logic.

So in the earliest flourish of western linguistics we can trace the source of our original metaphor. In the way a child growing up in our culture develops his ideas about language, in the folk linguistics of home and school, we can recognize these two distinct cognitive styles. The child's shift of perspective, from an unconscious awareness of language as doings, as a way of achieving by acting on others, to a conscious scrutiny of language as norms, or rulings, has its counterpart in the shift of perspective from language as rhetoric to language as logic in the ideology of the ancient Greeks.

The changed conception of grammatical structure, from a config- uration of functions defined **within** language to a bracketing of constituents representing functions defined **outside** language (in logic), symbolizes the beginnings of a split between ethnographic and philosophical linguistics which has persisted to the present day.

We can follow these two strands throughout the subsequent history of ideas about language in the west. The one stems from Aristotle; it is "analogist" in character, based on the concept of language as rule, and it embeds the study of language in philosophy and logic. The other has, for us today, less clearly defined origins, but it can probably be traced to Protagoras and the sophists, via Plato; it is "anomalist" in character, and has a marked element of Stoic thought in it. It is not philosophical (the Stoics were the earliest scholars explicitly to separate linguistics from philosophy, and grammar from logic) but rather descriptive or, to use another term, ethnographic; and the organizing concept is not that of **rule** but of **resource**.

Let me try to summarize these two traditions, as they have persisted through the ages. In doing so, I shall inevitably be grossly over- simplifying; in particular I would disclaim any suggestion that every school, every scholar and every work must belong squarely to one tradition or the other. Most of them combine ideas, in various measure, from both. But this may perhaps give some impression of a pattern that is to be found recurring throughout the history of ideas about language in western thought.

We can identify, broadly, two images of language: a philosophical- logical view, and a descriptive-ethnographic view. In the former, linguistics is part of philosophy, and grammar is part of logic; in the latter, linguistics is part of anthropology, and grammar is part of culture. The former stresses analogy; is prescriptive, or normative, in orienta- tion; and concerned with meaning in relation to truth. The latter stresses anomaly; is descriptive in orientation; and concerned with meaning in relation to rhetorical function. The former sees language as thought, the latter sees language as action. The former represents language as rules; it stresses the formal analysis of sentences, and uses for purposes of idealization (for deciding what falls within or outside its scope) the criterion of grammaticality (what is, or is not, according to the rule). The latter represents language as choices, or as a resource; it stresses the semantic interpretation of discourse, and uses for idealization purposes the criterion of acceptability or usage (what occurs or could be envisaged to occur).

The degree and kind of idealization involved is a key point of difference between the two perspectives. In philosophical linguistics the level is set very high; language has to be reduced as nearly as possible to an artificial logical language – hence the improbable examples used by philosophical grammarians, such as the famous *Socrates albus currit bene* 'white Socrates runs well' of medieval modistic grammar. Ethnographic linguistics, by contrast, keeps as close as possible to real language, spoken or written; when the linguist has to construct examples, he takes care to make them convincing.

It does not seem very difficult to discern that the two views are in no way contradictory. Yet they are often made to appear so. Throughout the history of western linguistics they have drifted now closer, now further apart; the last two decades has seen a very sharp polarization between them, but now the gap is closing once again. For most of the time the dominant strand has been the philosophical one. It appears in medieval linguistics in the theories of the Modistae, who laid the foundations of formal syntax; in their successors the French "rationalist" school of Port-Royal, with its Aristotelian conception of scientific knowledge; and in the Chomskyan structuralist-transformationalist theory of today. Philosophers of language tend to have a very explicit view of the nature of a theory, and of what constitute valid modes of reasoning; they tend to dismiss the ethnographers as non-theoretical, because their theories are not of the right kind. Chomsky's dismissal of Hockett for being right for the wrong reason is strikingly reminiscent of Aristotle's dismissal of the sophists for knowing things in an 'accidental' way. Both formulations mean simply that the two ideologies differ as regards what they consider to be an explanation.

Ideologically, philosophical linguists tend to be absolutists, while ethnographic linguists tend to relativists. The relativists of the ancient world were of course the sophists, who held that truth was relative to the time, the place and the individual subject; but this was a general philosophical outlook. Relativism as a specifically **linguistic** viewpoint appears only in the modern post-Renaissance period, when linguists first began to describe more than one language. Describing different languages is a relatively recent preoccupation; and with it the difference of ideology appears in a new guise, as an issue between language universals and language variables. When languages come to be seriously compared with one another, the question arises: are all languages alike, or are they different?

Presumably everyone agrees that there are certain respects in which all languages are alike. All languages consist of meanings, wordings and sounds; they all have names for things; they all have melody, rhythm and syllabic articulation. Equally, everyone agrees that there are certain respects in which languages differ: not only do they obviously have different names for things, they also construct these names differently, have different kinds of melody and rhythm, and different ways of wording and of sounding. The issue is, simply, which is to be the more emphasized, the uniformity or the variety. This is really the old "analogy-anomaly" controversy metaphorized into a modern form; but it is a critical issue. Philosophers of language stress the universals; they make all languages look alike. Ethnographers stress the variables; they make all languages look different. When new languages came to be described by European linguists, from the early seventeenth century onwards, first the modern European languages and then languages from further afield, both these two opposing tendencies became apparent. Either every language is treated as a version of Latin, or each language is described in its own terms.

The consequences of this are still with us today. Transformational linguistics made extreme claims about universals. Since these claims were couched in terms of a formal theory, they could not be empirically invalidated: if, for example, it is claimed that in all languages the subject precedes the predicate (the prior assumption being of course that all languages have subject and predicate), then if a language turns up in which the subject follows the predicate all one need do is to set up an abstract representation in which the subject precedes the predicate and derive the other one from it. This is a harmless enough exercise. What is not harmless, however, is the nature of the chosen universals. The features to which this universal status is assigned are largely features of English, which has replaced Latin as the huntingfield of philosophical linguists; or at best features of what Whorf called "Standard Average European". They are not any longer the crude and easily penetrated absurdities of a century ago, when the pluperfect subjunctive was likely to be foisted on to a language such as Indonesian or Chinese; they are much more subtly disguised – but they are European all the same. Modern philosophical linguistics is distressingly ethnocentric. It presents all languages as peculiar versions of English. In this situation it is not enough for the ethnographers simply to go on with their own work, of describing each language in its own terms. This cuts no ice at all. What they need to do perhaps is to turn the tables – to describe English in terms of categories derived from other languages, to interpret it as a peculiar version of Chinese, or Hopi, or Pitjantjatjara. With an effort of this kind universal linguistics might come to be freed from ethnocentricity and begin to make a serious contribution to the understanding of human cultures.

It is not easy to penetrate under the skin of another language, especially one from a culture that is very remote from one's own. On the surface, of course, there should be no problem, since whatever meanings are expressed in the other language can also be expressed in one's own, allowing for the invention of new names where necessary. But what matters most in a language is not what **can be** expressed but what **is**; and even more, what is coded – what meanings are systematized, and how these meanings are organised in their contrasts and combinations. Structural descriptions of sentences do no more than scratch the surface of language, and even here the very strength of the philosophers' insights into logical structures has distracted attention from the real nature of structural relations in language.

Our linguistics today is still very close to a folk science. We have progressed very little, in these two-and-a-half thousand years, from common sense everyday knowledge. Even our interpretations of the best described languages of our own culture are very limited in scope, and still more limited in imaginative power. In this context it is interesting to see what happened in the sixteenth century when western linguists first found themselves faced with exotic languages, and what was the impact of this on their own ideas about language. What happened, for example, when they were faced with the writing system of Chinese?

Perhaps the greatest single instance of the folk linguistic genius is the evolution of writing. In order for a language to be written down (to be "reduced" to writing, in the very appropriate folk linguistic metaphor), it must at the same time have been analysed to a rather sophisticated level. In modern times this is often a conscious process, as happens when missionaries or other language planners design alphabets for unwritten languages; but in the past it was usually unconscious, the cumulative effect of a number of small steps taken over a long period of time. In the course of this process (unlike the conscious efforts, which are often subject to the fads and fashions of linguistics of the time), a language usually gets the sort of writing system it deserves. So in the ancient world languages with rather tight syllabic structure tended to develop syllabaries; those with looser syllabic structure ended up with alphabets; and those with consonantal roots, the Semitic ones, evolved something in between the two. Of course the process is often affected by historical accidents; once a writing system evolves it takes on a life of its own and can be borrowed by others. Such 'accidents' range from trivial distortions like the demise of Old English "thorn" (the *th* sign), which the Norman scribes could not write, to massive effects such as the adoption of the Chinese writing system for Japanese, a language to which it was quite inappropriate. Interestingly, Japanese ended up with a script which, though extremely complicated, represented rather well the complex pattern of language that resulted from large-scale borrowing – a symbiosis of two very different sub-systems, one indigenous and the other imported from Chinese.

Chinese is unusual in having a phonological structure that is not well suited either to syllabic or to alphabetic writing; the only natural analytic unit is the hemisyllable, and this did form the basis of Chinese phonological theory, in which the primary elements were 'initial' and 'rhyme'. But Chinese is very well suited to another kind of writing system altogether, one in which the written symbol represents, not any unit of sound but a unit of wording, the morpheme. The morpheme (it has no non-technical name in English, though it has of course in Chinese) is the elementary particle of lexicogrammar, the thing out of which words are built (the English word *kindness* consists of two morphemes, *kind* and *ness*). Chinese writing is morphemic. For a language like English, a morphemic script would be a monstrosity; but for Chinese it works very well. Now in classical Chinese, unlike the modern language, most **words** consisted of only one morpheme; so, taking the script as the representation of the classical language, which was the language of most written texts up to this century, it is not too far out to interpret it in terms of western categories as a word-symbolizing, or "logographic" script ("lexigraphic" would be more accurate). One thing that it is **not** is ideographic; indeed the notion of an ideographic script is self-contradictory, since a visual communication

103

system becomes a script only when its symbols are mapped on to the elements of a language, and ideas are not linguistic elements. Ideographic symbols belong to that stage in the evolution of writing before it has **become** writing, though of course people may always continue to use ideograms for a range of special purposes.

European scholars knew nothing of Chinese writing until the mid-sixteenth century. At that time, reports and specimens of it began to filter through (see Firth 1946; reprinted in Firth 1957d: 92–120, esp. 104 n. 3). The problem of understanding what kind of a script it was presented an unfamiliar challenge to their ideas about language.

In 1588 Timothy Bright published his book *Characterie, an arte of shorte, swifte and secrete writing by character*. In it he put forward a new writing system, or "charactery", a highly original venture out of which two distinct intellectual traditions were to emerge, one of shorthand, the other of "universal character". Introducing his system, Bright related it to an interpretation of Chinese writing: "Upon consideration of the great use of such a kind of writing, I have invented the like: ... every character answering a word" (Firth 1957d: 103). Bright's interpretation of the nature of the Chinese script was essentially right.

In contrast with Bright's formulation "every character answering a word" is the following account by Francis Bacon written some fifteen years later in the *Advancement of Learning* (1605): "the Chinese write in characters real, which express neither letters nor words, ... but things or notions". Bacon's interpretation was wrong.

Matteo Ricci, the Jesuit scholar and missionary to China, wrote in his *Journals 1583–1610*, published in Latin translation in 1615, "[in Chinese] every word, just as every object, is represented by its own ideograph, or symbol, used to represent a thought ... every object has its own appropriate symbol" (Ricci, trans. by Gallagher 1953: 27). Ricci seems to have been uncertain, though inclined towards the wrong interpretation.

So Bright's original insight was lost, and a mistaken view of the nature of the Chinese script became part of western folklore about China. It is intriguing to find the same issue raised over 200 years later in a lengthy dispute between the American philosopher Peter du Ponceau, who published *A Dissertation on the Nature and Character of the Chinese System of Writing* (Philadelphia, 1838), and Samuel Kidd, the first Professor of Chinese in the University of London, whose book *China, or Illustrations of the Symbols, Philosophy, Antiquities, Customs, Superstitions, Laws, Government, Education and Literature of the Chinese* appeared in London in 1841.

Kidd expressed himself somewhat sarcastically at du Ponceau's expense; but in fact du Ponceau was right (he actually used the term "lexigraphic"), while Kidd was simply repeating the folk view of Chinese writing which prevailed, then as now, in the west (Firth 1949, reprinted in Firth 1957d: 156–72, esp. 163; Halliday, this volume, p. 55.

Not surprisingly, the folk linguistics of Chinese provides an unambiguous clue to the nature of the Chinese script. Just as, in English folk terminology, the word *letter* meant the written symbol **and** what it stands for in the language (an element in the sound system, roughly a morphophoneme) so in Chinese the term *zi* means both the written symbol (the character) **and** what it stands for in the language (in this case a morpheme – Chinese folk linguistics contains no term for 'word'). But the Europeans did not have the advantage of knowing Chinese, let alone Chinese linguistics. They lacked certain relevant information, such as the fact that Chinese characters have unambiguous readings, that synonyms are not written alike, and so on. So if Bright's insight was lost, this was partly through lack of evidence. More significant, however, was the fact that the ideographic fallacy fitted in perfectly with the mainstream of humanist thinking about language.

We must try to put ourselves back in the context of those times (Salmon 1966). The demise of Latin had left Europe without a lingua franca, just at a time when one was most needed; people were, obviously, going to speak in their own tongues, and the hope was that at least a written language might be found that was truly international. As Robert Boyle put it in a letter to Samuel Hartlib in 1646, "I conceive no impossibility that opposes the doing that in words that we already see done in numbers" – in other words, we write a figure 5 but read it *cinque* or *cinq* or *fünf* or *five*; why should we not write a unified symbol for tree and read it *albero* or *arbre* or *Baum* or *tree*, with everyone (in Cave Beck's words) "reading out of one common language their own mother tongue"? It seemed a reasonable goal.

But there was much more at issue than the need for international communication. The deeper concern was with the nature of knowledge itself, and in particular the nature of systematic organized or scientific knowledge. The demand for a "universal character" was a quest for the 'universal' in the medieval sense of a universal order of things, for a system of all there is to be known. The early humanist linguists inherited an intellectual tradition which contained, over and above the christianized Aristotelian philosophy and Ptolemaic cosmology of the establishment, a rich assortment of less reputable sources, including the art of memory and its associated cosmological theories. The medieval art of memory goes back to Simonides and the rhetoricians, who evolved it as a mnemonic device, the use of images as a way of remembering complicated lists of facts, as was necessary for example in the conduct of a lawsuit; but it had become interpenetrated with the hermetic tradition, with cabbalist and other mystical systems, and so tended to be regarded with some suspicion by the spiritual authorities. These systems introduced not only elements of sorcery, in which verbal magic played an important part, but also cosmologies which challenged the established view. Giordano Bruno, whose *Shadows of Ideas* and *Art of Memory* were imaginative developments of the thirteenth century *Grand Art* of Raymond Lully, with its Homeric "golden chain" linking all things to each other and heaven to earth, was burnt as a heretic in Rome in 1600 (Yates 1964). Other well-known examples at the time were the "memory theatre" of Giulio Camillo, and the "method" of Peter Ramus (Pierre de la Ramée) (Ong 1958). Ramus rejected the classical use of images as the basis of memory, regarding it as accidental and unsystematic, and took the art of memory out of rhetoric into logic, where "every subject was arranged in 'dialectical order'" – that is, taxonomically (Yates 1966: 232). Frances Yates writes of him (*ibid*: 234):

> Though many surviving influences of the old art of memory may be detected in the Ramist "method" of memorizing through dialectical order, yet he deliberately gets rid of its most characteristic feature, the use of the imagination. No more will places in churches or other buildings be vividly impressed on the imagination. And, above all, gone in the Ramist system are the images, the emotionally striking and stimulating images the use of which had come down through the centuries from the art of the classical rhetor. The "natural" stimulus for memory is now not the emotionally exciting memory image; it is the abstract order of dialectical analysis, which is yet, for Ramus, "natural", since dialectical order is natural to the mind.

Not surprisingly, Giordano Bruno thought Ramus another arch-pedant, like Aristotle, and he attacked them both vigorously.

So the new scientific mode of thought was expected to pursue the same goal that had fired the medieval imagination, that of providing the golden chain, the key to the organization of knowledge. And such a venture needed a systematic notation. This was where the significance of the Chinese script came in. The seventeenth-century philosophical grammarians, men like Cave Beck, Francis Lodowick, Samuel Hartlib,

Seth Ward and above all George Dalgarno and John Wilkins in England (many of them founder members of the Royal Society), as well as Mersenne in Paris, Bisterfeld at Weissenberg and, subsequently, Leibniz, who faced the problem of organizing, codifying and transmitting scientific knowledge, saw this clearly as a linguistic problem: knowledge was organized and stored in symbols. But they also inherited an immense suspicion of ordinary language, which in prevailing humanist ideology was regarded as at best arbitrary and at worst downright deceitful. Bacon had been one of the fiercest critics of language, deploring "the false appearances that are imposed upon us by words". Vivian Salmon comments: "It is difficult to say when this distrust of words first appeared" (1966: 386); but it is a recurrent theme of humanist scholarship. In part, no doubt, it was a reaction against what were regarded as the excesses of late medieval grammar, which like other aspects of medieval scholarship tended to become rather rarefied: the University of Paris had attempted to proscribe the teaching of grammar in 1515 (the year Ramus was born). But it was also a deeply felt attitude to language itself.

Words were dangerous; not only because they were ambiguous, and led to strife, though this is a familiar complaint, but also because they were seductive. They presented a false appearance of reality, and had to be cleared out of the way so as to expose the true reality which lay beyond. Scientific endeavour could be advanced only by attending to **things**, and to the logic of the relations between things: by observation, not by talk. Ideally it should have been possible to do away with words altogether, and put things in their place; and this must have been a contemporary impression of what it was that was being propounded, because the attitude is caricatured by Swift. In the *Voyage to Lagado* Gulliver visits the School of Languages, where he finds

> ... a Scheme for abolishing all Words whatsoever ... since Words are only Names for *Things*, it would be more convenient for all Men to carry about them, such *Things* as were necessary to express the particular Business they are to discourse on.

> *Gulliver's Travels*, Collins edn (1953: 203–4)

The passage continues:

> And this Invention would certainly have taken place, to the great Ease as well as Health of the Subject, if the Women in Conjunction with the Vulgar and Illiterate had not threatened to raise a Rebellion, unless they might be allowed the Liberty to speak with their Tongues, after the

Manner of their Forefathers: Such constant and irreconcileable Enemies to Science are the common People.

Since, however, we have to put up with words, the best we can do is to reduce their arbitrariness. Words should match things, in some way or other representing their true nature. For this purpose, a "universal character" (that is, a writing system) was not enough; there had to be constructed a new "philosophical language" in which words would represent things in some natural, non-arbitrary manner. This is a recurrent aspiration of those who reflect on language – the hope of finding some natural connection between meanings and sounds; it is one of the two opposing views on linguistic evolution that are put forward by Plato in the *Cratylus*. It is often ridiculed by linguists, who insist (rightly) on the essential arbitrariness to be found at this point in the system. Yet it is less absurd than it might seem – there can be varying degrees of non-arbitrariness built in to the linguistic coding process. One of those who thought it possible to create such a connection was Mersenne, who searched for precedents in existing languages in the form of what today would be called "phonaesthetic" patterns, where a particular sound is regularly associated with a particular area of meaning, like the *-ump* in *hump, bump, lump, rump, plump, stump* and *clump*. Phonaesthetic series display a kind of non-arbitrariness, and they happen to be a particular characteristic of English. Nevertheless it is difficult to create a whole vocabulary along these lines; and what those who were inventing new languages in fact set out to do was to construct words so that they reflected the relations between things (the "dialectic order" of Ramus). This is a notable feature of the two most successful philosophical languages that were actually constructed, those by George Dalgarno (*Ars Signorum*, 1661) and Bishop John Wilkins (*An Essay towards a Real Character and a Philosophical Language*, 1668). It did not seem to occur to the proponents of such schemes, however, that there was any conflict between this activity of inventing new languages, which if successful would have required considerable time to be spent in learning them, and the desire to avoid wasting time on language, expressed for example by Bishop Wilkins himself in what he had written a quarter of a century earlier: "that great part of our time which is now required to the learning of words might then be employed in the study of things" (*Mercury, or the Swift and Secret Messenger*, 1641).

Most of the "real character" projects stopped short of constructing words – that is, of giving phonetic values to the symbols, and rules for their combination; but they did represent conscious attempts at a universal symbolism, with (in the words of Seth Ward) "symbols . . . for every *thing* and *notion*". And this idea is in a direct line of descent from the classical and medieval memory systems. Frances Yates comments (1966: 378):

> . . . a whole group of writers . . . laboured to found universal languages on "real characters" . . . The universal languages are thought of as aids to memory and in many cases their authors are obviously drawing on the memory treatises. And it may be added that the search for "real character" comes out of the memory tradition on its occult side. The seventeenth-century universal language enthusiasts are translating into rational terms efforts such as those of Giordano Bruno to found universal memory systems on magic images which he thought of as directly in contact with reality.

And when Leibniz formed his project for the "Characteristica", a universal language with a calculus associated with it, he explicitly referred to the Cabbalist and Lullist systems, as well as to Chinese writing, which he described as pictographic and "in the nature of memory images". (Despite the interest in pictographic symbols, and in the "natural" relation between words and things, it is noteworthy that the characteries that were actually devised – including the earliest, that of Timothy Bright – showed little tendency to employ iconic symbols, pictorial or otherwise. The symbols themselves were entirely abstract and conventional. What was 'natural' was their taxonomic arrangement into primary signs, for genera, and secondary signs and diacritics for the descending subcategories.)

As a systematization of all knowledge, Wilkins' monumental universal language must be counted a failure. It was not a description of knowledge at all. But it was a description of meaning. It was in fact a brilliant essay in lexical semantics, revealing the principles on which languages organize names for things. As such it had a considerable impact on our ideas about language – not least because it was the basis on which Peter Mark Roget constructed his *Thesaurus* 150 years later. It is in a way ironical that the fundamental insights of an intellectual movement that explicitly sought to minimize the role of language in scientific thought should turn out to be, first and foremost, insights into language itself, into the taxonomic principles of naming which form an essential element of semantic structure. And both these aspects of the movement's ideology have gone into our present-day ideas about language: the understanding of the organization of word meanings on the one hand, and on the other hand the curious image of language as distortion of reality, as a barrier to the clear-sighted apprehension of **true** relationships which are relationships among things. One only has to consider modern attitudes on the subject of language in education to realize how deeply this second, negative view has penetrated into our thinking about language.

French rationalist grammar, which was a continuation of the scholastic tradition, and English universal semantics, with its origins in a rather different strand in medieval thought, represent two of the main trends in linguistics in seventeenth-century Europe. In the eighteenth century, the picture was beginning to change. The ethnographic approach was now coming to the fore, as linguists turned their attention to the vernacular languages of Europe and to the languages of Asia, Africa, the Pacific and the New World; and by the nineteenth century this had become the dominant perspective on language. It was primarily the ethnographic interpretation that was elaborated in the major European schools of the first half of the present century – the Prague school, the London school, and also the highly theoretical "glossematic" school of Copenhagen – as well as in the anthropological linguistics of Boas and Sapir in America. The development of American structuralist linguistics – a movement that was notably different from what was called "structuralism" in Europe – began to reassert the philosophical approach; and when Chomsky, bringing to bear the methods of logical syntax, showed that it was possible to formalize the American structuralist model of language, in what was the first successful attempt at representing natural language as a formal system, this became once again the dominant perspective. Linguistics became philosophy of language, as it has done from time to time throughout its history; and grammar became logic.

If Chomsky had admitted that he was building on the work of his predecessors, the ensuing dialogue between philosophers and ethnographers of language could have been very fruitful and rewarding. Instead he presented his theories in the form of a violent polemic aimed directly at those whose model of language he was taking over; in the course of this he so misrepresented the work of his other contemporaries and forerunners that for the following decade and more it was impossible for the two groups to engage in any dialogue at all. Probably never before in the history of ideas about language have the two views, of language as resource and language as rule, been made to seem so incompatible. The difference between the two was presented as an opposition between a concern with language as system and a concern with language as behaviour (competence and performance, in the Chomskyan terminology). In fact, however, both approaches are equally concerned with the system – with explaining the fundamental nature of language. Where they differ is in how they see the relation **between** system and behaviour. It soon came to be realized that the price to be paid for the Chomskyan type of formalism was much too high; it required a degree of idealization so great as to reduce natural language back to the status of an artificial syntax. Once its claims for psychological reality could no longer be sustained, transformation theory lost its original glamour; and today we are witnessing a retreat from these extreme positions (the field of child language studies provides a striking instance of this) and an attempt to reconcile the philosopher's demand for being explicit with the ethnographer's demand for being relevant. There is still, however, a long way to go.

One of the most significant theoretical developments of twentieth-century linguistics since Saussure is what is known as variation theory – significant because, among other things, it involves the discovery of new facts about language. This derives from the highly original work of William Labov in the field of urban dialectology, the study of the speech patterns of big city communities, which he started in New York in the early 1960s. The essence of variation theory is the notion that language is inherently a variable system, so that even within one individual speaker variation is the norm rather than the exception. This theory is throwing new light in some unexpected quarters, particularly on certain fundamental processes involved in linguistic change (1974). As might be expected, there are two versions of the theory; one (that of Bailey and Bickerton) philosophical, rule-based, deterministic and couched in terms of what people know, individually; the other (that of Cedergren and the Sankoffs) ethnographic, resource-based, probabilistic and couched in terms of what people can do, socially. And again as throughout history, it is the rule-oriented thinker who insists that the two are incompatible; who says, in effect, 'You may agree with me, but I don't agree with you.' As in the history of the individual, so in the history of ideas it is the secondary, restructured reality that has to be made to exclude the primary one, not the other way round.

So it is made to appear by the successors to the formal tradition that, in order to accept language as rule, one has to reject language as resource. This lack of symmetry between the two ideologies is very striking. The softer view can accommodate the harder – the rhetorician can believe in logic, the anomalist in analogy, the empiricist in reason – but not the other way round. It is as if the rule-giver, the tough-minded member of the pair, has to maintain as part of his conceptual framework the view that his is the **only** valid model of the universe, the sole truth about the nature of human knowledge and scientific enquiry.

But there is another angle. We can recognize a thread of ideas that, whether or not it will serve for any kind of a synthesis, at least avoids the schizophrenia that seems to characterize modern thinking about language. Let us make one final brief excursion into classical times. There was one mode of thought in the ancient world which perhaps more than any other provides the ideological foundations of modern linguistics, that of the Stoics. (The point has been made that their founder, Zeno, was not a native speaker of Greek, and so had been through the chastening experience of learning Greek as a Second Language.)

The records of Stoic thought are scanty, preserved only in the writings of others; but enough remains to show that they achieved a new perspective on language. They did so by specifically focusing on language as an object of investigation, while simultaneously placing it in a broader intellectual context. Here is Robins' summary:

> The Stoics ... regarded language as a natural human capability, to be accepted as it was, with all its characteristic irregularity. They took a broader view of what was good Greek than the analogists, and were interested in linguistic questions not principally as grammarians and textual critics; they were philosophers for whom language served as the expression of thought and feeling and for whom literature held deeper truths and insights veiled in myth and allegory.

The Stoics interpreted language in its own terms. They took the written symbol, and analysed it into three aspects; it had a shape, a value and a name. The first letter of the alphabet, for example, has a written shape α, a phonetic value [a], and a name 'alpha'. They then used this analysis as a metaphor for the interpretation of linguistic form, and identified the three aspects of a linguistic sign: the sign itself, in its outward manifestation; the value, or meaning; and the thing meant (σημαῖον, σημαιομένον, πράγμα – later the term σημαῖον was taken over to mean the whole complex of form and meaning, 'sign' in the modern sense, and the form, now in the sense of 'wording', was designated by λεκτόν).

In introducing the notion of the sign the Stoics opened the way to an interpretation of language in terms of what we would now call semiotics. In the early years of this century the Swiss linguist Ferdinand de Saussure took the **sign** as the organizing concept for linguistic structure, using it to express the conventional nature of language in the phrase "l'arbitraire du signe". This has the effect of highlighting what is, in fact, the **one point** of arbitrariness in the system, namely the phonological shape of words, and hence allows the **non**-arbitrariness of the rest to emerge with greater clarity. An example of something that is distinctly non-arbitrary is the way different **kinds** of meaning in language are expressed by different **kinds** of grammatical structure, as appears when linguistic structure is interpreted in functional terms.

A distinctive feature of the present decade has been the development of semiotics as a mode of thinking, not just about language but about all aspects of culture. From the semiotic standpoint culture is, as Keith Basso expressed it, "a body of knowledge which members use to interpret experience and to structure behaviour". A culture is a meaning potential of many modes; it comprises many semiotic systems, ranging from kinship systems and modes of commodity exchange through dance and music, modes of adornment and display, architecture and art forms, imaginative literature, mythology and folklore. These are the symbolic resources with which people discover, create, and exchange meanings.

Semiotics is not a discipline, defined by subject-matter. It is a way of interpreting things. In Pyatygorsky's words "When I analyse anything from the point of view of what it means, this is a 'semiotic situation'"; and such an analysis becomes more significant the more we are able to find similarities among different semiotic systems. Umberto Eco wrote, in his book *Absent Structure*,

> the hypothesis from which [semiotics] starts is that all cultural phenomena are really systems of signs ... it should perhaps be considered as an interdisciplinary domain within which all cultural phenomena are analysed against the background of an "obsession" with communication.

(I should rather say, with meaning.)

Semiotics evolves out of the investigation of language as object. It began to evolve in the west when the Stoics replaced the earlier view of language as **instrument** (an instrument for the study of something else, either rhetoric, with the sophists, or logic, with Aristotle) by one of language as **object** – as an object of study and interpretation in its own right. This opens the way to an understanding of meaning, and of systems of meaning with varying modes of realization. Once the semiotic perspective develops as an intellectual stance, it can be so to speak turned back on language, so that language is thought of as one among the many semiotic systems that constitute the culture. Its real uniqueness then begins to emerge. Language is a special kind of semiotic system in that it typically functions in the realization of other semiotic systems; it is a "connotative semiotic", in Hjelmslev's terms.

This is certainly the context in which language evolved. At the same time, however, once having come into existence in this way, language takes on an independent reality and creates new meanings of its own. In particular, it creates a new type of phenomenon, a new order of reality, called information, which then becomes a commodity to be exchanged. We live in an age in which the exchange of information is fast replacing the exchange of goods-&-services as the primary mode of social behaviour.

So much could be made to follow from this point that it should perhaps have been the beginning of this exploration rather than the end. Instead of beginning again, however, I shall make three final observations. The first is, that the semiotic perspective enables us to see language in the context of the social construction of reality. Language is the principal means through which we create the world in which we live. This is of course a world of multiple realities, in Alfred Schutz' terms, each with its own "finite province of meaning". And this, in turn, is the significance of seeing language as a variable system. Variety in language is functional, not only directly but also symbolically; it serves both as vehicle and as metaphor for the manysidedness of the cultural reality (Douglas 1973).

Secondly, related to this is the goal of understanding the diversity of human languages; not seeing them all as deviations from some one idealized logic, that of western culture, but as each embodying its own logic, and also its own rhetoric, and its own esthetic. At the end of 1974 UNESCO held a Symposium, in Nairobi, on interactions between linguistics and mathematical education. Linguists and teachers of mathematics, mainly from countries of Africa, came together to discuss questions of learning mathematics in languages with very different natural logics and semantic styles – different from those of European languages; and it became obvious how ineffective it could be simply to translate textbooks from English into Yoruba or Swahili or Bemba, textbooks which were unconsciously based on the folk mathematical concepts that exist in English, instead of designing new approaches based on the rather different mathematical concepts which are embodied in these languages.

114

Finally, discussion of ideas about language should not be thought to suggest that these ideas are isolated from ideas about everything else. Our picture of language is part of our picture of the world. In particular it is part of our picture of the world of meanings; and the value of the semiotic interpretation is that it shows us how the world of meanings is structured and what its constants are. We started with the child, so we will end with the child. Long before he can **talk about** meaning, a child is a engaging in **acts of** meaning; even before he has a mother tongue, he is using language to organize his view of the world (and himself), and to interact with the people around him. By the age of eight or ten months he has a very rich idea of what he will be able to achieve through learning to mean. It is to be hoped that our adult ideas about language will be rich enough in turn, so that they help rather than hinder him in his efforts towards that goal. For what, as the Red Queen said, is the use of a child without any meaning?

Chapter Five

LANGUAGE AND THE ORDER OF NATURE
(1987)

1 Order out of language

Out of the buzz and the hum in which mankind has been evolving – itself a kind of conversation, to our present way of thinking – has emerged what Rulon Wells once called the "distinctively human semiotic": a special form of dialogue powered by a system we call language. With this we talk to each other; and in the process we construct the microcosmos in which each one of us lives, our little universes of doing and happening, and the people and the things that are involved therein.

And in the course of this semiotic activity, without really becoming aware of it, we have also been construing the two macrocosmic orders of which we ourselves are a part: the social order, and the natural order. For most of human history, these deeper forms of dialogue have depended on substantially the same resource: ordinary, everyday, spontaneous, natural spoken language – with just some "coefficient of weirdness" such as Malinowksi found in the more esoteric contexts of its use (1935; see the section entitled 'An ethnographic theory of the magical word').

All this dialogic construction is, by definition, interactive. At the micro level, we get to know our fellow-creatures by talking to them and listening to them; and they respond to us in the same natural language. At the macro level, the "dialogue with nature", brilliantly scripted by Prigogine and Stengers in their book *Order out of Chaos* (1985: esp. 41–4), is also interactive; but in another guise. When we want to exchange meanings with physical or biological nature we have

First published in *The Linguistics of Writing: Arguments between Language and Literature*, edited by N. Fabb *et al.* Manchester University Press, 1987, pp. 135–54.

to process information that is coded in very different ways, and that may need to go through two or three stages of translation before we can apprehend it.

We have always assumed that it can be translated: that the information coming in can in the last resort be represented and transmitted through the forms of our own natural languages. In fact, up until the last few millennia, no conceivable alternative could ever present itself; because language was beyond the range of our conscious reflection. It was simply part of ourselves – the label "natural" language is entirely apt. Herbert Simon, in his *Sciences of the Artificial*, classified language among the artificial phenomena (1969: 5); but he was wrong. Language is as much a product of evolution as we are ourselves; we did not manufacture it. It is an evolved system, not a designed system: not something separate from humanity, but an essential part of the condition of being human. These natural languages, then, sufficed to enable us to interpret both facets of our wider environment, the social order and the natural order; these were, after all, construed by generalizing and abstracting from the microenvironments in which language had evolved all along.

It is just within the last hundred generations or so that some element of design has come into natural language; and just in certain cultural historical contexts, those in which language has come to be written down. Writing has been an inherent part of the process. In these contexts the dialogue with nature has begun to take on new forms; we have learnt to measure, and to experiment; and to accompany these new semiotic modes, our languages have spawned various metalanguages – the languages of mathematics and of science. These are extensions of natural languages, not totally new creations; and they remain in touch. Even mathematics, the most 'meta-' of all the variants of natural language, is kept tied to it by an interpretative interface – a level one metalanguage which enables mathematical expressions to be rendered in English, or Chinese, or other forms of distinctively human semiotic.

2 Does language cope?

Now and again some part of the dialogue breaks down, and then it becomes news – like London Bridge: as long as it stays up it is not news, but when it falls down it will be. Yet what is really newsworthy about language is how rarely it does fall down. The demands that we make on the system are quite colossal; how is it that it so seldom gets overloaded?

117

As far as the social order is concerned, we can watch language at work construing this from a child's earliest infancy, because from the moment of birth language intercedes, mediating in the dialogue between an infant and its caregivers. This kind of language, which is language for loving and caring rather than for knowing and thinking, would seem to have no great demands being made on it, and only in pathological cases is it likely to break down. Since here language is not being required to refer, its success is judged other than referentially. But this least referential kind of discourse is in fact actively enrolled in constructing the social order. Predictably, since the social order is highly complex, the language that is creating it is also highly complex. Only, the two complexities are not related in a straightforward referential fashion. Languages create society; but it does so without ever referring to the processes and the structures which it is creating (Hasan 1986: 125–46; esp. 134 example 6).

This appears surprising only because we are obsessed with the referential properties of language. Yet language is "not constrained by the need to refer" (Butt 1984, 1988b): even if a mother was aware of the features of the social order that her dialogue was bringing into being, her baby could scarcely be expected to understand them. She cannot talk to her child about social values, statuses and roles, decision-making hierarchies and the like. Yet all these are brought into being by her use of the grammar, as Hasan has convincingly demonstrated (1987a); and this is why when people want to change the conditions of the dialogue, and the structures it is setting up, they do so by changing the grammar – thus illustrating how well the grammar is doing its job. The complaint is not that the language is not functioning properly, but that it is functioning all too well – it is the social order construed by it that is being objected to. But mostly the design for change is drawn up only at the surface of the language, rather than at the much less accessible, cryptotypic level of patterning by which the structures are really installed.

When we come to consider how language creates the **natural** order, we might expect matters to be different. This is an order of happenings, and things, and language is our primary means of reflecting on these. Here, presumably, the essential function of language is to refer – to make contact with what is "out there". But this too we shall have to call into question.

In this sphere there have been from time to time complaints of a different kind. It is often objected that language is letting us down; and this especially at certain times in history, when the pace of the dialogue is quickening and knowledge is accumulating very fast. At such times there arise proposals for improving language, making it a more effective tool for recording and extending our knowledge.

Thus the precursors and contemporaries of Newton set about remodelling language: first simply as shorthand, then as universal character (a script that would be the same for all languages, based on the logographic principle of Chinese), then as "real character" (a new universal written language, with its own realizations in speech – the famous systems of Cave Beck, Dalgarno and John Wilkins), and finally conceived of as a calculus, a semiotic not so much for recording and transmitting knowledge as for creating it – a tool designed for thinking with, like the mathematical calculus newly invented by Leibniz and by Newton himself. (This last was never realized; nor were any of the earlier systems that were realized ever used.)

Since 1900 the call has been heard again, heralded perhaps by de Broglie's famous observation that "physics is in suspense because we do not have the words or the images that are essential to us". We can follow this motif through Einstein, Bohr and Heisenberg, down to the present day as it becomes increasingly specific (Heisenberg 1958; esp. ch. 10, 'Language and reality in modern physics'). David Bohm devotes a whole chapter to language, in which he objects that "language divides things into separate entities", and so distorts the reality of "undivided wholeness in flowing movement"; and he proposes a new form of language called the "rheomode", which gives the basic role to the verb rather than the noun (1980: esp. ch. 2, 'The rheomode – an experiment with language and thought').

We shall return to these objections in a moment. But despite the shortcomings which the natural scientists of these two periods have found in the languages they had to work with, science has continued to progress – and to change direction fundamentally on both occasions. Languages have not given way beneath its weight, nor are there any very obvious signs of overload. By and large, the dialogue has worked. One thing that Bohm and his predecessors may have overlooked is that you do not need to keep engineering a language in order to change it; it will change anyway – because that is the only way it can persist.

3 Language as dynamic open system

Every language is constantly renewing itself, changing in resonance with changes in its environment. But this is not an incidental fact about language; it is a condition of its existence as a system – and without language as system there could be no dialogue at all.

The earliest linguists of India, Greece and China all recognized that languages change in their expression – in their phonetics and morphology. These effects have now been shown to be statistical (Sankoff and Laberge 1978; Horvath 1985, esp. ch. 5, 'Analytical methodology'): variation sets in, from a variety of sources, internal and external; and this variation can either become stablilized, so that the system becomes inherently variable at that point, or a "variable rule becomes categorical" and we say that sound change has taken place. The terminology ("variable rule", and so on) is unfortunate, since it leads people – or perhaps confirms their inclination – to look for hidden variables, so that all variable rules can be reduced to categorical status. But the data resist such interpretations; it is simply not the case that if we knew everything there was to know then we could predict every instance. In other words, variability in language is not a limitation of the observer; it is a feature of the system, and hence the statistically defined behaviour of the micro particles of language – for example the realization of a particular vowel as a fronted or a backed variant – can induce the system to change.

Such expression variables are alternative realizations of some higher level constant (e.g. 'the phoneme /a/'), which therefore constitutes the entry condition to that particular little system. To understand changes in the meaning potential of language we need to consider analogous statistical effects on the content plane (Nesbitt and Plum 1988). Consider a grammatical system such as past/present/future primary tense in English, interpretable semantically as deictic reference to a linear scale of time (the traditional description was "time relative to the moment of speaking"). In any instance of the context which serves as entry condition to that system – in grammatical terms, any instance of a finite clause – each term has an inherent probability of occurring. A speaker of English 'knows' these probabilities; having heard, by the age of five, say, about half a million instances he has a statistical profile of the lexicogrammar of the language. It is by the same token (more specifically, by the same set of tokens) that he knows the lexical probabilities: that *go* is more frequent than *grow* and *grow* is more frequent than *glow*. Now, grammar and lexis are simply the same phenomenon looked at from two different ends; but one difference between them is that the patterns we treat as grammatical are those which are buried much deeper below the level of people's consciousness, and so these patterns, and the probabilities associated with them, are much harder for people to become aware of – many people reject grammatical probabilities when they are told about them: they feel insulted, and take them as affronts to the freedom of the individual. Lexical patterns are nearer the surface of consciousness: hence lexical probabilities are quite readily recoverable, as a sense of 'this word is more frequent than that', and are therefore found easier to accept. (Logically, of course, there is no reason why being told that one is going to use *go* more frequently than *glow* should be any less threatening than being told one is going to use past more frequently than future; but these observations tend to provoke very different responses.)

Now, just as, when I listen to the weather report every morning, and I hear something like 'last night's minimum was six degrees, that's three degrees below average', I know that that instance has itself become part of, and so altered, the probability of the minimum temperature for that particular night in the year – so every instance of a primary tense in English discourse alters the relative probabilities of the terms that make up the primary tense system. Of course, to make these probabilities meaningful as a descriptive measure we have to sharpen the focus, by setting conditions: we are not usually interested in the average temperature at all times anywhere on the surface of the globe (though this is a relevant concept for certain purposes), but rather in the probable daily minimum on Sydney Harbour at the time of the winter solstice. There are various dimensions conditioning grammatical probabilities: we might specify the context of situation – for example, the discourse of weather forecasting, which will considerably increase the weighting for future tense;[1] or we might specify a number of other concurrent grammatical features, such as whether the clause is declarative or interrogative. (There are also the transitional probabilities of the text as a stochastic process.) The more local the context, of course, the greater the moderating effect of a single instance.

Lemke (1984d) has pointed out that many human systems, including all social-semiotic systems, are of a particular kind known as "dynamic open systems". Dynamic open systems have the property that they are metastable: that is, they persist only through constant change; and this change takes place through interactive exchanges with their environment. In the course of such interaction, the system exports disorder; and in the process of exporting disorder, and so increasing the entropy of its environment, the system renews itself, gains information, imports or rather creates order and in this way continues to function. The system exists only because it is open. But it is now no longer itself; for such a system, the state of being is one of constant becoming. Language – natural language – is certainly a system of this general type.

Language (like other social semiotic systems) is a dynamic open system that achieves metastability through these statistical processes. Instances affect probabilities: from time to time probabilities thus rise to one or fall to zero, so that quantitative effects become qualitative and the system maintains itself by evolving, through a process of constant change.

In an ideal system, one having two states that are equiprobable, there is no redundancy. Once we depart from equiprobability, redundancy sets in. In all open systems the probabilities are skewed, so that the system carries redundancy. Lemke shows that a semiotic system is one that is characterized by redundancy **between (pairs of) its sub-systems**: what he refers to as "metaredundancy". To illustrate from the classic Hjelmslevian example of the traffic lights: the system has certain states, red, yellow and green. Since these are not equiprobable there is redundancy among them, at that level; but this simple redundancy is relevant only to the engineer who designs and installs them. There is then a ***metaredundancy*** between this system and the system of messages 'stop/go': this is the first order metaredundancy that defines the signifier and the signified. There is then a second order metaredundancy: this in turn 'metaredounds' with the system of behaviour of drivers approaching the signal: they stop, or else they drive on. And so on.

In other words: what the system 'says' (the wording: red/green), redounds with what it 'means' (the meaning: stop/go), which in turn redounds with what it does. But 'it' is a human system: it is people who drive the cars, people who construe the semantic opposition of stop/go, and people who switch on the lights, or at least programme the machine to do it for them. Traffic lights are in fact part of the social semiotic, even though I am using them here simply as an analogy for discourse that is 'worded' in the more usual sense – that is, in the form of lexicogrammar.

4   The emergence of metalanguages

Thus viewed as a social semiotic, language is a dynamic open system, probabilistic, and characterized by metaredundancy. These *n*-order metaredundancies define the levels, or strata, of the system: the relationship of metaredundancy is the general relationship whose manifestation in language we are accustomed to referring to as "realization". Such a system is good for thinking with and good for doing with, these being the two complementary facets of all human semiosis.

When either of these facets comes under pressure, the system responds by creating special varieties of itself to meet the new demands. So in a period of rapid growth of science and technology new metalanguages appear. These new forms of language are both created by and also create the new forms of knowledge — since what we call knowledge is simply a higher level of meaning, still linked to the grammar by the chain of metaredundancies. But it is at this point that the functioning of language starts to become problematic.

Let me refer again to David Bohm's *Wholeness and the Implicate Order*. Bohm is dissatisfied with the way language (as he sees it) fails to meet the demands of the new dialogue with nature, and he proposes the "rheomode" — a form of language that would represent the flux of things, and construe experience as dynamic rather than static. His suggestions are simplistic and confined to a few variations in derivational morphology: for example, to get away from a "language structure in which nouns are taken as basic, e.g. 'this notion is relevant'" we reinstate the verb *to levate*, meaning 'the spontaneous and unrestricted act of lifting into attention any context whatsoever'; we then introduce the verb *to re-levate*, 'to lift a certain context into attention again', whence irrelevation, levation and so on (p. 34). But the motive is clear: a new language is needed to encode a new view of reality.

There have been frequent assertions, throughout the history of quantum mechanics and the physics that derived from it, that it is impossible to talk about quantum ideas in language as it was received. The language of physics is under stress; and some of the more far-fetched notions such as the 'many worlds' interpretation proposed by Everett and Wheeler — that there are as many alternative realities as there are quantum events — might be used to illustrate the incapacity of our natural language-based metalanguages to cope with these new semiotic demands. The metalanguages are too determinate, too rigid, too unable to accommodate complementarities. They cannot tell us "that *all* is an unbroken and undivided whole movement, and that each 'thing' is abstracted only as a relatively invariant side or aspect of this movement" (p. 47).

Before examining these charges further, let us note an interesting paradox. When logicians and philosophers complain about language, their usual complaint is that it is too vague. When scientists find language letting them down, it is generally because it is too precise, too determinate. In part, no doubt, this reflects their two different ideologies. For the logician, if two things conflict they cannot both be true – so languages should force them to reject the one or the other; and if language does not do this, then it is too loose, too vague. For the scientist, on the other hand, if two things are both true they cannot conflict – so the language should help them to accommodate both, and if it doesn't, it is too rigid, too determinate. (What I am labelling "the logician", and "the scientist" are of course two different ideologies – not the individual members of these two respected professions.)

But they are also probably talking about different languages. The logicians are thinking of non-technical natural language, from which their artificial languages, including mathematics, were first derived. The scientists are thinking of their own technical metalanguages that have been constructed on the basis of natural language: the various registers of physics, for example. And these scientific metalanguages are among the more designed varieties of human language – hence, like all designed systems, they do tend to be rigid and determinate. These are the very features which make such metalanguages unsuitable for just that purpose for which they were in fact designed: the dialogue with nature, for which it is essential to be able to mean in terms that are dynamic, non-compartmental and fluid – and above all, that do not foreclose.

The irony is, that that is exactly what natural language is like: dynamic, non-compartmental and fluid. But it has got smothered under the weight of the metalanguages that were built upon it.

5 Levels of consciousness in language

Let me begin this section with a quotation from Prigogine and Stengers' book *Order out of Chaos* that I referred to at the outset:

> [In quantum mechanics] there is an irreducible multiplicity of representation for a system, each connected with a determined [i.e. decided upon by the investigator] set of operators.
>
> This implies a departure from the classical notion of objectivity, since in the classical view the only "objective" description is the complete description of *the system as it is*, independent of the choice of how it is observed ...

124

The physicist has to choose his language, to choose the macroscopic experimental device. Bohr expressed this idea through the principle of complementarity ...

The real lesson to be learned from the principle of complementarity, a lesson that can perhaps be transferred to other fields of knowledge, consists in emphasizing the wealth of reality, which overflows any single language, any single logical structure. Each language can express only part of reality.   (p. 225)

Here Prigogine and Stengers are of course talking about "languages" in the sense of conceptual constructs; and they go on to say:

No single theoretical language articulating the variables to which a well-defined value can be attributed can exhaust the physical content of a system. Various possible languages and points of view about the system may be complementary. They all deal with the same reality, but it is impossible to reduce them to one single description.

It is my contention that natural language – not as it is dressed up in the form of a scientific metalanguage, but in its common-sense, everyday, spontaneous spoken form – does in fact 'represent reality' in terms of complementarities; and that these are complementary perspectives in precisely the sense in which Bohr was using the term.[2] Only, it does so non-referentially. Just as language construes the social order without referring to the system it is constructing, so likewise language construes the natural order – through the unconscious, cryptotypic patterns in the grammar, which create their own order of reality independently of whatever it is they may be being used to describe.

I shall illustrate the complementarities inherent in this "de-automatized" sphere of the grammar in just a moment. But first we must recognise a problem. The features I am referring to in natural language are features of the "cryptogrammar"; they function way below the usual level of consciousness. And the problem is, that when we start reflecting on them, bringing them up to our conscious attention, we destroy them. The act of reflecting on language transforms it into something alien, something different from itself – something determinate and closed. There are uses for closed, determinate metalanguages; but they can represent only one point of view about a system. The language of daily life, which shapes our unconscious understanding of ourselves and our environment, is a language of complementarities, a rheomode – a dynamic open system. The question is whether we can learn to use it to think with consciously. It may be impossible. I don't

125

mean that it is impossible to understand the cryptogrammar of a natural language, but that its reality-generating power may be incompatible with explicit logical reasoning.

I have tried out a simple strategy for exploring the more unconscious features of the grammar. I selected a text – the headlines of a news broadcast, which I had taken down verbatim from the radio; I read it aloud to a group of students, and asked them to recall it. They gave me the motifs: death, disaster, violence and the like. I pressed them further: what was actually said? This time they gave me words: a list of the lexical items used, recalled with considerable accuracy although most of them had not figured in their first responses. Let me call the motif level zero, and the lexical responses level one. I pressed them for a more specific account (still without reading the passage again), and they gave me the more exposed parts of the grammar: the word, group and phrase classes, the derivational morphology and so on. This exposed grammar we will call level two. I pressed them once more; and this time – since they were students of linguistics – they began to get to level three, the hidden grammar (the cryptotypes, in Whorf's terminology): the transitivity patterns, the grammatical metaphors and so on.

In our normal everyday concern with language we simply attend to the motifs. We are not concerned with wordings, and do not trouble even to remember them. We behave as if the metaredundancy – the realization of meanings in lexicogrammar – is simply an automatic coding. If asked to reflect on the wording, we focus on the lexical end of the spectrum: the words, or rather the lexical items – since this is the edge that is nearest the domain of conscious attention. It takes much more effort to attend to the more strictly grammatical zone, especially to its more cryototypic regions. And when we get there, we find ourselves back at the motifs again; but this time with a greatly heightened understanding, because now we can see why the text meant what it did, and we can appreciate the deeper ideological content of the discourse – the messages we had received without becoming aware of them.

The process of reflecting on natural language can be modelled in terms of these four levels of consciousness:

'meaning' (semantic level)   level 0: 'motifs'

'wording' (lexicogrammatical level) { level 1: 'words'
                                       level 2: 'phenotypes'
                                       level 3: 'cryptotypes'

where the spiral (cryptotypes as hidden motifs) in turn represents the dialectic of metaredundancy. Or, to put this in more familiar semiotic terms: the signified constructs the signifier (by "realization" – grammar in its automatized function), and the signifier constructs the signified (grammar, especially the cryptogrammar, in its de-automatized function). The problem of turning the cryptogrammar of a natural language into a metalanguage for reasoning with is that it has to become automatized – that is, the grammar has to be made to describe, instead of constructing reality by not describing, which is what it does best.

6 Everyday language as a theory of the natural order

I will try to enumerate some features of natural language, as embodied in our everyday informal discourse from earliest childhood, that constitute for us a theory of reality. They are features common to all languages, but in respect of which each language presents its own particular mix; I make one or two references to English, but in the main they are set out in general terms that could be applied to all.

- Clausal structures: the organization of meanings in lexicogrammatical form (as **wordings**). The gateway through which meanings are brought together and realized in ordinary grammar is the clause; and the clause nucleus is a happening (Process + Medium, in systemic terms). So natural languages represent reality as what happens, not as what exists; things are defined as contingencies of the flow.
- Projection: the general relation underlying what grammarians call "direct and indirect speech". The system of projection construes the whole of experience into two different kinds of event: semiotic events, and other events; the latter can then be transformed into semiotic events by processes of consciousness.
- Expansion: logical-semantic relationships between events. Two events provided they are of the same kind (as defined by projection) may be related to one another by one of a set of logical-semantic relations, such that the second one defines, extends, or in some way (such as time or cause) correlates with the first.
- Transitivity: the theory of processes (i). Natural languages construe experience out of different types of process; this plurality is universal, though the details of the system vary. English sets up 'outer' processes, those of the world perceived as external; 'inner' processes, those of (human-like) consciousness; and processes of attribution and representation. All are distinguished in the cryptogrammar.

- Transitivity: the theory of processes (ii). With regard to (at least) the 'outer' processes, natural languages incorporate two models: the transitive, which interprets 'mechanically', in terms of transmission, and the ergative, which interprets 'scientifically', in terms of causation. These two are complementary; the generalizations they make contradict each other, but every clause has to be interpreted as both.
- Tense and aspect: the theory of time. Similarly, natural languages embody two models of time: a theory of linear, irreversible time, out of past via present into future (tense), and a theory of simultaneity, with the opposition between being and becoming, or manifested and manifesting (aspect). Languages have very different mixtures (English strongly foregrounds linear time): but probably every language enacts both, and again the two are complementary in the defined sense.

In these and other features of their 'hidden' grammars, ordinary languages in their everyday, common-sense contexts embody highly sophisticated interpretations of the natural order, rich in complementarities and thoroughly rheomodal in ways much deeper than Bohm was able to conceive of. To be more accurate, we would say that it is these features **in a system of this dynamic open kind** that construe reality for us in this way. The system itself must be a metastable, multi-level ("metaredundant") system – that is, a human semiotic – with the further property that it is *metafunctional*: it is committed to meaning more than one thing at once, so that every instance is at once both reflection and action – both interpreting the world and also changing it.

We have been reminded of "the impossibility of recovering a fixed and stable meaning from discourse". Of course this is impossible; it would be a very impoverished theory of discourse that expected it. But it is entirely possible – as we all do – to recover from discourse a meaning of another kind, meaning that is complex and indeterminate. The reason it is hard to make this process explicit is that we can do so only by talking about grammar; and to do this we have to construct a theory of grammar: a "grammatics", let us call it. But this *grammatics* is itself a designed system, another scientific metalanguage, with terms like *subject* and *agent* and *conditional* – terms which become reified in their turn, so that we then come to think of the grammar itself (the real grammar) as feeble and crude because it doesn't match up to the categories we've invented for describing it. But of course it is the grammatics – the metalanguage – that is feeble and crude, not the grammar. To borrow Whorf's famous simile, the grammatics (grammar as metalanguage) is to the grammar (the language) as a bludgeon is to a rapier – except that a better analogy might be with the hand that wields the rapier. If the human mind can achieve this remarkable combination of incisive penetration and positive indeterminacy, then we can hardly deny these same properties to human language, since language is the very system by which they are developed, stored and powered.

7 The need for plurality of language

To quote Prigogine and Stengers again: "Whatever we call reality, it is revealed to us only through active construction in which we participate" (p. 293). But, as they have already told us, "the wealth of reality … overflows any single language, any single logical structure. Each language can express only part of reality."

I have suggested that our natural languages do possess the qualities needed for interpreting the world very much as our modern physicists see it. But from the time when our dialogue with nature became a conscious exercise in understanding, we have come to need more than one grammar – more than one version of language as a theory of experience. Rather, we have needed a continuum of grammars, from the rheomodal pole at one end to something more fixed and constructible at the other. For our active construction of reality we had to be able to adopt either a dynamic, 'in flux' perspective or a synoptic, 'in place' perspective – or some mixture of the two, with a complementarity between them.

So our language began to stretch, beginning – as far as the West is concerned – with the explosion of process nouns in scientific Greek from 550 BC onwards (e.g. *kinesis* 'movement', from *kineo* '(I) move'), and culminating (so far!) in the kind of semantic variation found in pairs such as:

experimental emphasis becomes concentrated in testing the generalizations and consequences derived from these theories	we now start experimenting mainly in order to test whether things happen regularly as we would expect if we were explaining in the right way
1-attic	1-doric

Let me label these two styles the attic and the doric. The attic mode is not of course confined to abstract scientific discourse; 2-attic is from a television magazine:

129

he also credits his former big size with much of his career success	he also believes that he succeeded in his career mainly because he used to be big
2-attic	2-doric

Represented in this new, 'attic' style, the world is a world of things, rather than one of happening; of product, rather than of process; of being, rather than becoming. Whatever metaphor we use to label it with – and all these paired expressions capture some aspect of the difference – the emergence of the new attic forms of expression added a new dimension to human experience: where previously there had been one mode of interpretation, the dynamic, now there were two, the synoptic and the dynamic – or rather, two poles, with varying degrees of semantic space possible between them. There are now two ways of looking at one and the same set of phenomena.

The two are complementary, like wave and particle as complementary theories of light. Any aspect of reality can be interpreted either way; but, as with wave and particle, certain aspects will be better illuminated with the one perspective and others with the other. The doric style, that of everyday, common-sense discourse, is characterized by a high degree of grammatical intricacy – a choreographic type of complexity, as I have described it (1986): it highlights processes, and the interdependence of one process on another. The attic style, that of emergent languages of science, displays a high degree of lexical density; its complexity is crystalline, and it highlights structures, and the interrelationships of their parts – including, in a critical further development, **conceptual** structures, the taxonomies that helped to turn knowledge into science.

There was thus a bifurcation in the metaredundancy pattern, leading to the duality of styles that Rulon Wells (1960) spoke about at the conference whose aftermath we are celebrating here (he referred to them as "nominal and verbal styles", but the distinction is really that of nominal and clausal). Between the doric, or clausal, style and the attic, or nominal, style is a complementarity that itself complements the various first-order complementarities that we have already seen to be present within the doric system. But this second-order complementarity is of a somewhat different kind. The two perspectives are not on equal terms. The dynamic mode is prior; it comes first.

The dynamic mode is phylogenetically prior; it evolved first, along with the human species, whereas it is only in the last few millennia that the synoptic mode has come into being. It is also ontogenetically prior; it is what we learn as children – and carry with us throughout life.

Whenever we are speaking casually and unselfconsciously, in typically human dialogic contexts, we go on exploiting the dynamic mode, which as we have seen embodies the deep experience of the species in cryptogrammatic form. The synoptic mode, on the other hand, embodies the more conscious reflection on the environment that is stored in scientific knowledge; historically it is derived from the dynamic by the processes of grammatical metaphor. Of course, once in existence it can enter daily life; there is nothing very abstruse or formal about *every previous visit had left me with a feeling of discomfort* ... Nevertheless it is a metaphoric derivative; the agnate *whenever I'd visited before I'd ended up feeling uncomfortable* ... is a prior form of semiosis. So how does the more synoptic mode, the attic style arise?

Thanks to the metaredundancy principle, it is possible to introduce variation at any one level of language without thereby disturbing the patterning at other levels of the system (that is, without catastrophic perturbations; the consequences are seen in continued gradual changes such as I described earlier). It is even possible to replace an entire level of the system in this way; and this is what happened with the development of writing. Writing provided a new mode of expression – which could "realize" the pre-existing content patterns without disrupting them. At the same time, it provided a new interface, another kind of instantiation through which changes in the system could take place.

Writing evolved in the immediate context of the need for documentation and recording. But it opened the way to an alternative theory of reality.

8   The effects of writing

Conditions arise in history – essentially those of settlement – where experience has to be recorded: we need to store knowledge, and put it on file. So we invent a filing system for language, reducing it to writing. The effect of this is to anchor language to a shallower level of consciousness. For the first time, language comes to be made of constituents – sentences – instead of the dependency patterns – clause complexes – of the spoken mode. And with constituency comes a different form of the interpretation of experience.

It is important not to oversimplify the argument at this point. Both language itself, and the dimensions of experience that are given form by language, are extremely complex; and instead of hoping to gain in popularity ratings by pretending all is simple we do well to admit the complexity and try to accommodate it in our thinking. Let me take just three steps at this point.

Writing brings language to consciousness; and in the same process it changes its semiotic mode from the dynamic to the synoptic: from flow to stasis, from choreographic to crystalline, from syntactic intricacy to lexical density. Note that this is **not** saying that writing imposes organization on language. On the contrary: there is every bit as much organization in spoken language as there is in written, only it is organization of a different kind. Written language is corpuscular and gains power by its density, whereas spoken language is wavelike and gains power by its intricacy. I am not, of course, talking about writing in the sense of orthography, contrasting with phonology as medium of expression; but about *written language* – the forms of discourse that arise as a result of this change of medium (by a complex historical process that is based partly on the nature of the medium itself and partly on its functions in society). Similarly in talking about spoken language I mean the forms of discourse which evolved over the long history of language in its spoken mode; the mode in which language itself evolved.

Writing puts language in chains; it freezes it, so that it becomes a **thing** to be reflected on. Hence it changes the ways that language is used for meaning with. Writing deprives language of the power to intuit, to make indefinitely many connections in different directions at once, to explore (by tolerating them) contradictions, to represent experience as fluid and indeterminate. It is therefore destructive of one fundamental human potential: to think on your toes, as we put it.

But, secondly, in destroying this potential it creates another one: that of structuring, categorizing, disciplinizing. It creates a new kind of knowledge: scientific knowledge; and a new way of learning, called education. Thus writing changed the social semiotic on two levels. Superficially, it created documentation – the filing of experience, the potential to 'look things up'. More fundamentally, it offered a new perspective on experience: the synoptic one, with its definitions, taxonomies and constructions. The world of written language is a nominalized world, with a high lexical density and packed grammatical metaphors. It is these features that enable discourse to become technical; as Martin has shown, technicality in language depends on, not writing as such, but the kind of organization of meaning that writing brings with it (Martin 1986b; Wignell 1987). Until information can be organized and packaged in this way – so that only the initiate understands it – knowledge cannot accumulate, since there is no way one discourse can start where other ones left off. When I can say

> the random fluctuations in the spin components of one of the two particles

I am packaging the knowledge that has developed over a long series of preceding arguments and presenting it as 'to be taken for granted – now we can proceed to the next step'. If I cannot do this, but have to say every time that particles spin, that they spin in three dimensions, that a pair of particles can spin in association with one another, that each one of the pair fluctuates randomly as it is spinning, and so on, then it is clear that I will never get very far. I have to have an 'expert' grammar, the kind of grammar that is prepared to throw away experiential information, to take for granted the semantic relations by which the elements are related to one another, so that it can maximize textual information, the systematic development of the discourse as a causeway to further knowledge. That kind of grammar shuts the layman out.

It would take too long to demonstrate in detail how this written grammar works. Let me refer briefly to its two critical properties: nominalization, and grammatical metaphor. Most instances involve a combination of the two. For example,

> such an exercise had the potential for intrusions by the government into the legitimate privacy of non-government schools

Apart from *had*, the clause consists of two nominal groups: *such an exercise* and *the potential for intrusions by the government into the legitimate privacy of non-government schools*. The second of these displays one of the principal devices for creating nominal structures: nominal group *non-government schools* embedded inside prepositional phrase *of non-government schools* embedded inside nominal group *the legitimate privacy of non-government schools* embedded inside prepositional phrase *into the legitimate privacy of non-government schools*; another prepositional phrase *by the government*; the two both embedded in the nominal group *intrusions by (a) into (b)*, itself embedded inside the nominal group *the potential for . . .* And most of these embeddings involve grammatical metaphor: *potential*, nominal expression of modality 'be able to', perhaps even a caused modality 'make + be able to'; *instrusions*, nominal expression of process 'intrude'; *privacy*, nominal expression of quality 'private'; *legitimate*, adjectival expression of attitudinally qualified projection 'as they could reasonably expect to be', and so on. (That these are marked, metaphorical realizations in contrast to unmarked, **congruent** ones is borne out in various ways: not only are the congruent forms developmentally prior – children typically learn to process grammatical metaphor only after the age of eight or nine – but also they are semantically explicit, so that the metaphorical ones can be derived from them but not the other way around. But note that the 'metaphor' is in the grammar; there is not necessarily any lexical shift.)

So to the third step. Writing and speaking, in this technical sense of written language and spoken language, are different grammars which therefore constitute different ways of knowing, such that any theory of knowledge, and of learning, must encompass both. Our understanding of the social and the natural order depends on both, and on the complementarity between the two as interpretations of experience. I sometimes ask teachers about this question: whether there are things in the curriculum they consider best learnt through talking and listening, and other things best learnt through reading and writing. They have seldom thought about this consciously; but their practice often reveals just such a complementarity – processes and process sequences, such as sets of instructions, and including logically ordered sequences of ongoing argument, are presented and explored in speech, whereas structures, definitions, taxonomies and summaries of preceding arguments are handled through writing. Thus the complementarity of speech and writing creates a complementarity in our ways of knowing and of learning; once we are both speakers and writers we have an added dimension to our experience.

Having proclaimed the complementarity, however, I shall now take a fourth step – and end up by privileging speech. Again I stress that I am not talking about the channel; we can all learn to talk in written language, and a few people can manage the harder task of writing in spoken. I am talking about the varieties – spoken language and written language – that arose in association with these two channels. So by speech I mean the natural, unself-monitored discourse of natural dialogue: low in grammatical metaphor, low in lexical density, high in grammatical intricacy, high in rheomodal dynamic. This is language as it evolved as a dynamic open system; these are the features that keep it open, in the far-from-equilibrium state in which it enacts, and so construes, the semiotic parameters of our social, biological and physical levels of being. The frontiers of knowledge, in a post-quantum *nouvelle alliance*,[3] need a grammar of this kind to map them into the realm of 'that which can be meant'. But this mapping does not depend on reference, with the grammar being used in an automatized way to describe. If quantum ideas seem inexpressible, this may be because we have tried too hard to express them. They are almost certainly there already; what we must learn to do is to think grammatically – to recognize the ideological interpretant that is built into language itself.

9 Linguistics as metatheory

We have been saying that natural language is a theory of experience. But it is clear that language is also **a part** of human experience. Thus the system has to be able to include itself.

Lemke has pointed out that a social-semiotic system of this kind is not subject to the Gödelian restriction on self-reference (1984d: 71–3). Such a system can include itself in what it is describing – because it is a theory of praxis, of practices which operate irreversibly, ordered in time. Thus a grammar can also be, at the same time, a theory of grammar. I do not pretend to understand the argument at that point. But it is clear that, since we are interpreting language as it functions to create the natural and social order, and since it is itself part of that order, it must include itself in the description. And if we insist that linguists (*inter alios!*) should reflect on their own praxis as linguists, it is not just because such reflexivity is fashionable these days, but because we have learnt from quantum mechanics that the observer is an essential component in the total picture.

At the same time, as linguists we have learnt to be aware of the dangers of naïve scientism. We have heard at length – and with justice – of the superficial importation of Darwinian concepts into nineteenth-century historical comparatism; and there is a danger in the present situation too. Because we can see in post-quantum and far-from-equilibrium physics exactly the intellectual environment that is needed to make sense of language as we – independently – know it to be, we may all too easily latch on to these ideas and misinterpret them. And I am not claiming that, just by being aware of the danger, I have therefore avoided it myself.

Yet there are still two points to be made. One is that, for all its deflections and superficial applications where it did not fit, the Darwinian perspective was a fundamental one. Language has to be understood in a historico-evolutionary context, as part of evolutionary processes; the mistake is to apply these notions at places that are far too concrete and specific, instead of seeing them as the essential interpretative framework for our endeavours. And the same goes this time round, when all that comes from the sciences of nature resonates so sweetly with everything we as linguists have learnt to expect.

And secondly, it is not, in fact, the same scenario as before. History does not repeat itself – or only on the surface of things. This time, the communication is going both ways. We have become accustomed to accepting the privileged position of the natural sciences, which got their act together first: the nature of a scientific fact, notions of evidence and experimentation, and above all the relationship of the **instance** to the general principle – these were established first in physics, then in biology, and only a very late third in the social sciences.[4] So it was natural that physics should become the model for all the others.

Now, however, there are signs of a reversal. I quote David Bohm again: "the speed of light is taken not as a possible speed of an object, but rather as the maximum speed of propagation of a signal" (p. 123). In the quantum world, events are explained not in terms of causality but in terms of communication, the exchange of information. This is what used to be called "action at a distance" (Gribbin 1985: 182). And from Prigogine and Stengers once more:

> A new type of order has appeared. We can speak of a new coherence, of a mechanism of "communication" among molecules. But this type of communication can arise only in far-from-equilibrium conditions ...
>
> What seems certain is that these far-from-equilibrium phenomena illustrate an essential and unexpected property of matter: physics may henceforth describe structures as adapted to outside conditions ... To use somewhat anthropomorphic language: in equilibrium matter is "blind", but in far-from-equilibrium conditions it begins to be able to perceive, to "take into account", in its way of functioning, differences in the external world ...
>
> The analogy with social phenomena, even with history, is inescapable.
> (p. 14)

All this points us in a new direction. From now on, the human sciences have to assume at least an equal responsibility in establishing the foundations of knowledge. Their coat-tailing days are over. But if so, our practitioners will surely have to learn to behave responsibly, instead of squandering themselves in the wasteful struggle for originality in which everyone else must be deconstructed so that each can leave his (or her) mark. We have to learn to build on our predecessors and move forward, instead of constantly staying behind where they were in order to trample them underfoot.

More importantly, it means that we have to examine our basic concepts in the light of their more general relevance to the sciences of life and of nature. And as soon as we begin to do this, one thing stands out: that, among the human sciences, it is linguistics that finds itself inescapably in the front line. Partly because its object, language, is more accessible than those of sociology and psychology: more readily problematized, and seen to be opaque, than other forms of human behaviour. But more because, if we are to take seriously the notion that the universe is made of information, then we shall need a science of information – and the science of information is linguistics.

Why linguistics, rather than information science as at present constituted? Because natural language is the one non-designed human communication system, on the basis of which all other, artificial systems are conceived. It is presumably not a coincidence that, as technology has moved from the steam engine to the computer, so scientific explanations have moved from causality (limited by the speed of light) to communication (limited by the entropy barrier) (Prigogine and Stengers, p. 295). My colleague Brian McCusker observed that the universe was now "one, whole, undivided and *conscious*", so that the science of sciences had to be psychology (McCusker 1983: 239). I think he should have said "one, whole, undivided and *communicative*". The source of interpretation of the universe as a communication system, in so far as this can be brought within the constraints of our understanding, has to be sought in grammar – the grammar of natural language, since that is where our understanding is born, and that is the means whereby we act and reflect on ourselves and our environment. If there is to be a science of sciences in the twenty-first century it will have to include linguistics – as at least a partner, and perhaps the leading partner, in the next round of man's dialogue with nature.

Notes

1. Based on an analysis of weather reports in the *New York Times* and *Chicago Tribune*, May–June 1985 (Halliday and Matthiessen, forthcoming).
2. Cf. Briggs and Peat (1985: 54): "Bohr approved of the uncertainty principle itself, believing it was an aspect of a deeper idea he called "complementarity". Complementarity meant the universe can never be described in a single, clear picture but must be apprehended through overlapping, complementary and sometimes paradoxical views. Bohr found echoes of this idea in classical Chinese philosophy and the theories

of modern psychology." He would have found them also in the grammar of natural languages.

3. The title of the original French version of Prigogine and Stengers's *Order out of Chaos* was *La Nouvelle Alliance*.

4. Culler (1977) identifies Durkheim, Freud and Saussure as those primarily responsible.

Chapter Six

NEW WAYS OF MEANING: THE CHALLENGE TO APPLIED LINGUISTICS
(1990)

In 1984 in Brussels, Francisco Gomes de Matos opened the Sixth World Congress by reviewing the history of previous congresses and assessing how far in those twenty years applied linguistics could be said to have progressed towards maturity. He referred to the first one in the series, the Premier Colloque International de Linguistique Appliquée held at Nancy in 1964; and noted the doubts then expressed by the organizers about holding a colloquium devoted to applied linguistics (1984: 1736–79). Rereading the preface to that Nancy volume, by Bernard Pottier and Guy Bourquin (1966: 7–8), I was struck by what they had selected as the initial theme, that of "semantic information":

l'information sémantique en linguistique et en traduction mécanique

to which, with some hesitation, they had added another, that of foreign language teaching;

nous avons ... risqué l'entreprise, en adjoignant au thème initial celui de la pédagogie des langues vivantes: ...

This, they explained, was why the book seemed to lack unity:

d'où l'incohérence apparente du contenu de ce volume.

Those times have changed. In Sydney, at the Eighth World Congress in 1987, out of 548 papers submitted for consideration about one half were on some aspect of second language teaching and learning; while the "initial theme" from the Nancy colloquium was hardly represented at all. Very soon after Nancy, machine translation largely disappeared

First published in *Journal of Applied Linguistics* 6 (*Ninth World Congress of Applied Linguistics Special Issue*). Greek Applied Linguistics Association, 1990, pp. 7–36.

from the academic scene in Western Europe and North America; meanwhile "semantic information" was shifted to the domains of computational linguistics and artificial intelligence, and these had their own international forums and events. It is quite natural that our efforts should constantly be regrouped into new and different formations. We have already seen the generalized concept of educational linguistics emerging during this time. We have not yet reached a comparable stage with clinical linguistics; this has still not become a unified concept, although there are major achievements in particular areas, and the theoretical base in neurolinguistics is certainly gaining strength (Peng 1985; McKellar 1990). And the other major area that has developed during this period is that of language policy and planning. At the same time, however, it is noticeable that with all the varied activities that go under the name of applied linguistics we have still not really achieved a transdisciplinary perspective. I say "transdisciplinary" rather than "inter-" or "multi-disciplinary" because the latter terms seem to me to imply that one still retains the disciplines as the locus of intellectual activity, while building bridges between them, or assembling them into a collection; whereas the real alternative is to supersede them, creating new forms of activity which are thematic rather than disciplinary in their orientation.

A discipline is defined according to its content: what it is that is under investigation. The study of life forms, for example, constitutes the discipline of biology; and such disciplines split up into taxonomies as their domains become more and more subdivided: first biology, then zoology, then invertebrate zoology, entomology and so on. A theme, on the other hand, is defined not by content but by aspect, perspective or point of view. Perhaps the earliest theme to emerge in European scholarship was mathematics. If I measure anything systematically I am doing mathematics; it does not matter what it is I am measuring. The 'content' of mathematics does not exist in the material world; it is created by the activity of mathematics itself and consists of ideal objects like numbers, square roots and triangles. In the nineteenth century, history became transformed into a theme, in the form of evolution: any phenomenon could be studied from the standpoint of how it evolved. The twentieth century then countered this with the theme of structuralism: any phenomenon studied from the complementary standpoint of how it is organized and held together. This gave us our sense of language as "un système où tout se tient",[1] to use Meillet's famous phrase that Firth so vigorously objected to. Sometimes the theme may appear without its name being taken up, like cybernetics for

140

phenomena considered as circular, self-regulating systems; or more recently cladistics, for phenomena studied from the standpoint of how they change, whether by evolution, by growth or by individuation. For students of language it seems to me that the most important theme to emerge in this half century has been semiotics: any phenomenon investigated from the standpoint of what it means – anything considered as information, if you prefer. Not everyone likes the associations of this term – I myself do not accept the implication that the study of meaning must be grounded in some theory of the sign. But it serves to make explicit the perspective that some of us try to adopt, not only towards language but towards many other human activities as well.

We have recognized for a long time that activities such as teaching a foreign language involve more than the content of any one discipline: at the very least, they involve psychology and sociology as well as linguistics. Our academic courses – MA in Applied Linguistics, and its equivalents in other educational systems – have always been inter-disciplinary in this sense. Now I am not suggesting that such programmes can be underwritten by a single theme, any more than they can be by a single discipline; they are much too complex and many sided to be looked at from any one perspective alone. But I think in the future such activities will benefit as much from the complementarity of different themes as from the summation of different disciplines. Our practice as language teachers depends more on our being able to adopt the complementary perspectives of two conflicting themes, that of 'learning' and that of 'meaning', than on putting together pieces from linguistics with pieces from psychology and sociology. The reason learning a foreign language can be so extraordinarily difficult for an adolescent or adult who has not grown up multilingual is that there is a real-life contradiction between these two modes of processing language: that of learning it for future use, and that of using it. They can no longer both learn language and 'mean it' at the same time. The teacher cannot resolve this contradiction, but has somehow to transform it from a constraint into a condition which enables, and even enforces, the learning process.

Another activity that has become a major concern of applied linguistics – and which is no less complex, as regards the themes that are involved, than language teaching – is that of language policy and planning. I do not know at which of our congresses this first emerged as a separate section; there were thirty-one papers in the proceedings of this section at Brussels, as well as references to language planning in papers of many other sections, and we have had a Scientific Commission in this field from the start. Language planning is a highly complex set of activities involving the intersection of two very different and potentially conflicting themes: one, that of 'meaning', common to all our activities with language, and other semiotics as well; the other theme, that of 'design'. If we start from the broad distinction between designed systems and evolved systems, then language planning means introducing design processes and design features into a system (namely language) which is naturally evolving. This is bound to be a highly complex and sensitive task.

The greater part of language planning activity is institutional rather than systemic: that is to say, it has to do with planning not the forms of a language but the relationship between a language and those who use it.[2] The main issues are what languages to use for what purposes in the community and how to ensure that people in the community have access to the languages they want. This aspect of language planning involves formulating policies, getting them adopted, and making provision – primarily educational provision – for ensuring that they are carried out. These measures provide, in their turn, the institutional context for work in second language teaching; and also for work in mother tongue teaching for purposes of language maintenance and vernacular literacy.

They also provide the context for language planning of the systemic kind; in which the aim is to design the language itself, so as to expand its potential for meaning. Typically this kind of planning is undertaken when a language is being developed for use in new registers – new functional contexts in which it has not previously served. Almost always the main effort is directed towards expanding the **lexical** resources: planning consists in establishing principles for the creation of new terms, and applying these principles so as to develop systematic technical taxonomies in specific registers defined by field, or discipline. An example of this is the development programme for Swahili, as reported by S. J. Maina of the Kiswahili Council of Tanzania (1987). Discussing the enrichment of Kiswahili, Maina notes that "much of the effort is being specifically directed towards enrichment of Kiswahili terminology". He refers to the "three main processes [generally] used for the enrichment of terminology in a language", namely compounding, derivation and borrowing; and gives examples from Swahili of all three, specifying the types of compounding and derivation that are used and the sources of borrowed words. The policy context for this work is

Kiswahili as a medium of instruction: Maina notes that "there is a definite move towards the adoption of Kiswahili as a language of instruction in Secondary Schools".

Maina also notes some of the objections that have been raised, mainly to new terms whose taxonomic relationship is obscure (e.g. the words suggested for *hydrophily*, *hydrophyte* and *hydrotropism* have no common element corresponding to the *hydro-*); and some of the difficulties that arise with compounds that "carry a heavy semantic load" but which are not yet felt as single words. "A high frequency of usage will hopefully make users forget looking at the components of the words and accept the single lexical unit."

If we now turn to the grammar, then apart from the grammatical processes involved in the formation of new words, which may need minor adjustment, very little attention in language planning is devoted to developing the grammar of the language. Not that the planning agencies neglect grammar; but the effort here is directed towards standardization and the correction of errors, not to the development of new grammatical patterns. This naturally raises the question: why? – or rather, why not? Why does enriching the language not connote also the enrichment of the grammar? The answer, presumably, would be either that it is not necessary or that it is not possible; or perhaps some combination of the two, such as that it would be desirable but is too difficult.

To say that the grammar is not planned means that no one intervenes in its evolution by design. It does not imply that no grammatical changes take place; they clearly do. Newspapers in countries with rapidly developing languages frequently carry complaints that the language does not read like itself any more; it reads like English, or whatever is the predominant external source. Typical examples given are various kinds of **voice** pattern: that is, clause types analogous to passives, derived equatives (clefts and pseudo-clefts) and so on, which function to distribute the balance of information in the clause, along lines comparable to Theme + Rheme and Given + New in English. It is hard to say whether the patterns that seem alien to the speakers of the language have been "borrowed", by loan translation, or have been "coined" in the language itself; that line is virtually impossible to draw. Since the contexts in which they are used are contexts that are already associated with English (science and technology, bureaucracy and administration), and since their discourse functions are already defined in English discourse, such patterns will tend to seem English (that is, foreign) anyway, whether or not the forms themselves bear any great resemblance to English syntax. It is the overt semantic style that seems imported.

But whether or not it is possible to trace the **source** of particular changes, there may be significantly different views on what underlying general **processes** are taking place. Let me try and summarize these views in their canonical forms, recognizing that those who incline towards one view or another would often hold some modified version of it. One view would be that all languages are the unchanged products – unchanged, that is, except on the surface – of a semantic development that took place early on in human history, determining the overall structure and content of the semantic system, which is therefore universal to all humankind. The grammar is the arbitrary, or conventional, representation of a pre-existing reality, or a pre-existing cognitive model of such reality. Of course, new things are constantly being created, new objects, institutions and abstractions, and these get names; but naming new things (in this view) does not by itself perturb the semantic environment – hence if new grammatical forms arise in the course of technical development, they have been borrowed. In this view the lexicon is kept clearly distinct from the grammar, and the grammar is concerned only with ideational meaning, interpersonal functions being excluded. Enriching a language, in this view, means creating new terms which operate, or could operate, within existing contexts of use. I think Labov's perspective would be fairly close to this one.

A second view would be that language is continually evolving, and that this includes the semantic system, which is not constant for all times and places but differs from one time and one place to another. The material and non-material conditions of a culture are reflected in the grammar of its language, which is not arbitrary; when these change the language changes in response. The language thus optimizes itself in relation to its environment: new forms will arise when called for – they do not need to be borrowed. An explicit version of this view was articulated by N. Ya. Marr and his associates in the Soviet Union in the 1930s and 1940s, based on a simplified Marxist interpretation of history, with language as part of the superstructure erected on the economic base; language changed through stages, or "stades", corresponding to primitive communist, slave, feudal and capitalist modes of production. As an example Marr cited the ergative structure in transitivity, which he thought reflected a way of explaining

144

phenomena arrived at before an understanding of causality had been reached.[3] Put in more general terms, this view would hold that language reflects reality through the intermediary of human cultures; hence in the long run the grammar changes in response to the patterns of cultural change, even if the process is a very gradual and indirect one.

There is obviously much room for intermediate positions between these two extremes. But there is also a third view which is different from either of them: the view formulated by Whorf, following on from Sapir, and also, against rather different intellectual backgrounds, by Hjelmslev and by Firth. In this view language does not passively **reflect** reality; language actively **creates** reality. It is the grammar – but now in the sense of lexicogrammar, the grammar plus the vocabulary, with no real distinction between the two – that shapes experience and transforms our perceptions into meanings. The categories and concepts of our material existence are not 'given' to us prior to their expression in language. Rather, they are **construed** by language, at the intersection of the material with the symbolic. Grammar, in the sense of the syntax and vocabulary[4] of a natural language, is thus a theory of human experience. It is also a principle of social action. In both these functions, or metafunctions, grammar creates the potential within which we act and enact our cultural being.[5] This potential is at once both enabling and constraining: that is, grammar makes meaning possible and also sets limits on what can be meant.

I shall adopt this third view: that our "reality" is not something ready-made and waiting to be meant – it has to be actively construed; and that language evolved in the process of, and as the agency of, its construal. Language is not a superstructure on a base; it is a product of the **conscious** and the **material** impacting each on the other – of the contradiction between our material being and our conscious being, as antithetic realms of experience. Hence language has the power to shape our consciousness; and it does so for each human child, by providing the theory that he or she uses to interpret and to manipulate their environment.[6]

But, by the same token, since language evolves out of the impact between the material and the conscious modes of being, it follows that as material conditions change the forms given by language to consciousness also change. Grammar construes reality according to the prevailing means and relations of production – or what we wrongly call "production" (I shall return to this at the end). But these are not constant; they have **evolved** through different forms at different times and places. The meaning-making potential of language – the grammar, in our current sense of the term – has evolved along with them. It is also not the same throughout the courses of human history.

But the relationship of the grammar to these changing material conditions is an extremely complex one. Semogenic processes – processes of constructing meaning – cannot be understood **outside of** their historical contexts; but neither can they be **derived from** these contexts by any simple relation. Let us put it this way: language is at the same time a part of reality, a shaper of reality, and a metaphor for reality. Once any form of language – any grammar – has come into being, it participates itself in the shaping of historical processes, including those which constitute the means and relations of production. First, as a part of reality it makes it possible for people to coordinate material practices and it constructs the social relationships that go with them. Secondly, in enabling these forms to evolve it also, as the 'construer' of reality, both ensures and at the same time constrains their evolution into something else. Language constrains their evolution because the reality that the grammar enacts is that of the prevailing socioeconomic order; hence language will tend to be conservative – the way things 'are' **is** the way they are. But it ensures that the forms will evolve, because the grammar can never be either fixed or monolithic; it also contains all the prevailing contradictions and complementarities, both those that exist **within** the material, socioeconomic domain, and those that inhere in the impact that engendered language in the first place, that **between** the material domain and the conscious one. And so, thirdly, as a metaphor for reality language re-enacts, simultaneously, in its own internal system-and-process, through multiple fractal formations, the various contradictions and complementarities that it imposes on the reality that it is construing.

So while any language can create new names overnight, its semantic base – what Stalin, in demolishing Marr, called its grammatical system and basic lexical stock – under typical conditions[7] change only very slowly. The mechanism of such change has to be sought in the dialectic between the *system* and the *instance* (Halliday 1987: 135–54). But such change is not random (here Marr was right): it is a function of changes in the material conditions of the culture. The history of language is **part** of human history; it is not some mysterious surrogate process that goes bubbling along on its own. Thus major upheavals in human history are also linguistic upheavals. Grammar, since it is internal to language (not located at either material interface), can to a certain extent 'take off' on

146

its own; but since it is the powerhouse for construing experience there can never be a total disjunction between the symbolic forms and the material conditions of their environment.

What are the major upheavals in human history that seem to have also been critical in what we might call semohistory? One is, almost certainly, settlement: the gradual transition from moving around after food to staying in one place and raising it. A second is probably the "iron age" of classical Greece, India and China – although these two could be seen as the initiating aspect and the culminating aspect of a single complex transition. A third would be the so-called "renaissance" in Europe, culminating in the industrial revolution. And we should now add a fourth, namely the present: the move into an age of information, if you like, although we may need to think of it in rather different terms. Let me try to focus on these as changes in the semiotic construction of reality: not seeing them in terms of any of our western ideological constructs – neither with eighteenth-century 'fall from grace' romanticism, nor with nineteenth-century 'all for the better' progressivism, nor with twentieth-century 'nothing ever changes' ostrichism; but recognizing that they were transformations in the human condition which took place in some places and not others, among some peoples and not others, for a variety of complex historical and geographical reasons. There was nothing inevitable about them; rather, they arose as a potential which on some occasions was taken up.[8]

A significant component in these historical upheavals, I am suggesting, is a change in ways of meaning.

1 With settlement, the shift from hunting and gathering to pastoral and agricultural practices, there developed a new semiotic mode, namely writing; but the importance of writing lies in the grammar that develops along with it. This is a grammar in which **things** are construed as commodities; they take on value, and can be itemized and drawn up in lists. This work is done by the nominal group: nouns are measured into quantities, they are assigned qualities along various scales, and organized into taxonomies of classes and sub-classes. It is also a grammar in which social relations are transformed into institutions. But the main source of **abstract** meaning seems to shift from the interpersonal towards the ideational – from, for example, the rights and duties of kinship to generalizations about the phenomena of experience;[9] and within the ideational, from processes towards things. This shift into 'settlement' semantics is of course masterminded by the grammar, but it is also constituted iconically by the shift into the

147

written medium, whereby discourse itself becomes a thing and the abstractions – the written symbols and their arrangements – are transformations of processes into things. It is important to stress, however, that writing is not a cause; we are not talking about causal relationships but about realizational ones, whereby in the impacting between the material processes and the processes of human conscious-ness the grammar construes the reality of a settled agricultural existence, in which activities lead to products, and the space-time flux of experience is overlaid by constructions of objects having fixed location in space. Overlaid, but not obliterated: the pre-settlement grammar is still there in the language – but it is no longer the predominant mode of meaning. We could perhaps give an analogy with the history of a late twentieth-century individual: in the course of learning to read and write, the child takes on the grammar of the primary school, with its different construction of meanings – but the grammar of home and neighbourhood is still there underneath it.

2   In the classical, iron age culture of the Eurasian continent, the grammar became further transformed, taking up and expanding those options by which phenomena became "objectified", so that other domains of experience, hitherto construed as process-like, could be modelled in terms of things. As techniques evolved into technologies, discourse too became technical: the grammars of ancient Greek, Chinese and Sanskrit construed processes and properties as nouns, like 'movement', 'force', 'change', 'volume', 'line'; and created long mathematical nominal groups, like this one from Aristarchus of Samos:

> The straight line subtending the portion intercepted within the earth's shadow of the circumference of the circle in which the extremities of the diameter dividing the dark and the light portions of the moon move ...

– all of which is merely the Subject of the clause.[10] If we continue the educational analogy, these are the ways of meaning the student will meet in the middle school, where educational knowledge becomes technical and the disciplines begin to emerge.

3   Then, with the "advancement of learning" that led to what we, in the west, were brought up to think of as the "modern" age, the grammar was restructured once again, this time through a **meta-phorical** upheaval which resulted in the kind of language now used at congresses of applied linguistics, or indeed at congresses of all kinds and in many other contexts as well. Reality has been reconstrued in the learned, bureaucratic and technocratic mode that we are all so familiar with today; for example,

> What we seek is a capability for early initiative of offensive action by air and land forces to bring about the conclusion of battle on our terms.

– naïvely, we want to be able to attack first to make sure we can win.

It would be a gross oversimplification to present all our semohistory as a relentless march towards what one might call "thinginess". The semiotic processes involved are highly complex, and they lead to syndromes of all kinds of features which coexist in coteries, complementarities and contradictions. Moreover the grammar of every language is a mix of semiotic modes, whether or not it has been through these various upheavals. But the particular mix that characterizes the elaborated tertiary styles of the Eurasian world languages, from Japanese and Chinese at one end of the continent to English, French and Spanish at the other, is the result of the layering, one on top of another, of all these various 'moments' in their history through which experience has been ongoingly reconstrued in successively more abstract and objectified terms.

I hope by now we are beyond the point where we have to pretend that everybody's world view is alike, just in order to protect ourselves from a foolish accusation of prejudice by those who cannot distinguish between 'different from' and 'better (or worse) than'. The task for applied linguistics here is to **interpret** the grammatical construction of reality: to use our theory of grammar – let us call it our "grammatics" – as a metatheory for understanding how grammar functions as a theory of experience. This means taking account both of those features that are apparently found in all languages, and so constitute the construction of the essential human experience, and those that are specific to particular forms and phases of the human condition.

It is a difficult task, which tends to get pushed off the agenda; it is so hard to do and so easy to decry. Let us try and locate ourselves somewhere in between two extreme opposing points of view. One extreme would be: all grammatical patterning, whether invariant or varying between languages or within one language, is random and arbitrary, and has no bearing whatever on how people interpret experience. At the other extreme would be the view that all grammatical patterning, invariant or varying, contributes directly to the construction of reality. Now, everything we know about language, and also about human systems, suggests that neither extreme is likely to be valid: we should expect that some kinds of patterning will be relevant but not all, and some kinds more relevant than others. Two criteria suggest themselves. One is that such significant semantic effects will be achieved not by any single grammatical features, but only by syndromes, assemblies of features from different parts of the grammar which typically co-occur, in part reinforcing each other and in part contradicting each other, but constituting as a whole a distinctive meaning style. The other criterion is that such features are likely to be covert rather than overt; they will be found among the cryptotypic patterns of the grammar which typically remain beyond the limits of our conscious attention. Only the interplay of diverse semantic forces, largely hidden from view, would be powerful enough to slant us towards one rather than another among the 'possible worlds' into which our experience could be construed.

If we look at the world as a whole it is clear that different reality constructions can and do coexist. There are a few communities, now highly at risk, whose meaning styles are those of a hunting-gathering, non-settlement culture; there are large areas of peoples who mean in a settled but non-urbanized, agricultural mode; and a fairly massive portion of the globe dominated by industrialized, urban semantic patterns. These groups are not insulated from one another; there is constant mixing and interpenetration of the different modes. We cannot work with the traditional disjunction between sociology and anthropology, or its counterpart in literacy theory, according to which there are two human populations, the writers and the non-writers, with a clear dichotomy between them. Rather we should envisage a multidimensional space within which human beings construe experience, with certain regions within that space being taken up preferentially by different groups to resonate with the different conditions of their material existence.

But since these conditions were in fact ordered in time – thus the industrial age followed the agricultural age and not the other way round – there is an implicational scaling here: a settlement grammar has evolved through a non-settlement grammar, but not vice versa. Hence the layering of meaning styles referred to earlier: the different models of reality coexist within one language, features of the earlier phase persisting in very much the same way that features of the earlier material conditions continue to be part of the total experience. (A word of caution here. It is important not to be seduced by the analogy of the individual mentioned earlier. The individual child may, up to a certain point, recapitulate the history of the semantic system as he moves through primary, middle and tertiary education. But this pattern of change is one of growth, not one of evolution; if we say the earlier phases "persist" this is in a very different metaphorical sense.) But if different models of reality coexist within one language, what is to ensure that every group takes up the same set of options, construing their experience according to the same semantic priorities? The person who put this question on the agenda was Basil Bernstein, who showed that within our western societies there were in fact distinct modes of meaning by which the two major social classes construed reality – and that while the members of the working class typically selected for one mode, those in the middle class did not just select for the other but ranged over both. This is just the pattern that we should expect if the two modes derive from different phases in the evolution of the system. This is not to suggest that Bernstein's "restricted code" is the language of pre-industrial societies; that would be absurd – and in any case impossible, given the nature of evolutionary change. What it is saying is that the forms of discourse that Bernstein identified under the heading of restricted code (notably the orientation towards the particular in ideational meanings and towards the implicit in interpersonal meanings) constitute semantic styles which, while continuing to evolve, have not taken up the specific options that construe experience according to the changed conditions of late capitalist society – as it is construed, that is, by those who orchestrate the changes.

Bernstein ran head-on into the greatest disjunction of all: that a class-supported culture cannot admit the reality of social class. He was vilified from all sides, his professional standing arraigned; even today he is being labelled "class chauvinist", by people who have never read what he wrote and, to their shame and disgrace, will casually (that is, in a 'to be taken for granted' manner) guillotine a scholar who dares to break their sacred taboos. What Bernstein understood was that, given a single grammar, the potential of that grammar can be taken up in consistently different ways by different groups of people, selecting with different probabilities in the same system and so in effect construing different forms of social relationships and different models of experience. Bernstein's original and very practical concern was to show how one of the two groups was consistently disfavoured by this process – a semiotic process which turns out to be the fundamental mechanism by which oppressed groups in society contribute to the status quo of their own oppression.

151

Since we cannot quantify 'same or different', it is largely a matter of our own angle of approach whether we say that restricted and elaborated codes, or coding orientations, construe different realities, or the same reality seen from different ends. What we need to recognize is that, while the **system** of the language construes the ideology of society as a whole, the **deployment of resources within the system** differentiates among different groups within a society. There is nominalization in both codes; but that in the elaborated code is both more abstract and more general, and abstraction times generalization equals power. There is grammatical metaphor in both; but that in the elaborated code tends to be ideational, that in the restricted code interpersonal – and ideational metaphor equals power. The elaborated code is not merely the code in which the genres of power are written; it is the code in which material and social reality are construed from the standpoint of those who dispose of it.

One of the few of Bernstein's contemporaries who understood what he was saying was Mary Douglas, who saw that he was (as she put it) "cutting the middle classes down to size". But Bernstein's linguistic data base was limited, and it is only now that we have a large-scale study where it is shown by systematic linguistic analysis, clause by clause, of over 20,000 clauses (the full sample is three times as large) that he was right. Ruqaiya Hasan, in her study of the natural conversations that take place between mothers and their three-year-old children, has demon-strated that in an Australian urban society there are systematic and regular semantic differences in the way mothers talk to children, according to two social factors: one, the sex of the child, and two, the class of the family (Hasan 1990; Hasan and Cloran 1990).

Now everyone recognizes – well, perhaps not yet everyone; but very many people recognize – that the resources of the grammar as they are typically deployed in the discourse of settlement languages construe the world from the angle of the male, whether in encoding social norms, in naming and addressing, in assigning transitivity roles or a variety of other such enactments (Poynton 1987; on assignment of agency roles see Thwaite 1983; for an example of the linguistic construction of sexist ideology see Hasan 1986; see also Threadgold and Cranny-Francis 1990). We have a Scientific Commission on Language and Sex to deal with the situation (and note in this connection that it is **assumed** that by working on the language you can change social reality, which makes sense only if you accept that reality is construed in language). But why have we no Scientific Commission on Language and Class? When Hasan shows that mothers of boys use a different code from mothers of girls, she is praised for having added a new dimension to our understanding of language and sex. When she shows by the same linguistic techniques that working class mothers use a different code from middle class mothers, she is criticized on the grounds that there are no such things as social classes, and (somewhat self-contradictorily) that anyway mothers and children do not belong to them. It is not difficult to see why, although the explanation may sound very obvious. It is acceptable to show up sexism – as it is to show up racism – because to eliminate sexual and racial bias would pose no threat to the existing social order: capitalist society could thrive perfectly well without sex discrimination and without race discrimination. But it is not acceptable to show up classism, especially by objective linguistic analysis as Hasan has done; because capitalist society could not exist without discrimination between classes. Such work could, ultimately, threaten the existing order of society.

If language merely 'reflects' our experience of what is out there, by correspondence with the categories of the material world, it is hard to see how we could threaten or subvert the existing order by means of working on language. But this is what we are doing when we plan the grammar in order to combat sexism. That this makes sense is because language does not correspond; it construes. We are not easily aware of these effects because they are quantitative and gradual; and, as Paul Ehrlich has pointed out, as a species we are not biologically predisposed to recognize and respond to gradual effects, the "innumerable small momenta" so aptly labelled by Whorf. We recognize and respond to catastrophes; but the evolution of meaning is not usually catastrophic (except when a Shakespeare or a Newton comes along), and we do not naturally attend to the steady, infiltrating linguistic processes by which our ideological constructions are put in place.

For the same reasons, it is hard to illustrate these effects from text examples; if we represent them *instantially*, we need very large samples of discourse to bring them out. By the same token, however, we can represent them *systemically* – as features of the system rather than of the instance. (That is, as *langue* rather than as *parole* – except that we have first to deconstruct that dichotomy, in order to show that they are not distinct phenomena, but complementary aspects of the same phenomenon.) Let me cite two examples of meaning construction from languages in the Eurasian culture band which did not participate in the original western shift to capitalism and industrial technology: Urdu, and Tagalog. Hasan (1984a) has shown that Urdu has very many "implicit devices": that is, grammatical contexts in which no reference is made to the entity (person or thing) that is involved in a particular process because the context of situation makes it clear. Taken by itself, this could be an arbitrary fact of the grammar; the significant point is, however, that Urdu speakers positively favour the "implicit" option wherever it is available. To be an Urdu speaker "is to believe that your addressee knows what you are on about; it is to assume that the chances of ambiguity are so low as to be almost negligible". The listener can construe the text because of participating in the same culture, in which so much is taken for granted about social relationships and about possible roles. And this brings out the dialectic between the system and the instance: the grammar provides the potential, the systemic options, for implicit reference; these options resonate with the prevailing patterns of the culture; they are taken up as the most frequent options in everyday discourse; this feature is thus reinforced as part of the grammatical system. Thus the instances constitute the system, and the system defines the potential for each instance.

In the grammar of Tagalog, Martin (1988) identifies three key motifs that are critical for the cultural construction of reality – he refers to them as "grammatical conspiracies"; these are the motifs of face, family and fate. For each of these Martin presents syndromes of features that 'conspire' to construe experience and enact social relationships in certain ways which he then contrasts with comparable features in English. Thus in the *family* motif, "the basic theme ... is that of "togetherness": doing things together or having things in common". Martin relates this to Hasan's 'taking things for granted' in Urdu, identifying ten features in the grammar which collectively construct togetherness; and contrasts it with English grammar's construction of individuality. *Face* "has to do with appearances: respecting other persons' positions, possibly at one's own expense"; this 'appearance' is contrasted with the English orientation to 'reality', and is construed by a further ten grammatical features. The "basic theme of the *fate* conspiracy is that of events taking place outside of an individual's control – things simply happen; one cannot really determine one's fate". Martin finds nine features sustaining this "fatalistic" construction, and this he contrasts with the "deterministic" construction of English.[11]

The kinds of meaning style described by Hasan and by Martin tend to be characteristic of cultures where the members are close-knit and homogeneous, and share many of the same assumptions and values. It is an extension of family language, a semantics for contexts where only a small proportion of one's total discourse would involve interacting with strangers. Of course this kind of discourse occurs among speakers of English too; and presumably in every language in the appropriate interpersonal contexts. But what Hasan and Martin are saying is that this cultural reality is actively constructed by regular and systematic features of the grammar of the languages concerned. And here we find a significant contrast with English. Mathesius (1928) had already drawn attention over fifty years ago to certain changes that took place in Late Middle/Early Modern English, coinciding with the spread of printing and hence with the cultural upheaval of the renaissance. These seem to make up a syndrome which, interpreted in systemic terms, realigned the metafunctional priorities as between the textual and the ideational elements in the structure of every clause.

Following up Mathesius' observations we can identify certain features entering into this 'conspiracy', for example: (i) the shift from the bonding of Subject with Actor to the bonding of Subject with Theme, e.g. *I was accosted by a stranger* rather than *a stranger accosted me* or *me a stranger accosted,* leading to much more frequent use of the passive voice; (ii) the shift from mental process forms *methinks, melikes* etc. to *I think, I like,* (iii) the proliferation of phrasal verbs, with a shift from *I'll raise the matter* to *I'll take the matter up,* from *how can we solve this equation?* to *how can we work this equation out?,* getting the verb at the end of the clause; (iv) the pairing of expressions like *take the tailor this cloth* and *take this cloth to the tailor,* or *play the devil at cards, play cards with the devil,* where the difference between *the tailor* and *to the tailor,* or *the devil* and *with the devil,* has nothing to do with the transitivity functions (the part played by *the tailor, the devil* in the **process**, which is the same in both variants) but signals different roles in the information structure of the clause; (v) the spread of thematic equatives ("clefts and pseudo-clefts") permitting any distribution of the elements of the clause into thematic and informational values. All these patterns conspire to construe the discourse first and foremost in terms of Theme + Rheme and Given + New, with one element clearly signalled as Theme at the beginning of the clause and the main item of news having an unmarked location at the end. And there are other features associated with these in rather deep and complex ways; for example the shift from *dined, nodded, sounded, erred* to *had dinner, gave a nod, made a noise, made a mistake;* from *her hair is long, my arm is broken* to *she has long hair, I have a broken arm;* and the predominance of verbs displaying the ergative-type voice system, such as *the door opened/she opened the door, a new method evolved/they evolved a new method, he never changes his ideas/his ideas never change.* These features evolved as part of the newly emerging standard spoken English; and they lead to a form of discourse in which the dominant patterns in the grammar, in the sense of those which determine primarily what options are taken up, are the *textual* patterns of theme and information rather than – or at least as much as – the *ideational* patterns of transitivity. In other words, the ways of meaning of the listener are precisely **not** taken for granted. This kind of discourse can be spoken to a stranger, who shares neither the norms of interaction nor even necessarily the context of situation; likewise it can be written in a book that is going to be printed in multiple copies. These are the things a standard language is for; and they need a grammar in which the organization of the message, and the information value of each of its parts, will **typically** be rendered explicit.

At the same time as this general, non-technical grammar was settling in place in English there were evolving in the major languages of Europe (among which English was emerging as one) the new technical registers of science and of learning, destined to form the leading edge in construing the new reality. Both in the Italian of Galileo and in the English of Isaac Newton we find more or less identical syndromes of grammatical features constituting the semantic character of scientific discourse. Let me enumerate the most important of these, drawing for Galileo on the work of Maria Biagi (1989; see also Zanarini 1982; for the language of Newton see Halliday 1988a).

(1) Abstract nouns as *technical* terms, from ancient Greek via classical and medieval Latin:

velocità; mutazione	incidence; proportion

(2) *Metaphorical* nouns as nominalizations of processes and properties, *non–technical*:

il toccamento dell'acqua con la barca	the diverging and separation of the heterogeneous rays

(3) Nominal groups expanded with words functioning as *Epithet* and *Classifier* (pre-Head in English, post-Head in Italian); such words often derived from processes and properties by (2) above:

il moto generale diurno	several contiguous refracting Mediums

(4) Nominal groups expanded with *phrases* and *clauses* functioning as *Qualifier* (post-Head in both languages), such phrases and clauses often derived likewise from (2) above:

156

| il mobile cadente lungo il piano | the Whiteness of the emerging Light |
| quegli animaletti volanti con pari velocità | the Motion of the Ray generated by the refracting Force of the Body |

(5) **Metaphorical** verbs as verbalization of logical relations ('causes', 'proves', 'follows' etc.):

| risulta da; succede | arises from; is occasioned by |

(6) Ways of chaining abstract participants through the text.
(7) Long hypotactic and paratactic clause complexes, especially in the description of experiments.

The last two would require long passages of text for their illustration. But the following short extract from Newton (1952: 282) will exemplify a number of the features listed above:

> In this Proposition I suppose the transparent Bodies to be thick; because if the thickness of the Body be much less than the Interval of the Fits of easy Reflexion and Transmission of the Rays, the body loseth its reflecting power. For if the Rays, which at their entering into the Body are put into Fits of easy Transmission, arrive at the farthest Surface of the Body before they be out of those Fits, they must be transmitted. And this is the reason why Bubbles of Water lose their reflecting power when they grow very thin; and why all opake Bodies, when reduced into very small parts, become transparent.

Neither Galileo nor Newton was inventing new forms of language. Probably all the grammatical features of their discourse already existed in Italian, or in English. What they did was to reconstruct the probabilities of the system; and in doing so, to create a new register – not alone, of course, but in conjunction with others taking part in the activity of science. This carried still further the trend towards thinginess that had started in ancient times. But while evolving as clearly distinct varieties, they were in no way insulated from other forms of the standard language, including its spoken forms; thus scientific English both depended on and contributed to the standardization process and the new trends and patterns in the grammar that went with it.

Newton and his contemporaries were well aware that they needed to create new forms of discourse for codifying, transmitting and extending the new scientific knowledge. By Newton's time there had already been a century or more of language planning in various countries of Europe, notably France and England; at first concerned just with writing – shorthands and universal character systems (for writing all languages in the same form, like numbers); then lexical taxonomies (for scientific classification of natural phenomena); and finally artificial 'languages' based on general logical principles of word formation. Such efforts were concentrated on designing the more accessible features of language – the lexis and morphology; and none of the designed systems was ever in fact used.[12] The grammar in its more hidden aspects was not planned; we can be virtually certain that neither Newton nor Galileo before him were at all aware of the important grammatical developments that characterized their work. But it was the grammar that provided the critical resources for constructing the new discourse: in Newton,

(1) complex tactic patterns, based on those of speech, for the description of experiments, e.g.

> I found moreover, that when Light goes out of Air through several contiguous refracting mediums as through Water and Glass, and thence goes out again into Air, whether the refracting Superficies be parallel or inclin'd to one another, that Light as often as by contrary Refractions 'tis so corrected, that it emergeth in Lines parallel to those in which it was incident, continues ever after to be white. (p. 129)

(2) elaborate postmodified nominal groups for the mathematical expressions, for example:

> The Excesses of the Sines of Refraction of several sorts of Rays above their common Sine of Incidence when the Refractions are made out of divers denser Mediums immediately into one and the same rarer Medium, suppose of Air, are to one another in a given Proportion.
> (p. 130)

(3) and most of all, perhaps, a newly emerging clause type 'happening *a* caused happening *x*' where two nominalized processes are linked by a verb expressing the logical relationship between them, e.g.

> ... all Bodies by percussion excite vibrations in the Air, ...

– or with the logical relationship itself also nominalized, e.g.

> ... the cause of Reflexion is not the impinging of Light on the solid impervious parts of Bodies, but ... (p. 283)

The text thus follows a complex grammatical dynamic, in which experience is first construed in the form of clauses, as a world of happening which can be experimented with; and then reconstrued in the form of nominals (nouns, nominal groups, nominalizations), as a world of things, symbolically fixed so that they can be observed and measured, reasoned about, and brought to order.[13]

But there was, as there always is, a price to pay. For various reasons – partly textual, the Theme–Rheme/Given–New pattern referred to earlier; partly experiential, the need to construct technical taxonomies – the second, nominalizing forms soon came to dominate scientific writing (see for example Joseph Priestley's *The History and Present State of Electricity*, 1757; and even more John Dalton's *A New System of Chemical Philosophy*, 1827). The reality construed by this form of discourse became increasingly arcane and remote from the common-sense construction of experience as embodied in the spoken languages of daily life. Within a hundred years it had already come to be felt as alienating; a world made entirely of things, things which became more and more abstract and metaphorical as time went on, was not the world of experience a child grew up in, and there was a widening gap between the daily language of home and neighbourhood and the increasingly elitist language of the learned disciplines. But there were other problems with this register besides its alienation. The difficulty with a reconstructed reality is that it may become too far out, too committed; by the beginning of the present century the scientists themselves were becoming dissatisfied with their own scientific metalanguage, and this motif is enunciated particularly by quantum physicists and their successors, from de Broglie, Bohr and Heisenberg to David Bohm and Ilya Prigogine.[14] It seems that these scientists are not aware that the problem lies with the metalanguage of their own design; they blame natural language for 'distorting' reality by making it fixed and determinate instead of fluid and probabilistic. But it is scientific language that has these properties; whereas natural language in its everyday spoken form, non-settled, non-written, non-elaborated, has precisely the flux and fluidity, the playful quality (i.e. elasticity, with lots of 'play' in it), the indeterminacy and the complementarity that the scientists say is required to construe the universe in its post-quantum state, in which chaos rules and there is a continuum of communication and consciousness stretching all the way from inanimate nature to ourselves and whoever may be out there beyond.

We should not forget, of course, that the everyday spoken language is still a **construction** of reality, even though it may be **less** contrived, less rigid and determinate, than what is 'written'. There is no clear line between language as it evolved with human consciousness and is learnt as 'mother tongue' by a child, and language as it underpins the most abstract and abstruse scientific theories about the universe. As I put it earlier, the grammar of every language in its everyday form is a theory of experience. But as our linguistic construction of experience becomes more and more elaborated, and its grammar increasingly remote from its origins in everyday speech, the high prestige, elitist discourse which it engenders becomes available for ideological loadings of all kinds. We are all familiar with the bureaucratic discourse that derived from it, with examples like:

> Discharge is a redundancy severance, the circumstances of which do not attract payment of the retrenchment benefit.

The move towards "Plain English" for documents addressed to the public is a reaction against obscure wordings of this kind. But much more threatening is technocratic discourse; this combines the bureaucratic with the scientific forms which, while obscuring the issues at stake, by the same token contrive to persuade us that, since the issues are obscure, we cannot hope to understand them and so we should leave every decision to the experts. Lemke (1990b) quotes the following:

> Many large-scale sociological and economic studies show weak and inconsistent associations of educational outcomes with school-resource proxy variables such as expenditures per student and school size, and relatively moderate and consistent amounts of variance associated with student background variables such as socioeconomic state (SES) and family size (McDermott 1976). Other research suggests that specific and alterable behaviors of parents toward their children such as intellectual stimulation in the home environment are still more strongly predictive of cognitive development than are such proxy variables as family SES and size (Walberg and Marjoribanks 1976).

Lemke comments:

> We are told [here] that money spent on education has relatively little to do with students' learning and that lower class students don't do much worse than upper middle class students in school. The authority of 'many large-scale ... studies' is offered for these assertions. A critical reader might offer the absurdity of the studies' conclusions as authority for doubting the reliability of social science research.

Thus there are some ways in which the nominalizing, metaphorical grammar of late-twentieth-century prestige varieties of English has become dysfunctional, at least from some points of view. In the technical, scientific contexts in which it first evolved it construes the world after a fashion which, although forward-looking at that historical 'moment', has now become excessively abstract, objectifying and determinate. And when extended into other contexts it helps to perpetuate an outmoded social structure and is co-opted to promote the anti-democratic ideology that goes with it.

So when planning a language, applied linguists are **not** engaged in forging some passive, ideologically neutral instrument for carrying out a prearranged policy. They are creating an active force which will play its part in shaping people's consciousness and influencing the directions of social change. With this in mind, let us take a look at the present global context within which applied linguists are now holding their Ninth World Congress (1990).

We live – we are constantly being told – in an information society. What this means is that the dominant mode of economic activity that human beings engage in is no longer that of exchanging goods-&-services, as it has been since the beginning of settlement, but that of exchanging information. And information is made of language. It is an applied linguistic world, in which even numbers, and numerical data, become significant only in the context of discursive constructions.

But there has been another, rather less publicized, change in the human condition: that our demands have now exceeded the total resources of the planet we live on. Within a microsecond of historical time the human race has turned from net creditor to net debtor, taking out of the earth more than we put in; and we are using up these resources very fast. This is so little publicized that we might suspect what we are living in is really a **dis**information society.

I took some cuttings from one day's newspaper, the day on which I happened to be writing this section of the paper. Here is an extract from one news article. The article is headed "Air travel's popularity to soar to new heights" and, like most news nowadays, it is about what someone had to say, in this case the "annual aviation market forecast of the US plane manufacturer Boeing":

> Its forecast, regarded as one of the most reliable indicators of aviation trends, says airlines will buy 9,935 jet aircraft of all types over the next 15 years at a cost of A$834 billion.
>
> It says airline traffic to, from and within the Pacific area will lead the growth with rates unmatched anywhere else in the world.
>
> The study says the rationale for a more optimistic outlook includes prolonged air travel expansion driven by continued growth in discretionary income and a decrease in the real cost of travel.
>
> *Sydney Morning Herald*, 12 March 1990

Everything here, and in countless other such texts repeated daily all round the world, contains a simple message: growth is good. Many is better than few, more is better than less, big is better than small, grow is better than shrink, up is better than down. Gross National Products must go up, standards of living must rise, productivity must increase.

But we know that these things can't happen. We are using up the capital resources – not just the fossil fuels and mineral ones, which we could (*pace* Boeing) do without, but the fresh water supplies and the agricultural soils, which we **can't** live without. And at the same time as we are consuming we are also destroying. We are destroying many of the other species who form part of the planet's life cycle; and we are destroying the planet itself, through global warming and general poisoning with carbon dioxide and methane; through ozone depletion; through acid rain; and most of all by increasing our population at a rate of almost a hundred million new people a year – at a time when humankind is already using up nearly half of the total productive capacity of the globe (Suzuki 1990).

Paul Ehrlich, one of those who (along with David Suzuki and Edward Goldsmith) are doing most to make us aware of these things, made a point that I referred to earlier, and that is fundamentally important to us as linguists. Human beings, he said, have evolved so that they are not equipped to deal with the kinds of change that are happening now. We are good at recognizing and responding to sudden, catastrophic changes; but bad at recognizing and admitting to ourselves what he calls "slow notion crises" formed by gradual trends and shifts of probabilities. Even a massive change, provided it takes place slowly enough, will simply pass us by.

Ehrlich's observation on this is that we have to "change the way in which we perceive the world". He sees this as an exercise in information: educating people to respond to trends, graphs and numbers – not just to be able to follow them, but to take them seriously, to treat them as 'news'. He suggests that "some important environmental state report should be shown every night on the media". But let us look at the situation from a linguistic point of view. What I have been suggesting is that the same sort of gradual, stealthy processes as take place in the environment also take place in language; and we are equally unaware of them – more so, in fact, because they are beyond the range of our conscious attention.

It is not difficult to become aware of obvious verbal anomalies, like the following cartoon caption quoted by Charles Birch from the *Los Angeles Times*:

> Eventually we will run out of food to feed ourselves and air to breathe . . . this is something we must learn to live with!

Such explicit motifs, especially where self-contradiction is built in, are the most easily accessible to our conscious awareness. And we can fairly easily train ourselves to react to wordings like "the survey painted a bleak picture, saying that the number of business failures would continue rising" and "there will be relatively stable fuel prices in the long term and no US or world recession in the foreseeable future" – although we usually fail to perceive any contradictions unless they are thrust before us in adjacent sentences.

Still reasonably accessible to reflection – at the next level down in our consciousness, so to speak – are the lexical effects: single words with affective loadings of one kind or another and regular, more or less ritualized collocations, like *inflationary pressures, prospects sliding, optimistic outlook, unmatched growth rates, business climate improving, early stages of recession*. It does not take much work to show how our world view is constructed by expressions such as these. When we read *output fell sharply*, it is obvious that all our negative loadings from childhood come into play: falling is painful, sharp things are dangerous, and both (especially together!) are to be avoided. On the other hand *traffic is expected to grow* calls up all the comfortable smiles of the admiring aunts who told us how we've grown, as well as the positive relation of growth to consumption – eat your meat and you'll grow into a big girl/boy. And we only have to mention a word like *shrink* to be aware of its pejorative connotations: shrunken bodies and heads, the one who shrinks heads (the psychiatrist), and so on. Some people have tried to maintain the positive value of *grow* but reconstrue it in expressions like *zero population growth* and *negative growth*; but the *zero* and the *negative* sabotage the effort – how can anything that is 'zero' or 'negative' be a desirable goal? (Others have tried to find negatively charged words for growth, like gigantism and elephantiasis; but these don't work either – the words themselves are too elephantine, and even if giants are baddies elephants are definitely goodies.) It might be more effective to redefine growth as a failure to shrink. Since we are going to have to reduce the GTP (gross terrestrial product), should we not exploit the power of words by making *shrink* the positive term and labelling 'growth' very simply as *negative shrinkage?* This is using the power of the grammar: in this case the device of reversing the marking. How much more effective it would be, for example, if those who are ecologically aware, instead of letting themselves be called *greenies*, in marked contrast to ordinary people, became themselves the unmarked category and the rest of the population were reconstructed as *baldies*.

A little way beyond these is the outer layer of the grammar: the morphological construction of words, types of concord, and closed system or "function" words like prepositions and pronouns. This third level is where much of the work of anti-sexist language planning is done: engineering the third person forms *he/she, his/her*; reconstructing words like *chairman, manpower, salesgirl*; taking out the markedness from pairs like *author/authoress, nurse* and *male nurse*; redesigning concord structures like *everyone knows his job* to *everyone knows their jobs*, and so on. On the other hand, of the semantics of growthism relatively little is construed at this level – and there is even some countersuggestion that small is beautiful, in the form of diminutives, although this tends to be neutralized by their patriarchal combination of sexism and childism.

But if we probe into the inner layer of the grammar, to the cryptogrammatic fourth level that people are least aware of, here we find a gradual, clause by clause synthesizing of a world view, a hidden theory of experience on which we unconsciously base our actions and our strategies for survival. There is a syndrome of grammatical features which conspire – in Martin's term – to construe reality in a certain way; and it is a way that is no longer good for our health as a species. Let me try and identify four of these, beginning with one that is familiar and easy to access.

1 Whorf pointed out many years ago how, unlike the American Indian languages he knew, "Standard Average European" languages like English make a categorial distinction between two kinds of entity: those that occur in units, and are **countable** in the grammar, and those that occur in the mass and are **uncountable.** (More accurately, the latter can be counted; but when they are, the count refers to 'kinds of', not 'units of', e.g. *soils*.) Our grammar (though not the grammar of human language as such) construes *air* and *water* and *soil*, and also *coal*, and *iron*, and *oil*, as 'unbounded' – that is, as existing without limit. In the horizons of the first farmers, and the first miners, they did. We know that such resources are finite. But the grammar presents them as if the only source of restriction was the way that we ourselves quantify them: *a barrel of oil, a seam of coal, a reservoir of water* and so on – as if they in themselves were inexhaustible.

2 Among the properties construed by the grammar as gradable, most have a negative and a positive pole: for example, with 'good' and 'bad', 'good' is construed as positive. So the *quality* of a thing means either 'how good or bad it is' or 'the fact that it is good', but never 'the fact that it is bad'. In the first sense we can say *how do you rate the quality of these chocolates, good or bad?* In the second sense, the manufacturer can refer to them as *chocolates of quality* without worrying that this could ever mean 'bad quality'. Similarly *size* means both 'how big?' and 'being big' (*look at the size of it!*); *length* means both 'how long?' and 'being long', and so on. There are various manifestations of this asymmetry throughout the grammar; but the significant point is that quality and quantity are always lined up together (as they are also in that expression). The grammar of 'big' is the grammar of 'good', while the grammar of 'small' is the grammar of 'bad'. The motif of 'bigger and better' is engraved into our consciousness by virtue of their line-up in the grammar.

3 In transitivity, the part of the grammar that construes our experience of processes − actions and events, mental and verbal processes, relations of various kinds − the entities that take part in processes of a material kind are arranged by the grammar along a continuum according to their potential for initiating such processes: how likely they are to perform the action or to cause the event to take place. Naturally human beings come at the most active, agentive pole, with inanimate objects located at the other end. Such things are acted upon but do not act, and they stay where they are until disturbed. The only environment where inanimates regularly figure as agents is in catastrophic contexts, where (at least if they are big enough) they can become Actor in a process of the 'destroy' subcategory of material processes; and even here they are often metaphorized events, e.g. *the earthquake destroyed the city*; cf. *fire damaged the roof, a branch fell on the car*. The grammar does not present inanimate objects as doers, certainly not in ongoing, constructive or conservative processes. So we have problems with David Suzuki's formulation *all the kinds of things that forests do*. In English if I say of an inanimate object *what's it doing?* it means 'why is it there? − remove it!' So *what's that forest doing?* implies 'clear it!' rather than expecting an answer such as that it's holding water in store, it's cleaning and moistening the atmosphere, it's stopping flooding, it's stabilizing the soil, harbouring life forms and so on. The language makes it hard for us to take seriously the notion of inanimate nature as an active participant in events.

165

4 There is one particular point on this continuum where the grammar introduces a sharp dichotomy, making a clear division of phenomena into two classes. This is often referred to as human versus non-human, but it isn't that; it's conscious versus non-conscious – those entities that are treated as endowed with consciousness and those which are not. English constructs this dichotomy at various places all over the grammar. The most obvious manifestation is in the pronoun system, where conscious things are *he/she* while non-conscious things are *it*. More far-reaching, however, is the fundamental distinction made by the grammar of mental processes, where the Senser is always a conscious being: thus a clear line is drawn between entities that understand, hold opinions, have preferences, etc., and those that do not. Non-conscious entities can be a source of information, but they cannot project an idea (we can say *my watch says it's half past ten,* but not *my watch thinks it's half past ten*). This binary theory of phenomena has obviously been important for our survival, in the stage of history that is now coming to an end. But it imposes a strict discontinuity between ourselves and the rest of creation, with 'ourselves' including a select band of other creatures that are in some semantic contexts allowed in – the most typical of these being first our farm animals and now our highly destructive pets. And, of course, it totally excludes the concept of Gaia – of the earth itself as a conscious being. The grammar makes it hard for us to accept the planet earth as a living entity that not only breathes but feels and even thinks: that maintains its own body temperature despite massive changes in the heat that it receives from the sun, and that dies slowly but inevitably as each of the living species that compose it is destroyed. Let us at least try re-writing that last description: the earth as a living entity that ... maintains her own body temperature despite massive changes in the heat that she receives from the sun, and that dies, slowly but inevitably, as each of the living species that compose her is destroyed (we have to choose male or female, and Gaia was a goddess, the 'mother Earth') (Lovelock 1989).

A grammar, I have suggested, is a theory of experience; a theory that is born of action, and therefore serves as a guide to action, as a metalanguage by which we live. The particular grammars that we live with today are the products of successive 'moments' in the space-time of human history. Much of their meaning potential will no doubt continue to be valid; we are unlikely to demand a sudden, catastrophic reconstruction of reality. But at the same time there are disjunctions, contradictions and overdeterminacies which ensure that it must

166

continue to evolve. A language is a metastable system, which can only persist by constantly changing in interaction with its environment. The slowest part of it to change is the grammar, especially the inner layers of the grammar, the cryptogrammar, where the real work of meaning is done. The lexis is much more accessible; indeed we already have our slogans for the new age, based on words like *sustain*; what we need now, we are told, is *sustainable development*. We have an American professor lecturing in Australia on *global sustainability* (note here level two at work: everything is possible, by nominalizing the potentiality morpheme – *sustain, sustainable, sustainability*). But, by the same token, the lexis is rather easily co-opted:

> INSECTS may provide the vital factor in making Australia a world leader on sustainable development.
>
> (*Australian*, 10 March 1990)

– and we are back at leading, being out in front, and so once again to growth. You cannot on the other hand co-opt the grammar in this way; certainly not its inner layers.

But, again by the same token, neither can you engineer it. I do not think that even the language professionals of AILA can plan the inner layers of the grammar; there is an inherent antipathy between grammar and design.[15] What we can do is draw attention to it; to show how the grammar promotes the ideology of growth, or growthism. This may suggest in a fragmentary way what the alternatives might be like. But – and this brings me to my final motif – I think that this could only be done effectively under certain conditions. Let me summarize at this point some of the strands in this rather peripatetic discourse.

I started with one of our central concerns, language planning; and more specifically systemic language planning. Although language is an evolved system, not a designed system, it may become necessary to manage it at certain times and places in history: typically, where a language has rapidly to take on new functions, especially technical functions. This is not the management of information; it is the management of the system out of which information is constructed.

Such language planning is thematic not disciplinary: that is to say, it is concerned not with language as object but with systematically extending the power to mean, typically in the context of particular 'fields', or types of social activity. Institutionally, such language planning may involve all the major components of applied linguistics: computational linguistics and artificial intelligence, first and second language teaching, even clinical linguistics, as well as the more obvious concerns of sociolinguistics, multilingualism, and language in relation to culture.

To understand these processes, and especially to be able to intervene in them, we have to theorize about how language constructs reality: how language evolved as the resource whereby human beings construe experience. The lexicogrammatical continuum, from the vocabulary (the part showing above the surface of consciousness – the tip of the iceberg, so to speak) to the inner layers of the grammar, is the key component, the central processing unit for construing ideational meanings and mapping them on to meanings of the other primary kind, the interpersonal meanings which construct and enact social relationships.

But besides the more familiar contexts for language planning there are certain other spheres where language has become problematic. One was the register of scientific discourse, which scientists themselves began to find constricting: its highly nominalized grammar construed a world of fixed, determinate, discrete and abstract objects and could not cope with the flux, the indeterminacy and the continuity that they now saw as the deeper mode of reality. At the very least, such a distinct variety, with its highly metaphorical construction of the resources of the grammar, created a division between esoteric, technical knowledge and the common-sense knowledge of daily life, a division that is certainly dysfunctional in a modern democratic society.

The other problematic sphere is that of language and prejudice. Here while sexist and racist attitudes are clearly constructed in language it is not any particular variety that is at issue, nor the system of the language as a whole, but the deployment of resources within the system. Thus sex roles are construed by such things as mothers taking up different grammatical options in answering questions asked by boys and by girls; different interpersonal choices made in forms of address and reference; and different transitivity roles assigned to men and women in narratives. Sexual difference, racial otherness, social inequalities of all kinds are engendered and perpetuated by varying the probabilities in the selection of options within the grammar of the everyday language.

Social class is likewise construed in language, and transmitted by parents from different classes favouring different selections within the grammar. But it is a more 'slow motion' and cyptotypic process than the construction of gender or race: a long-term quantitative effect of orientation towards one 'quarter' rather than another within the overall semantic space described by the language (Hasan and Cloran 1990).

168

Perhaps because of the pervasive effect of different attitudes towards generalization and abstraction, the two 'feel like' competing realitites.[16] The theory of "codes" attempts to locate the linguistic basis of classism at the point where the system and the instance meet (where **parole** becomes **langue** – except that we have to redefine **langue** and **parole** for this to make sense), showing that the different coding orientations of the two classes are **not** different systems but different deployment of resources within the system: different enough, however, such that the contradiction which is construed in this way has not yet been historically transcended.[17]

The system itself is constantly open to change, as each instance slightly perturbs the probabilities; where such perturbations resonate with changing material and social conditions the system is (more or less gradually) reshaped. Thus in renaissance English there evolved a syndrome of features which collectively reoriented the grammar away from preoccupation with the experiential towards greater concern with the textual – from the clause as representation of a process towards the clause as organization of a message. In relation to the grammar as a whole this reorientation was very slight; but it was sufficient to nudge the system so that it could become more technical, more attuned to a specialized division of labour, less dependent on the particulars of shared experience. The everyday grammar thus provided a point of departure for, while still remaining in contact with, the alienating discourses of modern technology and science.

Meanwhile, according to some scientists, a deeper crisis is at hand, no less than the threatened destruction of the entire planet as a habitable environment. This too we can investigate linguistically as a site for possibly deconstruing reality through the grammar. We might be able to work on specific issues at the outer layers of the grammar, replacing war discourse (the language of the Pentagon) by peace discourse, the discourse of borrowing (the language of commercialism and credit capital) by that of saving, the discourse of building (the language of megacontracts) by that of keeping under repair. We might put certain key words in the dock, words like *production* and *growth*. Production is a major semantic confidence trick; as Goldsmith has pointed out, we don't produce anything at all – we merely transform what is already there into something else, almost always with some unwanted side effects. (Just as a cow does not 'produce' meat: it transforms grass into meat, churning out vast quantities of methane in the process.) We could perhaps relexicalize the semantic domain of 'production'. Growth means evolving or maturing, but it also means getting fat; we have noted the collocational and morphological support for the motif of 'small is beautiful' – but also that much of it is suspect as being patriarchal. But all these are relatively minor issues, semantically somewhat 'localized' in their scope. The main issue is that of growthism in the grammar; and we saw how deeply engrammatized are the motifs of growth versus shrinkage, of the unboundedness of our material resources, of the passivity of the inanimate environment and of the uniqueness of humankind instead of our continuity with the rest of creation. These and other features of the language system construe our experience in such a way that we believe we can expand for ever – our own numbers, our own power and dominance over other species, our own consumption and so-called "standard of living". Whereas in fact, as Suzuki has shown us, even at present population levels the rich 20 per cent will have to live far more frugally if the poorer 80 per cent are to be able to live at all.[18]

You may think that by now I have left language behind, and am talking simply of social and political issues. But I don't think I have. My point is that such issues are also linguistic ones. Growthism and classism are our two major ideological menaces; and ideologies are constructed in language.[19] But the linguistic perspective suggests one further consideration: that we shall not solve one of these problems without also solving the other. Both growthism and classism were positive and constructive for a certain moment in our history; both have now become negative, the means of self-destruction by division among ourselves and by division between ourselves and the rest of creation. So much we must accept. Now we have seen that, as a general principle, it is the **linguistic system** (things about which we have no choice) that divides us from everything else; whereas it is the **choice of options within the system** (taking up different probabilities) that divides us among ourselves. To come back to gender again: what construes our sex roles is not the inherent sexism in the forms of the language (such things are useful for making people conscious of the problem, but in themselves are trivial – some of the most sexist societies have no trace of gender morphology in their languages) but the way the resources of the language are deployed, how the meaning potential is taken up in the construction of the subject in the family, the media, popular literature and elsewhere. In other words those things which all humans share, or at least all the members of a primary culture band, are construed for them by the forms of the grammar; while those which divide them, which discriminate one group over another, are construed by systematic variation in the choices made within the grammar – what Hasan refers to as *semantic variation*.

But there is no insulation between these two, because the system **is** the set of its probabilities, in the same way that climate is the set of probabilities in the weather. Climate and weather are one phenomenon, not two; but interpreted within different time depths. So if the linguistic *system* (that is, our long-term slow motion semiotic praxis) construes us as lords of creation, our shorter-term but no less systematic praxis, the regular exercise of **choice within** the system, construes a fractal pattern whereby some of us are lords over the rest. The one construct that lies nearest the point of complementarity – that is, that can be equally well interpreted as long-term patterns of choice within the system or as a rather ill-defined system of its own (either as long-term weather patterns or as a temporary kind of climate) – is that of social class. It will be difficult to deconstrue growthism without also deconstruing classism, especially now that class has become a world phenomenon, so that what were previously regions of the city are now regions of the globe. The linguistic evidence suggests that these two transformations will have to take place together; that the hegemony arrogated by the human species is inseparable from the hegemony usurped by one human group over another, and that neither will come to an end as long as the other still prevails.

Now that our friends and colleagues from the heart of the Eurasian continent are leaping out of the socialist frying-pan into the capitalist fire; and we ponder whether, with Fukuyama, history is about to end[20] or, with Marx, it is (after all) still not ready to begin; and we realize that, long before we reach the (by now proverbial) one square metre of ground per human being, we have to learn to educate five billion children (and **that** is an applied linguistic task if ever there was one!) – at such a time it is as well to reflect on how language construes the world. **We** cannot transform language; it is people's acts of meaning that do that. But we can observe these acts of meaning as they happen around us, and try to chart the currents and patterns of change.[21] Suzuki says "the planet may soon become unlivable – it's a matter of survival". Let us formulate this in terms of possible outcomes: there is no historical necessity that this plant will survive in a habitable form, such that we (among others) can continue to live on its surface – this is merely one of the possibilities for the future. What I have tried to suggest is that the things which may rule out this possibility and which we ourselves have brought about – classism, growthism, destruction of species, pollution and the like – are not just problems for the biologists and physicists. They are problems for the applied linguistic community as well. I do not suggest for one moment that we hold the key. But we ought to be able to write the instructions for its use.

Notes

1. What Meillet wrote was "un langage forme un système très delicate et très compliqué ou tout se tient rigoureusement" (*Année Sociologique* 8, 1903/4: 641). For Firth's rejection of this "monosystemic principle" see the first few paragraphs of 'Sounds and prosodies', and also 'Personality and language in society', Chapters 9 and 14 in J. R. Firth (1957d).

2. The very useful concept of "institutional linguistics" was introduced many years ago by Trevor Hill (1958).

3. After Marr's death his views and those of his successors such as Meščaninov were rejected outright by Stalin (or whoever wrote 'On Marxism in linguistics' on Stalin's behalf) in the linguistics controversy in *Pravda* in May–July 1950: see Ellis and Davies (1951). Stalin asserted that language was not part of the superstructure, and that it changed (not by revolutionary changes but) only very gradually over time, particularly its grammatical system and basic lexical stock.

4. Including morphology, of course, in those languages where words display morphological variation.

5. For the notion of 'metafunctions' in systemic theory see my *Language as Social Semiotic: The Social Interpretation of Language and Meaning* (1978b esp. chs 2 and 10). There is an excellent summary in Christian Matthiessen's (1989) review of my *Introduction to Functional Grammar*.

6. We see language arising out of the impact of the material and the conscious from another perspective in the ontogenesis of language. The first symbolic acts occur at the time of the initial bodily engagement with the environment (reaching and grasping); protolanguage, shared with other mammals, accompanies crawling; and language, uniquely human as far as we know, is associated with walking.

7. That is, conditions other than creolization and decreolization. The former is a more or less catastrophic disruption, the latter an accelerated revival.

8. And sometimes perhaps was not taken up. For example, it is said that conditions in China in the southern Sung dynasty were very similar to those of Europe in the fifteenth century (see for example Mark Elvin (1973: esp. Part Two, 'The medieval economic revolution')). Yet in spite of this the transition to capitalism did not take place and the Ming empire settled into a small town market economy.

9. Cf. for example Stephen Harris' observation (1980) on what is explicitly

172

taught to children in Australian Aboriginal societies: there is no instruction in experiential matters (e.g. field skills), which are learnt by imitation and so do not need an abstract educational discourse; but a great deal of instruction in interpersonal matters.

10. From Proposition 13 of Aristarchus 'On the sizes and distances of the sun and moon'. See Sir Thomas Heath (1981).

11. Martin's discussion of the place of grammar is particularly insightful. Note that Martin is not taking English as a norm; in each case he specifies the corresponding features of English grammar which point the other way although, of course, the relevant clusterings, or syndromes, of English would have to be separately established.

12. But the experience of constructing them, especially the lexical taxonomies, influenced people's conception of the nature of language, and also their understanding of their own languages. One interesting output of this exercise was the appearance in England, nearly 150 years later, of Peter Mark Roget's *Thesaurus of English Words and Phrases*, one of the best-selling applied linguistic publications of all time. For a full account see Vivian Salmon (1979).

13. All extracts taken from Sir Isaac Newton (1952). The treatise was first published in 1704, the original manuscript (itself the output of twenty years' work) having been destroyed by fire in 1692.

14. See especially David Bohm's discussion of the "rheomode" (1980 Ch. 2).

15. This is not to deny the achievements in designed languages ("artificial languages") such as Esperanto. But these are based on existing grammars; they do not attempt to change the grammar's construction of reality.

16. As suggested by Michael Puleston, in 'An Investigation into Social Class Differences among School Pupils in Answering Interview Questions'. Unpublished MA dissertation, University of Sydney, 1979.

17. In other words, the system (the more or less permanent, invariant features of the language) construes the meaning styles, value systems and ideologies that constitute the culture as a whole; it does not represent the perspective of any one group within the culture – not even that of a 'ruling class'. If the system is hegemonic, this is because it defines the potential within which meanings can be meant. It is the deployment of resources within the system that differentiates social groups within the culture.

18. These scientists may be wrong. But the main argument that I have seen advanced against them is that prophets of doom have always been wrong in the past. This seems irrelevant.

19. Important work on language and ideology has recently been appearing in Australia, by (among others) Ruqaiya Hasan (1984a), J. R. Martin (1986a), William McGregor (1990); see also Threadgold *et al.* (1986); Birch and O'Toole (1988).

20. See Francis Fukuyama, 'End of history and the triumph of liberalism . . .', *Washington Post*, December 1989. Fukuyama's argument is summed up by

Peter Munz as "one tautology and one tacit platitude" (*Guardian Weekly*, Vol. 142, no. 6, February 11, 1990, p. 2). For capitalism as "the closing chapter of the prehistoric stage of human society" see Karl Marx, *A Contribution to the Critique of Political Economy* trans. by N. I. Stone, Chicago: Kerr (1904), Preface.

21. As always, language also works by its example – the metaphoric processes by which language itself displays the features it is construing. Thus the patterns of change we observe amount to a form of growthism in language.

PART TWO

LINGUISTICS AND LANGUAGE

EDITOR'S INTRODUCTION

At the outset of "A brief sketch of systemic grammar", which first appeared in *La Grammatica; La Lessicologia* (1969), Professor Halliday makes clear that the fundamental concept in the grammar is 'system' – "the system that formalizes the notion of choice in language". In "Systemic background", published in the proceedings of the Ninth Systemic Workshop (1985), Halliday writes, "the description of language is a description of choice". System networks – the grammar – specify the possible combinations of choices, which are subsequently 'realized' as structures. There are different types of structure, expressing different kinds of meaning: the experiential metafunction represented by constituency; interpersonal meaning by field-like structures; and texture by "the periodic, wave-like pattern of discourse". In "Systemic background", Professor Halliday acknowledges those who have influenced his own way of thinking, among them, his teacher, J. R. Firth, from whom the concept of 'system' was derived; and others of his seniors, immediate precursors, and contemporaries. Also discussed are three of the salient motifs of the fifteen years between "A brief sketch" and "Systemic background" which provided part of the context of systemic work: language and social reality, language and human development, and language in the machine. "The value of a theory", writes Professor Halliday in "Systemic background", "lies in the use that can be made of it." Systemic theory is described as "a way of thinking about language and of working on language – and through language, on other things". Addressing the theme of the Ninth Systemic Workshop, 'The Applications of Systemic Theory', Halliday emphasizes the social accountability of linguistics and linguists, noting that "Systemic theory is designed not so much to prove things as to do things."

In "Systemic grammar and the concept of a 'science of language'" (1992), Professor Halliday enumerates "certain principles and practices" followed by linguists working in systemic-functional linguistics. His aim, as he explains, is not to prove that linguistics, whether systemic or any other model, is a science. In fact, he regards "'a science of language', or a science of semiotic systems" as "still some way off in the future". This, however, does not preclude linguists from "doing science" as they endeavour to construct theories which will enable them to understand, describe and explain human language. In his opening lecture to the 1992 Congress of the Applied Linguistics Association of Australia, "Language in a changing world", Professor Halliday replies to those who would argue for a 'theory-free' approach to engaging with language, "There is no such thing as theory-free engagement with language, whether one is actively intervening in the linguistic practices of a community or systematically describing the grammar of a particular language." Grammars are theories – they are never neutral, always evolving. Linguistic theory is a grammar about grammar. Like any other theory, it has evolved "under pressure of work to be done, and the pressure is such that their evolution is tempered by design; they are so to speak semi-designed linguistic semiotics. But their design is that of the culture in which they operate, embodying its values, its styles of meaning, and the conflicts and tensions within it."

"A recent view of 'missteps' in linguistic theory", published in *Functions of Language* (1995), is a review of John M. Ellis' *Language, Thought and Logic* (1993). While crediting Ellis for having "engaged frontally with the movement that has dominated this half century's linguistics, countering its intellectual arguments and pointing up its errors and its misrepresentations", Professor Halliday nevertheless takes issue with what he characterizes as an americocentric view of the discipline in which "those working outside the Chomskyan paradigm have thereby become invisible". Instead, he argues, "there has always been a strong current in linguistics that did not merge with or get swamped by the Bloomfield-Chomsky tide", included among them Firth and Hjelmslev, and those who have since continued to build on the foundations they provided.

In sharp contrast to the strongly framed vision of language and linguistics characterizing the Chomskyan paradigm, the two final papers in this section, "Linguistics as metaphor" (1997) and "Is the grammar neutral? Is the grammarian neutral" (2001) offer a broader under-standing of language as "a meaning potential", and a theory of language as being "rather closely analogous to what it is theorizing about". Like language, a theory is also "enabling and constraining". Like language, linguistics is "a mode of action, a way of intervening in social and political processes". Instead of theorizing about language "as an autonomous intellectual game", the goal should be to "evolve a grammatics which will enable us to theorize about language – and to describe languages – as resource: as a potential wherewith we construct experience and intervene in social processes."

Chapter Seven

A Brief Sketch of Systemic Grammar
(1969)

I should like to describe to you in outline something of the work that my colleagues and I have been doing in the realm of grammatical description and theory. I hope to make six points about the grammar. The name "systemic" is not the same thing as "systematic"; the term is used because the fundamental concept in the grammar is that of the *system*. A system is a set of options with an entry condition: that is to say, a set of things of which one must be chosen, together with a statement of the conditions under which the choice is available.

First, then, the grammar is based on the notion of choice. The speaker of a language, like a person engaging in any kind of culturally determined behaviour, can be regarded as carrying out, simultaneously and successively, a number of distinct choices. At any given moment, in the environment of the selections made up to that time, a certain range of further choices is available. It is the system that formalizes the notion of choice in language.

The system network is the grammar. The grammar of any language can be represented as a very large network of systems, an arrangement of options in simultaneous and hierarchical relationship.[1] The network is open-ended. To the left of each arrow is the entry condition; to the right, joined by a brace, is the set of two or more options which make up the choice. So for example given the entry condition *clause* there are three simultaneous choices to be made: from transitivity, mood and theme. (For speech a fourth choice is added: information.) There are various ways in which selection in one option may serve as a condition of entry to another. In addition to the simple entry condition (if restricted then either intransitive or transitive) there are two types of

---

First published in *La Grammatica; La Lessicologia*. Bulzoni Editore, 1969.

junction: conjunction (if both non-middle and identification then either active or passive) and disjunction (if either modulated or modalized is selected, then there is a choice from both uncommitted/committed and neutral/oblique).

Second, the description of a sentence, clause or other item may be just a list of the choices that the speaker has made. The system network specifies what are the possible combinations of choices that could be made; each permitted path through the network is thus the description of a class of linguistic items. Thus the description of a linguistic item is the set of features selected in that item from the total available. Such a description is at the same time a statement of its relationship to other items: reference to the grammar shows that *John threw the ball* relates to *did John throw the ball?*, *the ball John threw, the ball was thrown by John*, etc., which differ from it, and from each other, in respect only of certain specified options.

Third, the term **structure** has not yet been mentioned, and in fact considerations of structure are delayed till the latest possible. By "structure" we may understand the representation of an item in terms of its constituents, with the linearity that such a representation implies: if *John threw the ball* is said to "consist of" a subject *John* and a predicate *threw the ball* it is implied that one comes before the other, or at least that their relation is expressible in terms of linear sequence. Obviously the description of a language must at some stage take cognizance of succession in real time; the problem is at what point to introduce linearity into the description. The linear arrangement of the parts of a sentence does not figure, here, in the most abstract representation of that sentence; structure is treated as a mechanism whereby the speaker realizes or makes manifest the choices he has made. The concept of realization has been familiar in linguistics for a long time, though it has been called by different names; in English, exponence, implementation, manifestation as well as realization. The options selected by the speaker are **realized** as structures; and there are two aspects to a structure, the bracketing and the labelling, each of which needs to be considered.

Fourth, then, two principal types of bracketing have been used in linguistics, which we might refer to as "maximum bracketing" and "minimum bracketing". The former is what is known as "immediate constituent" analysis; the latter has been called "string constituent" analysis and is often associated with the "slot and filler" account of structure. With minimum bracketing the fewest possible layers of structure are introduced into the description: the tree has a much smaller number of levels in it. In a systemic description the bracketing is minimal, for three reasons. First, any bracketing more than the necessary minimum is redundant, because the information it contains is recoverable from the systemic part of the description: its function is to show how sentences are related to one another and this is shown in terms of options. Second, the significance of the bracketing is that it indicates where a new set of options is open to the speaker: each node is the point of origin for a set of systems, so that again the determining factor is that of choice. Finally, non-minimal bracketing tends to be self-contradictory. The clause *John threw the ball*, minimally bracketed, is a three-element structure, and this represents its structure as the realization of options in transitivity, Actor Process Goal. If we then consider its structure as a message, assuming one possible reading in which *the ball* is marked out by intonation as **new** information and *John threw* as **given**, the clause will be structured into two constituents: Given (*John threw*) New (*the ball*); and if we introduce another dimension of structure, that of theme-rheme, we shall need a third analysis: Theme (*John*) Rheme (*threw the ball*), still in two parts but with the break at a different place. Thus any item may have not just one structure but many. Since there may be a number of simultaneous structures superimposed on one another in this way, minimal bracketing is the most neutral; in the present example, only a tree corresponding to the first bracketing is an adequate representation of all three.

Fifth, and closely related to the last point, is the question of labelling. There are two ways of labelling: according to structural function, and according to class. Functional labelling will indicate for example that the structure is one of Actor–Process–Goal, or Theme–Rheme, or Modifier–head and so forth. Class labelling will indicate such things as noun phrase, verb phrase, noun, verb, adjective or adverb. It is not always obvious what the difference between the two is. In terms of the present grammar, they are interpretable by reference to the underlying notion of choice. A class is a statement of 'choices now open'; for example the label "noun phrase" means that there are options of singular/plural, count/mass, specific/non-specific and so on. A function is a statement of 'choices already made': thus "subject" means that indicative has been selected, "goal" means that transitive has been selected, etc. The two types of labelling thus as it were face different ways in relation to the concept of choice. Since structure is fully predictable, being derived from the systemic representation, the primary labels used here are functional ones. But the analysis of structural function is componential; in *John threw the ball*, *John* has a composite function of Actor and Given and Theme and Subject and possibly others as well. Thus the element of a structure, the constituent, is a complex of structural functions each of which represents some choice that the speaker has made in the planning of that sentence.

Sixth, since the structure is regarded as the realization of systemic choices, the grammar has to indicate how the particular choices made by the speaker are realized in structural terms. To the systemic options, such as indicative, imperative etc., we may append a realization statement showing the contribution made by the selection of that option to the structure of the sentence: for example, the realization statement accompanying the option *indicative* would be "subject is present in the string". These are thought of as statements of relationship rather than as rules.

A realization statement may take various forms. Certain options are realized by the presence of a particular function in the structure, like indicative above, or *restricted* realized by the presence of the function "actor". But other options have the effect of mapping two structural functions one on to the other: of conflating them into a single element. For example in *John threw the ball*, John is both Subject and Actor (the definition of "subject" lies outside the present discussion, but it is treated here as a modal function, whose position in sequence varies with the choice of mood: declarative *John threw*, interrogative *did John throw*); but there is no need for the Subject and the Actor to be the same element – we could have the passive form *the ball was thrown by John* in which *the ball* is now Subject though it is not Actor but Goal. There must therefore be a particular option whereby the speaker decides to conflate the roles of Actor and Subject: this would be the option *operative*. The realization statement of the feature "operative" specifies that Subject and Actor form a single element. There are altogether five types of realization statement which are needed to relate the structure of sentences to the options selected. A complete structure is thus a sequence of elements, composed of functions any of which may extend across more than one element; it is bracketed at each rank and where there is recursion, where an option provides for going round a loop and returning to an earlier choice.

The six points I have made could be summarized as follows. One, the underlying notion in the grammar is that of choice, and this is represented through the concept of a system, which is a set of options together with a condition of entry. Two, the description of any sentence or other item in the language takes the form of a statement of the options that have been selected in that sentence. Three, the structural representation of a sentence is derived by realization from the systemic one, so that the latter is the more abstract ("deeper"). Four, the structural representation is minimally bracketed. Five, the structural labelling is functional and componential, the element of structure being a complex of functions realizing different options. Six, the systemic and the structural descriptions are related by realization statements which show the structural contribution of the options in the grammar.

Notes

1. System networks for English (Kress 1976b) are included as an appendix to Section 1 of Volume 1 in this series.

Chapter Eight

SYSTEMIC BACKGROUND
(1985)

The theme of the workshop [The Ninth Systemic Workshop] is "Applications of Systemic Theory", and this suggests to me that it is in the context of what can be done with the theory that we shall be seeking to exchange ideas. The theory has evolved in use; it has no existence apart from the practice of those who use it. Systemic theory is a way of doing things. If the English language permitted such extravagances I would name it not with a noun but with an adverb; I would call it "Systemically". I have never found it possible, in my own work, to distinguish between the activities of working on the theory and using the theory to work on something else. The interesting diversification of ideas that shows up when systemicists get together is not so much a taking of different positions on abstract theoretical issues as a diversity in the kinds of activities in which they are engaged. The debate that arises from these differences of perspective is very much more positive and fruitful than the rather sterile confrontation that takes place when people take a stand on some theoretical point largely as a means of establishing their individual identity.

There are a lot of different doings represented at this workshop, and enumerating some of these will perhaps give a flavour of what systemic theory is about:

- interpreting the nature, the functions and the development of language
- understanding the role of language in expressing, maintaining and transmitting the social system, in home, neighbourhood, school and other domains of the context of culture
- helping people to learn language, whether mother tongue or other

First published in *Systemic Perspectives on Discourse*, Vol. 1: *Selected Theoretical Papers from the Ninth International Systemic Workshop*, edited by James D. Benson and William S. Greaves (*Advances in Discourse Processes* 15). Ablex Publishing, 1985, pp. 1–15.

languages, whether children or adults; and to use language effectively as a means of learning and in a variety of contexts of situation

- helping people to overcome language disorders, educational or clinical: 'slow learners', 'backward readers', aphasics, the mentally handicapped, etc.
- understanding the nature of discourse, and of functional variation in language (*register*); studying particular types of discourse (classroom, medical, etc.) for practical purposes such as the training of teachers and of specialists in the field
- understanding the nature of 'value' in a text, and the concepts of verbal art, rhetoric, and literary genres; gaining access to literature through the careful study of such texts
- using computers to analyse and generate discourse; developing a grammar for decoding and encoding, and a semantic representation to direct and interpret the grammar
- exploring a range of practical activities where language is involved: forensic issues, readability and complexity measures, communication in institutional settings and so on
- relating language to other semiotic systems and to the ideological patterns of the culture

This is a rather broad spectrum of doings, and it reflects the broad foundation on which systemic theory is built. The workshop brochure refers to the theory as being "neo-Firthian"; and although I have never used that label myself, I have always made it clear that the most important influence on my own thinking came from my teacher J. R. Firth. Those who know Yorkshire – once described by Mary Abercrombie as "the Texas of England" – will recognize the significance of the fact that we are both Yorkshiremen, and indeed grew up in the same home town (but in fact you do not need to have heard of Wharfedale in order to take this point – you only need to have heard of Whorf). It is from Firth, of course, that the concept of **system** is derived, from which systemic theory gets its name; and unlike most of the other fundamental concepts, which were common to many groups of post-Saussurean linguists, particularly in Europe, the system in this sense is found only in Firth's theoretical framework.

Firth himself always emphasized his debt to the work of others. Among his predecessors and contemporaries, he held Hjelmslev in particularly high regard (though he thought Saussure overrated); he spoke admiringly of Trubetzkoy, Benveniste, Whitehead, Wittgenstein;

186

but above all he acknowledged what he owed to Malinowski. Hasan (1985a) traces the genesis of the Malinowskian element in Firth's thinking, especially the origins of contextual theory, which was the foundation of Firth's functional analysis of meaning as "serial contextualization". I would like to take the story a little further by referring to the work of my own seniors and immediate precursors, who obviously were not part of Firth's inheritance but from whom I have learnt the greater part of whatever I have been able to apply. I feel I should apologize for expressing this in personal terms as a kind of catalogue of 'these have influenced me'; this is done partly to keep it short, but also because to represent it in third person language as 'the origins of systemic theory' would be to impute a questionable objectivity to something that is inevitably more in the nature of autobiography.

First, then, I would like to mention Firth's own younger colleagues, especially W. S. Allen, R. H. Robins, Eugenie Henderson and Eileen Whitley. Eugenie Henderson's work showed what it meant to be "polysystemic", and demonstrated how to describe the phonology of a language in prosodic terms. Allen showed how to describe grammar, as well as phonology, in a Firthian way, and how to compare systems across languages. Robins built up a coherent picture of system-structure theory and – uniquely at that time – placed it in another contextual dimension, that of the history of linguistics. Eileen Whitley developed a deep insight into prosodic analysis; and also, very importantly, into Firth's conception of a text.

Of those on the western side of the Atlantic, the names that were most familiar to us were those of Sapir, Bloomfield and Fries: Sapir as the leading exponent of anthropological linguistics, Bloomfield mainly for his descriptive work, especially his Menomini studies, and Fries for his clearly stated methodology and for his interest in, and influence on, language education. The more immediate impact, however, came from their successors: from Hockett, who examined the foundations of structuralist linguistics, questioned them and was thus prepared for the developments to come; from Harris, who showed just how far one could go with these assumptions and where they could lead no further; from Gleason, who presented a systematic overall model for students and teachers, and then developed his own stratal viewpoint and his theory of narrative; and from Pike, who provided a solid foundation in phonetics, a functional theory of grammar and an explicit commitment to the cultural context of language.

But the one who had the most profound effect on my own thinking was a linguist whom of course I never met, Benjamin Lee Whorf. Whorf, developing concepts derived from his great predecessor Franz Boas, showed how it is that human beings do not all mean alike, and how their unconscious ways of meaning are among the most significant manifestations of their culture. Whorf's notion of the cryptotype, and his conception of how grammar models reality, have hardly yet begun to be taken seriously; in my opinion they will eventually turn out to be among the major contributions of twentieth-century linguistics.

Next I would like to mention five other scholars from whom I gained rich and, to me, new and exciting insights into language. Walter Simon, Professor of Chinese at London University, taught me what linguistic scholarship meant: to focus on language as an object of study, to take the text seriously, and to combine honesty with imagination in the construction of a theory. In China, Luo Changpei gave me a diachronic perspective and an insight into a language family other than Indo-European; and Wang Li taught me many things, including research methods in dialectology, the semantic basis of grammar, and the history of linguistics in China. When I first tried to teach linguistics, in a very disorganized way, David Abercrombie provided a model of how it should be done; he also provided a lucid and totally unbiased account of the principles of speech and of writing, and placed these studies in their historical perspective. Angus McIntosh demonstrated the scope and direction of a humanist linguistics, one that neutralized the opposition between arts and sciences; this he backed up in his own work by a farsighted commitment to a long-term programme of structured research (something I have never been able to achieve), which is now coming to a notable culmination.

At the risk of turning this into too much of a personal statement, I would like to round this part off by referring to some of my own contemporaries. I shall not try to make reference to those with whom I have been most closely associated in the work on systemic theory; it would take far too long to give even a remotely adequate account, and most are, happily for me, present on this occasion. But there have been a few other special acquaintances with whom I have interacted over the years, exchanging ideas when possible and always learning from them in the process.

Jeffrey Ellis was my first trackmate in exploring the (to me) unknown terrain of linguistics. Many years ago we wrote an article together, on temporal categories in the Chinese verb, which would have been my first academic publication; but the journal editor who had accepted it died suddenly, and it was rejected by his successor and so never appeared. Through Ellis I knew the late Denis Berg, who worked on conceptual-functional grammar when no one else would hear of it; and Jean Ure, who introduced the notion of register and has subsequently developed it in a systemic framework in the teaching of English to speakers of other languages. Trevor Hill initiated me into what would now be called sociolinguistics, and Kenneth Albrow worked with me on intonation and rhythm; both Hill and Albrow mastered Firth's prosodic phonology and wrote simple introductions to it, a thing which none of Firth's own colleagues ever felt the necessity to do. Peter Strevens organized the field of applied linguistics into a coherent and powerful domain of language study, in which we have continued to collaborate at a distance. And Ian Catford provided a unique under- standing of human speech production, as well as a broad comparative knowledge of languages of different parts of the world.

Further afield, I came to know Sydney Lamb; at our first talk, in a Georgetown bar masquerading as a pub, where we drank the beer from his home state, it became obvious that our ideas were compatible, and we have maintained the intertranslatability of systemic and stratifica- tional theory ever since. He reawakened my interest in the computer as a research tool in linguistics, which had been aroused when I had worked with Margaret Masterman and Frederick Parker-Rhodes in the Cambridge Language Research Unit in the late 1950s. Sydney Lamb was the first to show that it is possible to make grammar explicit and computable without discarding the achievements of descriptive linguistics and the understanding of language that grew out of them.

At about the same time I came to know Basil Bernstein, philosopher and thinker, and the first social theorist to build language into his explanatory scheme. From him we have learnt just what it is that is achieved through language – the transmission, maintenance and modification of the patterns of a culture – and hence what we, as linguists, have to be able to explain by means of our own theories. From Bernstein I learnt also, for the second time in my life, that linguistics cannot be other than an ideologically committed form of social action.

Thirdly during the 1960s, I began working closely with language educators; and at University College London, in the Programme in Linguistics and English Teaching, a team of primary and secondary teachers combined with linguists to work on problems of language development in school, from initial literacy through to multifunctional

English in the upper forms of high school. There were two of the team who participated from start to finish: David Mackay, and Peter Doughty. Peter Doughty brought a conception of English in secondary education which was so far ahead of his time that now, twenty years later, we are at last seeing some of his ideas introduced as innovations. David Mackay transformed an impoverished notion of 'reading' into a rich conception of language development in the infant and junior school; his work was followed up by the creation of the "Centre for Language in Primary Education" of the Inner London Education Authority, an institution which might justly have been named after him.

My concern here is with the systemic background; it would be impossible in this space to review work in systemic theory itself, which in any case is the substance of most of the present volume. But in order to bring the background up-to-date, let me refer briefly to three of the salient motifs of the past fifteen years which have provided part of the context for recent systemic work. These are: language and social reality, language and human development, and language in the machine.

George Herbert Mead (1932) regarded talk as one of the two forms of social action – the other one was play – by which an individual built up his identity; and in a series of penetrating and sympathetic studies Erving Goffman described the regulation and maintenance of this identity, under both normal and pathological conditions. Harvey Sacks came nearer to showing how language actually served these functions in a number of brilliant (but unpublished) *explications de texte*, which still however made no reference to the language system. Meanwhile Berger and Luckmann (1966) had described what they called the "reality-generating power of conversation". The work of Gunther Kress and his collaborators, in language and ideology (Kress and Hodge 1979; Fowler, Hodge, Kress and Trew 1979), and of Benjamin N. and Lore M. Colby, in the study of culturally pregnant texts such as religious narrative, have shown the potential of systemic theory as a theory of text and system for interpreting texts as ideological documents, bringing out their significance for the construction of the social semiotic.

Advances in developmental linguistics have introduced a new dimension into language education, especially in the early and middle childhood years. Educators such as Kenneth and Yetta Goodman, Jerome Harste and Martha King have been focusing explicitly on language development in their approach to reading and writing and to all aspects of the learning process, and Sinclair and Coulthard (1975) have shown how the linguistic analysis of the classroom throws light on educational practice. In Britain, Canada, the United States and Australia there is ongoing collaboration between linguists and educators using systemic theory, for the study of classroom discourse and of children's conversation, oral narrative and writing. Jay Lemke's (1982) work on science education uses a close linguistic analysis to reveal the underlying ideological structures of the education process.

The main contribution from linguistics to these activities is the study of discourse, and what makes systemic linguistics particularly relevant is its orientation towards the text. From the start it has been used in text analysis projects, such as the coding of the Nuffield Foreign Languages Teaching Materials Project Child Language Survey (Hasan 1965, Hanscombe 1966), the OSTI Programme in the Linguistic Properties of Scientific English (Huddleston, Hudson, Winter and Henrici 1968), as well as in stylistic and literary studies of register variation (e.g. Benson and Greaves 1973). A recent extension is its use in text generation by computer. Systemic theory had been employed before in artificial intelligence research (Winograd 1972, Davey 1979); but to use a systemic grammar as the basis of a text generation program would be uneconomical (since it is difficult to write systemic minigrammars) unless such a program was intended to become an exportable system that could be adapted to the needs of any user. This however is what William Mann set out to achieve, in the "Penman" project at the Information Sciences Institute of the University of Southern California; and there for the first time a comprehensive systemic grammar of English is being implemented on computer. This is reported on in another paper in this volume, by Mann and Matthiessen (see also Mann 1983; Mann and Matthiessen 1983). Eventually it should be possible to test the thesis that such a grammar is invertible, by constructing a systemic parsing program on the lines first sketched out by B. N. Colby and Mark James.

These very sketchy references will perhaps serve to bring out what I think is a salient feature in the evolution of systemic theory: its permeability from outside. By "outside" I mean not only outside itself, from other theories of language such as tagmemics and stratification theory, but also from outside linguistics, from disciplines for which language is not the object of study but rather an instrument for some other purpose – where this other purpose may be, in turn, either the study of some other object, such as human development or culture, or a body of praxis such as the teaching of foreign languages. Systemic theory has never been walled in by disciplinary boundaries;

191

this is not to imply that the concept of a discipline is vacuous, but that a discipline is defined not by what it studies but by the questions it seeks to answer, so that in order to understand language, which is what the questions of linguistics are about (the noun *language* is of course a grammatical metaphor – Peter Doughty preferred to talk about *languaging*, to show that our object of study is more process than entity), we have to study many other things besides, and hence a linguistic theory has to be a means of intersemiotic translation, interfacing with other theories of social meaning and so facilitating the input of findings from elsewhere.

The value of a theory lies in the use that can be made of it, and I have always considered a theory of language to be essentially consumer-oriented. In many instances the theorist is himself also and at the same time a consumer, designing a theory for application to his own task; in others he may be working together with a group of consumers, designing a theory for their particular needs. (Sometimes he may set up as 'pure' theorist on his own, without any particular consumers in mind; or thinking of a particular target group but without actually consulting them – the fate of "constrastive linguistics" is a good example of how this tends to limit the usefulness of the work.) Since there are so many tasks for which one needs a theory of language, any particular theory is likely to be, or very quickly to become, a family of theories – still on speaking terms, one hopes, and with a personal rather than positional family role system. This is why there is no orthodox or 'received' version of systemic theory, such as may arise with self-contained systems that are impervious to influences from outside, when some sort of 'standard' version comes to be defined by the stance adopted vis-à-vis certain issues that are identified from within.

Systemic theory is more like language itself – a system whose stability lies in its variation. A language is a 'metastable' system; it persists because it is constantly in flux. This does not mean that we cannot characterize a particular language, but that our characterization of it has to incorporate this feature. Similarly we can state certain essential characteristics of systemic theory (cf. Fawcett 1983). Let me try to enumerate some of those that are most central to our present theme.

1   A language is not a well-defined system, and cannot be equated with "the set of all grammatical sentences", whether that set is conceived of as finite or infinite. Hence a language cannot be interpreted by rules defining such a set. A language is a semiotic system; not in the sense of a system of signs, but a systemic resource for meaning – what I have often called a **meaning potential** (Halliday 1971). Linguistics is about how people exchange meanings by 'languaging'.

Part of the synoptic representation of a semiotic system is an account of its structure, the organic part-whole relationships that are known in linguistics as constituency. Because of the historical association of linguistics with writing – linguistics begins when a language is written down, and so made accessible to conscious attention; so grammar evolved as a grammar of written language – constituency has tended to occupy the centre of attention; so much so that my early (1961) paper 'Categories of the theory of grammar' was entirely misread (by Paul Postal 1964) as a theory of constituent structure, and the same mistake was made by Terence Langendoen in his book *The London School of Linguistics* (1968), which makes no reference at all to Firth's concept of system. In systemic theory, constituency is treated as a small, though essential, part of the total picture; and it is treated in a specific way, using ranks (which are the folk-linguistic notion of constituency, incidentally, and also that which is embodied in writing systems) instead of immediate constituents for the bracketing, and functions instead of classes for the labelling. These are not arbitrary choices; there are good reasons why philosophical theories of language, which tend to be formal and sentence-oriented, use maximal bracketing and class labels, whereas ethnographic theories, which tend to be functional and discourse-oriented, use minimal bracketing and functional labels.

What distinguishes systemic theory is that its basic form of synoptic representation is not syntagmatic but paradigmatic; the organizing concept is not structure, but system (hence the name). Since language is a semiotic potential, the description of a language is a description of choice. The various levels, or strata, of the semiotic 'code' are interrelated networks of options. The constituent structure is the realization of these options, and hence plays a derivative role in the overall interpretation.

2   Closely allied to this is the fact that constituent structure at the "content" level is part of an integrated lexicogrammar (as distinct from a syntax with lexicon attached) seen as natural, i.e. non-arbitrary. There are two distinct, though related, aspects to this non-arbitrariness, one functional the other metafunctional. (i) Every structural feature has its origin in the semantics; that is, it has some function in the expression of meaning. (This is unaffected by whether semantics and lexicogrammar are treated as one stratum or as two.) (ii) The different types of structure tend to express different kinds of meaning, as embodied in the

193

metafunctional hypothesis; and constituency is simply one type of structure, that which typically represents the experiential metafunction – the reflective component in our meaning potential. But whereas our experience is largely organized into particulate forms of representation, our interpersonal meanings – the active component – are expressed more prosodically, as field-like structures; and the texture is provided by periodic, wave-like patterns of discourse, in which prominence is achieved by beginnings and endings (of clauses, paragraphs and so on). Like the water I was contemplating at Niagara Falls, language is at once particle, wave and field (cf. Pike 1959); and depending on which kind of meaning we want to be foregrounded, so our representation of its structure needs to adapt to the appropriate mode.

3   The heart of language is the abstract level of coding that is the lexicogrammar. (I see no reason why we should not retain the term "grammar" in this, its traditional sense in linguistics; the purpose of introducing the more cumbersome term *lexicogrammar* is simply to make explicit the point that vocabulary is also a part of it, along with syntax and morphology.) A lexicogrammar is not a closed, determinate system; and this fact has three consequences for systemic theory and practice. First, grammar cannot be modelled as new sentences made out of old words – a fixed stock of vocabulary in never-to-be-repeated combinations. On the one hand, we process and store entire groups, phrases, clauses, clauses complexes and even texts; this is a crucial element in a child's language development. On the other hand, we constantly create new words, and even now and again new morphemes. The higher the rank, the more likely a given instance is to be in some sense a first occurrence; but there is nothing remarkable about that. Secondly, and closely related to the last point, the lexicogrammatical system of a language is inherently probabilistic. It has been readily accepted that the relative frequency of words is a systematic feature of language, but this principle has not generally been extended to grammatical systems; yet it is a fundamental property of grammar that, at least in some systems, the options are not equiprobable, and this can be built in to the representation of a grammatical network. The principle is an important one because it is likely that one of the significant differences between one register and another is difference of probabilities in the grammar (this again is to be expected, since it is clearly true of the vocabulary – different registers display different lexical probabilities). Thirdly, grammar is indeterminate in the sense that there are often two or more possible grammatical interpretations of an item, each of which relates it to a different set of other items, thus making a particular generalization of a paradigmatic kind. This may affect anything from an entire system – transitive and ergative interpretations of English transitivity would be a case in point – to a single instance, where alternative analyses can be suggested for some item in a particular text.

4 A fourth assumption of systemic theory is that language is functionally variable; any text belongs to some register or other. (Dialect variation is also functional, of course, as the symbolic vehicle of social structure; but the term "functional variety" refers to register). The different kinds of situation that collectively constitute a culture engender different kinds of text; but if we understand the semiotic properties of a situation we can make predictions about the meanings that are likely to be exchanged, in the same way that the interactants make predictions and in so doing facilitate their own participation. The notions of field, mode and tenor, together with the subsequent distinction into personal and functional tenor, provided an initial conceptual framework for characterizing the situation and moving from the situation to the text; and much current work in systemic theory is directed towards the construction of an adequate model of register and genre, taking into account the context of situation, the rhetorical structure of the text and the higher-level semiotics that make up the context of culture. This is an essential step in any adequate interpretation of language as a social semiotic, within the tradition that I referred to above as 'ethnographic' as opposed to 'philosophical' linguistics; but it also has important educational applications, for example in the development of children's writing (Martin and Rothery 1980/1). In general, as remarked above, differences among different registers are likely to be found in the relative weightings assigned to different systems: the orientation towards different metafunctions and different options in semantics. In some instances, however, more clear-cut distinctions emerge; for example the different kinds of complexity associated respectively with speech and writing.

5 Systemic theory accepts the Saussurean concept of how the system is represented by the observed *actes de parole*. But, as I see it at least, this has to be interpreted as Hjelmslev interpreted it; first in the framework of system and process, where the process (text) **instantiates** the system, and secondly, with a distinction between instantiation and realization.

The latter refers to the stratal organization of the system (and therefore also of the process) whereby the expression is said to **realize** the content.

To take the latter point first: we assume that language is stratified. The number of strata ("levels", in Firth's terminology) that we recognize, and the kind of relationship between strata, will tend to depend on the questions we are asking and the problems we are trying to solve. For example, for certain purposes we may want to work with the Hjelmslevian model of content and expression, the only stratal boundary being the Saussurean line of arbitrariness; this is a way of pushing the grammar so far towards the interface as to incorporate the semantics within it. For other purposes, such as the study of language development, especially the move from protolanguage to language, we may want to interpret the lexicogrammar as a third, purely abstract, level of coding that gets 'slotted in' between the two interface levels of semantics and phonology. We may want to add other, higher-level strata to accommodate a theory of register, or to represent the knowledge base in a text generation program. It is the basic concept of stratification that is important.

Secondly, whereas Saussure, in separating *langue* from *parole*, drew the conclusion that linguistics was a theory of *langue*, systemic theory follows Hjelmslev in encompassing both. For a linguist, to describe language without accounting for text is sterile; to describe text without relating it to language is vacuous. The major problem perhaps is that of interpreting the text as process, and the system as evolution (its ontogenesis in the language development of children): in other words, of representing both the system and its instantiation in dynamic as well as in synoptic terms. Dynamic models of semiotic systems are not yet very well developed, and this is one of the problems that theorists of language now have to solve.

6 It is a general feature of semiotic systems that they develop and function in a context, and that meaning is a product of the relationship between the system and its environment – where that environment may be another semiotic system. For language, the context of the system is the higher-level semiotics which it serves to realize; hence it is the stratal representation that allows us to interpret the context of the system (Malinowski's "context of culture"). It is in this sense that semantics is an interface ("interlevel", in earlier terminology), namely when we are considering it as the relationship between lexicogrammar and some higher-level semiotic. The context of a text, on the other hand, is Malinowski's "context of situation": the configuration of semiotic processes that are constitutive of its rhetorical structure and shape its ideational, interpersonal and textual characteristics. Systemic theory has always been explicitly contextual, in both these senses, offering contextual explanations for such problems as how children learn language from what goes on around them and how language provides a grid for the construction of models of experience.

7 Finally, given the tradition to which it belongs, it is to be expected that those using systemic theory have tended to take a particularist rather than a generalist position with regard to linguistic categories. In part, this has been to avoid claiming universality for categories such as "cases", or phonological features, that seemed far too specific to bear such a theoretical load, but equally, perhaps, from the knowledge that, while no one is likely to question the identity of all languages at a sufficiently abstract level, for most purposes for which linguistic theory is used it is **differences** among languages that need to be understood – while in those applications where only one language is concerned, the universality or otherwise of its categories is irrelevant.

I am not suggesting for a moment that these observations are acts of faith to which all 'systemicists' subscribe; but that it is an inclination to adopt viewpoints such as these that leads people to explore the potential of systemic theory. What is perhaps a unifying factor among these who work within this framework is a strong sense of the social accountability of linguistics and of linguists. Systemic theory is designed not so much to prove things as to do things. It is a form of praxis. I have often emphasized that language, both in its nature and in its ontogenetic development, clearly reveals a dual function; it is at once, and inseparably, a means of action and a means of reflection. Linguistics, as metalanguage, has to serve the same twofold purpose. Systemic theory is explicitly constructed both for thinking with and for acting with. Hence – like language, again – it is rather elastic and rather extravagant. To be an effective tool for these purposes, a theory of language may have to share these properties with language itself; to be non-rigid, so that it can be stretched and squeezed into various shapes as required, and to be non-parsimonious, so that it has more power at its disposal than is actually needed in any one context.

Systemic theory, then, is a way of thinking about language and of working on language – and through language, on other things. But it is also a symbolic system; and, as every infant knows, symbols do not affect things, only people. Thus 'applying' linguistics is using a linguistic

197

theory to act on people. But thinking about language is also, of course, thinking about people, since there is no language other than is people's acts of meaning; so that action and reflection in linguistics are not very clearly separated activities. Just as, in the evolved adult language, mood and transitivity are mapped into a single clause, so that one cannot mean in one way without also meaning in the other, so in reflecting on how people communicate we are likely to be also acting on their communicative processes. It seems to me that this is a perspective which most systemicists share.

Chapter Nine

SYSTEMIC GRAMMAR AND THE CONCEPT OF A "SCIENCE OF LANGUAGE" (1992)

Those who study language have often been concerned with the status of linguistics as a science. They have wanted to ensure that their work was objective and scientifically valid. The natural way to achieve this aim has been to use other, earlier developed sciences as a model: theoretical physics, evolutionary biology, chemistry – some discipline that is currently valued as a leader in the field of intellectual activity. It is assumed that, if we investigate language using the same principles and methods that have proved successful in these other domains, we shall have made our linguistics equally "scientific".

There are two problems here. One is perhaps a fairly obvious one: that the phenomena we are trying to understand – those of language – are phenomena of a rather distinct kind. Certainly there are, at a very abstract level, features in common to systems of all kinds, whether physical, biological, or social; and we can add to these also the fourth kind, semiotic systems, which are those which construe meaning – the kind of system to which language belongs. But there are also significant differences; and what constitutes "science", or scientific inquiry, is not likely to be the same thing in all cases. A science of meaning is potentially rather different from a science of nature, or of society.

The other problem may be less obvious. As I see it, the concept of "science" refers to scientific practice: to what scientists actually do when engaged in their professional activities. But this is not always the same thing as what they say they do; it is certainly not the same thing as what other people say they do, and it is still further away from what other people say they ought to do. We have tended to derive our concept of

First published in *Waiguoyu* (*Journal of Foreign Languages*), No. 2 (General Series No. 78), 1992, pp. 1–9.

science from studying the models constructed in the name of philosophy of science, rather than from observing scientists at work. But these models are highly idealized; even when they set out to be descriptive (as opposed to normative) they present a picture that is far removed from scientific daily life. I share the view of colleagues such as Victor Yngve and Claude Hagège, that in so far as we want to emulate those working in the more established sciences, it is the working practices of the scientists themselves that we need to be aware of – how **they** construct theories to explain the phenomena **they** are studying. These are what count for us; not the philosophical interpretations of science, which are theories constructed to explain how scientists work (Yngve 1986; Hagège 1988).

As an illustration of this point, consider how linguists have constructed the notion of "counterexamples". If anyone offers a generalization, others immediately start hunting after counterexamples, in the belief that this is how you test a hypothesis: if you find one counterexample you have demolished it, and it has to be abandoned. But this is an idealization; it is not how people actually work. What you do with a generalization is to apply it, and when you find it doesn't work a hundred percent of the time (which it never will do), you try to improve it, to define the limits of its applicability, and seek further generalizations to back it up. (Grimm's law was not abandoned; it was shown to apply only in certain cases, and then backed up by the addition of Verner's law.) In order to escape from this trap, linguists have had to invent the concept of the "prototypical". But they would never have needed such an escape hatch if they had not dug the hole for themselves to fall into in the first place.

I would like to enumerate, in this paper, certain principles and practices which I think are usually followed by linguists working in systemic-functional linguistics. These are not derived from any idealized model of scientific endeavour. They seem to me to correspond fairly closely to the sort of things that scientists do, and the general positions they adopt, in their everyday working lives. But I am not setting out to prove that linguistics, whether systemic or in any other model, is a science. My aim is simply to characterize how some linguists go about their work: what they adopt as their working principles. It is useful, I think, to try to make these principles explicit. (For the concept of 'doing science', see Lemke 1990a.)

1 Categories that are used in the analysis of language are general concepts which help us to explain linguistic phenomena. They are not "reified": that is, they are not endowed with a spurious reality of their own.

For example: we do not start with a ready-made concept like **Theme**. We start with a particular problem, such as "why does a speaker of English choose to put one thing rather than another in first position in the clause?" To explain this, we have to set up a long chain of explanation; this involves certain abstract categories, through which we relate this question to a large number of other phenomena in the language. "Theme" is the name that we give to one particular link in this chain of explanations, embodying a generalization about the structure of the message.

Two points should be made. One is that the name is not a definition. We try (following a traditional practice in linguistics) to give names that suggest the typical "purport" of a category, in Hjelmslev's term: hence grammatical categories get names that are interpreted semantically (and likewise phonological categories get names that are interpreted phonetically). But we do not then argue: "this instance does not fit my name: therefore it is not a member of this category". The name just helps us to remember where we are on the map.

Secondly, we do not use the name to impose artificial rigour on a language. Linguistic phenomena tend to be indeterminate, with lots of ambiguities, blends and "borderline cases". The categories of the analysis take this into account, allowing us to treat it not as something exceptional or dysfunctional, but as a natural and positive feature of an evolving semiotic system.

2   The categories used in the analysis are of two kinds: theoretical, and descriptive. Theoretical categories are those such as **metafunction**, **system**, **level**, **class**, **realization**. Descriptive categories are those such as **clause**, **preposition**, **Subject**, **material process**, **Theme**.

Theoretical categories are, by definition, general to all languages: they have evolved in the construction of a general linguistic theory. They are constantly being refined and developed as we come to understand more about language; but they are not subject to direct verification. A theory is not proved wrong; it is made better – usually step by step, sometimes by a fairly catastrophic change.

Descriptive categories are in principle language-specific: they have evolved in the description of particular languages. Since we know that all human languages have much in common, we naturally use the descriptive categories of one language as a guide when working on another. But, if a descriptive category named "clause" or "passive" or "Theme" is used in describing, say, both English and Chinese, it is redefined in the case of each language. (See Hu, Zhu and Zhang 1989, *passim*.)

201

So, for example, while *system* itself is a theoretical category, each instance of a system, such as *mood*, is a descriptive category; similarly, *option* (or *feature*) in a system is a theoretical category, while each particular instance of an option, like *indicative* or *declarative*, is descriptive.

Descriptive categories are thus of a lower order of abstraction. They can be defined in such a way as to make them subject to verification. For example, if in defining "passive" we include morphological criteria, saying that passive is distinguished from its alternative ("active") by systematic variation in the morphology of the verb, then it becomes possible to say that a particular construction in a given language is not a passive, or that there is no passive in the given language at all. (Note that, if it is claimed that some descriptive category is a "universal" of language, such a claim can only be evaluated if there is some explicit formal definition of this kind. A universal feature is different from a theoretical category: it is a descriptive category that is being said to be present in every language.)

3 Within both these types, theoretical and descriptive, the categories are defined not individually but in relation one to another. For example, "Theme", in English: this is defined not only in relation to Rheme (through the structural configuration *Theme* + *Rheme*) but also in relation to the category of *clause*, to other functions in the clause like *Subject*, to the system of *mood*, its various options such as *declarative*, and so on.

There is no ordering in such definitions; we do not **first** set up one set of categories and **then** derive other ones from them (we may have to express the description in an ordered way, since Chapter 1 has to precede Chapter 2 in the grammar book; but that is a question of presentation). The only ordering is that of delicacy: more specific categories depend on those that include them (i.e. that precede them in generality, as *indicative* precedes *declarative* and *interrogative*). But even this is not a definitional ordering. For example, *past, present, future* are defined as options in the English system of *tense*, which is a system of the *verbal group*. But, equally, the *verbal group* is defined as the entry condition to the system called *tense* whose options are *past, present* and *future*.

4 All descriptive categories are identified from three perspectives: those of (i) the higher level, (ii) the same level, (iii) the lower level. This is sometimes referred to as (i) "from above", (ii) "from around" and (iii) "from below". For example, in English the Subject is that which

(i)   has special status in the interpersonal structure of the clause, being the element on which the argument is made to rest (by reference to which the proposition is laid open to argument);
(ii) is mapped on to certain elements in the experiential and textual structural (e.g. Actor in active material process, Senser in one type of mental process; Theme in declarative mood, etc.);
(iii) is the nominal group that accompanies the Finite operator and is taken up pronominally in the declarative mood tag.

This enables us to express the difference between functional and formal grammars. All grammars, of course, are concerned both with function and with form; the difference is one of orientation. In a formal grammar, perspective (iii) has priority; (i) is derived from (iii), and may not be stated at all (e.g. in some formal grammars the category corresponding to Subject in English would have no interpretation from above). In a functional grammar, such as systemic grammar, (i) has priority, and (iii) will typically be derived from it.

Since criteria from the different perspectives often conflict, there may be a substantial difference between formal and functional grammars in how the descriptive categories are aligned, and even in the categories themselves. Categories that are relatively clearly identifiable from above may be very complex to describe from below (e.g. the different types of process in English, which may simply not be recognized in a formal grammar). Again, however, it must be emphasized that the priority is not absolute: no category is fixed from one perspective alone. The description is always a compromise among all the three perspectives.

5   In a functional grammar, perspective (i) is that which **explains** (this is what is meant by saying that a functional grammar is one which offers functional explanations – a kind that is not recognized as explanations in a formal grammar). What is **to be explained** is some pattern identified from the vantagepoint of perspective (iii). For example: "why does a particular one of the nominal elements in an English declarative clause turn up again pronominally in the tag?" (and cf. the question "why does a particular element come first in the clause?", cited in 1 above). The explanation will be given from the vantagepoint of perspective (i), e.g. "this is the element which the speaker selects in order to carry the weight of the argument – the one that is held 'modally responsible' for it". In other words, a functional grammar is one which explains the forms of the language by referring to the functions they express.

203

Now consider the case of ***comparative*** description: that is, using the categories set up for one language as tools for exploring another. Here the direction of inquiry is typically reversed. Instead of beginning with a question seeking to explain the formal pattern in (iii), we begin with what was originally the answer to such a question, namely the functional generalization under (i). So, for example, if we are using the concept of Subject to investigate the grammar of Chinese, we don't say "Is there a nominal element in the clause that accompanies the Finite operator and also turns up pronominally in the tag?" – which would not be very helpful, since we would first have to find Finite operators and mood tags in Chinese before we could ask the question! We say "Is there a nominal element that has special status in the interpersonal function of the clause, as being the one on which the argument is made to rest?" The assumption is that, if there is any such element, it will be recognizable somehow or other (that is, identifiable from perspective (iii)), although not the way it is in English.

In other words, the comparison is made from the vantagepoint of perspective (i). We look at the meaning of some category in the language of reference, and then ask if there is any category in the language under description that has a comparable function taken in the context of the whole. Almost all descriptive work today is in this sense comparative; and this is reasonable, since there is no point in pretending, when we come to describe a language, that no other languages have been described before, or that we cannot learn anything from those that have. Ideally – but let me say clearly that this is not what is usually done! – each language should be described twice over: first comparatively, using categories drawn from other language as guides, and then ***particularly*** – entirely in its own terms, as if no other language had been described before. This is the only way to ensure that it will not be misrepresented. Historically, the second one was the way the ancient Indian and Greek grammarians proceeded; first they described the forms, perspective (iii), and then they questioned why these forms arose: why is this noun in this particular case? why are there two sets of forms for certain verbs? and so on. This was the origin of syntax. The reason why syntax never evolved in China is that Chinese has no morphology; so questions of this kind were never asked.

6 We have said that comparative description begins from the vantagepoint of perspective (i): we look for categories which are comparable when viewed "from above". But by itself this could be misleading. We do not, in fact, start out by trying to identify individual categories, single elements of structure, like "Subject", or single options in a system, like "passive". The basis of any comparative description is the system (a point made very many years ago by Sidney Allen; see Allen 1956).

Thus, if we are using English categories to explore Chinese, we do not ask whether there is a Subject, or whether there is a passive; we ask whether there is a comparable system, in each case. For example, the category of Subject in English realizes choice of mood; so instead of asking whether or not Chinese has a category of Subject, we first ask "Is there a system of mood? – that is, a system for exchanging information and goods-&-services, one through which speakers are enabled to argue." There is; so then we ask about its options, to see whether they can be interpreted by reference to categories of declarative, interrogative and so on. Step by step we come to the question whether there is a particular nominal element which has a special function in the clause with respect to the system of mood. There is – but not the same as in English. The Subject in English does two jobs in the mood system: it takes responsibility for the proposition, and it also plays a part in realizing the distinction between one category of mood and another. There is a nominal element in Chinese which does the first job but not the second – and since it is not required for making the distinction between declarative and interrogative, it is often "not there" where the Subject would be in English. (The temptation then is to say that something in the Chinese has been "dropped" or "omitted". But this is where the comparative approach becomes pathological. Nothing has been omitted; that is a fiction created by looking at Chinese through English eyes.) The important question then becomes, what is the difference in meaning between a clause which makes explicit this modally responsible element and one which does not. It could be a matter of ellipsis (i.e. the element is presumed from elsewhere – note that there is still a difference in meaning between putting it in and leaving it out, albeit a subtle one); or it could be realizing some other systematic semantic opposition.

7   So it is the theoretical category of the *system* that enables us to use the comparative principle in describing different languages. But the question still remains, how do we decide what is or is not the same category?

This, however, is simply a question of naming. What we are asking is: how much alike must two things be for us to call them by the same name? And there is no way of answering this, because there is no way of measuring functional similarity across languages. The only principle is, that since there is a limit to the number of names that are available it seems sensible to reuse existing names if we can. (Of course there is no limit to the number of new names we could create; but they soon become an awful nuisance to remember.) The danger in this is that they have to be reinterpreted each time they are applied to a new language; and the best way of dealing with this situation, in my view, is to ensure that the metalanguage (the language of description) is always created in the language that is **under** description. Of course, we write grammars of Chinese in English; and we write grammars of English in Chinese. But the English term "Subject" will be prototypically defined according to the category of Subject in English; so the equivalent Chinese term *zhuyu* will be prototypically defined according to the category that it labels in the grammar of Chinese.

However, given the system as the fundamental category for comparison, we can develop a principled approach to the question of 'same or different'. Let us take a different example: say the category of passive in English, as a concept for explaining Chinese. We could reason like this. In any clause with two or more participants, there is a system in English whereby their textual status may be reversed: typically, this involves switching between thematic prominence (Theme) and informational prominence (New). Example: *the rain obscured my vision/my vision was obscured by the rain*, where the first has *the rain* as Theme and *my vision* as New, the second has *my vision* as Theme and *the rain* as New. We call this system "voice". In the voice system, one option is unmarked, the other marked; we call the unmarked option "active", the marked option "passive". The active voice assigns to the most "active" participant the status that is typically associated in the clause with that of Theme.

We can then compare this system with a system in another language, point by point: first the notion of a system with some comparable function of this **textual** kind, constructing the participants into different values in the message; then the scope of that system – which classes of clause possess the option; then the particular textual systems with which the choice is associated; the question whether there is also an experiential difference in meaning (as in English between Agent coded as Actor and Agent coded as Manner); evidence for the opposition of a marked versus and unmarked term and so on. It seems reasonable to label a system in another language which lies similarly at the intersection of transitivity and theme by the familiar name of "voice".

This would not necessarily demand that its options should be labelled "active" and "passive"; for this we might insist on some more specific features in common, such as the relative marking and the association of "active" with some relative value on the scale of agency. The terms do matter, because they carry a load of semantic baggage along with them (this is one of the reasons for insisting on constructing the metalanguage in words from the language under description – their semantic loading is different). But more important is using this kind of strategy as a way of exploring more deeply into the grammar of the language in question.

8 Even if a category has been **established** comparatively, by reference to something that was first set up in another language, it is **explained** by reference to other categories in its own language. Thus even if we have arrived at a category of "Subject" in Chinese by recognizing a system comparable to the English system of mood, and within that same function realizing special status in the argument, the thing we are calling "Subject" in Chinese will still be defined and explained **within the system of Chinese grammar**.

As already emphasized, such explanations are not single steps; they involve long chains of internal relationships, typically ranging across more than one metafunction. Thus, what we call "Theme" in English is explained by reference not only to the flow of information, with the speaker-listener axis as the source of energy (hence as a component within the Theme + Rheme, Given + New of the textual meta-function), but also to the mood system, and the role of Subject, in the interpersonal metafunction, and to the various clause types and participant roles in transitivity. Whichever part of the grammar we are explaining, we are constantly making references to all the other parts.

In comparative and typological studies based on formal grammars, it is common practice to take single features and compare them across a number of different languages. But when a feature is detached from the environment in which it actually functions, the basis for the comparison is rather different; it is not clear whether the things that are being compared are actually comparable in meaning.

Sometimes we are able to bring in the historical dimension to our explanations, if we have some evidence of changes that have taken place in the past. For example, in the evolution of so-called "phrasal verbs" in English: we can relate the development of this construction to textual and experiential factors combined. If there were two participants, the Process (verbal group) came to occur almost always between the two, while the focus of information was most typically located at the end of the clause. Thus, if the speaker wants to focus the information on the Process he splits the verbal group into two parts, so as to get one part at the end of the clause; e.g. *you left the best part **out***, instead of *you **omitted** the best part*, where the focus is marked and disturbs the required balance of information. Functionally, we can now compare this with the *ba* construction in Chinese: the pre-verb *ba* fulfils a similar function, that of getting the verb at the end of the clause, which in Chinese, as in English, is the typical location of the information focus. Hence Chinese *ni ba zuihao-di yi bufen **wangdiaole***, rather than *ni **wangdiaole** zuihao-di yi bufen*. (Would we therefore give the same name to the two systems: the choice between (e.g.) *omit* and *leave out* in English, and that between a non-*ba* clause and a *ba* clause in Chinese? We might feel here that, although the two are similar from the vantagepoint of perspective (i), from the vantagepoint of (ii) and, especially, (iii) they are rather too different. As always, what matters is that we are aware of the relationship between them.)

9   The data on which description rests are real language texts, instances of spoken and written language. In my opinion, texts of spontaneous speech are the most revealing, because it is in spontaneous speech that linguistic systems are most richly explored and exploited, and the meaning potential put under the greatest pressure to expand.

It is now at last possible to assemble and process large quantities of natural text, in the form of a computerized corpus. Spoken language still takes a long time to collect and transcribe; but it is not impossible to include it, even if not in its most spontaneous form – the radio is a valuable source. Such corpuses have a dual function. On the one hand, they enable us to base the grammar on what people actually say and write, in real contexts of situation; this is a great deal more satisfactory than relying on our own invention. On the other hand, they enable us to undertake large-scale quantitative studies of grammatical patterns, and so to explain the grammar in terms of probabilities. Both these features, in my view, are fundamental to the future development of grammatical theory, and hence to the successful use of grammatical descriptions for applied purposes such as machine translation and language teaching (cf. Sinclair 1987; Halliday and James 1993).

10   Descriptive categories are set up to explain the phenomena that we find in languages. Hence they are described as explicitly as possible, in such a way as to link them clearly to their exponents. This does not mean, however, that such categories are directly manifested in spoken and written forms.

Occasionally we find a systemic or structural category which has an entirely regular and overt pattern of exponence. English secondary tenses, though complex (or perhaps just **because** they are so complex), are extraordinarily regular in their construction. Likewise the basic categories of mood, and of polarity, in the Chinese clause. But many of the most significant categories in the grammar of every language are likely to be more or less hidden from view ("cryptotypic", in Whorf's term). They are also likely to be indeterminate, with ambiguities ('could be either a or b, but must be one or the other'), blends ('could be either a or b – the difference is neutralized in this environment') and borderline cases ('lies on the borderline of a and b, with some of the features of both'). These features are inevitable in any complex semiotic system, because functional criteria conflict and it is impossible for all functional categories to be uniquely realized in formal terms.

No grammatical description, therefore, can be 100 per cent explicit; the cost of any such requirement would be to leave out much of what is important in the language. But **all systems have their realizations** (cf. 4 above); the aim is to state these as explicitly as possible, at least in respect of what are shown to be their typical properties ("prototypical", in current terms).

11 We make the categories of the grammar explicit by saying how they are realized. The most abstract categories of the grammatical description are the systems together with their options (systemic features). A systemic grammar differs from other functional grammars (and from all formal grammars) in that it is paradigmatic: a *system* is a paradigmatic set of alternative features, of which **one** must be chosen if the entry condition is satisfied. For example, in English: (for any major clause) "positive polarity or negative polarity"; (for any finite verbal group) "modal deixis or temporal deixis"; (if temporal, then) "past, present or future tense". The features are thus independent of considerations of structure. They are **realized** as structures – but not separately. All the features that are selected at a given point of origin (for example, all the choices that are made by the major finite clause) are realized together as a single structure, a configuration of functional elements.

In the description, we state what contribution each feature makes to this configuration: to the choice of elements, their ordering, their mapping one on to another ("conflation"), and so on. These functional configurations, or **structures**, are realized, in their turn, as sequences of classes; and the cycle of realization relates one rank in the grammar to the next – for example, the rank of **clause** to that of **phrase/group**. Thus, the system of **theme selection** in English is realized as a configuration of Theme + Rheme; the feature **unmarked theme** is realized by mapping Theme on to some element that is realizing a choice in the system of mood (if the mood feature **declarative** is chosen, then on to Subject); the conflation Theme/Subject is then realized by the class **nominal group**.

In this way the abstract categories of the grammar are made explicit, through various cycles of realization. By using a computer for generating and parsing we can test how close to being explicit they actually are.

12 Realization also relates the categories of one level (stratum) to those of another. Hence, the categories of the lexicogrammar are related "upwards" to discourse-semantics and "downwards" to those of phonology.

Realization is probably the most difficult single concept in linguistics. It is the relationship of "meaning-&-meant" which, in semiotic systems, replaces the "cause-&-effect" relation of classical physical systems. Unlike cause, realization is not a relationship in real time. It is a two-way relationship that we can only gloss by using more than one word to describe it: to say that wordings (lexicogrammatical formations) **realize** meanings (semantic formations) means both that wordings **express** meanings and that wordings **construct** meanings.

The core of a language lies in its lexicogrammar, and specifically in the way meaning is constructed (or, better, **construed** – that is, constructed in the semiotic sense) as a metafunctional complex, ideational, interpersonal and textual (cf. Matthiessen 1989). Just as, in describing particular categories within the grammar, we approach them from three perspectives, so in describing the grammar as a whole (i) we relate it to what it **realizes** (what is "above" it), the semantics; (ii) we describe it as a system **in its own terms**, and (iii) we relate it to what it **is realized by** (to what is "below" it), the phonology. Again, the interpretation of the grammar of a language will always involve a compromise among these three perspectives.

13 Because semiotic systems are built on the relationship of realization they are potentially multistratal. Just as the lexicogrammar "realizes" the discourse-semantics, so the semantics in its turn "realizes" the context of situation and of culture.

This makes it possible for language to construct both human knowledge and human society – in the complex ways we simply take for granted (Hasan 1990).

It is often said that language must be dependent on the underlying systems (e.g. "knowledge of the world") and underlying processes (e.g. inferencing) that are located in the brain, or in the mind; and that, therefore, language can only be explained by reference to these. I would not argue about the first part; but I would want to add that systems of knowledge and belief, and processes of cognition, are also dependent on language. But since the main evidence for knowledge systems and cognitive processes is linguistic evidence, I would try as far as possible to use language as the means of understanding them. Instead of explaining how people mean in terms of what they know, I am inclined to explain what they know in terms of how they mean. Rather than treating language as part of the domain of cognitive science, I would treat cognition as part of the domain of linguistic science.

This last is a personal view, and not all those working in systemic theory would share it (contrast, e.g. Fawcett 1980). But all would agree, I think, that with a powerful **grammatics** (theory of grammar), you can seek linguistic explanations for so-called "pragmatic" phenomena – inferencing and conversational implicatures, speech acts, intentionality and the like. If we ask a question such as "Is language working directly, or is it triggering our logical inferencing?", this implies that these would be two different phenomena; but I do not think they are – they are two different ways of modelling, or interpreting, a single complex phenomenon. Of course, we can look at it from either end; there is no one right way to describe it. But it is the task of linguists to extend linguistic theory as far as possible in exploring these important domains.

These thirteen points, as briefly sketched out here, are some of the ways in which we try to understand, describe and explain a system such as that of human language – a semiotic system, in other words. They are not identical with the ways in which systems of other kinds are described and explained, although they are not completely different either. It seems to me that, when we describe a language in this way, we are probably "doing science" in the sense that Lemke referred to. The question is worth considering, because it does involve the relationship between what we do and what many of our colleagues are doing, in other faculties and departments; it is also important that they should understand what it means to be "doing grammar" (about which they often have very erroneous ideas). I would also add that, in my view, there has to be a "science of language", or a science of semiotic systems, just as Saussure was saying almost a century ago – but more urgently needed now, because semiotic systems are taking the place of physical systems as the model that we use to think about all the rest. But that is still some way off in the future.

Chapter Ten

LANGUAGE IN A CHANGING WORLD
(1993)

My "text" for this occasion is taken from the first paper in Frances Christie's project report on *Teaching English Literacy*, in which Kevin McDonald (1991) is writing about "the context of language education today".[1] Referring to David Harvey's observation, in *The Condition of Postmodernity*, that "the production city has been replaced by the city of the spectacle", McDonald goes on to say:

> Postmodern theories of the city emphasize flux, uncertainty, image – the city represented in Scott's *Bladerunner*. These latter theories emphasize the extent to which our environment is a symbolic one.

He goes on to say that one of the things that "makes postmodernity different from the modernist movement" is

> ... the insistence that social life is constituted essentially by the medium of language, rather than by the medium of energy and the transformation of nature. Thus the postmodern theorists join with many theorists who argue that our society is first and foremost a system of meanings, a symbolic reality. (pp. 4,5)

We might comment here that every society is "a system of meanings, a symbolic reality"; there is nothing special about that. So it is the "first and foremost" we should attend to. What makes our "postmodern" society significantly more of a semiotic construction than societies in the past? It is not, I think, due to what Harvey describes as "reconstituting the city as an artificial environment of leisure". Replacing foundryland by Disneyland does not by itself change the relative balance between the material and the semiotic in human life; it was observed long ago that the technology of one era becomes the pastime of the next, whether hunting, or gardening, or riding around

First published in *Occasional Papers* 13. Applied Linguistics Association of Australia, 1993.

on steam trains, and if people in Los Angeles no longer produce material goods, people in Osaka and Shanghai certainly do. More to the point, perhaps, is that our culture is becoming trapped inside a kind of semiotic cycle, in which the environment that is **depicted** by the media is also one that is **created** by the media, so that if the semotechnology broke down all happening would come to an end. We become aware of this first as a feature of the leisure industry, because it is obvious that most of the spectacle we see on television exists only as television spectacle; but that is because it is performance, and all performance, whether technology intervenes or not, enacts its own semiotic reality. A better source of insight here, I think, is the semiotic construction of the news. News, presumably, is a record of what people do. People are doing things all the time; it is when their doings are transformed into meanings that they become news. In his little book *The Tongues of Men*, written in 1937, Firth gave an account of what was news in England at the time, and commented:

> As we have seen, language can be regarded as operator, switchboard, and wiring in control of our social currents and power. It is the nervous system of our society.   (p. 131)

His 'Revue' (Firth 1937) provides some contemporary examples of the "forces which language commands".[2]

What sorts of "doings" are typically transformed into news? On television, on radio, and in mass circulation print, there seem to be two dominant motifs: one is discourse, the other is death. Grammatically, most constituents of "news" texts are either projections – what somebody said, for example:

> "I will not stand down," said a defiant Mr. Greiner.

or else material process clauses of the "destruction" category, e.g.:

> Fourteen people were killed when a gunman opened fire in a Texas supermarket.

Very often one of these motifs is introduced as a subplot of the other: "Killers threaten further reprisals ..." A third motif, a little way behind these two, is that of money: discourse, death and dollars, if we want to complete the 3-D trilogy. And then, of course, come sports, corrupt politicians, sex scandals of the rich and famous, and statistics of all kinds (it does not seem to matter what the statistics are about).[3] But the first two, discourse and death, seem to predominate: partly no doubt because they are catastrophic rather than gradual, but more because, of all the areas in the transitivity system, verbal processes, and processes of violent conflict, are the most susceptible of ideological loading – not just lexically, but in their ideational and interpersonal grammar. It is much less easy to promote the capitalist values of individualism and enterprise, or to construe people into their archetypal roles, as hero, villain, victim and so on, if the news consists of the community's recent artistic achievements or the seasonal migrations of birds.

We know this because it is precisely in the "reporting" of pronouncements and speeches on the one hand, and of massacres, terrorist acts and nuclear disasters on the other, that linguistic analysis most clearly reveals the opposing ideologies that are being promoted in different organs.[4] Construing events as news is a highly political act. But it is also more than that. If we are able to take the news as a way of exploring the concept of society as text, this is because constructing the news is not simply the semiotic transformation of verbal or material happenings; it is also the **instigation** of these happenings. There is no clear line, in fact, between construing events into meanings and bringing these events about. We can argue for a long time about the "events" in Tiananmen Square in 1989 and their construal/construction by the western media – about "what happened" at all the various levels of agency. Whatever conclusion we reach (if any), our most powerful resource for investigating what happened will be an interpretation of grammar: a "grammatics", which is a theory about how a grammar is, among other things, a theory of events.

There is no need to prolong this illustration; but let me refer to another salient aspect of the discursive society, namely its construction of history, or news from the past. An important function of the Bureau of Historiography in the imperial Chinese civil service was to legitimize each new dynasty by writing up the history of its predecessor – there is nothing specially twentieth century about such procedures! But again in our semiotically constituted society they are raised to new levels of symbolic construction, both in language and in other semiotic systems. 1992 is the 500th anniversary of the European invasion of the Americas. After months of spectacle, including a "symbolic wedding", in Birmingham registry office, of Barcelona's Statue of Columbus with the Statue of Liberty, at which "thousands of tiny eternity rings will be placed with a statue-sized perspex eternity ring, a video about Columbus' life showing in place of the gemstone", on 12 October the Columbus Lighthouse will be inaugurated, in the Dominican Republic, and "the Pope and all the Latin American and Caribbean

Cardinals and Bishops will bless Columbus' reconstructed boats after their arrival from Spain".[5] Meanwhile, from the same source, comes this news from South America:

> On 16 December 1991 twenty Paez Indians were machine-gunned and killed as they sat down to their evening meal, and another twenty were seriously wounded. The Indians were attacked by sixty men with their faces covered with camouflage grease and hoods. The killers tied their victims up, made them lie on the floor and opened fire. There have been no arrests. ...
>
> The Indians who were killed had settled there recently, on land given to them by an old lady sympathetic to their plight. It is thought that drugs dealers from the nearby city of Cali wanted to steal their land to grow opium poppies.

This was in Colombia. As the writer comments, "Indigenous people of North and South America see little cause for celebration. ... An alternative programme of events has been organized to mark the anniversary, under the banner '500 Years of Resistance'." The native Americans have their own semiotic device, reproduced below.

They know what makes (**them**) news; and their defence against being reduced to the status of a text in European history is to make the nature of that text explicit. Note that they employ this same 3-D motif: discourse (the church), dollars, and death.

Figure 1 Symbol of the official celebrations of the 500th anniversary

Figure 2 'Church, Death and Money' symbol used by South American protesters

The construction of news, and its projection in time (as history), serves to illustrate one interpretation of society as text: the post-modernist one whereby social processes are understood as competing and conflicting discourses, and the hierarchic divisions of class, race, sex and generation as competing and conflicting semiotic constructions of reality. This kind of discursivism is offered as a corrective to classical Marxist explanations in terms of technology and relations of produc-tion. Like most reactions, it overreacts, overplaying the discursive at the expense of the material; whereas what we need to understand is the dialectic that is set up between the two. But my question here is, what are the implications for language itself, if it is true that in some sense language has gained even more control than Firth saw it had in 1937? Already, according to our grammatics, experience is construed in language and interpersonal relationships are enacted in language: what more can language achieve? – or rather, what more can people achieve with it? In asking the question we have already implied the direction in which to look for an answer: namely, that unless these various discourses are to fragment altogether (which is unlikely, although not inconceivable; we can see this tending to happen, with the growing gulf between specialist technical registers and the language of common sense), new frames of consistency must evolve which will accommodate the contradictions and the tensions; not by covering them over, as dominant discourses tend to do, but by encompassing them within some higher-order construct.

It may be objected that this sounds much too "meta" – too much like constructing a more abstract scientific theory to accommodate conflicting models of the universe. But the grammar of a natural language **is** a model of the universe, in the sense that it functions (among other things) as a theory of human experience; and as language has evolved it has ongoingly reconstrued experience in line with, and as a part of, changes in the human condition. There is no reason to suppose that this evolution has come to an end, that our grammars are frozen in their present contingent state. On the contrary; it seems very clear that what we think of as "modern English" is actually an assortment of many divergent components – a complex product of semantic creolization, in which conflicting models from different stages in our history (pre-settlement, agro-pastoral, iron age, scientific-technological) compete with and complement each other. When we understand cryptogrammar rather better than we do now, we may be able to sort out the various syndromes of features that construe these

217

different dimensions of our experience.[6] By the same token, then, the grammar should be able to accommodate the variety of discourses that coexist in our postmodern societies – the "diversity of identities that can communicate with each other", to quote McDonald again – not only the dominant discourse that has shaped our modern "standard languages" but the other, opposed discourses that have hitherto tended to be excluded. To get a sense of this sort of thing in progress, we could look at the semantic reconstrual of the NVEs ("New Varieties of English") that is taking place around the world as English is steadily being remoulded to service the numerous non-European, non-"modern" cultures that are using it for their own semiotic needs.

I will come back to this point later. But first we might reflect that only those who have had the privilege of being modern can afford the luxury of being postmodern. To put this another way: you only begin to emphasize flux, uncertainty and chaos when your unmarked state has been an expectation of order. If we in ALAA (Applied Linguistics Association of Australia) take seriously our Australian protestations about being part of the Asia Pacific region, then we should remember that our neighbours in Japan, China and elsewhere take the modernist rather than the postmodernist view of things. This does not mean that they would have to reject the concept that society is founded on text; but they would mean by it something rather different. In their contexts, to suggest that modern culture is a construction of meanings, far from implying disillusionment with the technological society, would be heard as a celebration of what technology has achieved. In other words, modern (as opposed to postmodern) societies are still technology driven; but the technology itself has changed. It has become a technology of semiosis. The catchword is that of the "information society": instead of using all our energies exchanging goods-&-services, we now engage primarily in exchanging information. Why? Because with advances in automation and robotics, machines take over production, and people spend their working time in meaning. Language is no longer just a mode of social control; it is also the mode of control over physical systems and processes.

The immediate impact here is the technologizing of language itself. Here we have a direct line of evolution from the printing press to the computer, via the telephone, typewriter and tape recorder. But the pattern of this evolution is a helical one: while the invention of printing maximized the distance between spoken and written language, the one folksy, mobile and fleeting, the other high-tech, static and permanent, twentieth-century technology has reversed the trend: speech can be immortalized on tape, writing scrolled ephemerally up the screen. Mixed modes engender mixed genres, as in electronic mail; and the writer's own control once more extends over the entire production of the written word, as we compose, revise, edit, print and publish our own outpourings of text. There is no need to predict the effect all this is going to have, because it's already there for us to see – although, having said this, I should add that the immediate effects are rather surface ones (the use of colloquialisms, for example) and the deeper impact is still to come, and will be the result not just of new text technology but also of more fundamental tendencies and changes.

Here is the Mayor of Osaka addressing his fellow citizens:[7]

> At the approach of the 21st century, Japan is becoming a great, information-oriented society of truly international character and cultural and economic diversity.
>
> At this significant time of change, the citizens of Osaka feel that their city ... must develop into a community making greater contributions to the world than ever before in a wider range of fields, embracing industry, economy and culture.
>
> To this end, the City of Osaka has been holding numerous discussions with experts from various circles and organizations, both academic and industrial, as to the most appropriate use of the vast space to be created in the coastal area of the city, the Hokko and Nanko districts. The ideas gleaned from these discussions have formed the conceptual basis of the Technoport Osaka Project. In this new urban complex of the 21st century, four main functions will work in concert: information communication, advanced technology development, world trade, and culture, recreation and residence. ...
>
> In order that we 20th century contemporaries may pass on a splendid urban asset to subsequent generations, I ask for your free opinions and constructive suggestions with regard to this project.

Now as we all know, the centre of a technoport is its teleport, where "numerous information-related companies will be brought together around a new communications centre with optical fibre networks and a satellite communication base, to reinforce the information transmission capacity and thereby enhance Osaka's economic and cultural vitality". The teleport will contain, among other things, a technological information centre, an overseas trade information centre, and a comprehensive distribution information system centre.

The teleport is a familiar enough concept to science fiction readers and computer freaks; but this one actually exists, as hub of the world-wide network of "international information cities" that Osaka hopes to lead. The map in the city hall shows about a dozen cities around the world that would have the privilege of being part of this grand design – including one in Australia, thought of as Sydney, or perhaps a Sydney-Brisbane megalopolis. Here is the Australian vision of this same grand design, now transported to an Adelaide suburb called Gillman:[8]

> The eventual plan is to construct a small city, interspersed with commercial sites, educational centres, high-tech research facilities and all the Buck Rogers mumbo-jumbo we have been hearing about for the past few years. At least, the "world university" and the bizarre plan to make Gillman an HDTV (high definition television) broadcasting centre to cover Asia appear to have bitten the dust.
>
> Just what it will actually look like remained even more of a mystery when the architect, Lionel Glendenning, gave an interview in which he was quoted as saying, "It's going to be an urban city [sic], a set of villages, the sort of place you go around the corner to buy a cappuccino. It will be a slice of a city like Venice, Paris or parts of Sydney [with] people living above pastry shops. We have turned the project on its head. Now we are creating an urban experience that gives everybody the opportunity to gain access to the Arcadian dream."
>
> Be that as it may, the only source of income (other than the taxpayer) the Multi Function Polis authority will have to actually build this dream is the sale of land – land on which houses and blocks of flats to accommodate a population of 40,000 will be built (the polis), and land on which those beloved high-tech businesses will be established (the multi function). Unfortunately, a quick scribble on the back of an envelope illustrates a major flaw.
>
> It will cost a developer (if the MFP's figures are right, and at least one consultant has commented on the "highly speculative" nature of some of their calculations) $600 million to develop the site – that's if the Government provides the land for nothing and charges nothing for the $250 million of services that will have to be put on. That comes to more than $1 million a hectare, or close to $100,000 for a standard building block.
>
> Now, this is Adelaide, remember, the capital of low-cost housing. A typical serviced block in a new outer suburb costs $15,000 to $20,000. You can get a two-bedroom apartment in a bayside suburb, or a nice little freestone cottage in leafy Malvern for $100,000. For that, in Gillman, you get a bare block next door to a rubbish dump, gas pipeline, toxic bloom, etc.

It is not hard to agree with Kevin McDonald when he says that "there can be little doubt that we live in a culture where the theme of progress is exhausted".

One might be tempted to say that anything with a name so inept as Multi Function Polis could not be expected to end up any other way than bogged down in an Adelaide swamp. It belongs with such triumphs of Japanese semiosis as Sweat (the name of a soft drink) and Creap (the powdered substitute for milk in coffee). In principle, of course, Japan's economic dominance is such that any Japanese innovation in English could be expected to catch on, whether in teleport or in supermarket or wherever (though there is one weakness, which may turn out to be critical: Japanese English has no basis in speech).

Whatever the nature and extent of the Japanese input, the language of the information society will be different, both ideationally and interpersonally: ideationally because it participates in new techniques of production, interpersonally because it participates in new relationships of power, or at least new manifestations of the power structure. What is much harder to predict is the outcome of the tensions between two conflicting pressures: (1) to be user-friendly, and hence a still not too alienized variety of natural language, and (2) to be technology-controlled, and hence increasingly remote from what anyone would say or write.

At times of rapid historical change, we become aware of the power of symbols; and this is not surprising, because the symbols themselves have taken on extra power – the changes are at once both material and semiotic, and cannot take place in one without the other. One question that then arises is: do we intervene? Do we try to import some design into these essentially evolutionary processes?

The problem is, we do not know how to do it; and the recent history of language planning is not notably encouraging. I suspect it is subject to the operation of the law of the failed first try, or FFT as we might call it. This states that, when human beings intervene in any evolving system and start to introduce theory-based design, the first attempt always fails. I first observed this law at work in the context of applied linguistics, having noticed how, whenever a new theory-driven practice was introduced for the first time into language teaching, the result was disastrous; people then had to back off and think about it for a generation or so before coming back to the same idea with new understanding (and of course a new name). Two examples were the "situational approach" and "language for special purposes". One might object that in neither of these cases was the underlying theory properly

221

understood by those who first applied it – but that is precisely a part of the story of FFT. Meanwhile the twentieth century has provided us with the textbook illustration of this principle for all time, in the failure of so-called communism. Here people tried for the first time to design history on a theoretical foundation; and we all know the result – the kind of peasant-dynastic state capitalism that went under the name of communism was a prototypical instance of FFT. No doubt we will have to wait at least a generation before the next attempt, which will not be called communism but something completely different, with a name perhaps taken from Tamil or Yoruba and certainly not "post-" anything.

This is not to say that introducing design into evolving systems and processes (like language) can never succeed; it obviously can, and does, under the right conditions. But one absolute precondition is to understand the process one is intervening in. If we want to design grammar, then we need to understand how grammars work: that means having some theory of grammar, some explicit grammatics.

Now a theory, of any kind, is very like a grammar; it is a semiotic system, a system of meanings. This applies to theories in every field, physical, biological or social, as well as to theories of language; what is different about a linguistic theory is that it is a grammar about grammar (hence this term "grammatics", just as language about language is called linguistics). Theories are interesting because they are in part instances of semiotic design: that is, they are systems of meaning that are explicitly deployed to carry out certain tasks. But theories are not, or only seldom, designed *in toto*. When we first move in to a new field of learning, we often have a sense of facing a solid, ready-made, immutable edifice of the theory, which will inevitably appear to us as if it had been designed as a whole, and will often seem arbitrary if not downright perverse. (I remember having this feeling when I started to study psychology, many years ago.) But although theories are "grammars" which have been influenced by design – that is what distinguishes a technical theory from a principle that has evolved as common sense – they are not designed as a whole, in one massive burst of semiotic energy; and they are not usually constructed for their own sake, despite the appeal a mathematical theory may have as an object of elegance. Like natural language grammars, theories also evolve, bit by bit; they evolve in particular historical contexts, in pursuit of particular tasks; and they continue to evolve as long as the context persists and the tasks remain on the agenda.

By way of example, in the early 1950s a small group of linguists, in Britain, were constituted the Linguistics Group of the British Communist Party. They needed a general linguistic theory. On the one hand, the party was actively interested in national language policies in newly decolonizing societies; in questions of standard and dialect, of the development of technical and other functional varieties, of literacy in first and second languages, of script reform, especially in China, and so on. On the other hand, the search for a "Marxist linguistics" in the (then) Soviet Union had led to the famous linguistics controversy in Pravda in 1950; Stalin had just demolished Marr and Meščaninov, for "telling fortunes in the teacup of the four elements", and restored comparative philology to the centre of the stage by requiring Soviet linguists to get on with their task of demonstrating the linguistic unity of the Slav nations.[9] In this particular context, or complex of contexts, we had to develop our own Marxist linguistics. We never thought of this as creating something new; on the contrary, we saw it as building on something already latent in the major European tradition. But we were also aware that it had to be a socially accountable linguistics, and this in two distinct though related senses: that it put **language** in its social context, and at the same time it put **linguistics** in its social context, as a mode of intervention in critical social practices.

It might be argued that, while these practices undoubtedly involve one in engaging with language, to do so does not require any abstract linguistic theory; such work can be done with an approach that is "theory-free". This always has a very seductive appeal: it gives the impression that one is being objective. Unfortunately, however, this impression is false. There is no such thing as theory-free engagement with language, whether one is actively intervening in the linguistic practices of a community or systematically describing the grammar of a particular language. The linguist who claims to be theory-free is like the conservative who claims to be non-political: they are both saying, to be impartial is to leave things as they are – only those who want to change them are taking sides.

Our party group was, of course, taking sides, trying to formulate linguistics which would (to put it in more modern-sounding terms) give value to the language of the "other": non-European languages, unwritten vernaculars, non-native varieties of English, non-standard dialects, restricted codes and so on. The agenda was changing all the time; but this motif has remained constant, as the main ideological input to what evolved into systemic theory. The theory has never been

223

neutral. It has also never stopped evolving. (One should not be misled into thinking that once something acquires a name it ceases to change!)

To say that a theory is not neutral does not mean that every metalinguistic activity is ideologically loaded or that all those who use the theory share a uniform political stance. A great deal of linguistic research is unconnected in any obvious way with any particular form of commitment, and if I want to study the syntax and morphology of Old Icelandic what I need is a powerful tool for the job. But these are not unrelated. You may be strongly committed, let us say, to working on the language of a small, threatened community as part of the effort to maintain their cultural identity; but to do this effectively, you need a comprehensive, cryptotypic account of its grammar – and hence, a powerful tool for the job. Of course, much of what may seem at first sight to be "pure" research is highly political activity – and may be conceived of by the researcher as such; the difference often lies in the time depth, whether the political goal is concrete and immediate or more abstract and still some distance off. In any case, engaging with language on these different levels puts increased pressure on theoretical resources, pressure to which a socially accountable theory has to respond.

So theories are grammars that evolve under pressure of work to be done, and the pressure is such that their evolution is tempered by design; they are so to speak semi-designed linguistic semiotics. But their design is that of the culture in which they operate, embodying its values, its styles of meaning, and the conflicts and tensions within it. Current frontier theories, whatever type of phenomenon they are concerned with, whether physical, biological, social or semiotic, partake in the prevailing mannerisms and preoccupations of the postmodern scene; so they tend to foreground chaos rather than order, the mixed rather than the pure, the cyclical rather than the linear, and communication rather than cause; and these features are then contextualized with reference to, and in opposition to, the modernist theories with their origins in order, boundedness, progress, and cause-and-effect. Now grammars, that is the content systems of natural languages, could be said also to evolve under pressure, the pressure of historical processes; but this is a pressure of a different kind, because they are themselves part of these processes, not "meta" to them – that is, they are not second-order grammars designed as theories to explain them. We usually take our own grammar, reasonably enough, for granted, and do not even reflect on it very deeply, let alone try to intervene in it by design. Indeed our survival, as small children, depended on mastering the grammar to the point where we **could** take it for granted, rather than having to attend to it in all our doings. But we would assume, if ever we thought about it, that the grammar was not going to crack under the strain, whatever the particular demands we might come to make on it.

There have been moments in history when people have felt the need to design language (it is perhaps useful to talk of "language design" instead of the more inclusive "language planning", because most language planning is institutional rather than systemic). Perhaps the best-known example in western history, certainly the history of English, is the attempt at designing a language of science in the sixteenth century. What is interesting about this, as I have pointed out elsewhere,[10] is that while the design efforts centred on writing systems and, latterly, on vocabulary – constructing systematic taxonomies of written symbols and technical terms – these efforts had almost no effect on semiotic practice; whereas at the same time there was taking place a fairly massive restructuring of the grammar which none of those taking part in were even aware of. (There was a later spin-off from the concept of lexical design, as we see reflected today in biological and chemical termino-logies.) The most striking contemporary example is the linguistic politics of feminism, which has shown that by forcing people to attend to symbolic inequalities in the grammar, and work on them, one can contribute to engineering social change; this lesson is now being applied to the linguistic deconstruction of other manifestations of "otherhood".

So what are the lessons here for us as applied (or "applying") linguists? I tried to suggest in the paper I gave at the World Congress two years ago that the concept of doing applied linguistics means, among other things, that one is involved in the semiotic history of the culture. The point I was making there was that our dominant grammars lock us in to a framework of beliefs that may at one time, when they first evolved in language, have been functional, and beneficial to survival, but that have now become inimical to survival and harshly dysfunctional: the motifs of bigger and better (all 'growth' is positively loaded), of the uniqueness of the human species as lords of creation, the passivity of inanimate nature, the unboundedness of natural resources like water and air, and so on. These are not features of technical languages; they are aspects of our most unconscious, deeply installed, everyday common-sense grammar; and they are now very destructive, at a time when we have to learn to break the rhythm of endless growth, to identify ourselves with other species as part of a living whole, and to recognize that our planet is not a repository of infinite wealth and abundance. And I see this as an applied linguistic concern: to draw attention to these features of our daily language, its growthism and its lordism; and perhaps even to explore the possibility of design, though this will be forbiddingly hard to make succeed.

What then can be said about our technical languages? The most obvious feature of these is their insatiable demand for new words. If we put together all the technical dictionaries of English and counted the words in them, how many would we find? Would we be approaching ten million, perhaps? But words are grammatical constructions too; one can capture them in a dictionary, but one cannot really count them – what are significant, rather, are the resources available for constructing them. We now have nanotechnology, and that will no doubt engender another huge harvest of words. Their real impact is felt, however, through the rest of the grammar that goes with them. The technical discourse of modernism is this highly nominalized language by which, through a whole series of metaphorical processes in the grammar, our world of experience has been reconstrued, over the past few hundred years, as a world made up of things, abstract objects which act and react like the concrete entities in whose likeness they are semiotically moulded. Thus, for example, the discourse of information technology from Osaka again:

> The comprehensive Distribution Information System, organically uniting inland, marine and air transportation systems, will provide efficient, highly reliable distribution information.

This language of 'events into things' was the major semiotic strategy for transforming technology into science. By the same token, it was a semiotic for capitalism, maintaining a clear distinction between "those in the know" and the rest while turning the domains and components of knowledge into commodities. It leached into the discourse of administration and commerce (or perhaps even evolved there simultaneously?); and from both these sources, the technical and the bureaucratic, into the language of common sense, the everyday discourse of family and neighbourhood, where it has so far been contained by the barriers of age and class: age because it is impenetrable to children before a certain stage of semiotic maturation, and class because (since it was the gateway into knowledge and power) it remained, by and large, a middle-class prerogative and preserve. And here these objectifying metaphors of experience conspire (in Martin's term) with metaphors of another kind, those in the interpersonal component of the grammar, by which are enacted middle-class forms of the social relationship, patterns of implicit control, and personal rather than positional family relationships, so that the two together form the dominant discourse of capitalist culture.[11] As linguists we can observe and explain these phenomena; and we can track them through into the present late capitalist period, noting the semiotic developments that underpin the information society, the cult of the consumer, the disneyfication of culture and so on.

Is there then a language of resistance? There are of course various kinds of partial anti-languages, like that used by players of computer games which provides a delightfully non-metaphorical oasis in the desert of documentation; here is a little specimen:[12]

> 1. When you wake up you should take the wood and go into the packing case and take the chandelier to invert the room. Go to the machine and push the button to make a copy of yourself and then exit the case and then take it. . . .
> 4. Once you have six possessions go back to the island to the near side and then throw six possessions. The tree then has no arms left so go under it. When you threaten to cut it down a wood nymph will appear and offer you an idol in return for its life. . . .
> 9. In the cavern room use the corpse as food for the jelly.
> 10. To go up the chimney you must wear the cold cream from the cupboard.
> 11. Use the potato to scare away the rat at the junction.
> 12. Use the nails and the hammer to close the coffin in the tower on the orc's nose.
> 13. Use the cracked pot in the cell to get some slime to trip up the goat on top of the statue so that you can get the horn. . . .
> 17. When the Roc takes you to his nest squeeze the caterpillar to get the rope to escape. Keep the caterpillar, as he is valuable.
> 18. The dwarf is important as she leads you to the orc that is very valuable.
> 19. Use the horn to scare away the advancing orc army when it arrives.
> 20. When you are out of the nest you can find a wisp that can be trapped in the miner's helmet and used instead of the wood. . . .
> 26. The flint that passes your nose will not be there if you get rid of the dragon. (This is in the six-exited room.)

The interesting point about this is that Steve Rambaron, who wrote it, is obviously a sophisticated user of computer software. Perhaps our technical discourse, while it must have its nominalizations in order to create systematic taxonomies, could nevertheless be nudged away from its obsession with pseudo-things, towards more democratic forms which lessen the semiotic distance – both the experiential distance, which makes the language of technical knowledge so remote from the experiences of everyday life, and the interpersonal distance, which separates those who have the knowledge from those who are left outside. I suggest that ALAA might explore the potential for a clause-based rather than a noun-based techno-grammar, as a contribution to postmodern, or better to post-postmodern, forms of educational discourse.

Meanwhile, we have to enable people to control the discourses that now surround them, and the energies of applied linguists are very much taken up with language education work of this kind. In this field the Sydney-based programmes that have been developed in recent years by Jim Martin, first in collaboration with Joan Rothery and Frances Christie and subsequently with the participation of colleagues from many different institutions, stand out for their powerful exploitation of linguistic theory as a force for learning. For the past ten years and more, first in the primary school stage of children's writing development and more recently in secondary subject-based curricula and in language in the workplace, they have shown how a grammatics can open up access to the elaborated discourses of education and employment; and in doing so have enriched the theory in its turn.[13]

The environment of prevailing educational theory and practice within which language educators in Australia have to work is a difficult one, embodying beliefs and practices from different phases of capitalist ideology, and tending to look towards and copy the least appropriate models from elsewhere. As James Gee of the University of Southern California has pointed out in his book *The Social Mind*, current "progressivist" education in the USA derives from a body of doctrine which locates all learning in the mental make-up of the individual, sets up a severe disjunction between cognitive and affective processes, and interprets cognition as a kind of information-processing phenomenon. This kind of exaggerated reaction against behaviourism (largely irrelevant to the rest of the world, where behaviourism never impinged) has, like all reactions, many of the features of what it is reacting against; and it embodies an extreme form of middle-class ideology, with its rejection of "knowing" in favour of "speculation about" and its hidden curricula of values and educational goals. Like the authoritarian model which it sought to supplant, it is a-social and a-semiotic. It is interesting to wonder why, if educators are casting round for capitalist models from elsewhere, they do not look at the relatively successful ones (for example from Japan, since that country is now exalted as a model in every other respect), rather than one that is noteworthy for its general record of failure.

Let me mention here the work of three specialists in language education. Professor Ronald Carter, from the University of Nottingham, is Co-ordinator of the LINC Project ('Language in the National Curriculum') in Britain. This is a teacher education project in which the primary focus is on language and explicit attention is paid to forms of discourse and principles of linguistic variation. These materials proved too rich for their governmental sponsors to digest; but this has not prevented them from circulating freely and effectively throughout the teaching profession. Professor Jay Lemke, of the City University of New York, in his major work on science education (which is appropriately called *Talking Science*), has provided a semiotic – that is, meaning-based – interpretation of the activities of doing, teaching and learning science, based on a penetrating analysis of the discourse of New York science classes. Professor Bernard Mohan, of the University of British Columbia in Canada, directs an important research and development project in Vancouver primary schools, whose linguistic makeup is comparable to what we are familiar with in Sydney and Melbourne. His emphasis, as brought out in his book *Language and Content*, is on the development of writing as a multimodal experience, exploring how meanings are construed from a variety of semiotic resources. What runs through all their work is the principle that, if knowledge is construed in language, then those who want to open up access to such knowledge not only must themselves understand, but also must enable the learners to understand, how it is that language does its work – how the grammar of every language provides the power for interpreting and acting on the world.

There is no question that learners must have access to the dominant discourses of society; that is what education means. It would be a strange interpretation of social accountability to say that because you do not like these discourses you do not teach them to children and to migrants. This does not prevent you engaging in political action to change them. But there is another side to this, for applied linguistics: our accountability to those peoples who are not, and never have been, part of the culture to which these dominant discourses belong. I referred earlier to the role of grammatics in the struggle to maintain, and give value to, the modes of meaning of the non-settlement cultures of native Americans and Australians. If it makes sense to say that "our society is first and foremost a system of meanings", then language must be at the centre of social change; and now is the time – and it will be the last time – when we can raise a more challenging question, asking not just how these semiotic modes may be preserved but how they may contribute to and become part of the collective human experience of the future. Are we so convinced of the rightness of our ways of meaning – whether modern or postmodern – that we do not need to explore those of people that our culture has pushed aside? I am not talking here of some romantic, idealized conception of this or that individual or social group; nor on the other hand of the random, local linguistic variations that were the subject-matter of the old typologies of language. I mean the modes of understanding and of doing – of construing experience and enacting interpersonal relationships – that are located deep within the cryptogrammars of these "other" languages. With due homage to Whorf, we still know very little of these; they may be different, in important ways, from our own; and it may well be in our own interest to try harder to understand them. There is no mystique about this; it is saying no more than that the dominant written cultures of Europe and Asia do not hold a monopoly of human wisdom. It would be a pity if their system of meanings was the only one to survive in a changing world.

Notes

1. The full title of McDonald's paper is "Cultural innovation and economic modernization: the context of language education today". It appears in Christie 1991.
2. From Firth 1937. The "Revue" chapter (Chapter 11) includes the words; "We live in an age of propaganda which everywhere encompasses us. It behoves us to study the language used for us and against us every day of our lives with that objective detachment and calm scrutiny which we are accustomed to give to the classics" (pp. 132–3).
3. I first observed this many years ago when finding examples such as the following presented as news: "Only one in nine of the inhabitants of Staffordshire owns a toothbrush"; "One out of six of the population of Glasgow was conceived in the cinema". (How do they know?)
4. A classic study of this kind was Tony Trew's chapter " 'What the papers say': linguistic variation and ideological difference", in Fowler et al. 1979.

5. See *Mazan Times: Newsletter of the Rio Mazan Project*, 4.3, Spring 1992. (This is an Anglo-Ecuadorian project "for forests and people of the Andes"; addresses 38–40 Exchange Street, Norwich NR2 1AX, England, and Casilla 844, Cuenca, Ecuador.) In the event, the Pope's visit was rescheduled.

6. Perhaps the clearest example one could cite here is that of the complex of features brought together under the heading of "experiential (or ideational) grammatical metaphor"; see Halliday and Martin 1993a; Martin 1992, esp. chs 5 and 6.

7. From *Technoport Osaka: Information-oriented International Urban Complex of the 21st Century*, published by City of Osaka Port and Harbor Bureau, no date (probably 1987).

8. See the feature article "The $2 billion creature on a black lagoon" by Ben Hills in the *Sydney Morning Herald*'s magazine *Good Weekend* of 27 June 1992.

9. See Stalin 1950. The original was in *Pravda* of June 20. For a contemporary appraisal see Ellis and Davies 1951.

10. See Halliday and Martin 1993a. For an account of the work in scientific language design, see Vivian Salmon, "Language planning in seventeenth-century England: its context and aims", in Bazell *et al.* 1966.

11. Identified by Bernstein in the early 1960s and named by him "elaborated code" (see his two articles in *Language and Speech* 5, 1962a and b).

12. From a popular British magazine for Atari users, of which I cannot now find the original source.

13. See, for example, numerous publications of the Metropolitan East Disadvantaged Schools Program, e.g. *Developing Critical Literacy, a Model of Literacy in Subject Learning, Teaching Factual Writing, Exploring Literacy in School Science* and other "Write It Right" publications. These are available from DSP Centre Marketing, cnr. Bridge & Swanson Streets, Erskineville, NSW 2043.

Chapter Eleven

A RECENT VIEW OF "MISSTEPS" IN
LINGUISTIC THEORY
(1995)

John M. Ellis. *Language, Thought, and Logic*. Evanston, Illinois: Northwestern University Press 1993 (ISBN 0 8101 1095 4).

I found this book a pleasure to read, and would like to share the pleasure. It is elegantly and flowingly written; it is beautifully produced; and it makes good sense. To achieve any one of these is rare enough; when all three metafunctional needs are satisfied, there is cause to celebrate. But celebrating by itself would not justify taking up precious meaning space; I would also like to make some critical comments, believing it is important to engage constructively with a book that has so much to offer.

The heart of Ellis' argument, presented in the first part of the book but informing the discussion throughout, is that there are three "initial missteps in theory of language" which have bedevilled philosophical enquiries – and hence also mainstream linguistics – in the middle and last part of the present century. These are "classical theoretical traps" that can "lead time and again to a complete theoretical impasse and breakdown". The three missteps are (1) "the assumption that the purpose of language is communication", (2) "the assumption that descriptive words like *square* or *cat* are simpler [and therefore more basic] than evaluative words like *good*", and (3) "the assumption that the ... categories of a language serve to group like things together". These assumptions sound harmless, being "built into what look like statements of the obvious that make no assumptions at all"; in fact they are "so subtle that those who take them never recognize that they have made any move at all, but so destructive and far-reaching that, once taken, they make it impossible to achieve a coherent theory of language"; moreover, "these missteps are virtually universal" (pp. 13–14).

First published in *Functions of Language* 2.2. Benjamins, 1995, pp. 249–67.

Under the first "misstep" Ellis brings together the conceptions of language as communicating information, as encoding messages, and as making truth claims by reference to some situation in the real world; all of which he interprets (rightly, in my view) as variants of the same intellectual stance, one that is characterized by a naive correspondence model of language and "reality". As he remarks, "virtually all organized schools of thought are permeated by it. It is pervasive in philosophy of language. It is ever present in the field of linguistics, whether one looks to the mainstream of the predominant school of thought, that initiated by Chomsky, to its heretical splinter groups, or even to those groups of linguists who reject Chomsky altogether" (p. 19). He cites in this connection Chomsky himself, the "antigenerativist" Wallace Chafe, Crystal's popular introduction to linguistics, and Barwise and Perry's *Situation and Attitudes*; together with (in its "language as code" formulation) Eco, Sebeok, the information theorists, and Lévi-Strauss. The only writers on linguistic theory who have "largely avoided this error" are said to be Wittgenstein, Saussure, Peirce and (in "a cryptic marginal note") Whorf.

The second misstep "has a form specific to language theory as well as a more general form that relates to inquiry in general". The former, as already noted, is the idea that "the easy starting point will be the descriptive words that appear to have clear correlations in physical reality – say, *round*, *square*, or *mile* – while evaluative words are the hard cases, to be approached only when the basic principles of how words work have been abstracted from the easy cases" (p. 20). Here Ellis simply reverses the priority; his view is that "words like *good* are prior to words like *square*; including here the sense of 'historically prior': "this hierarchy of words – descriptive words as simple, basic, and central; evaluative words as complex, difficult, and less central – will instantly seem dubious once we point to a single fact: the words that this model makes the more basic and simple of the two kinds are evidently *newer* than the others, while the second group must be very old indeed" (p. 24). Hence in the context of ethics and aesthetics "factual statements must be assimilated to evaluative ones, not the reverse" (p. 74). I shall return to this point below; meanwhile the latter, more general form of this second misstep is "the antiquated and long since discredited methodology of Descartes", whereby "one begins by taking simple cases and generalizes from them to derive principles that can then be used to break down the hard cases". This view, the basis of "the aggressively claimed 'scientific' status of generative grammar", is simply wrong, and the logical error at this general level can be readily diagnosed: "easy cases are easy because they do not test very much ... [they] do not challenge the current state of understanding and its assumptions".

At this general level too, therefore, the priorities have been the wrong way round – whereas "anyone who was really in touch with the daily life of scientists would have known that it is the unclear cases that are expected to provide fundamental new insight". And the result of this misstep has been to narrow down linguistics to no more than "the construction of grammars": to quote one of Ellis' (very few) infelicitous sentences, "the limitations imposed by a starting point that took and ran with those things that looked like 'clear cases' had now congealed into an extraordinarily limited view of the study of language itself, one that reduced significantly the intellectual ambitions of the field" (pp. 20–4).

The third misstep has to do with "the most central issue in linguistic theory: categorization". The fundamental error, the belief that categorization is "the grouping together of like things", is derived from a naive realism according to which the categories of language "correspond" to some pre-existing structure in the real world (pp. 25–7). Ellis devotes a special and rather forceful chapter to this issue, showing that linguistic categories are precisely the opposite: they are groupings of phenomena that are not alike, which enable speakers to treat them as if they were. Words are not inert labels; they are active constructs which categorize, abstract and simplify – they "assign a very large number of cases to a much smaller number of groups", they function "in analysing experience and in drawing out patterns in it", and they "reduce limitless complexity to an ordered and thus manageable state" (p. 29). And since there are indefinitely many ways of doing this, languages differ in the categories they impose; to imagine that they "represent natural kinds" is (here Ellis quotes Haas' words) "just a naive belief in the divinity of one's own language". (The variant notion, that they have their origin "in an inherent structure of the human brain", is equally problematic; "in the case of an English speaker, we can be sure that mentalese will turn out to have the categories of English".) "The equivalence created by the categories of language is a functional one", "the reflection of the collective purposes of the speakers"; it is "this distortion, this making equivalent of things that are not the same, which makes language *and knowledge* possible" (Ellis' italics) (pp. 32–5). (Again, I shall comment further on this below.)

234

The third, critical misstep could have been avoided if the work of Wittgenstein, Saussure, Peirce and especially Whorf had been understood and taken seriously – but only if their separate insights had been combined. "Wittgenstein gave us the idea of family resemblances, Saussure that of contrast and differentiation", while Peirce understood that "to know something is not to have a direct intuition of it but to classify it and relate it to other things". But each was writing in a particular context, relating his discourse to particular current issues in philosophy or in linguistics; each therefore presented only one facet of the total picture, and they remained as isolated fragments. "The most serious attempt to explore a functional view of categories and to relate the categories of language to human behaviour is that of Benjamin Lee Whorf, but Whorf did so without providing the logical grounding for this step" (pp. 38–42). Thus the fragmentation of the disciplines, and later scholars' blinkered obsession with local, short-term issues (of which Ellis cites some notable examples), meant that no coherent alternative was perceived; language theorists continued to return to the familiar default condition ("we have a word for cats because cats exist and we need to talk about them and communicate information about them" (p. 91)), the naive realism apparently "given" to us by language itself and legitimized in logical positivist thinking. This is the basis of all those "new beginnings" such as speech act theory and direct reference theory, as well as the whole edifice of formal grammars including Chomsky's own and the subsequent numerous attempts to shore it up.

By examining developments in the fields of ethics and aesthetics Ellis shows the effects of this series of missteps on twentieth-century philosophy: "... many intractable philosophical problems have been created and perpetuated by assumptions made about the logic of these problems which are essentially due to misconceptions about how language works" (p. 67). Central to this is the false hierarchization of factual and evaluative statements already referred to; whereas "the opposition of facts and values is actually a continuum" (p. 80), in which "evaluative statements are not complex judgments that everything else leads up to but instead simple and even crude beginnings" (p. 74). Similarly in epistemology and logic, where "much of the energy and attention ... has been absorbed by a single central problem, that of validity. How is knowledge to be distinguished from mere opinion?" Ellis comments that "only philosophers seemed to think there was a problem"; and that when attempts to solve it depended on examining "the alleged assurance of the existence of a physical world" (quoted from Richard Aaron in the 1986 Encyclopedia Britannica), this too seemed like "a problem that has to be invented in order to be found worth solving". As Ellis says, "to know is to categorize": "While undoubtedly something exists independent of the knower, to know anything about it is to have done something to it: to categorize it, to relate one situation to others, to place it among others, to situate the experience of it among other experiences" (pp. 83–6). Hence "Theory of knowledge should concern itself above all else with organization of meaning and the structure of categorization in languages". Instead, theory of knowledge has been vitiated by its "overblown concern with verification and truth", always falling back on "semantic primitives and uninterpreted facts". Instead of a recognition that knowledge is constructed in language, there is still the old myth about language getting in the way: "epistemological purposes are thought of as being thwarted by linguistic complexity or obscurity, and a process of purification is therefore advocated that will leave us face-to-face with a clear statement" (pp. 89–93). Formal logic is irrelevant to the understanding of language: not because of the limitations of language but because of the limitations of conventional logic.

But if these misconceptions have been harmful to philosophy, they have been nothing short of disastrous for linguistics. In a penultimate chapter on "The State of Linguistics", Ellis demolishes the myth of the "Chomsky revolution", showing how in bolstering his original claim for the autonomy and ascendancy of syntax Chomsky "carefully picked weak positions to argue against" – in rejecting the argument in favour of "correspondences" between grammar and semantics "Chomksy has not argued against it but only talked it into insignificance". Once grammar and semantics had been separated in this way they had to be brought together again; thus "Finding a solution to an imaginary problem now became the goal of an entire field" (pp. 98–100). Similarly imaginary problems were created by the whole series of dichotomies that Chomsky introduced, or took over unproblematized: not only syntax/semantics but also grammar/lexis, language/thought, competence/performance (of the last of these Ellis comments that "MIT linguists were actually using the distinction to get rid of those aspects of the linguistic system of a language that they could not deal with" (p. 105). Once these dichotomies had been set up, the problem arose of locating and maintaining the boundaries between them. After generative semantics tried (and failed) to repair the conceptual muddle they created, other heresies – such as Montague grammar, GPSG – all attempted "to wring success from the same flawed premises by taking them to greater extremes" (p. 109). All their protagonists claimed to be starting again from the beginning, not recognizing that the entire conceptual basis was impaired. Ellis sums up by saying there can be "only one verdict on the era it [sc. generative grammar] has dominated: this has been a most unproductive time in the history of linguistics" (p. 114).

In my opinion, the picture presented by Ellis is largely valid. When language is reduced to the status of an (imperfect) formal system, a "code" to be measured by its correspondence (or lack of it) to some supposedly independent reality, whether material or mental, by reference to which its meanings are judged to be (or else not to be) "true", the resulting vision is so impoverished that serious questions about language can hardly even be raised, let alone imaginatively pursued; and Ellis' diagnosis in terms of a syndrome of three related "missteps" – the ideas that language serves to communicate information, that in investigating language one proceeds from (simple) assertions to (complex) evaluations (itself an instance of a more general misconception about the nature of science itself), and that the categories of language reflect (objective) likeness rather than imposing functional analogy – is persuasive and well supported by the symptoms he points out in evidence. He is also surely right in relating this to the twentieth-century malady of the fragmentation of disciplines, in which scholars easily become blinkered and focus only on their own local issues and current trends, not looking beyond to see what others have had to say that might illuminate their chosen objects from a different angle – and in extreme cases arrogating to themselves the sole right to define what the relevant issues and approaches are. But precisely because this book does make its points so effectively, it seems important to take up any aspects of the argument that one finds to be problematic. My comments here fall under two heads: those relating to Ellis' account of recent history, and those relating to his own theoretical suggestions. I shall take up the latter first.

Ellis' own suggestions, summarized in a brief concluding chapter, amount, reasonably enough, to a correction of the various missteps he has identified, with "categorizing" as the main organizing concept – together with the principle that ideas must be assigned to the right place, otherwise "a 'truth' becomes in effect a falsehood" (p. 115). To quote just two brief extracts: "only when we understand that we cannot make sense of the notion of referring to a state of affairs without a language already being in place are we then able to see that [reference] cannot have the central place in theory of language that has been assumed. Theory only begins to take on a coherent shape when reference, communication, and information are assigned to a different place – one that comes *after* categorization. Accordingly, categorization must be the basic process of language." Furthermore, categorizing must be understood not in relation to the things categorized but "primarily in relation to the purposes of the categorizers" (p. 116). And this is critical not only for linguistics itself; Ellis commends A. J. Ayer for recognizing that "a proper understanding of how language works could produce far-reaching consequences in a number of different fields when applied rigorously to the central problems of those fields" (p. 117). The relevance of theory of language is not limited to any one discipline, even if only one, namely linguistics, is defined by having language as its object of study.

I have a slight misgiving about the "purposes of the categorizers" (cf. "the overall unity of the category lies in its purpose" (p. 37)). This is the sense in which the categories are being said to be "functional": ". . . linguistic categories are primarily the reflection of the collective purposes of the speakers of a language. . . . In other words, the equivalence created by the categories of a language is a functional one: . . ." (p. 34); ". . . the basis of linguistic categories must be functional: we distinguish one set of cases from another because we want to treat them differently . . . categories relate to our purposes primarily, and to the actual differences of the real world secondarily" (p. 36). This may be a harmless enough form of expression; but it does suggest an element of design – as if the intention to mean exists prior to its realization in meaning. I would prefer a formulation in terms more like the following. The history of language, it seems to me, is part – an integral part – of human history; and this "history" is a dialectic interplay of material and semiotic processes, whose impacting engenders the complex ecosocial systems that we know as human cultures (cf. Lemke 1993 for a powerful account). The grammar (rather, lexicogrammar) of every language construes the collective experience: that is, its categorizations (of process types, the configurations of elements that make up processes, the relations between processes, etc.) enable each member to share in the heritage of that history, both systemically (through the system as received) and epigenetically (by recapitulating, in part, its evolutionary trajectory in the course of learning it). "Categorizing", in this sense, means creating a multidimensional semantic having both spatial and temporal depth: with meanings from local to global – family, neighbourhood (clan, tribe), region, culture band, species; and from all the stages in its own past (a "history of histories" so to speak). What we encounter as "a language" forms a patch in the total mosaic, one that is relatively persistent and more or less clearly bounded in space and time. The critical feature of "a language", in this sense, is that it serves as a mother tongue: there are people for whom it functions in the (primary) construal of experience – for whom, as Ellis points out, its categories **are** the objective and the real, and its statements can be definitively evaluated as "true" or "false".

So while I would prefer not to characterize these properties in terms of "purposes of the speakers", I find no problem in talking of such categorization as "functional". But this raises a more serious question in Ellis' analysis. In refuting his second misstep, that of treating descriptive words as logically prior to evaluative ones, he insists that the priority should be reversed: that descriptive words are, historically, a "*specialized development*" (his italics (p. 24)) of evaluative ones. But there is no more evidence for this priority than for the other way round. On the contrary: everything we know about the ontogenesis of language strongly suggests that the two evolved simultaneously: that neither is derivative from the other. But in order to understand this fully we have to move to a deeper interpretation of the concept of "function" in language.

Let us first consider Ellis' own case. Giving as the examples of descriptive words *square* and *round*, Ellis observes "Geometric shapes have always been popular examples of descriptive words in these kinds of arguments: square, round, triangular. ... But what should have puzzled everyone, though it never did, is that words like *good* and *bad* have a very long history, while the vocabulary of science and geometry is newer and more artificial" (p. 24); cf. "... the prototype of all statements is much more likely to have been 'this is good' or 'this is dangerous' than it is to have been 'this is triangular'" (p. 75). Certainly. But this is because *learned* descriptive words are being compared with *commonsense* evaluative ones. If we compare like with like – say evaluative 'this is good/bad' with descriptive 'this is big/small', or descriptive 'this is square/triangular' with evaluative 'this is fertile/ infertile' – then the picture is far less clear. It is not at all obvious that either is prior to the other, whether historically, developmentally or analytically. And there is a certain inconsistency in Ellis' own argument, since he refers to "the most general categorical distinctions – that is, verb and noun" (p. 108); but if anything the verb/noun distinction (and the other grammatical categorizations he uses as examples, like "concatenations of words in phrase structures which order meanings and in doing so add extra dimensions to them" (pp. 107–8)), would typically construe descriptive rather than evaluative categories.

What is missing here is the concept of metafunction (Halliday 1967/ 68, 1994; Gregory 1987; Matthiessen 1989). Ellis' distinction "descriptive/evaluative" is a complex one which needs to be deconstructed in metafunctional terms. Meaning is construed not by words but by the lexicogrammar as a whole (which Ellis rightly characterizes as a continuum); and all construction of meaning – all discourse – functions simultaneously **both** as construal of experience **and** as enactment of interpersonal relations. Neither of these is prior to the other; ontogenetically, both develop in the transition from "child tongue" (protolanguage) to mother tongue (Halliday 1975a, 1993b; Painter 1984, 1989), and there is no reason to doubt that they co-evolved: that the entire meaning potential of language depends on the interplay of the experiential and the interpersonal. Making a statement (of any kind) is a form of interpersonal action; and it is one that presumably evolved fairly late, since children first learn the *mathetic mode* (rehearsing experience that the listener also shared) and only later the *indicative mood*, whereby they can exchange (give, or demand) "information" (that is, as a surrogate of non-shared experience) – information being something that does not yet exist until brought into being by language itself (as Ellis also points out; cf. Halliday 1984b: 27–30). In other words, declaratives such as *this garden is good* or *that cat is big* both enact a particular kind of interpersonal relationship (and the action is the same in both – and, more importantly, so is the action *potential*; cf. the (rather more plausible!) exclamatives *what a lovely garden!*, *what an enormous cat!*).

But, equally, there is no "action" without "reflection": that is, the (interpersonal) enactment of telling, or exclaiming, or whatever, in the *mood* system always combines with some (ideational) construal of experience in the *transitivity* system (the two coming together to form a *clause*). And it is here, in the transitivity system, that we find, in the potential for different *types of process*, one type of process that construes "affect" (or "affection", in its earlier sense): liking, disliking, fearing, despising, admiring and so on. Ontogenetically, as the transitivity system develops, "evaluative words" (e.g. *nice*, as in *nice dog*) and first person affective clauses (e.g. *I like banana*) do not appear earlier than "descriptive words" (e.g. *big*, as in *big dog*) or clauses of other types (e.g. *banana fell*). Thus it seems that Ellis weakens his own argument by insisting on the primacy of the evaluative over the descriptive. In metafunctional terms, experiential and interpersonal meanings co-evolve in the lexicogrammar: the two are mapped on to each other in the grammatical structure (as transitivity and mood in the clause), and their developmental origins, though complex, do not suggest that either is driving the other.

As so often happens, when we explore the issue in greater depth we find that the initial question has been wrongly posed. Researchers in neuroscience, more specifically in evolutionary neurobiology, have argued that the main reason why the brain of mammals evolved to become more and more complex in its structure was that as species evolved the organism needed more and more complex constructions of experience (Jerison 1973; Edelman 1992). I would want to modify that, again in metafunctional terms, by saying that that is one of the two main reasons, the other being that the organism needed more and more complex ways of interacting with its fellow-beings (and cf. Dunbar 1992, on the relation between brain complexity and living in social groups). But the point there is that, for those mammals who develop language (i.e. Edelman's "higher order consciousness"), a critical component of experience to be construed is the experience of their own consciousness (see Matthiessen 1991b, presenting arguments for the view that it is the grammar of conscious processes that forms the nucleus of the transitivity system). And in the protolinguistic phase (that of human "infancy"), the two motifs of 'I am curious about …' and 'I feel strongly about …' play equal and complementary parts in the critical separation of the self from the rest of what is "out there". So it is not a simple matter of reversing the hierarchy; rather, the simple dichotomy of descriptive (or factual)/evaluative has to be discarded (and Ellis himself recognized that "all [categories] are to a degree 'evaluative'" (p. 75)), in favour of a richer model of language and its modes of meaning – in particular, with "evaluative" being contextualized within the wider concept of the enactment of social process and of the self as defined thereby.

And this leads me into my final point. Ellis is setting out to engage with the mainstream of linguistics and philosophy, and he writes with established positions and established ideology in his sights. The chapter headed "The State of Linguistics", for example, deals exclusively with Chomskyan linguistics and its spinoffs. Fair enough. But Ellis himself

241

has criticized those who took no note of intellectual activity that was going on outside their own discipline or their own school; and I think one could reasonably point out that there has always been a strong current in linguistics that did not merge with or get swamped by the Bloomfield–Chomsky tide. Scholars such as Firth and Hjelmslev, in the mid-century period, held very different views, largely compatible with Ellis' own: they rejected the notion of language as a system of communication; they saw language as actively constructing reality not passively reflecting it; and they distrusted the pseudo-science and the spurious rigour of models from formal logic ("rigor mortis" was Firth's way of characterizing it). Firth disputed Saussure, particularly rejecting his *langue/parole* dichotomy, as well as his conception of the sign – but accepted his notion of meaning as "opposition", which he developed into the technical concept of the "system" (as in system-structure theory); he also acknowledged ideas taken over from Wittgenstein, whom he understood very well. Hjelmslev on the other hand developed Saussure's ideas (and those of Brøndal) into a highly coherent model; perhaps too complex for its time, and too mathematical to be readily applied – but he saw clearly the fundamental place of the realization relation in language and the essentially stratal organization of a higher order semiotic system.

Some linguists have continued to build on the foundations provided by Hjelmslev and by Firth, as well as on the work of Saussure and of Whorf, and others such as Mathesius, Trubetzkoy, Martinet; remaining outside the Chomskyan establishment because they disagreed with its dogma in very much the same way that Ellis disagrees with it himself. It is a very different interpretation of language that we find for example in the work of Lamb, of Hartmann, and of Hagège; note in this connection Hagège's own (1981) critique of generative grammar. Among American scholars of the structuralist generation, Gleason, Hockett and Pike all distanced themselves from the onesidedly formalist, syntactic approach to linguistic description and the anglo-centric "universalism" that pervaded generativist thought. (It is strange that the only alternative scholar mentioned by Ellis is Joseph Greenberg (p. 119).)

My own thinking was profoundly influenced by J. R. Firth, and many of Firth's key statements of position resonate strongly with observations that Ellis has made [page numbers in parentheses refer to the relevant passages in Ellis' book]. Firth explicitly rejected the definition of language as a means of communication and was highly critical of those who imported into linguistics a conception of language derived from communication theory (p. 20). Malinowski had already challenged the received view of language as expression of thought (1923, e.g. "language is a mode of action, not a countersign of thought"; 1935; cf. Hasan 1985a); Firth often expressed agreement with Malinowski's point of view (e.g. 1957a/1968), and was particularly scathing about early work in machine translation in which language was regarded as a "clothing" for "naked ideas" (1956/68) (p. 86). Firth cited approvingly certain professional writers for being far removed from "the naive approach to the meanings of words . . . which regarded them as if they were immanent essences or detachable ideas which we could traffic in" (1968, ch.1); neither he nor his colleagues subscribed to such "conduit" metaphors, in either their traditional or their contemporary form – language as cover-up or disguise for the reality that lies underneath (p. 91), or language as code for facilitating the transmission of ideas (p. 18). (An example of the "code" version was Whatmough's *Language: A Modern Synthesis* (1956); in reviewing this book (1959a), I asked the question "If language is a code, then where is the pre-coded message?") A more recent incarnation of this approach appears today under the rubric of "cognitive science", where in some instances language gets reduced to information processing and the brain to some kind of an all-purpose computer; I think most linguists whose work is more functionally orientated feel some disquiet with such a model of human semiosis – as indeed does one of the original founders of cognitive science, Jerome Bruner (1986, 1990). Matthiessen (1993a) has shown how this "scientific" concept of mind derives rather directly from folk linguistic origins: it is simply an elaboration (and a notably one-sided one, as Matthiessen suggests) of how the processes of human consciousness, in a typical SAE language such as English, are ongoingly construed in the grammar of daily life.

Firth consistently maintained that all study of language was a study of meaning; and meaning was function in a context, where the "context" was located both in the various strata of language itself and in its situational and cultural environment – all of which came within the compass of linguistic theory. Malinowski had stressed the functional basis of vocabulary (1935; Ellis uses one of the same examples that Malinowski had used, namely the definition of *weed*); subsequently linguists working within a meaning-based theoretical framework have extended and enriched the concept of "function" in language, developing for example in systemic theory a functional-semantic

243

approach to lexicogrammar as a whole which draws explicitly on Whorf's conception of meaning (pp. 42, 47–8) (Halliday 1967/68; Kress 1976a; Martin 1988).

This in turn is part of a wider perspective, also characteristic of Whorf's thinking, whereby language, instead of "corresponding" to some deeper reality that is independent and ready-made, is itself the active agency in reality construction (pp. 29, 53); as I have put it, it is language with which human beings construe experience, where *construe* means 'construct semiotically – that is, transform experience into meaning', and *experience* relates the process of construal to the experiencer rather than to the "real world" (cf. Ellis' notion of the "categorizers" (p. 116)) (Martin 1985; Halliday 1987; Hasan 1987b, c). Since language is, as Ellis observes, "a creation for which there was no blueprint in reality" (p. 19), it has to create a universe of its own, a parallel reality that is as it were made of meaning; it is this "textual" potential that enables language to be at the same time both a part of human experience and a model of it – a theoretical construction of that of which it is itself a critical part (Lemke 1984d; Matthiessen 1992a).

If human experience has to be construed in language, this is because, as Ellis asserts, there are no natural classes in the perceptual world (p. 32). Alternatively, one might say that there are far too many natural classes; phenomena resemble each other in indefinitely many ways, hence there are innumerable ways of categorizing, leading to variation not only between one language and another but also within one and the same language (p. 40) (Halliday, McIntosh and Strevens 1964; cf. on vernacular, expert and scientific classifications, Wignell, Martin and Eggins 1987). The resource for this construal is the lexicogrammar – which Ellis recognizes to be a single stratum (pp. 52, 107), as I myself have always represented it (1961, 1967/68; cf. Hasan 1985b, 1987c). Ellis remarks, of the grammar's construction of reality, that in reality there is only constant change: it is we who cut it up with our verbs and nouns, into processes and things – "a fluid world made to sit still" (pp. 51–2). He notes that the picture presented by the grammar may itself change over time (p. 48); this is in fact the central concern of my own work on the language of science, showing how the writers of scientific discourse, in modern Europe, reconstrued processes by transforming them grammatically into things – the fluid world had to be made to sit still while it was being observed and experimented with (Halliday 1987, 1988a).

I referred above to Ellis' observation that the lexicogrammatical construction of reality is "functional" in relation to the "collective purposes" of the speakers of the language concerned (pp. 32, 34). Hasan's account of "ways of saying, ways of meaning" in Urdu, and Martin's discussion of "grammatical conspiracies" in Tagalog, both demonstrate how the taken-for-granted assumptions underlying inter-personal communication in the respective cultures are established through lexicogrammatical patterns (Hasan 1984a; Martin 1988). Their work takes off from the position that Ellis is arguing for, but with the concept of "functional" defined broadly enough to cover the interpersonal as well as the experiential domain.

What Ellis has to say on theory of knowledge (p. 93), and on the relation of knowledge to action (p. 77), seems to tie in very closely with the metafunctional hypothesis, where "functions" are not ways of using language but rather ways of knowing and of acting that are brought about, or constituted, by language. As I see it, the ideational metafunction is a construal of experience, from which are derived modes of interacting with the environment; while the interpersonal metafunction is an enactment of personal relationships, from which is derived an understanding of social processes and the social self (Halliday 1993c). In this view "meaning", as a semiotic activity, constructs the unity of knowledge and action – proceeding in either direction, or rather in both directions at once. Without some such functionally rich conception of language it is not easy to explain the way language constructs society, reproducing, modifying and challenging the social order, as demonstrated in Bernstein's researches and theorized in his sociological theory (Bernstein 1971, 1990; Hasan 1973, 1995a); compare Hasan's powerful demonstration of how children build up their picture of the world, and of their own place in it, through everyday conversational interaction in the home (1991, 1992b, 1992c). The now very considerable body of work in language education that is based on functional models of language likewise depends for its effectiveness on having adopted from the start very much the sort of intellectual stance that Ellis is propounding (see, among many others, the work of Carter, Lemke, Martin, Mohan, Wells: e.g. Carter 1987, 1990a; Lemke 1990a; Martin 1993; Mohan 1986; Wells 1986). The wide-ranging discussion by de Beaugrande (1994) presents both a general picture of functionalist thinking during this period and a number of specific suggestions and findings that match closely with Ellis' views.

Many other pertinent observations are made, throughout the book, regarding the nature and organization of language and the require- ments for its theoretical modelling; such as that linguistic research needs to be based on real data (p. 107), and that language has to be seen as stratified (pp. 45–8), functionally variable (pp. 36, 89) and indeterminate or "fuzzy" (p. 95). Ellis' message is: this is how linguists ought to be looking at language. Those of us who do look at language this way, and have been theorizing it in these terms in our own work, are naturally chuffed when we find these ideas incorporated into a coherent philosophical framework, elegantly and convincingly pre- sented and backed up by strong supporting arguments. At the same time, we feel in something of a dilemma. There is nothing more objectionable than the response "we have been saying these things all along". But it has become so commonplace in recent years to dismiss a whole discipline in these monolithic terms, proclaiming that "linguists only do this", "linguists never consider that" as if there was only one voice in the arena (Ellis is by no means alone in giving this impression), that it seems wrong not to challenge this dismissive totalizing of the field.

In Ellis' view, the essence of the "Chomsky revolution" was that a new mythology was created, with the aid of mystifying terminology such as "generative" and "data-oriented": a mythology both about the school itself (Ellis remarks on its "obsessive self-congratulation" (p. 111), which was bolstered by "uncritical adulation" on the part of others – here he cites Lyons' (1970) book in the Fontana Modern Masters series (p. 100)) and about its predecessors, whose ideas were presented in a distorted form such that they could be either co-opted or ignored. But it almost seems as if Ellis himself has become trapped within this same mythology, in such a way that those working outside the Chomskyan paradigm have thereby become invisible. His book is perhaps addressed mainly to American readers, which could explain the notably americocentric view of the discipline that it offers. But there are many linguists around the world who never accepted this dogma, but tried simply to get on with their own work – not that they stayed behind where they had been in the 1950s, but that they moved forward in significantly different directions. So when Ellis writes that his aim is "to establish a new general picture of linguistic theory" (p. x), one has to demur; his picture is one which many others who investigate language have been seeking to establish for some time.

To say this, however, is not to imply that Ellis has achieved nothing new. On the contrary: he has engaged frontally with the movement that has dominated this half century's linguistics, countering its intellectual arguments and pointing up its errors and its misrepresentations. And he has sought to formulate a consistent philosophical position as a foundation for underpinning alternative theories of language. This is the "new general picture"; and it is a notable contribution.

Chapter Twelve

LINGUISTICS AS METAPHOR
(1997)

1 Introduction

The burden of this paper is something that I feel is really very simple; yet I have found it quite difficult to formulate. The argument runs like this. Language is a meaning-making system – let me refer to this property as *semogenesis*, the semogenic power of language. We can, I suggest, identify some particular features of language that are associated with this semogenic power (I shall enumerate five that seem to me to be significant). Now, a *theory* is also a semogenic system; this applies to all theories – they create meaning – and hence to all scientific theories, and hence to theoretical linguistics. Will we find these same features present in a scientific theory? In particular, since linguistics is theory about the making of meaning, will we find that a linguistic theory shares, or mimics, some of the semogenic properties of language itself? (cf. Matthiessen and Nesbitt 1996).

2 Language as meaning potential

I have always spoken of a language as a *meaning potential*; that was the motif behind the idea of a *system network*, which is an attempt to capture this potential. We try to construct networks for all the strata of language – perhaps concentrating particularly on the lexicogrammar since that is, as it were, the source of energy, the semogenic powerhouse of a language, but making it explicit that all strata participate in the overall construction of meaning. In a sense this central question underlies all the other questions we ask, at least at the present imperfect state of our knowledge: how do people mean? What is the

First published in *Reconnecting Language: Morphology and Syntax in Functional Perspectives*, edited by A.-M. Simon-Vandenbergen, K. Davidse and D. Noël. Benjamins, 1997, pp. 3–27.

real nature of this semogenic power, and how does it come to be attained by language – or, if you prefer, how is it that it comes to be attained by human beings through the forms of their various languages? I have always felt it important to try to view a language as a whole, to get a sense of its total potential as a meaning-making resource. This is not to imply that a language is some kind of a mechanical construct all of whose parts come together in a perfect fit, any more than if you try to see a human body as a whole you are conceiving of it as an idealized machine. Indeed it is precisely because the human body is not a mechanical assemblage of parts that it is important to view it paradigmatically as well as syntagmatically (to view it panaxially, if you like); and the same consideration applies to language.

In trying to construe, and to maintain, this general perspective on language as a semogenic resource, I have found it helpful to keep in focus the mutually constructive sets of relationships that I referred to as **metafunctions**: the ideational, whereby language construes human experience; the interpersonal, whereby language enacts human relation-ships; and the textual, whereby language creates the discursive order of reality that enables the other two. This gives some substance to the notion of meaning potential. Language construes experience by transforming it into the experience of meaning; it enacts interpersonal relationships by performing them as acts of meaning; in this way the world of semiosis unfolds alongside the material world, interpenetrat-ingly. The semogenic power of language derives from, and depends on, its constantly reasserting its connection with the material conditions of existence; the concept of metafunction allows us to interpret where, and how, these connections are being made.

I might perhaps mention here various more specific problems on which the metafunctional frame of reference has helped to throw some light, because these also relate to my general theme. One is the question of grammatical agnateness: how do we establish systematic patterns of predictable meaning relationship? Structural proportionalities provide evidence, but the underlying proportions are systemic, and located within metafunctionally defined regions of the grammar – which enable us to set up proportionalities such as these, from the region of modality in English:

I think [they're away]	:I don't think [they're here]
::it's possible [they're away]	:it's not certain [they're here]
::they must [be away]	:they can't [be here] ...

A second question is that of the relation of such patterns of agnateness to functional varieties – to variation in register, and hence to context of situation. And a third question, or set of questions, arises when we adopt a developmental perspective, seeing how small children build up their potential for meaning. The metafunctional framing makes it possible to approach these questions by setting up environments within the grammar, which can be (a) interrelated one to another and (b) related to the diatypic and diachronic environments within which the grammar is deployed and within which it is learnt.

And this leads me to one further point before I finish with the preliminaries. If we talk of semogenesis, this implies something that takes place in time. But in order to locate it, to contextualize it in a temporal perspective, we find ourselves operating not with a single time dimension but with three different time dimensions, each constituting one strand of semohistory. There is the history of the system, and of this or that particular subsystem – the phylogenetic dimension, where meaning **evolves.** There is the history of the language user – the ontogenetic dimension, where meaning **develops** in a pattern of growth and maturation, followed by senescence, decay and death. And there is the history of the text, the instance – the logogenetic dimension, where meaning **unfolds** in an individuated manner of progression. Thus, the potential; the instantial, or instantiated; and, in between as it were, the instantiator (and hence keeper of the potential) – the human brain.

3   Five critical features

In my abstract for ISFC21, which (as is inevitably the case) had to be submitted over half a year in advance, I committed myself to trying to identify and elaborate on those features of the grammar of a natural language that it seemed to me were really critical as the source of grammatical energy: features from which a language derives its semogenic power and is enabled to evolve and function as a self-organizing system. I came up with five headings: language is **comprehensive**, **extravagant**, **indeterminate**, **non-autonomous** and **variable**. Let me try to explain, now, why each of these seemed to me significant. One or two of the headings I can deal with fairly briefly; others will need a rather longer exegetical note.

3.1 Comprehensive

I referred just now to the ideational and interpersonal metafunctions: language as construing experience, language as enacting personal and social relationships. But what is striking about these is their coverage: language structures **all** of our experience, it enacts **all** of our interpersonal processes. Notice for example how from very early in their lives children's personal engagements are mediated, and modulated, through language; this is already well established at the stage of their protolanguage, even before they start learning a mother tongue. There are, of course, specialized registers or sublanguages which are by definition partial; but these are meaning-creating precisely because they are systematic variants within the comprehensive whole. (You could not start learning your mother tongue by learning some specialized variety of it.) Interpreted in quantitative terms, they are local resettings of the global probabilities of the system, and this gives them their semogenic power: they create new meanings by taking the non-specialized register (the discourses of commonsense knowledge) as their point of departure.

A language is able to be comprehensive because it is very big. I am surprised how seldom people ask the question "how big is a language?" – but perhaps it is because they are not accustomed to looking at a language globally as a meaning-making resource. Some years ago I gave a paper on this topic, and with that title, to a psychology department seminar: I think it is a question that can, and should, be taken seriously. Chomsky had said that a language was a finite system generating an infinite body of text; I prefer to reverse that principle and characterize a language as an infinite system generating a finite body of text, but replacing "infinite" by "indefinitely large" (mindful of Robert de Beaugrande's observation that linguists typically do not know what "infinite" means).

I illustrated this point, in another paper (1995), by presenting a network giving a partial representation of the English verbal group – the systemic potential open to a single verb, taken up to a certain moment in delicacy. It extended I think to about 75,000 possible selection expressions (alternative combinations of features); and that was nowhere near the end of the story: I had stylized (to use the term employed by phoneticians) many of the systems, such as those of modality and those realized by intonation; and I had included no systems involving a verbal group complex. We would soon find the output of such a network extending into the millions – still with one

251

lexical verb as the point of entry. Let me remind you here of Christian Matthiessen's (1994) discussion of system networks, in which he demonstrated that, while a network is a presentation of the potential that is already there (those sets of options that are currently being instantiated), it is also a model of the further expansion of that potential, thus showing it to be inherently open-ended. In other words, a language is not just a meaning potential; it is a **meaning potential potential**, if we follow through the full implication of its character as a semogenic resource.

Noticeably, however, this huge meaning potential is achieved by intersecting a rather small number of rather simple systems. After all, it only wants 25 independent binary choices to generate over 3×10^7 (thirty million) possibilities; and while the grammatical systems in a network are only patchily independent (Fawcett 1992), there are far more than 25 of them (over a thousand, in the COMMUNAL and Nigel computational systemic grammars), and by no means all of them are binary. So there is no great conceptual effort required to envisage a resource on such a scale.

Nor is it difficult to envisage that such a resource can afford to generate surplus power; and that leads me into the second of my five headings.

3.2 Extravagant

One of the clear signs of extravagance in language is its fondness for complementarities – for having things both ways. Whether or not our material practices are typically discrete (we have the impression that we are always either doing this or doing that, but that in turn may be the effect of having to categorize these practices in language), in semiotic practice, at least, we are often doing – or rather meaning – two different things at once. To put this in proverbial terms: in language you can eat your cake and have it (I notice that in current usage this has become "have your cake and eat it", which is a much blander form of wording, and also makes much less sense – the parataxis is linear: you eat your cake ... but then you still have it). I am not talking here about the discursive ambiguities of public and domestic rhetoric (although the potential for these is ultimately an aspect of the same phenomenon in language), but rather about the systemic complementarities in the way that language categorizes and "constructs reality". Kristin Davidse's theoretical work (1992, 1996) has highlighted for English one of the major complementarities that seems to pervade all languages in their systems of transitivity: that between the transitive and the ergative construal of (material and other) processes. If there are two participants involved in a process, is the one acting on the other, or is it causing the other to act? One might say: in any given instance it may be either, but the two are contradictory – the same phenomenon cannot be both. Yet the grammar wants to have it both ways: not only does the system as a whole accommodate both perspectives but many processes are construed as a tension between the two. In languages where the distinction is formally marked this dual perspective is often very clear. Another fundamental complementarity is that between aspect and tense as construals of time: is time a linear flow, out of past through present into future, or is it an emerging movement between the virtual and the actual? (This is ultimately related to the transitive/ergative nature of processes.) Again, it seems it cannot be both; yet the grammar insists that it is, in some mixture or other according to the language. (As you move across the Eurasian continent the balance tends to shift, with tense more highly systematized in languages at the western end and aspect in those at the eastern – and perhaps a more even mix in some languages in the middle, such as Russian and Hindi.) And in the construal of entities we find another complementarity, that between bounded and unbounded, or "count" and "mass".

What is characteristic of such complementarities is that they offer alternative models of experience, such that, while it would be possible to construe the entire range of the phenomena in question in just one of the two perspectives, when you bring in both the picture gains in depth. Then it turns out that certain features are better illuminated when the phenomena are viewed from one perspective, while other features show up more clearly from the other. The extravagance of modelling the same domain of experience in more than one way leads to a richer and more life-supporting account. Of course, this will always leave room for what Claude Hagège (1997) referred to as "unheeded contradictions", the leftover bits of language-building materials that continue to lie around; but the **principle** of contradictory construal is intrinsically a productive one.

Let me mention just two other examples of what I am calling extravagance in language. One is that of *redundancy*, in its technical, information theory sense. While some grammatical systems display roughly equal probabilities, others (such as positive/negative) are highly skew; and where probabilities are skew there is redundancy. The other is that of *metaphor*, the constant decoupling and recoupling between the semantics and the lexicogrammar that becomes possible once these evolve as separate strata. There are also forms of semiotic extravagance; and both are intrinsic to the working of language as a multifunctional semogenic system.

3.3 *Indeterminate*

From extravagance to indeterminacy is again a natural step. We are familiar enough with indeterminacies in the realization patterns of language: the puns (lexical and structural ambiguities) when we have to decide between two meanings, opting for either one or the other. Children start to play with these ambiguities from their earliest encounters with the mother tongue. But the more significant types of indeterminacy – significant because they create new meanings – are those which do not resolve by enforcing choice: the overlaps, the borderline cases, and the blends. Overlapping categories are things like behavioural processes in English, which have some of the features of material processes and some of the features of mentals. A borderline case is something that can be interpreted in either of two ways, with different consequences for agnation; e.g., in English, participant$_1$ + *get* + participant$_2$ + *to* + process (*we got it to stick*), either as simple causative, like *we made it stick* (cf. agentive *we stuck it*), or as causative modulation, like *we forced it to stick* (cf. two processes: *we forced it, so it stuck*). Blends arise when, in some paradigmatic or syntagmatic environment, features which would otherwise be kept apart tend to lose their clear-cut distinction and become neutralized. With English modal verbs, for example, whereas in their non-oblique forms such as *can* and *may* the meanings of probability, usuality, obligation and readiness are typically rather distinct, in the oblique forms such as *could* and *might* these become somewhat blurred: *he can be tough* means either 'is sometimes tough' or 'is capable of being tough [if he needs to be]' (one or the other); but in *he could be tough* there seems to be a blending of the two, and the listener does not find it necessary to choose.

Indeterminacy is bound to arise in language because the grammar is constantly juggling with conflicting categorizations, accommodating them so as to construe a multidimensional meaning space, highly elastic and receptive to new meanings. In doing so, the grammar adopts a kind of trinocular vision, giving it a threefold perspective on the categories and their configurations. In the first place they are viewed as it were from above – the phenomena are construed according to their significance in some higher order construct; and in the second place they are viewed from below, the phenomena being construed by reference to how they appear and become manifest. But there is also the third angle of vision, that from round about: all phenomena are construed as being agnate to other phenomena – no categories are set up in terms of themselves alone. The indeterminacy comes from reconciling the three perspectives of this trinocular vision: since all yield different pictures, the result will always be compromise. All grammatical description is the product of compromise.

3.4 Non-autonomous

I think there is little that need be said to explain this fourth heading. Language has evolved as part and parcel of human history, not as some mysterious epiphenomenon coming into being on its own. Thus, grammar is bound up with all the other aspects of the human condition, as part of the eco-social system constituted by a human community and its environment. It takes its shape from the other strata of language with which it interfaces, from the relation of "languaging" both to other semiotic and to social and material processes, and from the nature of those processes themselves. It is the outcome of the ongoing dialectic between the material and the semiotic in human life.

3.5 Variable

A language is a space defined by dialectal and functional, or "registerial", variation. I think it is useful here to stress the analogy between *dialect* and *register*, as names for **kinds of variation**. They are both mass nouns. When we move from the category of "dialect", as mass noun, to that of "a dialect", as a count noun, we are modelling the experience whereby only certain feature combinations within this variable space are actually found to occur; they therefore stand out as rather clearly bounded patches. It is the same kind of shift we are making when we derive from the mass noun "register" the count noun "a register". What we recognize as "a register" is a clustering of features – in this case, predominantly features of the content plane, rather than features of the expression plane as with "a dialect" – that can be observed to co-occur in a regular fashion: a local resetting of the global probabilities of the system, as I expressed it earlier. Like a dialect, a register comes to exist only because the great majority of possible feature combinations never occur at all; there are huge disjunctions, empty regions in a language's variable space.

Higher stratum at which variants are unified ("higher level constant")	semantics [content plane]	social context	[no higher level constant]
Stratum at which variation typically occurs	phonology [expression plane]	semantics	semantics
Type of variation	dialect	code	register

Figure 1   Types of variation in language

But there is also a third kind of variation within language, originally identified by Basil Bernstein (1971, 1996) and referred to by him under the name of *code*. Ruqaiya Hasan (1989) has interpreted "code", in terms of linguistic theory, as systematic semantic variation: that is, variation in the semantic features that are typically associated with a given social context. In other words, code variation (a) is **semantic** – and in this it is unlike dialect but like register; at the same time, (b) it is **variation against a higher level constant** – and in this it is unlike register but like dialect (cf. Figure 1). I would like at this point to follow up these notions a little further, as a way of exploring the consequences which arise from the characteristics I have been ascribing to language. All of these characteristics – its comprehensiveness, its extravagance, its indeterminacy, its non-autonomy, its variability – are going to be implicated in any domain of practice where language is involved (which means, in effect, all human domains). But in the context of our present deliberations, this seems an appropriate point of entry into the next phase of my argument.

4 Language as a constraining force

I have stressed the nature of language as semogenic resource: its character as "meaning potential", including in that characterization the potential for expanding itself – moving into new domains of construal and enactment, and refining the delicacy of those that are already in place. It is important, I think, in an age when the prevailing stance (on language, but also on other things besides) is the "critical" – and this often means only destructively critical – to place the enabling power of language clearly in the centre of the stage; otherwise, in our own praxis, whether educational, clinical, forensic or whatever else, we will come up only with problems, and never any solutions to them.

But it would be foolish merely to celebrate language as an enabling force without at the same time recognizing the other side of the picture: that while it is enabling, it is also constraining. As well as opening up, language also closes off; as well as liberating, it can also be enslaving. In part this is simply the general problem of *form*: to release the power that lies in anything – any substance, any process – you have to shape it, and in shaping it you also limit its scope. We see this most clearly perhaps in forms of art: generic structures and metric schemes in prose and poetry, composition forms in music, styles in architecture and so on, which first engender waves of creative artistry and then become rigid, stylized, stereotyped, and are discarded. In language, as in any semiotic mode, the "system" is what makes instantiation possible (that is in fact the definition of the system: the potentiality for being instantiated); by the same token, it sets limits, not only on what is possible – what can be instantiated – but also, no less significantly, on how whatever is instantiated will be interpreted and understood.

This property is inherent in any **system**. But there is more to the "constraining" aspect of language than this. Because the grammar sets limits on what can be meant (even though those limits are constantly being extended), it constrains the ways in which experience comes to be construed – to be "transformed into meaning", as I put it earlier. Our typical clausal grammars construe experience in the contexts of daily life; in doing so, they constrain our understanding, precluding us from becoming more deeply aware of the nature of everyday phenomena. Christian Matthiessen (1993b) has shown how the transitivity system of English (but with parallels in many other languages, at least those of Standard Average European), especially the grammar of mental processes, construes a picture of mind that is functionally effective in the situations of daily life but seriously flawed as a basis for scientific understanding.

When the semogenic resources of metaphor are deployed so as to overcome the limitations of the everyday grammar as a gateway to systematic technical knowledge, another form of constraint becomes apparent: that of limiting some people's access to certain realms of meaning. Consider in this connection the specialized languages of science. The **evolution** of the nominalized grammar of scientific discourse **enabled** the founders of experimental science to reason and to theorize – to construct technical taxonomies and chains of logical argument; but it **locked** them, or their successors, **into** a world that was objectified (modelled as objects) and determinate, a construal in terms of abstract and virtual **things** remote from the positive disorder of everyday life – and as it turned out rather less helpful for conceptualizing the fluid and indeterminate "reality" required by quantum physics. The **development** of the grammar, towards the end of childhood, **opens up** to adolescents the route to educational knowledge; but by the same token it **closes off** the childhood forms of experience that have been first construed in the conversations of home and neighbourhood. And these two effects taken together – the disjunctions created by the grammar, its distancing both of their day-to-day experience and of their own semiotic past – create the conditions for yet another form of constraint: that while the language creates new knowledge it also limits access to that knowledge. Not everyone is enabled to control the new ways of meaning; thus the grammar is liberating for some, but enslaving for others. The grammar is not neutral, as Basil Bernstein put it in his talk (1994).

Thus variation on the content plane, while it vastly increases a language's meaning potential, is not an "unmixed blessing". Let me return now to the concepts of register and code. Register variation is semantic variation **according to the social context**: different activities coevolve with different registers. It thus supports – enables – the social division of labour, while also constraining – consolidating the divisions. Code variation, on the other hand, is semantic variation that is not driven by the situation: it is variation **within "the same" social context.** The two are not sharply distinct in every instance – there are borderline cases; but the theoretical distinction is a fundamental one. Ruqaiya Hasan (1994) has shown what this means: investigating, for example, patterns of question and answer in mother–child dyads in the home, during ordinary routinized sectors of the daily round – mealtime, bathtime, bedtime and the like, she found statistically significant semantic variation which divided her subjects into clearly defined sub-groups, and always in one of two ways: mothers of boys versus mothers of girls, and middle-class families versus working-class families. Such differences are differences of code. In themselves, of course, all such variants are equally enabling: they open up for the child entry into the common-sense knowledge and values of the culture. But in their impact on the children's subsequent encounter with education, as Basil Bernstein had already discovered in the 1960s, one code may be vastly more constraining than another. Thus the phenomenon of code variation, together with the fact that a variant which is equally effective in one context may be less effective when transferred to another, brings out rather clearly the two opposing facets of language's semogenic power (cf. Sadovnik 1995, Part 3, 'The Sociology of Language and Code Theory').

As is well known, Bernstein labelled the predominant codes with the terms "restricted" and "elaborated", arguing that the restricted code was, typically, shared by all children, whereas the elaborated was accessible only to those who were privileged. The choice of these terms turned out to be unfortunate; Bernstein might have been better served by his own original nomenclature of "public and formal language". Even the term "code" itself was problematic, since it tended to reinforce the notion that language itself is a code – a thoroughly misleading notion with which it has nothing to do whatever. Like register variation, code variation does increase the total meaning potential of the language. Through it, the system organizes itself to favour (increase the probability of) just those meanings that are selected for by the relevant sub-culture, whether of social class, gender, provenance, age or any other. Hence it is the code selection which transmits the (sub-)cultural variation from one generation to the next; and this turns out to be the critical semiotic mechanism whereby social hierarchies are maintained and perpetuated, as Bernstein and Hasan have shown. By the same token, we know that the transmission process can be subverted so that new meanings arise at the disjunctions, new meanings whereby the social order can be, if not transformed, at least affected – sometimes unconsciously, sometimes prompted by design, or "linguistic engineering".

The problem for Bernstein, when he was researching these issues in the 1960s, was where to locate the codes in the luxuriant jungle of language (cf. Halliday 1990). At that time, the *system* of language and the *instance* had been forced apart by Chomsky's notions of "competence" and "performance" as if they belonged to different orders of reality – a dichotomy that did considerable harm to linguistics. Bernstein knew that the codes were not different linguistic systems; so he tried locating them in performance. But, equally clearly, they were not sets of random instances; so wisely, he gave up the attempt of mapping them into the Chomskyan framework. The problem, however, is a real one – not in terms of competence and performance, but in terms of system and instance: where do we model the codes on *the cline of instantiation*?

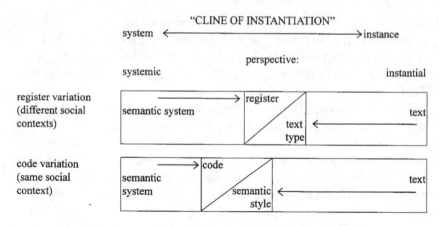

Figure 2   Code on the "cline of instantiation"

We can throw some light on this question by looking into the other type of semantically based variation, that of register. It might be worth noting here that the distinction between the language of commonsense knowledge and the language of educational and technical knowledge, as discussed by Jim Martin and myself in our book *Writing Science* (1993a), is also a difference of code, though one that is a little closer to variation of the register kind than are the original Bernstein codes. I have suggested elsewhere the reasons why I think that code is the most difficult kind of variation to model: because it lies near enough to the "system" end of the cline to be hard to typify instantially. Figure 2 makes this point in diagrammatic form. System and instance form a complementarity such that we can examine variation, as a phenomenon having to be located intermediately between the two, from either end. If we consider register variation first: viewing from the "instance" end, we can recognize a **text type** as a collection of similar instances. But when we shift perspective and see it as systemic variation, each of these text types appears as a **register**, a kind of subsystem which redounds with the properties of the context in terms of field, tenor and mode.

Likewise, we can look at code variation from the perspective of the instance. It is extremely difficult to do this, because it means recognizing different semantic styles (different "ways of meaning", in Hasan's terms) within one and the same language – which may appear, from above, as different ways of "meaning the same thing" (e.g. of grounding the reasons for a given judgment, or of interpreting a given complex class of experiences), but end up by creating different models of reality. The critical step here is to identify that which various instances have in common, such that the shared features constitute a code. Bernstein, having recognized that the commonalities and differences were not a product of chance, examined the resulting codes from the system perspective, and found in them a pattern of systematic variation which constructs and maintains an edifice of social hierarchy, with social class as the most significant variable. He also showed that this was not something that resided in a few lexical items, or overt grammatical markers; it was much more deeply enshrined in the cryptotypic regions of the grammar. At that time we had only a very partial picture of the grammar, and even less of a model of semantics; it was not yet possible to represent such particular orientations within the semantic system. Now that we have a more comprehensive account of the grammar, Hasan's work on mother–child interaction together with her theoretical modelling of semantic variation have been able to provide both a powerful demonstration of the principle of code variation and a further confirmation of the validity of Bernstein's original findings.

Today people like to refer to (actual and potential) text collectives as "discourses", again deriving a count noun from a mass one; it is not always clear whether they see "a discourse" as a collection of text instances or as a subsystemic meaning potential. Part of the problem is that we are often not told what lexicogrammatical or semantic features the exemplars of a particular discourse have in common that distinguish them from other discourses. And yet this is critical, if it is being suggested that such discourses act differentially in the construction of ideologies, in the distribution of political power and the like. The principle of code variation (like variation of any kind) is that it can be modelled in explicit linguistic terms; and when this is done, it helps us to understand one of the fundamental ways in which language, despite – or, in the final analysis, because of – its enabling power, also functions to constrain – liberating some while enslaving others, as I put it earlier. That, as I saw it, was the sense in which the grammar could be said to be not neutral.

And yet, when we step back and look at it in relation to the human condition as a whole, the grammar surely **is** neutral. It must be, if language has the enormous powers that we are constantly having to ascribe to it. The grammar is neutral in the same sense that technology, or scientific knowledge, is neutral. Language may be co-opted, unconsciously or even by design, in the service of some particular ideology, or some social and political power play; but it is as readily adaptable to one as to another. The grammar itself does not favour any one group, or any one interest, within a society. Where it does come to privilege one particular segment, this happens through the interaction between language and the historical processes which constitute its environment; not through any intrinsic properties possessed by a language as such.

The critical factor is, I think, what I had in mind earlier in saying that language evolved as part of human history. Let me make this more explicit, perhaps, by saying that language evolved as an aspect of the evolution of the human species. This is made clear by Gerald Edelman (1987, 1992), in his work on "neural Darwinism" – his model of the evolution of the human brain. Human beings, it seems uniquely, have what Edelman calls "higher order consciousness": this includes consciousness of self, of past and future, and of reportable subjective experience. This higher order consciousness is still the outcome of evolutionary processes operating in the physical universe; there is no need to postulate some mysterious form of disembodied mind. But it differs from "primary consciousness", that of (as far as we know) all other species that have consciousness at all, in that our brains have mappings, and then further mappings of these mappings, not only of previous experience but also of the values that further experience has assigned to it. The brain evolves in a specific historical context: that the organism requires increasingly complex construal of its experience in order to survive. Primary consciousness is efficacious in that it enables the individual to abstract and organize complex changes in an environment involving multiple parallel signals; but it is limiting in that it lacks a concept of self and so cannot model past and future to form a complex scheme – it is subject to what Edelman calls the "tyranny of the remembered present". This can be transcended only by the evolution of social symbols: that is, of language. Language is absolutely necessary for distinguishing self from non-self and for remembering beyond the small memorial interval which illuminates the present.

Like all biologists concerning themselves with language, at least as far as I am aware, Edelman recognizes only the ideational, experience-construing metafunction and ignores the equally important interpersonal metafunction – the fact that language evolves also in the context of enacting increasingly complex social (intraspecies) relationships. We may want to criticize him on these grounds. But his characterization of language would not need to be altered in order to account for this. In our terms, what Edelman ascribes to language demands a *stratified*

262

semiotic: that is, language in its prototypical post-infancy form. It could not be achieved by a system such as the human infant's protolanguage, which reflects the lower level of the evolution of consciousness – primary consciousness. Language in its evolved, higher order form depends genetically on certain morphological changes in the brain: specifically, on the evolution of the supralaryngeal tract. Edelman goes on to ask: "Can we account for language's evolutionary emergence without creating a gulf between linguistic theory and biology?" His answer is "Yes – provided we account for speech in epigenetic as well as genetic terms": that is, relating the developmental history to the evolutionary one. The child's development of language must follow a certain trajectory; and this trajectory in a deep sense copies or mimics the evolutionary trajectory of the system. This means, says Edelman, "abandoning any notion of a genetically programmed language acquisition device". Language develops epigenetically in a definable sequence, beginning as a non-stratified (or minimally stratified) pairing of meaning and sound – or let us say meaning and expression, since the expression may be sound or gesture; only later, with the move to higher order consciousness in the second year of life, does the stratum of grammar (lexicogrammar) appear – and its appearance depends on interaction with other human beings in the environment. Edelman again:

> This theory of speech is a nativist theory insofar as it requires the prior evolution of special brain structures. But it invokes no new principles beyond those of the TNGS [theory of neuronal group selection – MAKH]. It is not a computational theory, nor one that insists on a language acquisition device containing innate genetically specified rules for a universal grammar. Syntax is built epigenetically under genetic constraints, just as human faces (which are about as universal as grammar) are similarly built by different developmental constraints. The principles of topobiology ... apply to both cases.   (p. 131)

It is clear from Edelman's discussion that the evolution of language has been an integral and necessary component in the evolution of humankind; that language is a socially constructed system, leading to a socially constructed self; and that it is a stratified construct, with lexicogrammar as the latest phase. (It has always seemed to me problematic to claim that grammar could be innate, given that children begin by constructing a fully functioning protosemiotic that has no grammar in it at all, and then abandon this when they are ready to replace it by a stratified system of the adult kind.) It is of course this evolved adult system, social, stratified, and epigenetically as well as genetically developed, that I have been characterizing in these terms, as comprehensive, extravagant, indeterminate, non–autonomous and variable. Let me now in the final section turn to the question with which I started: to what extent are these features of language reflected in the ways in which we talk about language, in our linguistics and, more specifically, in our grammatics?[1]

5 Linguistics as metaphor

Regarding comprehensiveness, I think there are two points, related but still distinct, that need to be made. Since our present discipline-based structure of knowledge first became firmly institutionalized, a little over a century ago, each discipline has tended to fragment into separate "branches"; linguistics, apart from its traditional split into historical and descriptive, held together until fairly late, but it too has now become a collection of specializations. This carried with it all the usual dangers – plus some others that are unique to linguistics. Because language is a system that is at once physical, biological and social, as well as having its own special property of being semiotic (it is a system of fourth-order complexity, as I have remarked elsewhere), it is by nature open to interpretation from a maximum number of different standpoints; it seemed to me all the more important, therefore, that a theory of language was itself comprehensive, in the specific sense of accommodating these different modes of being. Otherwise, the parts of the picture are unlikely to fit together; and if it is argued that there is no reason why they should fit together, I would suggest that if they don't, then we create a very impoverished picture, one which could never explain, for example, how language comes to be learnt by a human child.

But there is a second sense in which our theory attempts to be comprehensive: that of viewing the grammar of a language (or any other stratum) in its entirety. I am aware that the formulation "language as resource" can easily come to sound like a pious slogan; but to me it has a quite substantive import. I think we can only fully understand particular features of a language with reference to the system as a whole; so we try to develop models, methods, and forms of representation which encompass the grammar as a totality rather than as a collection of discrete parts – as a network of systems, not as an inventory of structures. Otherwise, however elegant the exposition of one part of the grammar, it may fall apart, or at least it may fail to cohere, when it is put together with the rest. There is a natural metaphor here, between language and metalanguage: if the grammar is comprehensive enough to encompass the whole of human experience and human relationships, then could not our grammatics, given that (like the grammar) it accommodates variable delicacy, be comprehensive enough to model the whole of the grammar?

The notion that a theory might be extravagant is probably more controversial; but I have always seen this as a positive feature, in the sense that there are more conceptual resources available than are necessitated for any particular task. This seems, perhaps, to go against the usual demand for theoretical parsimony, for "the simplest solution that is compatible with the facts"; and it is true that I see no great virtue in simplicity – I prefer the criterion of "the best tool for the job". But the issue is a more substantive one. It is a common experience in working with language that what is locally simpler becomes globally more complex – and also the other way round. One meets with examples of this all the time; one that happens to be in the front of my attention is that of the relationship between intonation and grammar. It is clear that intonation is systemic: it construes meanings in regular and predictable ways. It might seem simpler, therefore, to treat intonation patterns as the direct realization of semantic features, without grammaticizing it along the way. If that is all you are interested in, and you ignore the rest of the language, it obviously is; but once you want to interpret intonation as part of a more general picture of the language, then it becomes vastly more complex to try to circumvent the grammar (among other things, the meaning of intonation choices depends on their grammatical environment), and setting up grammatical systems realized by intonation leads to what is ultimately the simpler account. Paul Tench's (1996) studies of English intonation put this very well in perspective.

The theory is also extravagant, I think, in ways that are analogous to the extravagance of language itself. As I suggested earlier, language often construes experience in terms of complementarities: models deriving from alternative perspectives which contradict each other and yet are both "true" (for example, many objects being both bounded and unbounded at the same time, like *rock, a rock*). Such complementarities also have a place in a theoretical modelling of language. A clear case is the complementarity of grammar and lexis: a paradigm is either a closed system ("grammatical") or an open set ("lexical"), but presumably the same paradigm cannot be both. What we find, however, is a continuum. At one end, there are paradigms that appear clearly closed, and at the other end are those that appear clearly open; so we write grammars, and we write dictionaries. But there is an extensive region in the middle where it is not clear which kind we are dealing with (prepositions in English, postverbal completives in Chinese, etc.); these we can look at from either of the two perspectives. Yet when we do this, it becomes clear that we can in fact look from either perspective at the whole of the lexicogrammar, and that we may gain considerable further insight when we do so. Hasan's (1996, ch. 4) 'Lexis as delicate grammar' shows how lexical items do form closed systems when treated as complexes of features; on the other hand, the COBUILD grammar (Sinclair *et al.* 1990), being "driven by" lexis, treats grammatical classes as open sets. There will always be more than one way to skin a category.[2]

Our theory is indeterminate, I think, again in two different ways. First, it celebrates the indeterminacy in language itself, instead of sweeping it under the carpet and then treading on it to force it into shape. What this means is that it becomes possible to operate with descriptive categories that are themselves fluid and unstable — that constitute fuzzy sets like the categories of language itself. Describing a language demands the same kind of trinocular vision that language has, and in a very specific sense that is defined by stratification: in setting up grammatical systems, for example, we are necessarily approaching them from above (semantic perspective: what meanings they realize), from below (morphological and phonological perspective: how they are realized) and also from roundabout (lexicogrammatical perspective: what are their patterns of agnation). This means that the categories themselves are inescapably the product of **compromise**, since the different perspectives locate the boundaries **between** categories at different places.

Secondly, the general theoretical framework offers ways of modelling indeterminacy. The most important of these, perhaps, is the notion of probability. Probability has been accorded rather little place in linguistics; but that is because mainstream linguistics is largely preoccupied with syntagmatic considerations, whereas probability is inherently a paradigmatic concept — it relates to system, not to structure. In a systemic grammar, probability has a central place: firstly as a feature of any given system, so that a system *a/b* is characterized not just as "either *a* or *b*" but as either "*a* or *b* **with a certain probability attached**"; secondly as a feature of the relationship (association) between systems, so that two systems a/b and x/y are not simply "either freely associated (simultaneous) or not at all" but "partially associated, such that $a + x$, $b + y$ are the favoured combinations" (cf. Halliday 1996). Another concept that allows for indeterminacy is stratification, and in particular the representation of the content plane. There is no doubt that the content plane requires to be modelled bistratally, with a distinction being drawn between lexicogrammar and semantics (without this separation there would be no possibility of metaphor). But the boundary between the two strata is not determinate, and it will be shifted "up" and "down" according to circumstances: in particular, the nature of the task and the state of knowledge about the language concerned (cf. Fawcett 1992; Hasan 1996, ch. 5).

That the theory is non–autonomous is I think obvious; since language is a semiotic system (no doubt the prototypical one, but nevertheless one among a wider class of systems), theorizing about language is an aspect of theorizing about meaning-making systems as a whole. My earlier formulation "language as social semiotic" was an attempt to make this approach explicit. In that sense, there is no way in which a linguistic theory could be expected to be independent of a general theory of meaning, as Saussure had already made clear.

But this lack of autonomy takes on an additional significance at a time when the structure of knowledge as a whole is changing, with transdisciplinary motifs or themes beginning to complement, or even to replace, subject disciplines as the organizing principle. There are two kinds of pressure under which this change is affecting linguistics. One is from the theoretical end: new understanding of the nature and typology of systems, and of processes of change. This makes it possible to comprehend language in terms of its place in a self-organizing, dynamic open system of the type referred to by Jay Lemke (1993) as an "eco-social system"; and to comprehend language evolution and development in terms of the more general kinds of history to which these belong – as well as in the context of new understanding of the nature and evolution of the brain (where evolution, in turn, is interpreted by Gerald Edelman as one instance of a more general category of "selective recognition" processes). The other kind of pressure comes from the applications end. Now that our understanding of language has come, or is coming, to be directed on a significant scale to enterprises in education, in medicine and in the law, these have generated new motifs of educational, clinical and forensic linguistics which have defined rather clearly certain contexts and directions in which theoretical studies of language need to be pursued. One might add here the enterprise of linguistic computing, now that it is becoming clear that a computer is not simply an engine for processing text and speech but one that, as Michio Sugeno (1995) has shown, needs to be driven and controlled by natural language. At such a moment in history it would be perverse to theorize about language as an autonomous intellectual game.

Coming to my final heading, "variable", it might be argued that linguistic theory has never been anything but variable, given the competing models and methods that have sprouted and, in some cases at least, flourished since the beginning of the present century. But I am concerned rather with variation within one general model, which is where it becomes interesting and potentially positive. Robin Fawcett has referred to "dialects" within systemic theory: variations in the way those using a systemic functional model interpret some domain of linguistic phenomena, such as exchange structure, or register and genre (Matthiessen 1993b), or the relation between grammar and semantics. Are these more like dialects, or more like registers? If they have arisen in the context of dealing with distinct problems and issues, they are more register-like; but if they are different ways of dealing with the same problems and issues they do resemble dialects – or even codes, depending perhaps on how many levels of abstraction one had to go through to reach what I referred to as the higher level constant (that which they have in common). It does not really matter where the analogy is drawn – except that, the more code-like the variation, the greater the danger that the parties will cease to communicate with one another, and that is something that does need to be borne in mind.

Given that any scientific theory forms a semiotic system, it is perhaps not surprising to find that a theory of language (language itself being, in turn, a semiotic system) should be rather closely analogous to what it is theorizing about. Basil Bernstein (1994, see this volume, pp. 271–2) has remarked that every theory in the semiotic and social sciences is essentially a metaphor; and I think this metaphoric quality is an important feature of our theoretical thinking. A theory is, inevitably, both enabling and constraining, just as I have tried to suggest that language is. Its constraints can still be a positive force for thinking with, provided the theoretical domain – in this case, language – is construed as a highly elastic space, in the same spirit in which language construes experience.

One might ask: why these preoccupations at this particular moment? In one sense, any moment would serve as an appropriate context: one can always ask the questions how language is able to achieve all the potency, both positive and negative, with which we credit it, and how we can most effectively model language in relation to this or that particular enquiry or application. But from another point of view the present is an especially appropriate moment. For the first time, we, as linguists, have access to adequate data (we might recall here Robert de Beaugrande's observations (1997) on the significance of the large-scale corpus); this will – or at least it should – transform much of the discipline, enabling us to get rid of some of the more mythical elements in our thinking. It will provide evidence for our system networks, allowing them to extend much further in delicacy while continuing to model language as a potential – one in which each instance, every clause in every text, nudges the probabilities of the whole. The output of the system is clearly finite (COBUILD's two hundred million words is no nearer to infinity than a single clause); but the semogenic power of the system is open-ended. The system operates, as de Beaugrande put it, by interfacing local constraints; in Christian Matthiessen's (1994) terms, creating instantial subsystems, copies of parts of itself with which to function as it goes along.

Ultimately, the overall power of our theory – the overarching metaphor, perhaps – attempts to replicate the power of language. With power, of course, comes responsibility: as David Rose (1993) has put it, if grammar has the power to construe experience, this means that it is charged with the responsibility of transmitting that experience – not just the categories and relations, but the categories together with their experiential value – across the generations. It cannot therefore be subject to random or trivial distortions, to the special interest of this or that section of society, however much they may control the material resources. Power groups try, of course, to control the semiotic resources as well: the Nazis were able to carry out some pretty effective lexical engineering (Klemperer 2000); but even they could not change the meanings of the grammatical categories of the everyday German language. As Paul Thibault (1991a) has observed, the meaning potential of a culture is not that of any ruling elite. Grammar, in its role as what I called the semogenic powerhouse of language, is essentially a democratic force. It takes a rather long-term view, and is largely out of reach of those who might try to manipulate it.

Claude Hagège (e.g. 1993) is one of the few linguists who has been sensitive to the power of language, drawing on a vast store of knowledge of languages from around the world. In talking of the power of language, I do not mean only its power as exploited in political contexts, but what it achieves at every institutional and personal level in human lives. What I find surprising, in this light, is the discrepancy between the potency of language and the trivial picture that is so often presented of it – not least by some of the folk who most strongly caution against its powerful effects. One wonders whether it is almost part of the programme of language to hide its potential under a clutter of superficial detail. It seems to me that however local may be our immediate focus in any one moment of professional activity, and whether we think we should be foregrounding the opening up or the closing off, the liberating or the enslaving, we do need to harbour the conception of a language's global semogenic force, and of the grammatical energy by which it is ongoingly powered. And, talking of linguistics as metaphor: it takes a lot of theoretical energy to cope with that.

Notes

1. See Martin (1996a) for a recent study (of a language other than English) illustrating very cogently many of the theoretical features that are being raised here.
2. For further work incorporating the notion of complementarity at the theoretical level see Martin and Matthiessen (1991), Martin (1996b).

Chapter Thirteen

IS THE GRAMMAR NEUTRAL? IS THE GRAMMARIAN NEUTRAL? (2001)

It seems to me that Michael Gregory's work in the Canadian law courts completed a cycle within his professional activities, by bringing to the fore his commitment to the social accountability of a linguist. One might try to capture this by saying that he has always seen linguistics as something to be applied; but somehow that is not the appropriate metaphor. If we think of "doing linguistics", then forensic linguistics in Michael Gregory's conception of it is not simply an extension of some prior given called "linguistic theory"; it is part and parcel of the total of linguistic doings. I think one could say the same about other so-called applications of linguistics, such as educational linguistics, clinical linguistics; for at least some of those involved (including Michael Gregory's former students and colleagues), these are just different aspects of being a linguist. Nor is this only a matter of their degree of social commitment; it means that linguistic theory itself is dependent for its continued progress on such ongoing engagements with language. If language is social semiotic, we shall understand it better if we not only observe the text but also intrude in it (cf. de Beaugrande 1996).

Work of this kind raises an important question, one which has surfaced as a motif at recent international systemic functional congresses: where does the grammar itself stand in the matter? (I am using "grammar" here to mean grammar, not grammatics; and with its usual extension to encompass the whole lexicogrammatical stratum.) Let me sum this up in a phrase (actually a clause, and the difference is significant) used by Basil Bernstein when he spoke to the 22nd

First published in *Communication in Linguistics*, Vol. 1: *Papers in Honour of Michael Gregory*, edited by Jessica de Villiers and Robert J. Stainton (*Theoria Series No. 10, 2001*). Toronto: Editions duGref, 2001.

International Systemic Functional Congress in Gent in 1994. Bernstein said, the grammar is never neutral. This was in the context of his own paper; and Robert de Beaugrande, commenting on this in his address to the subsequent Congress in Beijing (1995), said:

> Much of [the grammar's] apparent neutrality is a reflex of the formalist imposition carried over from antiquity and reinforced by the modern impositions in language policy, education, and science. Unless we wish to acquiesce or even become accomplices, we must reject such a neutrality and declare our partiality to the project of revealing the subtle and complex proportions of neutrality and non-neutrality in the lexicogrammar of the languages we describe, and of enabling the wider deployment of the lexicogrammar to enhance human equality.

At the same Congress, in Beijing, Erich Steiner raised the issue of the social accountability of a linguistic theory, and asked whether having a socially responsible linguistics was by itself enough to ensure that the activities deriving from it would in turn be socially responsible.

Let me refer briefly to the origins of my own thinking about language insofar as they relate to this same point. As a student in China, I had studied Chinese linguistics – Chinese grammar, dialectology, history of the Chinese language, and also the history of Chinese linguistics – with two outstanding linguists, Luo Changpei and Wang Li; and I had tried (not very successfully!) to combine these with what I could find out about Soviet "marxist" linguistics (which at that time meant the work of N. Ya. Marr and his associates) in trying to relate the Chinese language to Chinese history and culture. Back in Britain, I joined the Linguistics Group of the British Communist party, where I was able to exchange ideas with Jeffrey Ellis, Dennis Berg, Jean Ure, Trevor Hill, Peter Wexler, Robert Davies and others; we were struggling towards what we understood as a marxist approach to linguistics, one that would, as I put it in a much later formulation (1993a), "give value to the language of the other: to non-European languages, unwritten vernaculars, non-native varieties of English, non-standard dialects, restricted codes and so on". We saw this not as something decisively new but as a natural development of current European linguistics with its social and functional orientation: Firth and the London group, with their insistence on language in its social context, the Prague school, and the post-Saussurean tradition in France, Holland, Scandinavia and elsewhere. Firth was, of course, my other great teacher; he and I were agreed that "doing linguistics" was a highly political activity – in which as it happened we found ourselves on opposite sides. (Firth once remarked to me that he saw nothing in his approach to language which was incompatible with Marxist thinking; and I fully agreed with him. At the same time, his own political views were deeply conservative.)

This was in 1950, an interesting moment in the history of ideas about language. Stalin had just demolished the Marrists in the famous linguistics controversy in *Pravda*, denouncing their attempts to set up a specifically Marxist linguists (in which language was regarded as part of the superstructure of society, and hence as changing in response to changes in the economic base), and enjoining Soviet linguists to get on with "their task of establishing the linguistic unity of the Slav nations" (reasonably enough, seeing that the Russians had just taken them all over). We debated in particular two ideas, one from each side of the controversy: Marr's notion of convergence, as a corrective to the received comparative historical principle according to which languages tended always to diverge (and his rather obscure sense of the "unity of the glossogenic process") and from Stalin (or whoever wrote "On marxism in linguistics" on Stalin's behalf, later known to have been Chikobava) the conception of the "grammatical system and basic lexical stock" as that fundamental component of a language that persists through time and maintains its characteristic (or, in Prague theory, its characterological) continuity. These were relevant to two aspects of our own thinking at the time: one was the notion of how developing languages expand their meaning potential for operation in new domains (we were investigating the emergence of national languages in post-colonial societies); the other was the concept of functional variation in language, which Jean Ure first referred to (following Reed 1956) as "register" and which became the basis on which we theorized the relation of language to social context (Ure and Ellis 1974). I modelled the context in terms of field, mode and style (eg. 1961); Spencer and Gregory developed these concepts further, replacing "style" by "tenor" (1964), and Gregory presented a theoretically based categorization of the whole range of language varieties (1967).

In this perspective, linguistics was (like language itself) a mode of action, a way of intervening in social and political processes; and this has remained as a significant motif of work in systemic functional linguistics. To cite one example: systemic theory has been widely used in education: not so much in the teaching of foreign languages (though it has had some input there as a descriptive framework), but in what was at first called "language across the curriculum": language in the teaching of initial literacy (reading and writing), of composition, of science, history, literature and so on. In England in the 1960s I directed the

Programme in Linguistics and English Teaching (see Pearce *et al.* 1989), which produced *Breakthrough to Literacy*, a literacy programme developed particularly for use in schools in inner-city working-class and migrant communities where there was a high rate of educational failure; *Language and Communication*, an introduction to the study of language for middle schools; and *Language in Use*, an exploration of language and language varieties for upper secondary students. In Australia in the past two decades Jim Martin, Joan Rothery, Frances Christie, Geoff Williams and others have carried out numerous language education projects along with primary and secondary teachers; their experience shows that teachers are often highly motivated to engage seriously with language – including the study of grammar if they perceive that this has something to offer them in their work (Christie and Martin 1997). (The ones who really love doing grammatics are the children, expecially the younger ones.) What matters here is that the results of all these efforts are ongoingly fed back into the theory, which has always evolved in the context of activities of this and other equally "practical" kinds. Here again, the work that was set in train by Michael Gregory at Glendon College in Toronto played a critical role in the evolution of an educational linguistics (e.g. Benson and Greaves 1973, 1984; Cummings and Simmons 1983); in addition to integrating the study of grammar and register, this work was unique in being underpinned by one of the earliest systematic investigations of the spoken langauge of children in primary school (*Five to Nine*, 1972).

Linguistics who engage in professional activities of this kind are taking an interventionist view of their science, one where the scientist is an active participant in the social process and defines the concept of "doing science" in these inclusive terms. Such a grammarian is clearly not being neutral, and might go so far as to deny that neutrality was possible. But does this tell us anything about the grammar itself? If we subscribe to the view of language that has prevailed in western (including marxist) thinking, it does not; according to this view language merely reflects, often very imperfectly and with a kind of perverse distortion, the concepts and feelings that inhere, independently of language, in the mind of a speaking subject. The challenge to that view of language came from two sources; from Malinowski and Firth, who regarded language as "a mode of action rather than as a countersign of thought" and stressed its interpersonal and social rather than its referential functions (Malinowski 1923, 1935; Firth 1956, 1957a); and from Sapir and, especially, Whorf, who offered an alternative interpretation of the referential whereby

274

language does not passively reflect but plays an active part in reality construction – or, as I prefer to envisage it, in construing human experience. And it is here that we begin to see where the grammar, itself, may not be entirely neutral (Whorf 1956).

Given this perspective, the problem as I see it is to evolve a grammatics which will enable us to theorize language – and to describe languages – as resource: as a potential wherewith we construct experience and intervene in social processes. These two aspects are closely interconnected, in that on both counts language is understood to be an active participant, constructing and intervening rather than reflecting and conveying. This is language interpreted as social semiotic (cf. Gregory 1980; Halliday 1978b). At the same time, the grammatics should lead us to problematize these issues: to ask what it means to say that a semiotic system is "active" in this way. Let me back off a little at this point. There are in the universe two different and complementary types of phenomena: physicists call them "matter" and "information". These are, in the words of the evolutionary biologist George Williams (writing about genes):

> two more or less incommensurable domains: that of information, and that of matter ... These two domains will never be brought together ... Information doesn't have mass or charge or length in millimetres. Likewise, matter doesn't have bytes ... It doesn't have redundancy, or fidelity, or any of the other descriptors we apply to information. This ... makes matter and information two separate domains of existence, which have to be discussed separately, in their own terms.
> The gene is a package of information, not an object.
>
> Brockman (1995: 43)

To which of these two domains does language belong? If we are thinking of the heart of language, its lexicogrammatical system, this clearly belongs to the domain of information. But the outer reaches of language lie primarily in the domain of matter: at one frontier, the physical and biological systems involved in the transmission of speech sound and its production and reception in the human brain; at the other frontier, the eco-social conditions of human existence. Whether some aspects of these outer, largely material phenomena are considered to be part of language or not is not the issue here; this is a question of the perspective in which we choose to model and explain them. What is pertinent is that language evolved at the impacting of the outside world, via the world of sensation, on the human brain: as the species' interaction with its eco-social environment becomes more complex, so it comes to be mapped into a more and more complex information system. This process engenders language as each generation receives it today, as an interface, on two fronts, between the material and the informational domains.

But we can distinguish here two classes of information. One class of information is that typified by the genes: coded instructions whose presence marks the biological off from the physical within the material domain. The other class of information is that which takes the form of consciousness, as this is brought about within the brain. Let us refer to this latter class of information as "meaning", and to systems-&-processes of this kind as "semiotic". Language is a semiotic system; moreover, following Edelman (1992), who refers to human (post-infancy) consciousness as "higher-order consciousness", we can call it a higher-order semiotic. A higher-order semiotic is one which has a system of coded information (a lexicogrammar) at its core. This enables it to transform matter into information. The lexicogrammar is the powerhouse of language: the source of its semiotic energy.

One part of this semiotic energy enables language to serve as a theory – a theory of human experience. Language does not "reflect" our thought processes; it actively creates ("construes") the categories and relations with which we think. Here "transforming matter into information" means transforming our experience into meaning: both what we experience as "out there", in the world that lies round about us, and what we experience as "in here", as going on inside our own bodies and our own consciousness. Hence a theory of grammar (a "grammatics") is a theory of how language does this.

If that was all that the grammar achieved, we might say that it was just another system of information. But this is only one part of what the grammar does. As well as construing experience, the grammar also enacts our interpersonal relationships; and here it is not a mode of thinking – it is a mode of acting. When human beings evolved the resource of language, it served from the beginning not only as our means of information (the ideational function) but also as our means of interaction (the interpersonal function); and the two are inseparably bonded – you cannot have one without the other. Every act of meaning is both construal and enactment at one and the same time.

The cost of this, in terms of semiotic energy, is considerable. What it implies is that language has to create a parallel universe of its own: a world that is made of meaning, and hence instantiated in the semiotic process. This is what we have called the "textual" function of language. We are attuned to this in the form of the flow of discourse (this aspect of language has lately become familiar under the label "information flow" – a term which, as always, privileges the ideational component of meaning). The flow of discourse is what enables the ideational and the interpersonal currents of meaning to flow together – and, by the same token, constrains them from flowing apart; and, as we shall see below, it is in the interstices between the two that bias creeps in.

Let me at this point introduce a short passage of discourse (Text A). This text is of no importance in itself; I constructed it for a project in "intelligent computing" (Halliday 1998b). But it illustrates the initial point. Every utterance in it **means** in these three ways at once – even if it consists of only one word, like *Brake!* So, for example, *You should have* **braked** *before* **turning** construes a quantum of experience involving a participant (the pupil), a couple of actions (braking and turning) and a logical relation (of time) set up between them. But it also enacts a particular relationship between the speaker and the listener – a rather complex one, including something that we might perhaps gloss as 'I censure you: you failed your obligation: you must do better next time'. Figure 1 presents a skeleton structural analysis in systemic functional terms. It shows how these three functional motifs combine in the one "output" form.

Text A: Constructed dialogue
   [Driving instructor and pupil in car; on public roads, in urban traffic; pupil driving]
   [Pupil takes corner rather too fast]
   Instr.: You should have braked before turning. O.K.; go left here.
   [Pupil again takes corner too fast]
   Instr.: Now what did I tell you just now?
   Pupil: Sorry! You said I had to slow down at corners.
   [Bus pulls out in front]
   Instr.: Brake!!
   [Pupil stops car]
   [On three-lane highway; pupil repeatedly changes lanes]
   Instr.: Don't be in a hurry to overtake; it'll only slow you down.
            More haste less speed!
   [Bus appears from cross street; pupil swerves and misses it]
   Instr.: Why didn't you brake?
   [Pupil slows down and draws into kerb]
   Instr.: You can't stop here – go on!
   Pupil: But you told me to stop the car!

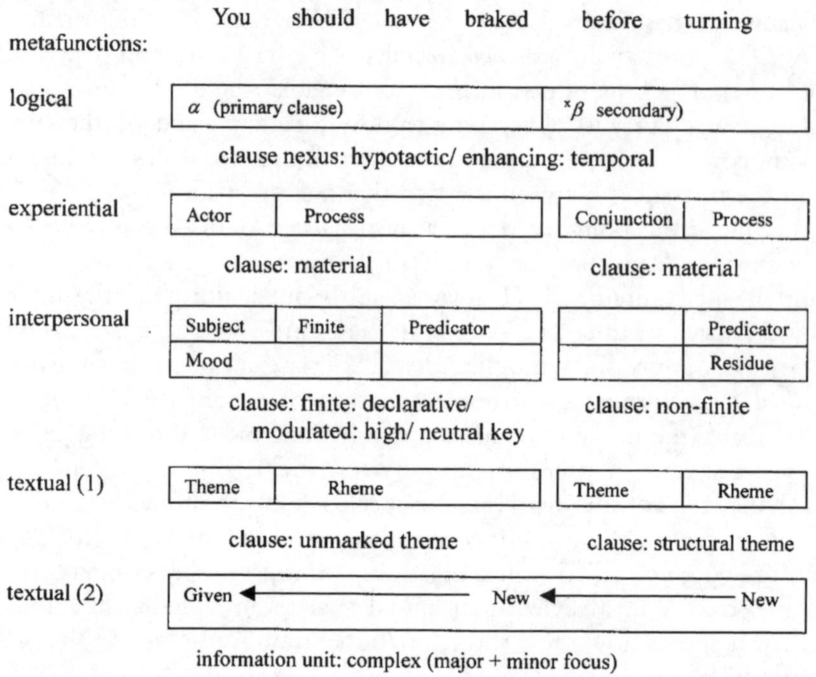

metafunctions:	You	should	have	braked	before	turning

logical

α (primary clause)	ˣβ secondary)

clause nexus: hypotactic/ enhancing: temporal

experiential

Actor	Process		Conjunction	Process

clause: material   clause: material

interpersonal

Subject	Finite	Predicator			Predicator
Mood					Residue

clause: finite: declarative/   clause: non-finite
modulated: high/ neutral key

textual (1)

Theme	Rheme		Theme	Rheme

clause: unmarked theme   clause: structural theme

textual (2)

Given ◄——————————— New ◄——————— New

information unit: complex (major + minor focus)

Figure 1 Metafunctional analysis of one clause nexus

A metafunctional analysis of this kind, deriving from a general model of the grammatical system (that is, where the structures realize selections of systemic features), is a mode of entry to the study of discourse, because it shows how the given text instantiates the systemic potential. A text is meaningful because there is a system behind it, a resource of meaning potential against which it is understood and interpreted. Of course, the analysis of the text is not confined to the stratum of lexicogrammar; the grammatical features in turn relate to a general model of language in which the analysis of grammar is one component. In particular, discourse is understood "from above", in its relation to cultural context – as Gregory remarks (1995: 69), "a discourse, like any organic whole, is considered to be more than the sum of its parts". Gregory's "phasal" descriptions are grounded in the "Communicating Community Context" and the "Generic Situation" (see also Gregory 1988; Malcolm 1985). Hasan (1995b) is a rich and penetrating discussion of (to borrow her own title) "the conception of context in text", and her own interpretation of context is further expounded in Hasan (1999). But the view of discourse "from above" does not displace the view "from below"; the two are complementary facets of the interpretative enterprise.

Many years ago I suggested that the linguistic analysis of text had an immediate goal, that of explaining how, and why, a text means what we say (or someone says) it does; and a higher goal, that of evaluating the text in relation to its situational and cultural context. The higher goal may be formulated as a straightforward question such as: how far does the text achieve what its context of situation demands (e.g. if it's a recipe, can you cook from it?). Or it may raise the problem of the value accorded to a sacred text or a work of verbal art. But we may also want to ask: does the text effect something other than what its immediate environment or its overt wording would suggest? Can we demonstrate its ideological force? And it is here that the question of the grammar's neutrality is broached.

In the 1970s Roger Fowler introduced the concept of "critical linguistics", using grammatics to reveal the political or other ideological constructs that were latent in the wording of a text; and this has been followed up in an impressive body of work in "critical discourse analysis" (Fairclough 1992). (Not all comparable efforts at critical analysis are equally successful or convincing; some writers barely engage with the text at all, and give little linguistic evidence for the interpretation that is being proposed.) Martin (Halliday and Martin 1993a: ch. 11), in a powerful critique of Derrida and other "anti-technical and anti-rational discourses", comments that "the real function of [these] discourses is an ideological one, which means they must be evaluated on political grounds". Martin adds (p. 266):

> The point of including [these texts] here has been to highlight the way in which pedagogic discourses of science and history are constructed for young apprentices in junior secondary school. These students need to learn to deconstruct both technical and anti-technical discourses, and abstract and anti-rational ones, [if they are] to succeed in tertiary education in the late twentieth century.

Texts, of course, come in quanta of any extent, and we can see the ideological force of the wording even in a single clause. Hasan (1986/ 1996) examines how children in a typical western society build up their picture of "work", such that if a woman stays at home and runs the household she is not considered to be working. Alison, at three years and eight months, asks her mother "Are you at work?" Her mother replies, "Oh, I don't work. I look after you." Of course, this motif will be reinforced by countless texts with different wordings and in different contexts; and while it does not need any analysis to bring out the ideological significance of that one instance, it does require both grammatical and semantic analysis to bring out the underlying patterns

– the commonalities and the contradictions – that run through a large body of discourse, such as, for example, the conversations that take place in a day or a week or a month between a three-year-old child and her mother in the home. It is the cumulative effect of the whole that construes the child's experience, by transforming that experience into meaning – an effect that is at once both qualitative and quantitative: on the one hand the momentum carried by hundreds and thousands of instances, combined with, on the other hand, the powerful thrust of a few that appear as salient, and may even end up in the child's long-term conscious memory as having made a critical impact at the time. This kind of large-scale grammatical and semantic analysis is what Hasan herself has carried out, in a research project in which she and her colleagues analysed over 22,000 messages of natural conversation between mothers and children in ordinary domestic situations. This research is the most thorough and penetrating study of the ontogenesis of ideology in early childhood that anyone has yet undertaken (Hasan 1989, 1991, 1992b; Hasan and Cloran 1990).

I have recently been studying the language of pain, the ways in which English speakers talk about the experience of pain in daily life (Halliday 1998a). Pain, presumably, is universally feared and detested; whatever moral or intellectual virtues may be ascribed to physical suffering, most of us do not like to be hurt. There is no doubt, one might think, about its status in the construal of experience. When we come to analyse typical expressions of pain, however, what stands out is the great variety of different grammatical patterns that are used. The number of different everyday words for 'pain' is not very great: the common ones are just four: *pain, ache, sore* and *hurt*. Yet the construal of pain in the grammar marks it out as a highly complex area of human experience: one that is unlike any other because it has something in common with all. If the 'pain' is construed as a process, using a verb like *hurt*, then hurting is a bit like doing (*my leg's hurting*), a bit like having it done to you, perhaps by some external agency (*I'm getting hurt, the rope's hurting me*), a bit like happening (*I'm hurting*); but it's also a bit like being – simply existing (*I hurt*); and it's also a bit like having something assailing our senses or impinging on our consciousness (*it hurts me*). But 'pain' may not be construed as a process at all; it may be a quality (*painful/sore*), which may be either attained or ascribed, to you (*I feel sore*), to a part of your body (*my leg's sore/painful*), to an injury (*the cut is painful*), or to some external action or event (*the fall was painful*). Or, again, 'pain' may be a thing, (*pain*), some entity which you acquire and keep (*I've got a pain*), or it can be given to you (*that gave me a pain*); but even though you have acquired it, no doubt against your will, you cannot give it away. All this complex ideological construction is laid down unconsciously by the grammar; and children – for whom pain is particularly threatening, because they do not know if it is ever going to end – master it all very early in their lives. Pain is one of the most deeply inscribed of all domains of experience.

We might contrast this with a very different domain, the mechanisms of late-twentieth-century capitalism, where the primary ideological motif is one of growth (Appendix 1, Text B). As Kenneth Galbraith has pointed out, it seems perverse to claim that capitalism is successful, given that it can survive only so long as the gross terrestrial product keeps on increasing; but if the claim for success is to be believed, then growth must be construed as 'good', and shrinkage must be construed as 'bad'. Here, unlike in the motif of 'pain', the semiotic work is mainly done by the vocabulary – the lexical end of the lexicogrammar, the part which is much nearer the surface of our consciousness; and the two motifs of 'bigger' and 'better' are linked to each other via the metaphor of 'up' and 'down' – naturally enough, since things that are getting bigger, like children and trees, grow upwards rather than downwards. So 'up' is good, and 'down' is bad; and the text shows how this works (this extract happens to be mainly about things going down). The words that are used here are all familiar enough:

fall	rise	lower	higher
shed	surge	down	up
be off	inch up		
slide	boost	weaker	strongest
drop	pick up		healthy
plunge	jump	decline	improve
tumble			

Note also the wordings *worst performance – a fall* and *better, just below the day's high*. Problems arise, of course, when the polarities have to be reversed. When enterprises have to sack people, in order to replace them with inanimate semiotic systems (like computer programs), they say they are *downsizing*, cancelling out the 'bad' meaning of *down* by the 'good' meaning of *size* (which equals 'being big'; compare the following, from an account of a media star in a television magazine: *He also credits his former big size with much of his career success*); and when, in the process, more people go out of work, we have the headline *French jobless at new high*, where the 'bad' of *jobless* is cancelled out by the 'good' of *high* (and also of *new*). There are other lexical motifs that also promote growthism: that of aggressive violence, with words such as *hardest hit, punished*; anxiety (the word *nervous*

281

is repeated several times), and solidity (*hardening, firming, tightening* and so on). Matthiessen (1995a) has shown how texts within this general register of discourse organize their thematic structure in such a way that the motif of 'growth' emerges as the most powerful unifying force.

Let me finally look briefly at a text expounding military strategy, the "Airland Battle Concept" put forward by the US Defence Department in 1986 (just towards the end of the Cold War) (Appendix 1, Text C). Here the effect is achieved both grammatically and lexically: the syntax and the vocabulary conspire together to construe a "star wars" type of scenario – a universe in which there are no people (the only human noun anywhere in the text is *the enemy*), and much of the discourse consists of equations set up between one set of virtual entities and another, e.g. *The Airland Battle Concept outlines an approach* . . .; *the Airland Battle Concept is designed to be the unifying idea which pulls all these emerging capabilities together so we can realize their full potential for winning.* In many instances these virtual entities simply appear, like holograms: *What emerges is a perception of the battlefield in which the goal of collapsing the enemy's ability to fight drives us to unified employment of a wide range of systems and organizations* . . .; or they are brought in as things to be considered: *Thirdly, it is important to consider now the number of systems entering the force* . . . . *Not just weapons of greater lethality and greater range, but automated systems and communication systems for more responsive command control* . . . . The text is a dense concentration of grammatical metaphor (Halliday 1998b), whereby a holocaust becomes a harmless non-event (not *weapons which kill more people* but *weapons of greater lethality*) and the purpose is so highly encrypted that we have to translate it to find out what it means: *What we seek is a capability for early initiative of offensive action by air and land forces to bring about the conclusion of battle on our terms* – in other words, our soldiers and airmen must be able to attack first so as to make sure that we can win.

This kind of metaphorical grammar is characteristic of those discourses by which our "reality" is reconstructed, in new and (in some cases such as this) quite unreal forms. This particular text, with its remarkable amalgam of the technical with the political and the bureaucratic, is just a rather extreme specimen of the elaborated kind of grammar with which uncommonsense written knowledge is construed. This is a grammar that is based on nouns, rather than on clauses as the spoken grammar is. It is found in a less exaggerated form in the registers of science and technology (Appendix 1, Text D, presents an example from a microbiology textbook); somewhat differently deployed in the social sciences and the humanities; and again in other variants in the registers of industry and commerce, of law and government, and all the professional and managerial activities that form the mainstay of modern capitalist society. It is an essentially **written** mode of meaning, that constitutes the definitive semiotic of the nation state: the "standard language" in its most highly elaborated guise. And this kind of grammar tends to take over, to replace the commonsense grammar of the mother tongue, even in everyday contexts such as media magazines, sports journals and the like. Where it does not take over, as a rule, is in casual and spontaneous speech – nor, as far as we can tell at present, in personalized electronic mail.

Such highly nominalized, metaphoric grammar is the kind of grammar about which it might reasonably be said, in Bernstein's words, that it is not neutral. But we need to be more explicit about what this means. We can approach this, perhaps, through the reciprocal notions of **enabling** and **constraining**. We might want to say, of this elaborated metaphorical grammar, that it is not neutral because it constrains: it limits people's access to certain kinds of knowledge (or rather, to certain modes of meaning, and these are the modes of meaning which afford entry to these kinds of knowledge) – that is, uncommonsense or esoteric knowledge; and hence to the power that is associated with it, and increasingly depends on it in our so-called "information society". I have been illustrating from English, where this grammar has evolved to a fairly high degree; but in fact it seems to be a feature of all languages having comparable functions and comparable status in the community. Historically it takes the place of a "standard language" in the older, dialect-based sense of the term, as the condition of entry to the control rooms of the nation state. And while we are constantly being told that capitalist society no longer depends on a division of the population into those who have and those who have not (rich and poor, upper class and lower class or whatever), it is hard to see any realistic evidence of this; the dividing line has not disappeared – but it has shifted, so that now it cuts across the globe. The standard language is now no longer a dialect; it has become what Bernstein identified as a "code".

Everyone can learn this kind of grammar, once they have emerged from childhood, even if they are being educated in a language other than their mother tongue – provided they have adequate access to it. (They also need motivation; but that applies equally to all learning.) The problem is that if you do not learn it as an adolescent it becomes significantly harder to catch up later on; so "school failures" tend to remain "failures" for life. There is a second sense, however, in which this grammar is not neutral; and that is in the meanings that it has evolved to construe. There are two aspects to this.

One is that, as we have seen, it is ideologically loaded; and the ideologies it constructs tend to be inimical to at least some human populations (and at the most to the whole of creation). They can of course be deconstructed; but one has to work at this – and one has to use language to do it: we have to invoke the power of grammar to deconstruct itself (that is, to use a grammatics to understand how the grammar construes and then reconstrues human experience). The second aspect is more problematic. Modern scientific and technical knowledge not only was first evolved but also is still being extended through this nominalizing metaphoric grammar, in which processes (actions and events), and the qualities and properties both of process and of things, are reconstructed as if they were things. *Planets move* became *planetary motion*; by the same token, *weapons which kill more people* become *weapons of greater lethality*. Now there is strong reason for thinking that this metaphoric reconstrual of experience in the grammar was a necessary step towards a more powerful understanding – towards theorizing that experience in what we would now call "scientific" terms. It made it possible to construct chains of reasoned argument leading from experimental observations to theoretical principles, and to distil the knowledge thus accumulated into taxonomies of theoretical concepts (cf. Halliday and Martin 1993a; Martin and Veel 1998). In other words, grammatical metaphor – the decoupling and recoupling of grammar and semantics – made scientific theory possible. (Of course, the scientists who evolved this grammar did so in response to the pressure to create new meanings, not by any conscious design.) But here again we meet this dual motif of enabling and constraining. The grammar imposed a new kind of order on experience, and so provided a powerful semiotic tool for thinking with; but by the same token it locks us in to this pattern of thought and we now find we need to break out of it, once again to re-form the structure of knowledge. This after all is the general problem of form: all form enables, whether in art, in science and technology or wherever – form is necessary in order to release energy and prevent it becoming dissipated. But this enabling also constrains; in time the initial momentum is lost and the form becomes primarily a constraint, preventing the emergence of a new semiotic or material order. Grammar is form; it releases semiotic energy (that is, it creates meaning); but in doing so it limits the meanings that can be created – and in that sense, it is not neutral. Our elaborated, second order grammar brings with it a particular model of the universe and of our own place in it.

So while in the immediate sense the grammar of any language is neutral, in that you can use it to produce discourse supporting every possible subject positioning and ideological stance, at another level it is highly partial: it construes the world from the standpoint of a given moment in history, and in ways that are geared to survival under those particular historical conditions. Our elaborated written grammar is an uncommonsense grammar, one that evolved out of the everyday, spoken, commonsense grammar of our mother tongues but reconstrued our shared experience in such a way as to favour a nation state, a scientific model of knowledge, and a capitalist order. In its time it generated a massive tide of semiotic energy – but at a cost; and its time may now be over.

But even while much of the discourse of adult life has been preempted by this elaborated, nominalized grammar, the mother tongue with its commonsense, clausal grammar has remained a part – perhaps the central part – of our everyday social being. After all it was the first in place: every adult began life as a child, and first made sense of the world through the grammar of a mother tongue. This grammar, moreover, is perfectly good to think with; the "grammatical logic" of a natural language is different from mathematical logic, but it serves equally well in constructing rational discourse (Hasan 1992b). Text E (Appendix 1) shows a child of around two years old using his grammar for reasoning (Halliday 1984a). The child will gradually accommodate to adult modes of meaning and adult discourse; but the synaptic traces of these early encounters are not likely to be wholly obliterated.

Yet even this grammar of daily life is scarcely neutral. It has been ongoing selected for, by the evolving brain, as the semiosis of human survival – more specifically, in the case of the world's dominant languages, the survival of the settlement culture of the main Eurasian continent. So it privileges humans as the lords of creation, and favours continual growth rather than steady state (cf. Halliday 1990/1992). And while the ideological loadings and interpersonal bias may be most noticeable in the discourses of the elaborated standard language (Martin and Veel 1998; Hunston 1993; cf. Bernstein's 1997 analysis of pedagogic discourse), the features that enable these effects – stratification (an abstract grammar decoupled from the semantics) and metafunction (ideational and interpersonal meanings independently variable, yet neither able to be instantiated without the other) – are features of human language as such, not a special characteristic of its elaborated variants. The systematic semantic variation (Hasan 1996: ch. 5, esp. pp. 115–6) revealed in Hasan's research, that so clearly constituted both gender and social class, was all contained in conversational exchanges with three-and-a-half-year-olds.

And yet – no language, and no variety of a language, is ineluctably tied to any one subculture, or to any one ideology or any one construction of reality. There is no semiotic construal that cannot be deconstrued. And here the most significant fact is that, whenever we deconstruct a text or critically analyse a discourse or unpack a latent ideology, we are not only using **grammatics** (that is, a **theory** of grammar) with which to do so; we are also using **grammar**. All theories, and this includes theories of language, are made out of meanings; and meanings are construed in the grammar. The fact that our grammar enables us to deconstrue the (non-neutral) grammars of commonsense or uncommonsense modes of discourse is the proof that, in the last resort, this grammar is neutral. But it takes work – grammatical energy – to keep it that way. So we, who are grammarians, cannot afford to be neutral.

Appendix 1

Text B: Financial report

Dow tumbles amid renewed rate fears

AMERICAS

Continued nervousness about future interest rate increases contributed to renewed losses among US shares at midsession, *writes Lisa Bransten in New York.*

At noon, the Dow Jones Industrial Average was off 57.79 at 6,553.26, its lowest level since January 3. The Standard & Poor's 500 had fallen 6.65 at 752.99. Volume on the NYSE came to 188m shares.

Technology shares were also weaker with the Nasdaq composite, which is weighted toward the sector, falling 8.17 to 1,208.76, 6 per cent below where it started the year and nearly 13 per cent off the high it reached on January 22. The Pacific Stock Exchange technology index, which contains Nasdaq and NYSE-quoted shares, shed 0.5 per cent.

Traders said that the market was expected to trade nervously ahead of tomorrow's release of March employment figures. Investors would be looking at those numbers for guidance about whether the Federal Reserve would raise interest

again in the near term. There was much debate among economists and investors about whether last week's move by the Fed to boost interest rates would be a one-off event, or the first in a series on monetary tightenings.

Cyclical shares, which had been among the hardest hit in the market's recent sell-off, performed modestly better than shares in consumer non-durable companies. The Morgan Stanley index of cyclical companies shed 0.6 per cent; while the counterpart index of consumer goods companies was off 0.7 per cent.

Du Pont was among the strongest performers in the Dow with a gain of $1¾ at $105¾.

Meanwhile, financial stocks continued to slide after posting modest gains on Tuesday. Among the three financial stocks in the Dow, JP Morgan lost $1¾ at $98, Travelers Group shed $1⅛ at $48¼ and American Express dropped $1¼ at $59¾.

Apple Computer, the troubled personal computer company, managed to buck the

falling market on news that the Saudi prince, al-Waleed bin Talal, had taken a 5 per cent stake in the company for about $115m. Shares in Apple, which had tumbled more than 50 per cent since the start of last year, added $⅜, or 2 per cent, at $17¼.

TORONTO moved lower from the opening bell in what dealers described as moderate activity. Selling pressure was not heavy, but there were very few supports for sentiment in the face of the renewed early weakness on Wall Street. At noon, the TSE-300 composite index was off 14.87 at 5,885.50.

Bre-X Minerals continued to hog the limelight. Trading in the troubled exploration group, hit by computer problems on Tuesday, resumed at the opening and by 11 am more than 4m shares had changed hands. The stock, which stood at C$15.50 a week ago, fell 65 cents to C$3.25. Among leading issues, Seagram fell 60 cents to C$52.60 and Newbridge Networks 35 cents to C$38.95. Toronto-Dominion Bank came off 10 cents to C$35.00. Barrick Gold hardened 70 cents to C$33.80.

EUROPE

The renewed downtrend in the Dow gave late-closing bourses a bad afternoon, but senior traders said that client business had been minimal, both yesterday and on Tuesday.

FRANKFURT was rated "paranoid and nervous" as the DAX index, which started higher, took a late slide to end 70.52, or 2.15 per cent, lower at 3,210.94, some 7.4 per cent down from last Thursday's intraday high.

Turnover dropped again, from DM13bn to DM11.7bn, but Allianz, a market leader, did not figure in the top 10 active stocks, although it put up the worst DAX 30 performance, with a fall of DM146, or 4.45 per cent, to DM3,134.

Mr Michael Geiger, German strategist at CS First Boston, said that Allianz was punished after a US lawsuit, filed in Manhattan on Monday, which alleged that European insurers, including Allianz, had cheated Holocaust survivors of billions of dollars. The company said that the implications of the suit were, as yet, unclear.

Other big fallers also had specific vulnerability. Bayernhypo, down DM2, or 3.6 per cent, at DM53.10, was

Financial Times, 5 April 1997

Text C: Operational concept for the airland battle

1.1 Purpose

The Airland Battle Concept outlines an approach to military operations which realizes the full potential of US forces. Two notions – extending the battlefield and integrating conventional, nuclear, chemical and electronic means – are blended to describe a battlefield where the enemy is attacked to the full depth of his formations. What we seek is a capability for early initiative of offensive action by air and land forces to bring about the conclusion of battle on our terms.

1.2 General

(a) This concept primarily deals with war in areas of the world where there are large numbers of relatively modern, well-equipped forces who use Soviet style operational concepts and tactics. Quite naturally, therefore, the threat against which the concept is designed is typified by the Warsaw Pact in Central Europe, the larger aggregations of mechanized forces in the Middle East, or the threat from the north in Korea.

(b) The concept emphasizes the all too frequently ignored or misunderstood lesson of history – that once political authorities commit military forces in pursuit of political aims, military forces must win something – else there will be no basis from which political authorities can bargain to win politically. Therefore, the purpose of military operations cannot be simply to avert defeat – but rather it must be to win.

(c) This concept does not propose new and radical ways to fight. Rather, it describes conflict in terms of an environment which considers not only conventional systems, but also chemical, nuclear, and electronic. It also forces consideration of this conflict in terms of reaching the enemy's follow-on echelons. Consideration of such a battlefield is necessary if we are to reinforce the prospects of winning.

(d) Extending the battlefield is not a new notion; it is a more descriptive term for indicating the full potential we must realize from our acquisition, targeting, and weapons systems. The battlefield and the battle are extended in three ways:

    (i) First, the battlefield is extended in depth, with engagement of enemy units not yet in contact to disrupt the enemy timetable, complicate command and control, and frustrate his plans, thus weakening his grasp on the initiative.

(ii) Second, the battle is extended forward in time to the point that current actions such as attack of follow-on echelons, logistical preparation and maneuver plans are interrelated to maximize the likelihood of winning the close-in battle as time goes on.

(iii) Lastly, the range of assets figuring in the Airland Battle is extended toward more emphasis on higher land Army and sister service acquisition means and attack resources.

(e) What emerges is a perception of the battlefield in which the goal of collapsing the enemy's ability to fight drives us to unified employment of a wide range of systems and organizations on a battlefield which, for corps and divisions, is much deeper than that foreseen by current doctrine. The word "doctrine" is used advisedly. It must be acknowledged at the outset that there is probably little set forth here which is not already being done and done well in some operational units. The purpose of the Airland Concept is less to suggest innovation than it is to pull together many good ideas for making extended attack an integral feature of our combat capability – in all units.

(f) In essence our message can be distilled in four primary notions:

(i) First, deep attack is not a luxury; it is an absolute necessity to winning.

(ii) Second, deep attack particularly in an environment of scarce acquisition and strike assets, must be tightly coordinated over time with the decisive close-in battle. Without this coordination, many expensive and scarce resources may be wasted on apparently attractive targets whose destruction actually has little payoff in the close-in battle. The other side of this coin is that maneuver and logistical planning and execution must anticipate by many hours the vulnerabilities that deep attack helps create. It's all one battle.

(iii) Thirdly, it is important to consider now the number of systems entering the force in the near and middle-term future. Not just weapons of greater lethality and greater range, but automated systems and communication systems for more responsive command control, as well as sensor systems to find, identify and target the enemy, and to assess the effectiveness of deep attack (Figure 1).

TRADOC Pam 525

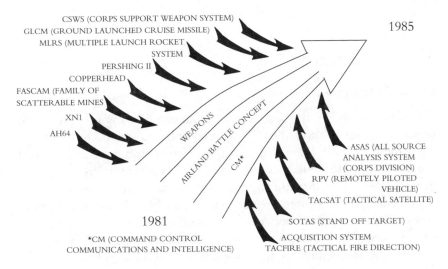

Figure 1 A substantial step toward future capabilities

(iv) Finally, the Airland Concept is designed to be the unifying idea which pulls all these emerging capabilities together so we can realize their full combined potential for winning.

(g) The Airland Concept is not a futuristic dream to remain on the shelf until all new systems are fielded. For instance, with minor adjustments, corps and divisions can and must begin to learn and practice fighting the Airland Battle now – during 1981. The payoffs in readiness for combat will be enormous; and implementing the concept today means that we are building the receptacle into which every new system can be plugged immediately, minimizing the build-up time to full capability.

(h) To insure that the Airland Battlefield is understood in the full context of the integrated conventional-nuclear-chemical-electronic and extended battlefield, this pamphlet will first review, in a broad sense, major aspects of the concept, then describe how, by attacking assaulting and follow-on echelons simultaneously, the prospects for winning increase dramatically.

1.3 Limitations

None.

From TRADOC Pamphlet 525-5 (1981: 2–4)

Text D: Osmotic tolerance

Osmotic tolerance

Osmotic tolerance – the ability of an organism to grow in media with widely varying osmolarities – is accomplished in bacteria by an adjustment of the internal osmolarity so that it always exceeds that of the medium. Intracellular accumulation of potassium ions (K^+) seems to play a major role in this adjustment. Many bacteria have been shown to concentrate K^+ to a much greater extent than Na^+. Moreover, there is an excellent correlation between the osmotic tolerance of bacteria and their K^+ content. For bacteria as metabolically diverse as Gram-positive cocci, bacilli, and Gram-negative rods, relative osmotic tolerance can be deduced from their relative K^+ contents after growth in a medium of fixed ionic strength and composition. Studies on *E. coli* have shown that the intracellular K^+ concentration increases progressively with increasing osmolarity of the growth medium. Consequently, both the osmolarity and the internal ionic strength of the cell increase.

The maintenance of a relatively constant ionic strength within the cell is of critical physiological importance, because the stability and behavior of enzymes and other biological macromolecules are strongly dependent on this factor. In bacteria, the diamine putrescine (Chapter 5) probably always plays an important role in assuring the approximate constancy of internal ionic strength. This has been shown through studies on *E. coli*. The concentration of intracellular putrescine varies inversely with the osmolarity of the medium; increases of osmolarity cause rapid excretion of putrescine. An increase in the osmolarity of the medium causes an increase in the internal osmolarity of the cell as a result of uptake of K^+; ionic strength is maintained approximately constant as a result of the excretion of putrescine. This is a consequence of the differing contributions that a multiply charged ion makes to ionic strength and osmotic strength of a solution; a change of putrescine^{2+} concentration that alters ionic strength by 58 per cent alters osmotic strength by only 14 per cent.

290

Changes in osmotic strength or ionic strength of the growth medium also trigger a cellular response that changes the proportions in the outer membrane of *E. coli* of the two major protein constituents, OmpC and OmpF. These changes are thought to be adaptive, but the mechanism by which they alter the cell's ionic or osmotic tolerance remains unclear.

From Roger Y. Stanier *et al.*, *General Microbiology*, 5th edn, Basingstoke and London: Macmillan Education (1987: 204–5)

Text E: Nigel at two years three months

Nigel was sticking pictures of trains in his scrapbook. He could now put the gum on by himself, turn the picture over, and stick it where he wanted it on the page. He had learnt to put the gum on the back of the picture; this was difficult, because it had been cut out of a magazine and there was often another picture on the other side; you had to decide which picture you wanted to be seen and then turn it over, without letting yourself be distracted by the one on the back. He called the back of the page the "second side", because turning it over was like turning over to the second side of a gramophone record.

"You did put the gum on the **sècond** side," he said proudly, "but not on the **ùnderground** train picture." He used *you* to refer to himself.

"That's very good," I said.

"You can put the gum on the **bàck** of the fast electric underground train **pícture**," he explained, "but not on the **bàck** of the fast electric underground train picture." In other words: you can turn the picture over once, to put the gum on; but you have to be careful not to turn it over again.

We came to a picture of a train that had been stuck in upside down. I pointed to it and looked at Nigel inquiringly.

"Did you stick it wrong way up because it doesn't **stìck** that **wáy**," he said. "You stuck it wrong way up because it doesn't **stìck** that **wáy**."

I looked puzzled.

"No the **tràin** is not wrong way **úp**," he reassured me. "It's the **pìcture** that's wrong way up. The picture won't fall off the **scrāpbook**."

In other words: it looks as if the train is going to fall off the rails. But it won't, because the train is really right way up. The picture is wrong way up. But being wrong way up doesn't make the picture fall off the

291

scrapbook. And I stuck the picture wrong way up because right way up it wouldn't fit in.

The interrogative meant 'I'm telling you something you don't know – you weren't there when it happened.' The declarative was for experience that was shared. Accents show the tone of tonic syllables: fall ↘, rise ↗, fall-rise ↷.

From M. A. K. Halliday (1984a)

PART THREE

LANGUAGE AS SOCIAL SEMIOTIC

EDITOR'S INTRODUCTION

Addressing the relation between the functions of language and language itself, Professor Halliday poses several questions in "The functional basis of language" (1973), appearing in Basil Bernstein's *Class, Codes and Control* (Volume 2): "If language has evolved in the service of certain functions that may in the broadest sense be called 'social' functions, has this left its mark? Has the character of language been shaped and determined by what we use it for? Is the social functioning of language reflected in linguistic structure – that is, in the internal organization of language as a system?" Noting Malinowski's conclusions on the functional origins of the language system based on his work with the language of young children, Professor Halliday maintains that "The internal organization of language is not accidental; it embodies the functions that language has evolved to serve in the life of social man." Language is evolving and the form that it takes has been determined by its uses. Understanding the 'uses of language' gives "insight into the way language is learnt and, through that, into the internal organization of language, why language is as it is." How the uses of language are linked with the formal system of language through its organization into functional components is explained further in "Towards a sociological semantics" (1973): "An amorphous and indeterminate set of 'uses of language' is partly reducible to generalized situation types, the social contexts and behavioural settings in which language functions. For any one of these situation types, we seek to identify a meaning potential, the range of alternatives open to the speaker in the context of that situation type; these are expressed as semantic networks with which meaning selections are made. The options in the semantic network determine the choice of linguistic forms by 'pre-selection' of particular options within the functional components of the grammar."

"Meanings are made by people who have meant before; they relate to prior acts of meaning; and their source is a meaning potential that has been transmitted, as a metastable system (one that persists by constantly changing, in interaction with its environment), over a very long time. The impact of a text is dependent on its location in this complex semo-history, at the intersection of the various dimensions of that history where we ourselves are located when we enact it or hold it up for investigation," writes Professor Halliday in "The history of a sentence: an essay in social semiotics" (this volume, Chapter 16), written to celebrate the history of the University of Bologna. Professor Halliday identifies four dimensions of history that contribute to a sentence becoming an act of meaning: intertextual; developmental; systemic; and intratextual. With examples ranging from "the grammatical history of the favourite scientific clause as it evolved from Newton onwards" to "a well-known contemporary political phenomenon – the 'disneyfication' of western man", Professor Halliday illustrates a critical approach to text from a social-semiotic standpoint – solidly grounded in a multidimensional "grammatics", as outlined in the Introduction to the present volume.

Speaking to the Georgetown University Round Table Meeting on Linguistics and Language Study (1992), Professor Halliday puts forward the argument that "The power of language is vested in the act of meaning". "The act of meaning" enumerates "some of the contexts in which the power of language is proclaimed:"

(1) language as a means of access . . . to particular domains, or spheres of social action;
(2) language as ideology;
(3) language and social inequality;
(4) language as metadiscourse (in the construction of reality);
(5) language as model (for understanding systems of other kinds).

The power of language resides in acts of meaning "because every act of meaning transforms it, however microscopically, from what it was into something else". Therein lies the promise of inherent potential for change. "You cannot redesign it;" asserts Professor Halliday, "but you can nudge it along by the innumerable small momenta (a phrase of Whorf's I never tire of repeating)." In discussing 'language as ideology', he addresses the question of the relation between language and culture, declaring "Language neither drives culture nor is driven by it; the old questions about which determines which can be set aside as irrelevant, because the relation is not one of cause and effect but rather (as Firth saw it, though not in these words) one of realization: that is, culture and

296

language co-evolve in the same relationship as that in which, within language, meaning and expression co-evolve."

Language is "not the outward and imperfect manifestation of some idealized entity called mind", nor can it be reduced to a communication code. Rather, argues Professor Halliday in "On language in relation to the evolution of human consciousness" (this volume, Chapter 18), "It is an evolving eco-semiotic system-&-process, constituting the most recent phase of evolution of the mammalian brain." Gerald Edelman's theory of "neural Darwinism" is presented "as an account of brain evolution which takes language as the critical manifestation of consciousness in its human form". Professor Halliday points out the need for a kaleidoscopic approach in linguistic research, "constantly turning language round and around, as it were, and examining it in different contextual alignments".

Chapter Fourteen

THE FUNCTIONAL BASIS
OF LANGUAGE
(1973)

1 Function and use

What do we understand by a "functional approach" to the study of
language? Investigations into "the functions of language" have often
figured prominently in linguistic research; there are several possible
reasons for wanting to gain some insight into how language is used.
Among other things, it would be helpful to be able to establish some
general principles relating to the use of language; and this is perhaps the
most usual interpretation of the concept of a functional approach.

But another question, no less significant, is that of the relation
between the functions of language and language itself. If language has
evolved in the service of certain functions that may in the broadest sense
be called "social" functions, has this left its mark? Has the character of
language been shaped and determined by what we use it for? There are a
number of reasons for suggesting that it has; and if this is true, then it
may be an important factor in any discussion of language and society.

There is one aspect of the relation between language and its use
which immediately springs to mind, but which is not the one we are
concerned with here. The social functions of language clearly
determine the pattern of language varieties, in the sense of what have
been called "diatypic" **varieties**, or *registers*; the register range, or
linguistic repertoire, of a community or of an individual is derived from
the range of uses that language is put to in that particular culture or sub-
culture. There will probably be no bureaucratic mode of discourse in a
society without a bureaucracy. The concept "range of uses" has to be

First published in *Applied Studies towards a Sociology of Language*. Vol. 2, *Class, Codes and
Control*, edited by Basil Bernstein. London: Routledge and Kegan Paul, 1973, pp. 343–66.

understood carefully and with common sense: there might well, for example, be a register of military diction in a hypothetical society that does not make war – because it observes and records the exploits of others that do. Its uses of language do not include fighting, but they do include historiography and news reporting. This is not a departure from the principle, merely an indication that it must be thoughtfully applied.[1]

But diatypic variation in language, the existence of different fields and modes and tenors of discourse, is part of the resources of the linguistic system; and the system has to be able to accommodate it. If we are able to vary our level of formality in talking or writing, or to switch freely between one type of context and another, using language now to plan some organized activity, now to deliver a public lecture, now to keep the children in order, this is because the nature of language is such that it has all these functions built in to its total capacity. So even if we start from a consideration of how language varies – how we make different selections in meaning, and therefore in grammar and vocabulary, according to the context of use – we are led into the more fundamental question of the relation between the functions of language and the nature of the linguistic system.

Hence, the interpretation of our original question which concerns us here is this: is the social functioning of language reflected in linguistic structure – that is, in the internal organization of language as a system? It is not unreasonable to expect that it will be. It was said to be, in fact, by Malinowski, who wrote in 1923 that "language in its structure mirrors the real categories derived from the practical attitudes of the child …".[2] In Malinowski's view all uses of language, throughout all stages of cultural evolution, had left their imprint on linguistic structure, although "if our theory is right, the fundamental outlines of grammar are due mainly to the most primitive uses of language".

It was in the language of young children that Malinowski saw most clearly the functional origins of the language system. His formulation was, actually, "the practical attitudes of the child, and of primitive or natural man"; but he later modified this view, realizing that linguistic research had demonstrated that there was no such thing as a "primitive language" – all adult speech represented the same highly sophisticated level of linguistic evolution. Similarly all uses of language, however abstract, and however complex the social structure with which they were associated, were to be explained in terms of certain very elementary functions. It may be true that the developing language system of the child in some sense traverses, or at least provides an analogy for, the stages through which language itself has evolved; but there are no living specimens of its ancestral types, so that any evidence can only come from within, from studying the language system and how it is learnt by a child.

Malinowski's ideas were rather ahead of his time, and they were not yet backed up by adequate investigations of language development. Not that there was no important work available in this field at the time Malinowski was writing; there was, although the first great expansion of interest came shortly afterwards. But most of the work – and this remained true until very recently, right throughout the second wave of expansion, the psycholinguistic movement of the 1960s – was concerned primarily with the mechanism of language rather than with its meaning and function. On the one hand, the interest lay in the acquisition of sounds – in the control of the means of articulation and, later on, in the mastery of the sound system, the phonology, of the language in question. On the other hand, attention was focused on the acquisition of linguisitic forms – the vocabulary and the grammar of the mother tongue. The earlier studies along these lines were mainly concerned with the learning of words and word-grammar – the size of the child's vocabulary month by month, and the relative frequency of the different parts of speech – backed up by investigations of his control of sentence syntax in the written medium.[3] More recently the emphasis has tended to shift towards the acquisition of linguistic structures, seen in terms of a particular psycholinguistic view (the so-called "nativist" view) of the language-learning faculty.

These represent different models of, or orientations towards, the language-learning process. They are not, however, either singly or collectively, adequate or particularly relevant to our present perspective. For this purpose, language acquisition – or rather language development, to revert to the earlier term; "acquisition" is a rather misleading metaphor, suggesting that language is some sort of property to be owned – needs to be seen as the mastery of linguistic functions. Learning one's mother tongue is learning the uses of language, and the meanings, or rather the meaning potential, associated with them. The structures, the words and the sounds are the realization of this meaning potential. Learning language is learning how to mean.

If language development is regarded as the development of a meaning potential it becomes possible to consider the Malinowskian thesis seriously, since we can begin by looking at the relation between the child's linguistic structures and the uses he is putting language to. Let us do so in a moment. First, however, we should raise the question of what we mean by putting language to this or that use, what the notion of language as serving certain functions really implies. What are "social functions of language", in the life of *homo grammaticus*, the talking ape?

One way of leading into this question is to consider certain very specialized uses of language. The languages of games furnish many such instances; for example, the bidding system of contract bridge. The language of bidding may be thought of as a system of meaning potential, a range of options that are open to the player as performer (speaker) and as receiver (addressee). The potential is shared; it is neutral as between speaker and hearer, but it presupposes speaker, hearer, and situation. It is a linguistic system: there is a set of options, and this provides an environment for each option in terms of the others – the system includes not merely the option of saying *four hearts* but also the specification of when it is appropriate. The ability to say *four hearts* in the right place, which is an instance, albeit a trivial one, of what Hymes explains as "communicative competence", is sometimes thought of as if it was something quite separate from the ability to say *four hearts* at all; but this is an artificial distinction: there are merely different contexts, and the meaning of four hearts within the context of the bidding stage of a game of contract bridge is different from its meaning elsewhere. (We are not concerned, of course, with whether four hearts is 'a good bid' in the circumstances or not, since this cannot be expressed in terms of the system. We are concerned, however, with the fact that *four hearts* is meaningful in the game following *three no trumps* or *four diamonds* but not following *four spades*.) We are likely to find ourselves entangled in this problem, of trying to force a distinction between meaning and function, if we insist on characterizing language subjectively as the ability, or competence, of the speaker, instead of objectively as a potential, a set of alternatives. Hence my preference for the concept of "meaning potential", which is what the speaker/hearer **can** (what he can mean, if you like), not what he knows. The two are, to an extent, different ways of looking at the same thing; but the former, "inter-organism" perspective has different implications from the latter, "intra-organism" one.

There are many "restricted languages" of this kind, in games, systems of greetings, musical scores, weather reports, recipes and numerous other such generalized contexts. The simplest instance is one in which the text consists of only one message unit, or a string of message units linked by 'and'; a well-known example is the set of a hundred or so cabled messages that one was permitted to send home at one time while on active service, a typical expression being *61 and 92*, decoded perhaps as 'happy birthday and please send DDT'. Here the meaning potential is simply the list of possible messages, as a set of options, together with the option of choosing more than once, perhaps with some specified maximum length.

The daily life of the individual talking ape does not revolve around options like these, although much of his speech does take place in fairly restricted contexts where the options are limited and the meaning potential is, in fact, rather closely specifiable. Buying and selling in a shop, going to the doctor, and many of the routines of the working day all represent situation types in which the language is by no means restricted as a whole, the transactional meanings are not closed, but nevertheless there are certain definable patterns, certain options which typically come into play. Of course one can indulge in small talk with the doctor, just as one can chatter idly while bidding at bridge; these non-transactional instances of language use (or, better, "extra-contextual", since "transactional" is too narrow – the talk about the weather which accompanies certain social activities is not strictly transactional, but it is clearly functional within the context) do not at all disturb the point. To say this is no more than to point out that the fact that a teacher can behave with his students otherwise than in his contextual role as a teacher does not contradict the existence of a teacher–student relationship in the social structure. Conversation on the telephone does not constitute a social context, but the entry and the closure both do: there are prescribed ways of beginning and ending the conversation.[4] All these examples relate to delimitable contexts, to social functions of language; they illustrate what we use language for, and what we expect to achieve by means of language that we should not achieve without it. It is instructive here to think of various more or less everyday tasks and ask oneself how much more complicated they would be to carry out if we had to do so without the aid of language.[5]

We could try to write a list of "uses of language" that we would expect to be typical of an educated adult member of society. But such a list could be indefinitely prolonged, and would not by itself tell us very much. When we talk of "social functions of language", we mean those contexts which are significant in that we are able to specify some of the meaning potential that is characteristically, and explainably, associated with them. And we shall be particularly interested if we find that in doing so we can throw light on certain features in the internal organization of language.

2   An example from child language

With this in mind, let us now go on to consider the language of the child, and in particular the relation between the child's linguistic structures and the uses to which he puts his language. The language system of the very young child is, effectively, a set of restricted language varieties; and it is characteristic of young children's language that its internal form reflects rather directly the function that it is being used to serve. What the child does with language tends to determine its structure. This relatively close match between structure and function can be brought out by a functional analysis of the system, in terms of its meaning potential. We can see from this how the structures that the child has mastered are direct reflections of the functions that language serves for him.

Figures 1 to 3 give an actual example of the language system of a small child. They are taken from the description of Nigel's language at age nineteen months; and each represents one functional component of the system – or rather, each represents just a part of one such component, to keep the illustration down to a reasonable size. The total system is made up of five or six functional components of this kind.[6] Figure 1 shows the system Nigel has developed for the instrumental function of language. This refers to the use of language for the purpose of satisfying material needs: it is the "I want" function, including of course "I don't want". Here the child has developed a meaning potential in which he can request either goods or services, the latter in the form either of physical assistance or of having something made available to him. We show some examples of these requests. In addition his demand may be in response to a question *do you want . . .?*, in which case the answer may be positive or negative; or it may be initiated by himself, in which case it is always positive. Furthermore, under one set of conditions, namely where the demand is initiated by himself and it is a demand for a specific item of food, there is a further option in the meaning potential since he has learnt that he can demand not only a first instalment but also a supplementary one, *more*. (This does not correspond to the adult interpretation; he may ask for more bread when he has not yet had any bread but has had something else. Note that he has not yet learnt the meaning 'no more'.) With toiletry, and with general demands for food, this option does not arise. In the system of "basic" versus "supplementary", therefore, the term "basic" is the unmarked one (indicated by the asterisk), where "unmarked" is defined as that which must be selected if the conditions permitting a choice are not satisfied.

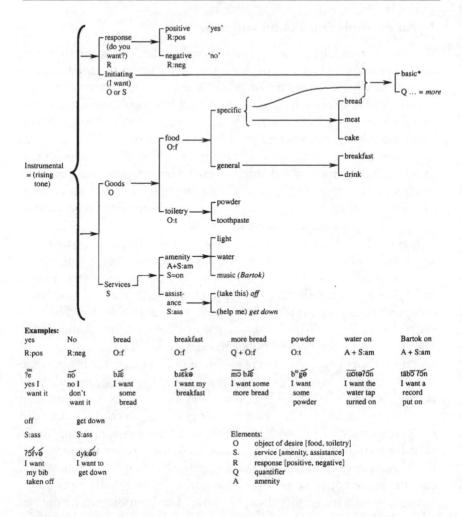

Figure 1 Nigel at nineteen months: part of the instrumental component

Each option in the meaning potential is expressed, or "realized", by some structure-forming element. In the instrumental component there are just five of these: the response element, the object of desire, the service desired, the amenity, and the quantifier. The selection which the child makes of a particular configuration of options within his meaning potential is organized as a structure; but it is a structure in which the elements are very clearly related to the type of function which the language is being made to serve for him. For example, there is obviously a connection between the "instrumental" function of language and the presence, in the structures derived from it, of an element having the structural function "object of desire". What is significant is not, of course, the label we put on it, but the fact that we are led to identify a particular category, to which a label such as this then turns out to be appropriate.

The analysis that we have offered is a functional one in the two distinct but related senses in which the term "functional" is used in linguistics. It is an account of the functions of language; and at the same time the structures are expressed in terms of functional elements (and not of classes, such as noun and verb). It could be thought of as a kind of "case grammar", although the structural parts are strictly speaking "elements of structure" (as in system-structure theory) rather than "cases"; they are specific to the context (i.e. to the particular function of language, in this instance), and they account for the entire structure, whereas cases are contextually undifferentiated and also restricted to elements that are syntactically dependent on a verb.

We have assumed for purposes of illustration a relatively early stage of language learning; at this stage Nigel has only one- and two-element structures. But it does not matter much which stage was chosen; the emphasis is here on the form of the language system. This consists of a meaning potential, represented as a network of options, which are derived from a particular social function and are realized, in their turn, by structures whose elements relate directly to the meanings that are being expressed. These elements seem to be more appropriately described in terms such as "object of desire", which clearly derives from the 'I want' function of language, than in any "purely" grammatical terms, whether these are drawn from the grammar of the adult language (like "subject") or introduced especially to account for the linguistic structures of the child (like "pivot"). I shall suggest, however, that in principle the same is true of the elements of structure of the adult language: that these also have their origin in the social functions of language, though in a way that is less direct and therefore less immediately apparent. Even such a "purely grammatical" function as "subject" is derivable from language in use; in fact, the notion that there are "purely grammatical" elements of structure is really self-contradictory.

The same principle is noticeable in the other two functions which we are illustrating here, again in a simplified form. One of these is the "regulatory" function of language (Figure 2).

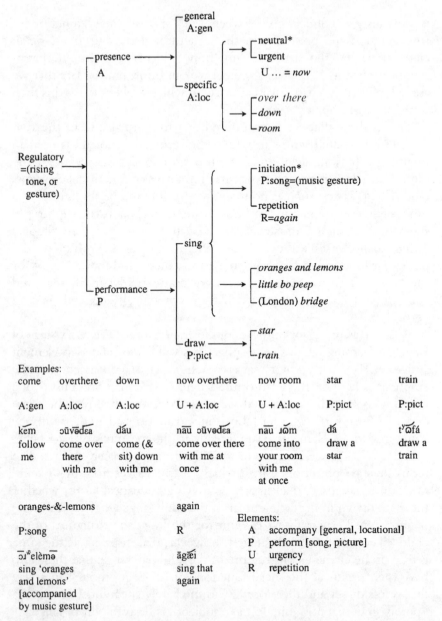

Figure 2 Nigel at nineteen months: part of the regulatory component

This is the use of language to control the behaviour of others, to manipulate the persons in the environment – the 'do as I tell you' function. Here we find a basic distinction into a demand for the other person's company and a demand for a specific action on his or her part.

306

The demand for company many be a general request to 'come with me', or refer to a particular location 'over there', 'down here', 'in the (other) room'; and it may be marked for urgency. The performance requested may be drawing a picture or singing a song; if it is a song, it may be new (for the occasion) or a repeat performance. It is interesting to note that there is no negative in the regulatory function at this stage; the meaning 'prohibition' is not among the options in the child's potential.

The third example is of the 'interactional' function (Figure 3). This is the child's use of language as a means of personal interaction with those around him – the 'me and you' function of language. Here the child is either interacting with someone who is present ("greeting") or seeking

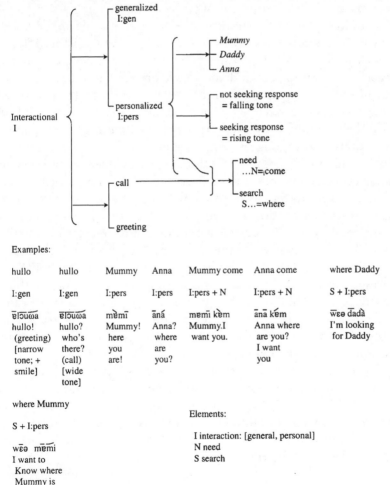

Examples:

hullo	hullo	Mummy	Anna	Mummy come	Anna come	where Daddy
I:gen	I:gen	I:pers	I:pers	I:pers + N	I:pers + N	S + I:pers
ēlɔuɵa hullo! (greeting) [narrow tone; + smile]	ēlɔuɵa hullo? who's there? (call) [wide tone]	mḛmī Mummy! here you are!	ānā Anna? where are you?	memī kḛm Mummy.I want you.	anā kḛm Anna where are you? I want you	w̄ɛə dadà I'm looking for Daddy

where Mummy

S + I:pers

w̄ɛə mḛmī
I want to
Know where
Mummy is

Elements:

I interaction: [general, personal]
N need
S search

Figure 3 Nigel at nineteen months: part of the interactional component

to interact with someone who is absent ("calling"). That someone may either be generalized, with *hullo* used (i) in narrow tone accompanied by a smile, to commune with an intimate or greet a stranger, or (ii) in wide tone, loud, to summon company; or it may be personalized, in which case it is either a statement of the need for interaction, ... *come!*, or a search, *where* ...? And there is here a further choice in meaning, realized by intonation. All utterances in the instrumental and regulatory functions end on a high rising tone, unless this is replaced by a gesture, as in the demand for music; this is the tone which is used when the child requires a response of any kind. In the interactional function there are two types of utterance, those requiring a response and those not; the former have the final rise, the latter end on a falling tone (as do utterances in the other functions which we have not illustrated here).

It would be wrong to draw too sharp a line between the different functions in the child's linguistic system. There is a clear connection between the instrumental and the regulatory functions, in that both represent types of demand to be met by some action on the part of the addressee; and between the regulatory and the interactional, in that both involve the assumption of an interpersonal relationship. Nevertheless, the functions we have suggested are distinguishable from one another; and this is important, because it is through the gradual extension of his meaning potential into new functions that the child's linguistic horizons become enlarged. In the instrumental function, it does not matter who provides the bread or turns the tap on; the intention is satisfied by the provision of the object or service in question. In the regulatory function on the other hand the request involves a specific person; it is he and no one else who must respond, by his behaviour. The interactional also involves a specific person; but he is not being required to do anything, merely to be there and in touch. There are, to be sure, borderline cases, and there are overlaps in the realization (e.g. *come* is sometimes regulatory, sometimes interactional in meaning); but such indeterminacy will be found in any system of this kind.

These extracts from the account of Nigel's developing linguistic system will serve to illustrate the types of structure that are encountered in the language of the very young child, and how they relate directly to the options that he has in his meaning potential. The networks show what the child can do, in the sense of what he can mean; the structural interpretations show the mechanism by which he does it – how the meanings are expressed, through configurations of elementary functions.

3   From functions to macrofunctions

In another paper (1969) I have suggested what seem to me to be the basic functions that language comes to fulfil in the early life of the child, listing the instrumental, the regulatory, the interactional, the personal, the heuristic, the imaginative and the representational. (The last was badly named; it would have been better called "informative", since it referred specifically to the use of language for transmitting information.) These are the generalized social functions of language in the context of the young child's life. When the child has learnt to use language to some extent in any of these functions, however limited the grammatical and lexical resources he can bring to bear, then he has built up a meaning potential for that function and has mastered at least a minimal structural requirement – it may be a "configuration" of only one element – for purposes of expressing it.

The social functions which language is serving in the life of the child determine both the options which he creates for himself and their realizations in structure. We see this clearly in the language of young children, once we begin to think of language development as the development of the social functions of language and of a meaning potential associated with them. However, although this connection between the functions of language and the linguistic system is clearest in the case of the language of very young children, it is essentially, I think, a feature of language as a whole. The internal organization of natural language can best be explained in the light of the social functions which language has evolved to serve. Language is as it is because of what it has to do. Only, the relation between language function and language structure will appear less directly, and in more complex ways, in the fully developed adult system than in children's language.

To say this is in effect to claim, with Malinowski, that ontogeny does in some respect provide a model for phylogeny. We cannot examine the origins of language. But if we can relate the form of the adult language system to its social functions, and at the same time show that the language of the child, in its various stages, is explainable in terms of the uses that he has mastered up to the particular stage, then we have at least opened up the possibility of interesting discussion about the nature and social origins of language.

It is characteristic, it seems, of the utterances of the very young child that they are functionally simple; each utterance serves just one function. If an utterance is instrumental in function, seeking the satisfaction of some material desire, then it is just instrumental and

nothing else. This represents a very early stage of language development. It is shown in our illustrations by the fact that each utterance is
totally specified by just one network: to derive *more bread!* we need only
the instrumental system network, which fully describes its structure.

The adult language bears the marks of its humble origins in systems
like these. But it differs in fundamental ways; and perhaps the most
fundamental – because this is what makes it necessary to develop a level
of linguistic form (grammar and vocabulary) intermediate between
meanings and sounds – is the fact that utterances in the adult language
are functionally complex. Every adult linguistic act, with a few broadly
specifiable exceptions, is serving more that one function at once.

One very familiar type of phenomenon which illustrates this fact is
that of denotation and connotation in word meanings. For example,
after the FA Cup Final match between Leeds and Chelsea a friend of
mine who is a Londoner greeted me with *I see Chelsea trounced Leeds
again*, using the word *trounce* which means 'defeat' plus 'I am pleased'.
But the functional utterance goes much further than is signalled by the
word-meaning of *trounce*. The speaker was conveying a piece of
information, which he suspected I already possessed, together with the
further information (which I did not possess) that he also possessed it;
he was referring it to our shared experience; expressing his triumph
over me (I am a Leeds supporter and he knows it); and relating back to
some previous exchanges between us. There is no simple functional
category from which we can derive this utterance, corresponding to
categories such as regulatory or instrumental in the linguistic system of
the young child.

The problem for a socio-linguistic theory is: what is there in the
adult language which corresponds to the functional components, the
systems of meaning potential, that make up the early stages in the child's
language development? Or, since that is a rather slanted way of asking
the question, what is the relation of the fully developed language system
to the social functions of the adult language? And can we explain
something of the form that languages take by examining this relation?

In one sense, the variety of social functions of language is, obviously,
much greater in the adult. The adult does more different things than the
child; and in a great many of his activities, he uses language. He has a very
broad diatypic spectrum. Yet there is another sense in which the adult's
range of functional variation may be poorer, and we can best appreciate
this if we take the child as our point of departure. Among the child's uses
of language there appears, after a time, the use of language to convey new

information: to communicate a content that is (regarded by the speaker as) unknown to the addressee. I had referred to this in a general way as the "representational" function; but it would be better (as I suggested above) if one were to use a more specific term, such as "informative", since this makes it easier to interpret subsequent developments. In the course of maturation this function is increasingly emphasized, until eventually it comes to dominate, if not the adult's use of language, at least his conception of the use of language. The adult tends to be sceptical if it is suggested to him that language has other uses than that of conveying information; and he will usually think next of the use of language to **mis**inform – which is simply a variant of the informative function. Yet for the young child the informative is a rather minor function, relatively late to emerge. Many problems of communication between adult and child, for example in the infant school, arise from the adults' failure to grasp this fact. This can be seen in some adult renderings of children's rhymes and songs, which are often very dramatic, with an intonation and rhythm appropriate to the content; whereas for the child the language is not primarily content – it is language in its imaginative function, and needs to be expressed as pattern, patterns of meaning and structure and vocabulary and sound. Similarly, failures have been reported when actors have recorded foreign language courses; their renderings focus attention only on the use of language to convey information, and it seems that when learning a foreign language, as when learning the mother tongue, it is necessary to take other uses of language into account, especially in the beginning stages.

What happens in the course of maturation is a process that we might from one point of view call "functional reduction", whereby the original functional range of the child's language – a set of fairly discrete functional components each with its own meaning potential – is gradually replaced by a more highly coded and more abstract, but also simpler, functional system. There is an immense functional diversity in the adult's use of language; immense, that is, if we simply ask "in what kinds of activity does language play a part for him?" But this diversity of usage is reduced in the internal organization of the adult language system – in the grammar, in other words – to a very small set of functional components. Let us call these for the moment **macro-functions** to distinguish them from the functions of the child's emergent language system, the instrumental, the regulatory and so on. These "macro-functions" are the highly abstract linguistic reflexes of the multiplicity of social uses of language.

311

The innumerable social purposes for which adults use language are not represented directly, one by one in the form of functional components in the language system, as are those of the child. With the very young child, "function" equals "use"; and there is no grammar, no intermediate level of internal organization in the language, only a content and an expression. With the adult, there are indefinitely many uses, but only three or four functions, or "macro-functions" as we are calling them; and these macro-functions appear at a new level in the linguistic system – they take the form of *grammar*. The grammatical system has as it were a functional input and a structural output; it provides the mechanism for different functions to be combined in one utterance in the way the adult requires. But these macro-functions, although they are only indirectly related to specific uses of language, are still recognizable as abstract representations of the basic functions which language is made to serve.

4 Ideational, interpersonal and textual

One of these macro-functions is what is sometimes called the representational one. But just as earlier, in talking of the use of language to convey information, I preferred the more specific term "informative", so here I shall also prefer another term – but this time a different one, because this is a very distinct concept. Here we are referring to the linguistic expression of ideational content; let us call this macro-function of the adult language system the *ideational* function. For the child, the use of language to inform is just one instance of language use, one function among many. But with the adult, the ideational element in language is present in all its uses; no matter what he is doing with language he will find himself exploiting its ideational resources, its potential for expressing a content in terms of the speaker's experience and that of the speech community. There are exceptions, types of utterance like *how do you do?* and *no wonder!* which have no ideational content in them; but otherwise there is some ideational component involved, however small, in all the specific uses of language in which the adult typically engages.

This no doubt is why the adult tends to think of language primarily in terms of its capacity to inform. But where is the origin of this ideational element to be sought within the linguistic repertoire of the very young child? Not, I think, in the informative function, which seems to be in some sense secondary, derived from others that have already appeared. It is to be sought rather in the combination of the personal and the heuristic, in that phase of linguistic development which becomes crucial at a particular time, probably (as in Nigel's case) shortly after the emergence of the more directly pragmatic functions which we illustrated in Figures 1 to 3. At the age from which these examples were taken, nineteen months, Nigel had already begun to use language also in the personal, the heuristic and the imaginative functions; it was noticeable that language was becoming, for him, a means of organizing and storing his experience. Here we saw the beginnings of a grammar – that is, a level of lexico-grammatical organization, or linguistic "form"; and of utterances having more than one function. The words and structures learnt in these new functions were soon turned also to pragmatic use, as in some of the examples quoted of the instrumental and regulatory functions. But it appears that much of the initial impetus to the learning of the formal patterns (as distinct from the spontaneous modes of expression characteristic of the first few months of speech) was the need to impose order on the environment and to define his own person in relation to and in distinction from it. Hence – to illustrate just from vocabulary – we find the word *bus*, though it is **recognized** as the name of a toy bus as well as of full-sized specimens, being used at first exclusively to comment on the sight or sound of buses in the street and only later as a demand for the toy; and the one or two exceptions to this, e.g. *bird* which was at first used **only** in the instrumental sense of 'I want my toy bird', tend to drop out of the system altogether and are relearnt in a personal-heuristic context later.

It seems therefore that the personal-heuristic function is a major impetus to the enlarging of the ideational element in the child's linguistic system. We should not however exaggerate its role *vis-à-vis* that of the earlier pragmatic functions; the period fifteen to twenty-one months was in Nigel's case characterized by a rapid development of grammatical and lexical resources which were (as a whole) exploited in all the functional contexts that he had mastered so far. The one function that had not yet emerged was the informative; even when pressed – as he frequently was – to 'tell Mummy where you went' or 'tell Daddy what you saw', he was incapable of doing so, although in many instances he had previously used the required sentences quite appropriately in a different function. It was clear that he had not internalized the fact that language could be used to tell people things they did not know, to communicate experience that had **not** been shared. But this was no barrier to the development of an ideational component in his linguistic system. The ideational element, as it evolves, becomes crucial to the use of language in all the functions that the child has learnt to control; and this gives the clue to its status as a macro-function. Whatever specific use one is making of language, one will sooner or later find it necessary to refer explicitly to the categories of one's experience of the world. All, or nearly all, utterances come to have an ideational component in them. But, at the same time, they all have something else besides.

When we talk of the ideational function of the adult language, therefore, we are using "function" in a more generalized sense (as indicated by our term "macro-function") than when we refer to the specific functions that make up the language of the young child. Functions such as "instrumental" and "regulatory" are really the same thing as "uses of language". The ideational function, on the other hand, is a major component of meaning in the language system that is basic to more or less all uses of language. It is still a **meaning potential**, although the potential is very vast and complex; for example, the whole of the transitivity system in language – the interpretation and expression in language of the different types of process of the external world, including material, mental and abstract processes of every kind – is part of the ideational component of the grammar. And the structures that express these ideational meanings are still recognizably derived from the meanings themselves; their elements are in this respect not essentially different from those such as "object of desire" that we saw in Figures 1–3. They represent the categories of our interpretation of experience. So for example a clause such as *Sir Christopher Wren built this gazebo* may be analysed as a configuration of the functions "agent" *Sir Christopher Wren*, "process: material: creation" *built*, "goal: effected" *this gazebo*, where "agent", "process", "goal" and their subcategories reflect our understanding of phenomena that come within our experience. Hence this function of language, which is that of encoding our experience in the form of an ideational content, not only specifies the available options in meaning but also determines the nature of their structural realizations. The notions of agent, process and the like make sense only if we assume an ideational function in the adult language, just as "object of desire" and "service" make sense only if we assume an instrumental function in the emergent language of the child. But this analysis is not imposed from outside in order to satisfy some theory of linguistic functions; an analysis in something like these terms is necessary (whatever form it finally takes for the language in question) if we are to explain the structure of clauses. The clause is a structural unit, and it is the one by which we express a particular range of ideational meanings, our experience of processes – the processes of the external world, both concrete and abstract, and the processes of our own consciousness, seeing, liking, thinking, talking and so on. Transitivity is simply the grammar of the clause in its ideational aspect.

Figure 4 sets out the principal options in the transitivity system of English, showing how these are realized in the form of structures. It can be seen that the structure-forming elements – agent, process, phenomenon etc. – are all related to the general function of expressing processes. The labels that we give to them describe their specific roles in the encoding of these meanings, but the elements themselves are identified syntactically. Thus, in the English clause there is a distinct element of structure which expresses the cause of a process when that process is brought about by something other than the entity that is primarily affected by it (e.g. *the storm* in *the storm shook the house*); we can reasonably label this the "agent", but whether we do so or not it is

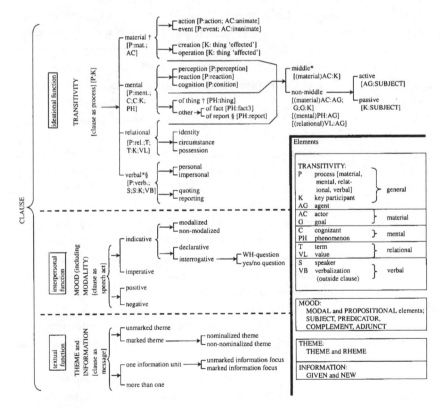

Figure 4 Summary of principal options in the English clause (simplified; structural indices for transitivity only)

present in the grammar as an element deriving from the ideational function of language.

The clause, however, is not confined to the expression of transitivity; it has other functions besides. There are non-ideational elements in the adult language system, even though the adult speaker is often reluctant to recognize them. Again, however, they are grouped together as a single macro-function in the grammar, covering a whole range of particular uses of language. This is the macro-function that we shall refer to as the *interpersonal*; it embodies all use of language to express social and personal relations, including all forms of the speaker's intrusion into the speech situation and the speech act. The young child also uses language interpersonally, as we have seen, interacting with other people, controlling their behaviour, and also expressing his own personality and his own attitudes and feelings; but these uses are specific and differentiated. Later on they become generalized in a single functional component of the grammatical system, at this more abstract level. In the clause, the interpersonal element is represented by mood and modality – the selection by the speaker of a particular role in the speech situation, and his determination of the choice of roles for the addressee (mood), and the expression of his judgments and predictions (modality).

We are not suggesting that one cannot distinguish, in the adult language, specific uses of language of a socio-personal kind; on the contrary, we can recognize an unlimited number. We use language to approve and disapprove; to express belief, opinion, doubt; to include in the social group, or exclude from it; to ask and answer; to express personal feelings; to achieve intimacy; to greet, chat up, take leave of; in all these and many other ways. But in the structure of the adult language there is an integrated "interpersonal" component, which provides the meaning potential for this element as it is present in all uses of language, just as the "ideational" component provides the resources for the representation of experience that is also an essential element whatever the specific type of language use.

These two macro-functions, the ideational and the interpersonal, together determine a large part of the meaning potential that is incorporated in the grammar of every language. This can be seen very clearly in the grammar of the clause, which has its ideational aspect, transitivity, and its interpersonal aspect, mood (including modality). There is also a third macro-function, the *textual*, which fills the requirement that language should be operationally relevant – that it should have a texture, in real contexts of situation, that distinguishes a living message from a mere entry in a grammar or a dictionary. This third component provides the remaining strands of meaning potential to be woven into the fabric of linguistic structure.

We shall not attempt to illustrate in detail the interpersonal and the textual functions. Included in Figure 4 are a few of the principal options which make up these components in the English clause; their structural realizations are not shown, but the same principle holds, whereby the structural mechanism reflects the generalized meanings that are being expressed. The intention here is simply to bring out the fact that a linguistic structure – of which the clause is the best example – serves as a means for the integrated expression of all the functionally distinct components of meaning in language. Some simple clauses are analysed along these lines in Figure 5.

What we know as "grammar" is the linguistic device for hooking up together the selections in meaning which are derived from the various functions of language, and realizing them in a unified structural form. Whereas with the child, in the first beginnings of the system, the functions remain unintegrated, being in effect functional varieties of speech act, with one utterance having just one function, the linguistic units of the adult language serve all (macro-) functions at once. A clause in English is the simultaneous realization of ideational, interpersonal and textual meanings. But these components are not put together in discrete fashion such that we can point to one segment of the clause as expressing one type of meaning and another segment as expressing another. The choice of a word may express one type of meaning, its morphology another, and its position in sequence another; and any element is likely to have more than one structural role, like a chord in a polyphonic structure which participates simultaneously in a number of melodic lines. This last point is illustrated by the analyses in Figure 5.

We hope to have made it clear in what sense it is being said that the concept of the social function of language is central to the interpretation of language as a system. The internal organization of language is not accidental; it embodies the functions that language has evolved to serve in the life of social man. This essentially was Malinowski's claim; and, as Malinowski suggested, we can see it most clearly in the linguistic system of the young child. There, the utterance has in principle just one structure; each element in it has therefore just one structural function, and that function is related to the meaning potential – to the set of options available to the child in that particular social function.

	this gazebo	was	built	by Sir Christopher Wren
IDEATIONAL material(action/ creation/(non-middle:passive))	G:K; effected	P:material/ action		AC:AG; animate
INTERPERSONAL declarative/non-modalized	Modal	Propositional		
	Subject	Predicator		Adjunct
TEXTUAL unmarked theme one information	Theme	Rheme		
unit: unmarked	Given			New

	I	had		a cat . . .
IDEATIONAL relational: (possession/middle)	T:K	P:rel-ational		VL
INTERPERSONAL declarative/non-modalized	Modal	=did	have Propositional	
	Subject	Predicator		Complement
TEXTUAL unmarked theme one information	Theme	Rheme		
unit: unmarked	Given	New		

	. . . the cat	pleased		me
ID.mental:(reaction/ fact/(non-middle: active)	PH:AG; thing	P:mental: reaction		C:K.
INT.declarative/ non-modalized	Modal	=did	please	Propositional
	Subject	Predicator		Complement
TEXT. unmarked theme one information	Theme	Rheme		
unit: unmarked	Given	New		

	such a tale	you	would	never believe
ID.mental:(cognition/ report/middle)	PH: report	C:K	P:mental: cognition	
INT.declarative/ modalized	Propo-.	Modal		-sitional
negative	Complement	Subject		Predicator
TEXT.marked theme: non-nominalized	Theme	Rheme		
two information units	New	Given		New

Figure 5   Analysis of clauses, showing simultaneous structures

In the developed linguistic system of the adult, the functional origins are still discernible. Here, however, each utterance has a number of structures simultaneously – we have used the analogy of polyphony. Each element is a complex of roles, and enters into more than one structure (indeed the concept "element of structure" is a purely abstract concept; it is merely a role set, which is then realized by some item in the language). The structure of the adult language still represents the functional meaning potential; but because of the variety of social uses of language, a "grammar" has emerged whereby the options are organized into a few large sets in which the speaker selects simultaneously whatever the specific use he is making of language. These sets of options, which are recognizable empirically in the grammar, correspond to the few highly generalized realms of meaning that are essential to the social functioning of language – and hence are intrinsic to language as a system. Because language serves a generalized "ideational" function, we are able to use it for all the specific purposes and types of context which involve the communication of experience. Because it serves a generalized "interpersonal" function, we are able to use it for all the specific forms of personal expression and social interaction. And a prerequisite to its effective operation under both these headings is what we have referred to as the "textual" function, whereby language becomes text, is related to itself and to its contexts of use. Without the textual component of meaning, we should be unable to make any use of language at all.

If we want to pursue this line of interpretation further, we shall have to go outside language to some theory of social meanings. From the point of view of a linguist the most important work in this field is that of Bernstein, whose theories of cultural transmission and social change are unique in this respect, that language is built into them as an essential element in social processes. Although Bernstein is primarily investigating social and not linguistic phenomena, his ideas shed very considerable light on language; in particular, in relation to the concept of language as meaning potential, he has been able to define certain contexts which are crucial to the socialization of the child and to identify the significant orientations in the behaviour of participants within these contexts. The behavioural options of the participants are, typically, realized through language; and with a functional interpretation of the semantic system we can begin to appreciate how it is that, in the course of expressing meanings that are specific to particular contexts of situation, language at the same time serves to transmit the essential patterns of orientation in the total context of the culture.

319

a SYSTEM

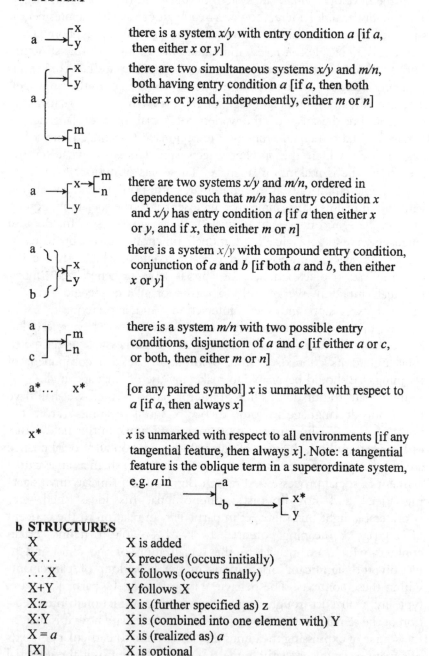

a ⟶ [ₓy]   there is a system x/y with entry condition a [if a, then either x or y]

a ⟨ ⟶ [ₓy] ... ⟶ [ₘn]   there are two simultaneous systems x/y and m/n, both having entry condition a [if a, then both either x or y and, independently, either m or n]

a ⟶ [x→[ₘn] y]   there are two systems x/y and m/n, ordered in dependence such that m/n has entry condition x and x/y has entry condition a [if a then either x or y, and if x, then either m or n]

a ⟩ [ₓy] **b** ⟩   there is a system x/y with compound entry condition, conjunction of a and b [if both a and b, then either x or y]

a ⟩ [ₘn] **c** ⟩   there is a system m/n with two possible entry conditions, disjunction of a and c [if either a or c, or both, then either m or n]

a*... x*   [or any paired symbol] x is unmarked with respect to a [if a, then always x]

x*   x is unmarked with respect to all environments [if any tangential feature, then always x]. Note: a tangential feature is the oblique term in a superordinate system, e.g. a in

⟶ [ₐb] ⟶ [x*y]

b STRUCTURES

X	X is added
X...	X precedes (occurs initially)
...X	X follows (occurs finally)
X+Y	Y follows X
X:z	X is (further specified as) z
X:Y	X is (combined into one element with) Y
X = a	X is (realized as) a
[X]	X is optional

Figure 6 Summary of notational conventions

This provides the backdrop to a functional view of language. In front of our eyes, as it were, are the "uses of language"; we are interested in how people use language and in how language varies according to its use. Behind this lies a concern with the nature of language of itself; once we interpret the notion "uses of language" in sufficiently abstract terms we find that it gives us an insight into the way language is learnt and, through that, into the internal organization of language, why language is as it is. Behind this again is a still deeper focus, on society and the transmission of culture; for when we interpret language in these terms we may cast some light on how language, in the most everyday situations, so effectively transmits the social structure, the values, the systems of knowledge, all the deepest and most pervasive patterns of the culture. With a functional perspective on language, we can begin to appreciate how this is done.

Notes

This chapter was based on a preliminary interpretation of some of my early records of child language development. I had begun working on linguistic ontogeny in the context of our "Breakthrough to Literacy" project, while at the same time continuing with the systemic functional analysis of the grammar of (adult) English. The account given here was considerably modified in the course of more detailed, corpus-based study on both these fronts; among other things, the development of linguistic functionality was reinterpreted in terms of three stages: micro-functions (in protolanguage), macro-functions (in the transition to mother tongue), meta-functions (in the mother tongue). My essays on child language development are collected in Volume 4. Volumes 1 and 3 are concerned with systemic functional theory; specific chapters on the grammar of English will appear in a later volume.

1. For diatypic variety in language, see Gregory 1967; Ellis 1966a.
2. Bronislaw Malinowski, 'The problem of meaning in primitive languages', Supplement 1 to Ogden and Richards 1923.
3. See for example Watts 1944.
4. Emanuel A. Schegloff, 'Sequencing in conversational openings', in Gumperz and Hymes 1972.
5. This was in fact a task assigned to the mothers in relation to the socialization of children in a study by Bernstein and Henderson, 'Social class differences in the relevance of language to socialization': they were asked to say how much more difficult it would be for parents who could not speak to do certain things with young children, such as disciplining them or helping them to make things. It should be borne in mind that in the present discussion we are using 'language' always to refer to the

meaning potential; we assume some means of expression, but not any linguistic forms in particular.

6. The analyses given in Figures 1 to 3 represent a provisional interpretation of the material. A full account of Nigel's language development from nine to twenty-four months is presented in Volume 4 of this series, *The Language of Early Childhood*.

Chapter Fifteen

TOWARDS A SOCIOLOGICAL SEMANTICS
(1972)

1 *Meaning potential* and semantic networks

We shall define language as "meaning potential": that is, as sets of options, or alternatives, in meaning that are available to the speaker-hearer.

At each of the levels that make up the linguistic coding system, we can identify sets of options representing what the speaker 'can do' at that level. When we refer to grammar, or to phonology, each of these can be thought of as a range of strategies, with accompanying tactics of structure formation.

There are also sets of options at the two interfaces, the coding levels which relate language to non-language. We use "semantics" to refer to one of these interfaces, that which represents the coding of the "input" to the linguistic system. The range of options at the semantic level is the potentiality for encoding in language that which is not language (cf. Lamb 1970).

The term "meaning" has traditionally been restricted to the input end of the language system: the "content plane", in Hjelmslev's terms, and more specifically to the relations of the semantic interface, Hjelmslev's "content substance". We will therefore use "meaning potential" just to refer to the semantic options (although we would regard it as an adequate designation of language as a whole.)

Semantics, then, is "what the speaker can mean". It is the strategy that is available for entering the language system. It is one form of, or rather one form of the realization of, behaviour potential; "can mean" is one form of "can do". The behaviour potential may be realized not only by language but also by other means. Behaviour strategies are outside language but may be actualized through the medium of the language system.

First published in the series of working papers and prepublications (14/C, 1972), edited by Centro Internazionale di Semiotica e Linguistica of the University of Urbino, 1972.

Let us take as an example the use of language by a mother for the purpose of controlling the behaviour of a child. This example is invented, but it is based on actual investigations of social learning – including, among a number of different contexts, that of the regulation of children's behaviour by the mother – carried out in London under the direction of Professor Basil Bernstein. In particular I have drawn on the work of Geoffrey Turner, who has undertaken much of the linguistic analysis of Professor Bernstein's material and shown how the networks of semantic options can serve as a bridge between the sociological and the purely linguistic conceptual frameworks (Bernstein 1971, 1973; Turner 1973).

The small boy has been playing with the neighbourhood children on a building site, and has come home grasping some object which he has acquired in the process. His mother disapproves, and wishes both to express her disapproval and to prevent him doing the same thing again. She has a range of alternatives open to her, some of which are non-linguistic: she can smack him. But supposing she elects to adopt linguistic measures, the sort of thing she might say would be:

(1) that's very naughty of you
(2) I'll smack you if you do that again
(3) I don't like you to do that
(4) that thing doesn't belong to you
(5) Daddy would be very cross

These represent different means of control, which might be characterized as (1) categorization of behaviour in terms of disapproval or approval on moral grounds; (2) threat of punishment linked to repetition of behaviour; (3) emotional appeal; (4) categorization of objects in terms of social institution of ownership; (5) warning of disapproval by other parent. And we could add others, e.g. (6) *you're making Mummy very unhappy by disobeying* (control through emotional blackmail), (7) *that's not allowed* (control through categorization of behaviour in terms of the operations of a rule), etc.

The mother's behaviour could also be described linguistically, in terms of grammatical systems of mood, transitivity and so on. For example, (1) is a relational clause of the attributive (ascription) type where the child's act is referred to situationally as *that* and has ascribed to it, in simple past tense, an attribute expressed by an attitudinal adjective *naughty*, the attribution being explicitly tied to the child himself by the presence of the qualifier *of you*. In (2) we have a

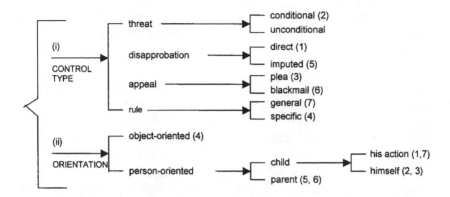

Figure 1 Semantic network for control options

hypotactic clause complex in which the main clause is a transitive clause of action in simple future tense with *smack* as Process, *I* as Actor and *you* as Goal, the dependent clause being a conditional, likewise of the actions type, with situationally-referring Process *do that* and Actor *you*.

But these two accounts of the mother's behaviour, the sociological and the linguistic, are unrelated, except in that they are descriptions of the same phenomena. In order to try and relate them, let us describe the mother's verbal behaviour in the form of a system of semantic options, options which we can then relate to the social situation on the one hand and to the grammatical systems of the language on the other.

Figure 1 is a first attempt at a semantic network for this context. It uses a simultaneous characterization of the options in terms of two variables: (i) the type of control adopted and (ii) the orientation of the control. System (ii) is redundant for the purpose of discriminating among the present examples, since all are uniquely specified in system (i); but it adds a generalization, suggesting other combinations of options to be investigated, and it specifies other features which we might be able to link up with particular features in the grammar.

2 Provisional version of a semantic network

This is the simplest form of such a network, specifying merely options and sub-options. It reads: "select threat *or* disapprobation *or* appeal *or* rule; *and either* object-oriented *or* person-oriented. *If* threat, *then either* conditional *or* unconditional", and so on. Numbers in parentheses indicate how these options relate to the examples that were given above.

Now there is probably no category of "threat" or "blackmail" or "object-oriented" to be found in the grammar of English. These are semantic not grammatical categories. But it may be possible to specify what are the grammatical realizations of semantic categories of this kind. For instance, "threat" is likely to be realized as a transitive clause of action with *you* as Goal, and with a verb of a particular sub-class as Process, in simple future tense. The combination of "disapprobation" and "person-oriented: action" leads us to predict an attributive clause type, in which the action that is being censured is expressed as the "Attribuend" (the Goal of the attribution) and the Attribute is some adjective of the attitudinal class. Thus the semantic options are relatable to recognizable features in the grammar, even though the relationship will often be a rather complex one.

A semantic option may, in addition, have more than one possible realization in the grammar. For instance, "threat" might be realized as a modalized action clause with *you* as Actor, e.g. *you'll have to stay indoors if you do that*. Where there are such alternatives, these are likely in the end to turn out to represent more delicate semantic options, systematic subcategories rather than free variants (see 6 below). But until such time as a distinction in meaning (i.e. in their function in realizing higher-level options) is found, they can be treated as instances of diversification. This is the same phenomenon of diversification as is found in the relations between other pairs of strata.

We have not expressed, in the network, everything that was included in the description of the forms of control; there is no reference yet to the category of "ownership", or to the fact that the disapproval is "moral" disapproval. It is not yet clear what these contrast with; they might be fully determined by some existing option. But they are expressed in the same way, by realization in linguistic forms, and there is no difficulty in adding them as semantic options once their value in the meaning potential can be established.

3 The semantic network as a statement of potential at that stratum

A network such as that in Figure 1 is a specification of meaning potential. It shows, in this instance, what the mother is doing when she regulates the behaviour of the child. Or rather, it shows what she **can** do: it states the possibilities that are open to her, in the specific context of a control situation. It also expresses the fact that these are **linguistic**

326

possibilities; they are options in meaning, realized in the form of grammatical, including lexical, selections.

These networks represent paradigmatic relations on the semantic stratum; so we shall refer to them as *semantic networks*. A semantic network is a hypothesis about patterns of meaning, and in order to be valid it must satisfy three requirements. It has to account for the range of alternatives at the semantic stratum itself; and it has to relate these both "upwards", in this instance to categories of some general social theory or theory of behaviour, and "downwards", to the categories of linguistic form at the stratum of grammar.

In the first place, therefore, we are making a hypothesis about what the speaker can do, linguistically, in a given context: about what meanings are accessible to him. In order to do this we need not only to state the options that are available but, equally, to show how they are systematically related to one another. This is the purpose of the system network, which is a general statement of the paradigmatic relations at the stratum in question, and therefore constitutes, at one and the same time, a description of each meaning selection and an account of its relationship to all the others – to all its "agnates", in Gleason's formulation.

From the network we can derive a paradigm of all the meaning selections. This is the set of well-formed *selection expressions* from the network in question, and the network asserts that these and no others are possible.

The network is, however, open-ended in delicacy. We take as the starting point the total set of possible meaning selections, and proceed by progressive differentiation on the basis of systematic contrasts in meaning. It is always possible to add further specification, but it is never necessary to do so, so we can stop at the point where any further move in delicacy is of no interest. For instance, if for the purposes of a particular investigation the social theory places no value on the distinction between different types of appeal in a control situation, there is no need to incorporate any subsystems of "appeal" into the semantic network.

We use the paradigm to test predictions about meaning selections that might be expected to occur. This can be illustrated from the same general context, that of parental regulation of child behaviour; but we will use a modified form of the network so that the illustration is kept down to a manageable size. Let us postulate the network of options in Figure 2.

327

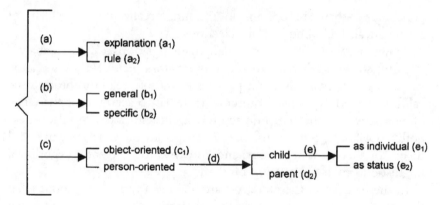

Figure 2   More generalized version of earlier network

This specifies that the following meaning selections occur:

$(a_1\ b_1\ c_1)$	$(a_1\ b_2\ c_1)$	$(a_2\ b_1\ c_1)$	$(a_2\ b_2\ c_1)$
$(a_1\ b_1\ d_2)$	$(a_1\ b_2\ d_2)$	$(a_2\ b_1\ d_2)$	$(a_2\ b_2\ d_2)$
$(a_1\ b_1\ e_1)$	$(a_1\ b_2\ e_1)$	$(a_2\ b_1\ e_1)$	$(a_2\ b_2\ e_1)$
$(a_1\ b_1\ e_2)$	$(a_1\ b_2\ e_2)$	$(a_2\ b_1\ e_2)$	$(a_2\ b_2\ e_2)$

We can construct a set of possible exponents, one for each:

$(a_1\ b_1\ c_1)$	playing in that sort of place ruins your clothes
$(a_1\ b_1\ d_2)$	grown–ups like to be tidy
$(a_1\ b_1\ e_1)$	it's not good for you to get too excited
$(a_1\ b_1\ e_2)$	boys who are well brought up play nice games in the park
$(a_1\ b_2\ c_1)$	all that glass might get broken
$(a_1\ b_2\ d_2)$	Daddy doesn't like you to play rough games
$(a_1\ b_2\ e_1)$	you might hurt yourself
$(a_1\ b_2\ e_2)$	you ought to show Johnny how to be a good boy
$(a_2\ b_1\ c_1)$	other people's things aren't for playing with
$(a_2\ b_1\ d_2)$	Mummy knows best
$(a_2\ b_1\ e_1)$	you mustn't play with those kind of boys
$(a_2\ b_1\ e_2)$	little boys should do as they're told
$(a_2\ b_2\ c_1)$	that tin belongs to somebody else
$(a_2\ b_2\ d_2)$	I told you I didn't want you to do that
$(a_2\ b_2\ e_1)$	you'll get smacked next time
$(a_2\ b_2\ e_2)$	you can go there when you're bigger

The paradigm seems to be valid. We have substituted just two types of control, "by rule" and "by explanation", each of which may be general or specific; and we have sub-divided "child-oriented" into the more significant system of "child as individual" versus "child as status".

As an example of a wrong prediction, if we kept the original (Figure 1) network, which had "child-oriented: child's action" versus "child-oriented: child himself", and showed this system in free combination with the four types of control, we should almost certainly have found gaps. It is difficult to see how we could have the combination "appeal" and "child's action"; one can disapprove of an action, or give rules about it, but can hardly appeal to it. The original network is thus wrong at this point, and would have to be rewritten.

Figure 3 is a rewritten version of it, corrected in respect of this error. In order to test it, we can write out the paradigm of meaning selections and for each one construct an example which would be acceptable as an exponent of it.

Here we have introduced two further conventions. The option "*either* child's action *or* child himself" depends on the selection of **both** "control type: positional" **and** "orientation: child"; there is an intersection at this point in the network. Secondly, this system is

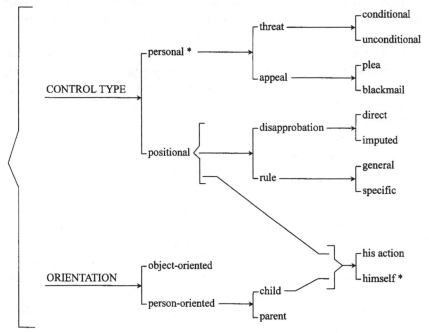

Figure 3 Revised version of Figure 1

characterized by the presence of an unmarked term, "child himself", indicated by the asterisk. An unmarked option is always unmarked "with respect to" some other option, here that of "personal" also marked with an asterisk. The meaning is: 'if the speaker selects the "personal" control type, then if the orientation is to the child it must always be to the "child himself"'. The unmarked option is that which must be selected if one part of the entry condition is not satisfied, some other feature being selected which then determines the choice.

4 The semantic network as realization of behaviour patterns

In the second place, as is shown by what was said above, the semantic network is an account of how social meanings are expressed in language. It is the linguistic realization of patterns of behaviour.

We have stressed at various points that a linguistic description is a statement of what the speaker can mean; and that "meaning", in its most general sense, includes both function within one level and realization of elements of a higher level. These "higher level" elements will, at one point, lie outside the confines of what we recognize as language.

In the sociological context, the relevant extra-linguistic elements are the behaviour patterns that find expression in language. It is convenient to treat these under two headings: social, and situational.

First, there are the specifically social aspects of language use: the establishment and maintenance of the individual's social roles, the establishment of familiarity and distance, various forms of boundary maintenance, types of personal interaction and so on. These are largely independent of setting, but relate to generalized social contexts, such as those of mother and child already referred to.

The social contexts themselves are in turn dependent for their identification on a social theory of some kind, for instance Bernstein's theories of socialization and social learning. From such a theory, we are able to establish which contexts are relevant to the study of particular problems. The behavioural options are specific to the given social context, which determines their meaning; for example, "threat" in a mother–child control context has a different significance from "threat" in another social context, such as the operation of a gang. This may affect its realization in language.

Secondly, there are the situation types, the settings, in which language is used. These enable us to speak of "text", which may be

330

defined as "language in setting". Here we are concerned not with behaviour patterns that are socially significant in themselves but with socially identifiable units – various kinds of tasks, games, discussions and the like – within which the behaviour is more or less structured. Mitchell's (1951) classic study "The language of buying and selling in Cyrenaica" provides an instance of a well-defined setting. The structure, in fact, may lie wholly within the text, as typically it does in a work of literature, or an abstract discussion; from the sociological point of view, these situation–independent uses of language are the limiting case, since the "setting" is established within and through the language itself.

The behaviour patterns that we derive from social contexts and settings are thus intrinsic to sociological theory; they are arrived at in the search for explanations of social phenomena, and are independent of whatever linguistic patterns may be used to express them. The function of the semantic network is to show how these "social meanings" are organized into linguistic meanings, which are then realized through the different strata of the language system. But whereas the social meanings, or behaviour patterns, are specific to their contexts and settings, their linguistic reflexes are very general categories such as those of transitivity, of mood and modality, of time and place, of information structure and the like. The input to the semantic networks is sociological and specific; their output is linguistic and general. The rationale for this is discussed in section 6 below.

This means that in sociological linguistics the criteria for selecting the areas of study are sociological. We investigate those contexts and settings that are socially significant, for instance those concerned with the transmission of cultural values. At the same time, it is not irrelevant that language has evolved in the service of social functions, so we may expect to take account of social factors in explaining the nature of language. There is therefore a clear **linguistic** motivation for studies of a sociolinguistic kind.

Here is an example drawn from a clearly defined setting, from the game of pontoon (vingt-et-un). This is a social context with closely circumscribed behaviour patterns, namely the rules of the game. These define what the participant can do. The semantic network does not describe the rules of the game; it specifies what are the verbalized options in play – what the participant "can mean", in our terms.

The form of play has been described by Bernard Mohan (1968), as part of an extremely comprehensive study in which he examines various possible methods in the relation of language and setting. Figure 4 is a semantic network showing the meaning potential for one move, by a player other than the bank.

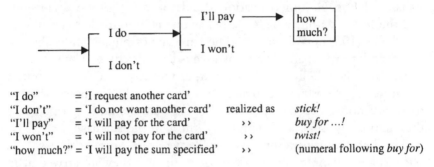

"I do"	= 'I request another card'		
"I don't"	= 'I do not want another card'	realized as	*stick!*
"I'll pay"	= 'I will pay for the card'	››	*buy for ...!*
"I won't"	= 'I will not pay for the card'	››	*twist!*
"how much?"	= 'I will pay the sum specified'	››	(numeral following *buy for*)

Figure 4   Network for move in pontoon

Now, having requested one card, the player has the option of requesting another. Is this an option in meaning, or merely a rule of the game? If we recognize it as part of the meaning potential, there is a recursive option in the semantic network (Figure 5).

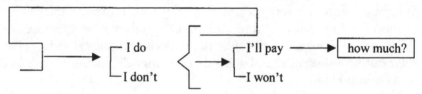

Figure 5   Pontoon move network showing recursive option

We might even think of extending this into the grammar: an example such as *buy for two, buy for two, twist, stick* would then form a single paratactic univariate structure. This would be somewhat uneconomical, though as a matter of fact there is some evidence in its favour. It would be uneconomical because we should have to build in to the grammar a number of special features associated with it: the absence of *and*, the possibility of interruption, and so on. The evidence for it is that the player does normally use the intonation pattern appropriate to co-ordination, e.g.

//3 buy for / **two** //3 buy for / **two** //3 **twist** //1 **stick** //

with the (normally non-final) tone 3 representing the **hope** that he will be able to request another card. The fact that the entire structure is not planned at the start is immaterial; this may be a general characteristic of univariate structures. It is interesting that in contract bridge many

332

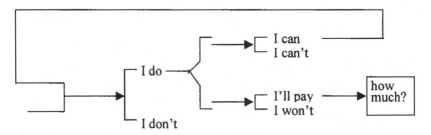

Figure 6   Revised version of Figure 5

players use this "non-final" intonation when bidding as a means of inviting their partner to make a higher bid. They distinguish

//3 three | **clubs** //'I want you to raise it'

from

//1 three | **clubs** //'and don't you go any higher!'

If we do recognize a recursive option in the semantics, we must also take account of the fact that the player has first to pass through the option "I can/cannot request another card", as in Figure 6. We add to this the condition that if on the third time round he still selects "I can" he must nevertheless proceed to "I don't", which is realized this time as *five and under.*

Here, then, there is some indeterminacy between the strata. Whether in fact we represented the whole of one "turn" in the semantic network would probably depend on the nature of the problem being investigated. But it is possible to do so, since the system can be reduced to a single complex expression of request.

It is, of course, the fall of the cards that determines whether the player has the **right** to request another card or not. But the conditions under which he may or may not do so are part of the rules of the game; they belong to a higher-stratum context. The semantics cannot specify what are the rules of the game.

Likewise we could make a flow-chart for another game setting, one that is reasonably closed (e.g. the bidding system of contract bridge), and construct an associated semantic network. For this it would be necessary to identify some unit that is appropriate as the domain of the semantic options. For pontoon, we suggested one turn; here it would probably be one bid. The semantics then specifies what is the set of possible bids. It does not specify the circumstances in which the player has the right to make a particular bid – still less those in which it would be a good one!

To summarize: grammar is what the speaker **can say**, and is the realization of what he **means**. Semantics is what he **can mean**; and we are looking at this as the realization of what he **does**. But it is "realization" in a somewhat different sense, because what he **can do** lies outside language (and therefore, as we expressed it above, semantics cannot tell us the rules of the game). Some of the behaviour potential, the "can do", can be expressed in sociological terms; not all, since not all language behaviour has its setting in identifiable social contexts, and much of that which has is not explainable by reference to the setting. In sociological linguistics we are interested in that part of language behaviour which **can** be related to social factors and stated in these terms. We examine areas which are relatively circumscribed; and we select those which are of intrinsic interest – noting at the same time, however, that the investigation of the socio-linguistic interface may also shed valuable light on the nature of language itself.

5   The semantic network as realized in the grammatical system

In the third place, the semantic network is the "input" to the grammar. The semantic network forms the bridge between behaviour patterns and linguistic forms.

We cannot, as a rule, relate behavioural options directly to the grammar. The relationship is too complex, and some intermediate level of representation is needed through which we express the meaning potential that is associated with the particular behavioural context. It is this intermediate level that constitutes our "sociological" semantics. The semantic network then takes us, by a second step, into the linguistic patterns that can be recognized and stated in grammatical terms.

In some instances, the semantic network leads directly to the "formal items" – to the actual words, phrases and clauses of the language. This is likely to happen only where there is a closed set of options in a clearly circumscribed social context.

Systems of greetings would often be of this kind. Figure 7 is a semantic network for a greeting system in middle-class British English. On the right are the items realizing the meaning selections; the colon is used *ad hoc* to show that these are on a different stratum.

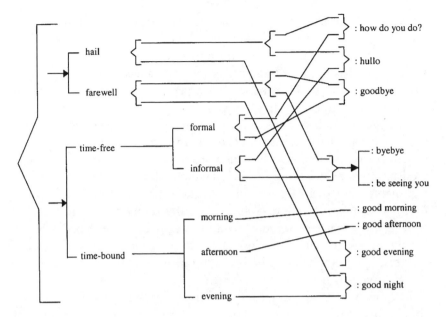

Figure 7 System network for greeting

[This display leaves out a number of factors, treating them by implication as behavioural (as "rules of the game") and not semantic. There are severe limitations on the use of time-bound forms, other than *good night*, as valedictions; they are used mainly in the conclusion of transactions, and are probably disappearing. The form *how do you do?* is used only in the context of a new acquaintance, a time-bound form being required in the formal greeting of old acquaintances. Such factors could be incorporated into the network, if they are regarded as part of the "meaning potential"; but for the present discussion it does not matter whether they are or not.]

In this instance, we can go straight from the options to the actual phrases by which they are realized, the "formal items" as we have termed them. There is no need for any intervening level of grammatical systems and structures.

A number of more specific social contexts, and recurrent situation types, are likely to have this property, that the formal items, the words and phrases used, are directly relatable to the options in the semantic network. Apart from games, and greetings systems, which have already been exemplified, other instances would include musical terms (*adagio*, etc.), instructions to telephone operators, and various closed transactions such as buying a train or bus ticket. If we ignore the fact that the formal items are in turn re-encoded, or realized, as phonological items ("expressions"), which are in turn put out as speech (or the equivalent in the written medium), these are rather like non-linguistic semiotic systems, such as those of traffic signs and care labels on clothing, where the meanings are directly encoded into patterns in the visual medium. There is a minimum of stratal organization.

In language such systems are rather marginal; they account for only a small fraction of the total phenomena. In order to be able to handle systems of meaning potential which are of wider linguistic significance we have to consider types of setting which, although they may still be reasonably clearly circumscribed, are much more open and also much more general. In sociological linguistics the interest is in linguistic as well as in social phenomena, and so we need to explore areas of behaviour where the meanings are expressed through very general features, features which are involved in nearly all uses of language, such as transitivity in the clause.

In other words, for linguistic as well as for sociological reasons we should like to be able to account for grammatical phenomena by reference to social contexts whenever we can, in order to throw some light on why the grammar of languages is as it is. The more we are able to relate the options in grammatical systems to meaning potential in the social contexts and behavioural settings, the more insight we shall gain into the nature of the language system, since it is in the service of such contexts and settings that language has evolved.

This is no more than to recognize that there is a *stratal* relation of the usual kind between grammar and semantics. In general the options in a semantic network will be realized by selections of features in the grammar – rather than "bypassing" the grammatical systems and finding direct expression as formal items.

We have exemplified this already in discussing the realization of semantic categories such as that of "threat". Let us return to this instance, and add further examples. The following are some possible expressions of "threat" and of "warning" as semantic options in a regulatory context:

I'll smack you		
Daddy'll smack you		
you'll get smacked		
I'll smack you	} {	if you do that again
Daddy'll smack you		if you go on doing that
you'll get smacked		

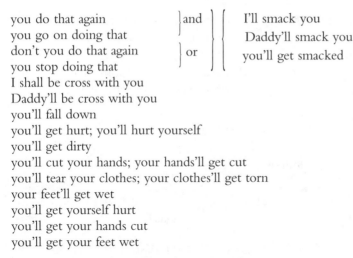

you do that again   ⎫ and   ⎫ ⎧   I'll smack you
you go on doing that   ⎬   ⎮ ⎮   Daddy'll smack you
don't you do that again   ⎭ or   ⎮ ⎩   you'll get smacked
you stop doing that
I shall be cross with you
Daddy'll be cross with you
you'll fall down
you'll get hurt; you'll hurt yourself
you'll get dirty
you'll cut your hands; your hands'll get cut
you'll tear your clothes; your clothes'll get torn
your feet'll get wet
you'll get yourself hurt
you'll get your hands cut
you'll get your feet wet

We suggested earlier, as a generalization, that "threat" could be realized by an action clause in simple future tense, having *you* either as Goal, or as Actor together with a modulation. We can now take this a little further, building up the network as we go.

The "threat" may be a threat of physical punishment. Here the clause is of the action type, and, within this, of intentional or voluntary action, not supervention (i.e. the verb is of the *do* type, not the *happen* type).

The process is a two-participant process, with the verb form a lexical set expressing "punishment by physical violence", roughly that of section 972 (PUNISHMENT) in Roget's *Thesaurus*, or perhaps the intersection of this with section 276 (IMPULSE). The tense is simple future. The Goal, as already noted, is *you*; and the clause may be either active, in which case the agency of the punishment is likely to be the speaker (*I* as Actor), or passive, which has the purpose of leaving the agency unspecified. It is not entirely clear whether, if the Actor is other than *I*, the utterance is a threat or a warning; but it seems likely that in *Daddy'll smack you* the speaker is committing another person to a course of action on her behalf, so we still treat it as "threat".

Figure 8   Network for agency in physical threat

Any one of these threats may then be accompanied by a condition referring to the repetition or continuation by the child of whatever he was doing, and here we can specify almost the entire form of the clause: action verb substitute *do that*, Actor *you*, Conjunction *if*, and either auxiliary of aspect (*go on*) or aspectual adverb (*again*).

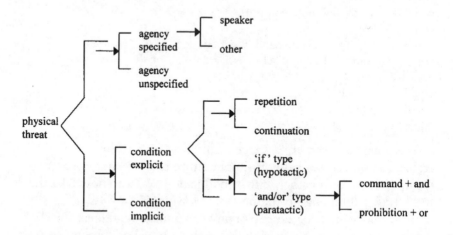

Figure 9 Network for physical threat

Probably all threats are conditional in this context, so the choice is between a condition that is explicit and one that is implicit. Note the alternative form of the condition – as an imperative clause (which must come first) in a paratactic: co-ordinate structure, either command with "and" or prohibition with "or". (The prohibition also occurs by itself as a form of regulatory behaviour, e.g. *don't you do that again!*; but that is left out here because it is not a threat.)

There are two other sub-categories of "threat" among the examples given. One has a relational clause of the attributive type, having as Attribute an adjective expressive of anger or displeasure (Roget section 900, RESENTMENT) and *I* or a committed other person as Attribuend. The other is an action clause with the action modulated by necessity (e.g. *must*, *have to*), *you* as Actor and a wide range of punitive states of which little more can be specified. Contextually the former constitutes a threat of mental punishment, the latter a threat of restraint on the child's own behavioural options.

Figure 10   Non-physical threat

Next, there is the distinct category of "warning". This also is inherently conditional; we have given only examples without condition but all of them could occur in an explicitly conditional form.

The warning specifies something that will happen to the child – something considered to be undesirable – if he does whatever it is he is being told not to do. The warning may relate to some process in which the child will become involved. Here the clause is of the "action" type; it is, however, always "superventive" – the child is involved against his own volition. The action in question may be one that is inherently unintentional, represented by a verb of the "happen" type; in this case the meaning is 'do involuntarily' and the voice is active (e.g. *fall down*). Otherwise, if the action is inherently intentional, with a verb of the "do" type (typically from a sub-set of Roget section 659 DETERIORATION, or section 688 FATIGUE), the meaning is 'have done to one, come in for' and the voice is non-active: either passive: mutative (e.g. *get hurt*) or reflexive (*hurt yourself*), according to whether or not some unspecified agency is implied that is external to the child himself.

Alternatively, the warning may specify an attribute that the child will acquire. Here the clause is relational: attributive, also in the mutative form (i.e. *get* rather than *be*), and the Attribute is an adjective of undesirable physical condition such as *wet, sore, tired, dirty* (in Roget section 653 UNCLEANNESS, section 655 DISEASE, section 688 or elsewhere).

In all these clauses, there is only one participant, and it is always *you*. This may be Actor, Goal or Attribuend; but it always has the generalized function of Affected.

So far it has been assumed that the warning relates to the child himself. But it may relate instead to a part of his body or an item of his **clothing** (e.g. *you'll cut your hands, your clothes'll get muddy*). And finally the consequence has been represented as something that will happen to the child (or, again, to his person) without any specified agency: *you'll fall down, you'll get dirty, you'll get hurt, you'll hurt yourself, you'll cut your hands, you'll tear your clothes*. (Note that the last two are still superventive; *you'll tear your clothes* means "your clothes will get torn", not "you will

339

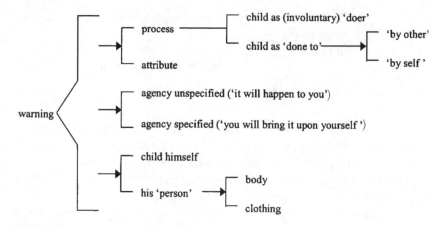

Figure 11   Network for warning

tear your clothes deliberately"; cf. *you'll hurt yourself*). But it may be represented instead as something which he will bring upon himself. In this case, the clause has the resultative form *you'll get your ...* (self, part of the body or item of clothing) *hurt*, *dirty*, *torn* etc.; here *yourself*, *your clothes* etc., function as Affected and *you* as Agent.

Figure 11 is the network of warnings at this point. In this network, we have shown the three options "process, or attribute; agency unspecified, or child's own agency; the child himself, or his person" as being independent variables. This asserts that all logically possible combinations can occur, including those formed with the sub-options dependent on "process" and on "his person"; there is a total paradigm of 4 × 2 × 3 = 24 meaning selections. But only some of these are given in the examples, and this illustrates once again the point made earlier, that the paradigm defined by a system network provides a means of testing for all possibilities. If, when the paradigm is written out, it is found that not all combinations can occur, the network needs to be amended.

Here it will be found that the primary options are in fact independent. But the sub-option of "child as doer, or child as done to", dependent on the selection of "process", turns out to be at least partly determined in all environments except one, that of "agency unspecified *and* child himself". In the environment of "child's own agency" it is fully determined – naturally: since the child is represented as bringing the consequence on himself, there is no distinction of how the process comes about. In the remaining environment, that of "agency unspecified *and* child's person", it is partly determined: the opposition "child as doer, or child as done to" is still valid, but the reflexive does not occur. This again is to be expected, since it is not the child himself but his person that is involved.

The final version of the network, showing both threat and warning, is therefore as in Figure 12.

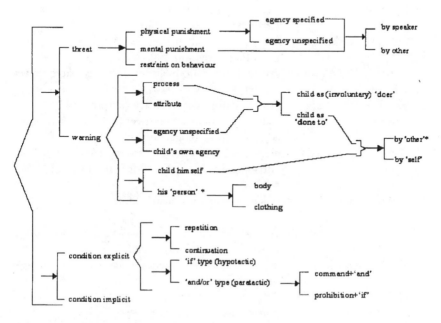

Figure 12   Revised network for threats and warnings

6   Semantic networks etc. grammar

In the last section we have been looking at the semantic network from the point of view of its relation "downwards", seeing how we get from it into the grammar. In particular, we were considering the question to what extend the grammatical and lexical properties of the sentences used by the speaker in the speech situation – in our example, the mother regulating the behaviour of her child – can be "predicted" from a semantics of behaviour, a semantics based on social context and setting.

Let us make this a little more specific by writing out the realization statements associated with the features in the network of threats and warnings:

1 threat	clause: declarative
2 physical punishment	clause: action: voluntary (*do* type); effective (two-participant): Goal = *you*; future tense; positive; verb from Roget section 972 (or 972 ^ 276)
3 agency specified	voice: active
4 agency unspecified	voice: passive
5 by speaker	Actor/Attribuend = *I*
6 by other	Actor/Attribuend = *Daddy*, etc.
7 mental punishment	clause: relational: attributive: Attribute = adjective from Roget section 900
8 restraint on behaviour	clause: action; modulation: necessity; Actor = *you*
9 warning	clause: declarative
10 process	clause: action: superventive (*happen* type)
11 attribute	clause: relational: attributive: mutative; Attribute = adjective from Roget section 653, 635, 688 etc.
12 agency unspecified	clause: non-resultative; Affected (Actor, Goal or Attribuend) = *you/yourself* or some form of "your person"
13 child as "doer"	voice: active; verb of involuntary action; Actor = *you*
14 child as "done to"	voice: non-active; verb of voluntary action; from Roget section 659, 688 etc.
15 child's own agency	clause: resultative; Agency = *you*; Affected = *yourself* or some form of "your person"
16 child himself	Affected = *you/yourself*
17 by "other"	voice: passive: mutative
18 by "self"	voice: reflexive
19 his "person"	Affected: some form of "your person"
20 body	"your person" = *your* + part of body
21 clothing	"your person" = *your* + item of clothing
22 condition explicit	clause complex; clause (1 or ß): action: effective; anaphoric: verb substitute = *do that*; Actor = *you*
23 repetition	aspect: *again*
24 continuation	aspect: *go on/stop* (in negative) ... *ing*
25 "if" type	clause complex; hypotactic: clause ß conditional: *if*
26 "and/or" type	clause complex: paratactic: clause 1 imperative
27 command + "and"	clause 1 positive; *and*
28 prohibition + "or"	clause 1 negative (including form with *stop*); *or*
29 condition implicit	(————————)

Two points suggest themselves immediately. The first is that in this particular example we have been able to generate a great deal of the grammar in this way. We have given some specification of many of the principal grammatical features of the clause or clause complex: paratactic complex with *and* or *or*, hypotactic complex with *if*, or simple clause; the clause type in respect of transitivity (action clause, relational clause etc.); whether positive or negative, in some cases; and something of the selection in mood and in modality and tense. We have also determined the items occupying some of the participant functions, especially the pronouns *I* and *you*. We have not been able to specify the exact lexical items, but we have been able to narrow down many of them fairly closely by using the notion of a lexical set as exemplified in Roget's *Thesaurus*. A significant portion of the clause, in this instance, can be related to its "meaning" in terms of some higher level of a socio-behavioural kind.

Secondly, the features that we have been able to specify are not marginal areas of the grammar but are categories of the most general kind, such as mood and transitivity. Nearly every clause in English makes some selection in these systems, and in this instance we were able to relate the choice to the social function of the utterance. For example in the "warning" network, where the mother makes explicit the nature of the consequence that will follow if the child continues or repeats the undesired behaviour, we were able to get to the core of the English transitivity system, and to see what lay behind the choice of active or passive or reflexive verb forms. We did not go very far in delicacy, and certainly there would be limits on how far we could go. But we did not reach those limits in this example, and in a more detailed study it would be possible both to extend and to elaborate the semantic network.

It must be made clear, however, that the example chosen was a favourable instance. We would not be able to construct a socio-semantic network for highly intellectuated abstract discourse, and in general the more self-sufficient the language (the more it creates its own setting, as we expressed it earlier) the less we should be able to say about it in these broadly sociological, or social, terms. Of the total amount of speech by educated adults in a complex society, only a small proportion would be accessible to this approach. Against this, however, we may set the fact that the instances about which we **can** say something, besides being favourable, are also interesting and significant in themselves, because they play a great part, almost certainly the major part, in the child's early language learning experience. They are in fact precisely those settings from which he learns his language, because both language and setting are accessible to his observation. He can see what language is being used for, what the particular words and structures are being made to achieve, and in this way he builds up his own functionally based language system. So even if with some adults the types of social context that are most favourable for socio-linguistic investigation become as it were "minority time" usages this does not mean they are unimportant to the understanding of the language system.

★ ★ ★

We need to say a little more here about the relation between the semantics and the grammar, or level of linguistic form. We began with an example of the simplest type of relation, one of *bypassing*, where the semantic options could be as it were wired directly into a small set of words and phrases, without our having to take account of any intervening organization. This situation does arise, but only rather marginally. In the more usual and more significant instances we have to go through a level of grammatical organization, in order to show how the semantic options are put into effect. This in fact is the definition of grammar – the term "grammar" being used, as always, for the level of linguistic form, including both grammatical (in the sense of syntax and morphology) and lexical features. Grammar is the level at which the various strands of meaning potential are woven into a fabric; or, to express this non-metaphorically, the level at which the different meaning selections are integrated so as to form structures.

We also express the grammar in networks, such as those of transitivity, mood and modality. The question is, then: what is the relation between the networks of the grammar and the semantic networks that we have been illustrating here?

We already have the notion of *preselection* between networks, in relating grammar and phonology. For instance, in the phonology of English there is a system of tone, which we show as a network at the phonological stratum. But the selection in this system is fully determined by the grammar: there is "preselection" of the phonological options. The pattern is rather complex, because there is no one-to-one correspondence between options in the grammar and options in the phonology; a large number of different grammatical systems are realized by means of selection in the phonological system of tone. But it is not impossible to find them out.

Between semantic and grammatical networks the same relation obtains. The grammatical options are the realizations of the semantic ones. Again, there is no one-to-one correspondence: there is what Lamb calls "interlocking diversification" (many-to-many). But, again, the relations can be stated: the selection of a given option in the

344

semantic network is realized by some selection in the networks of the grammar. Very often more than one grammatical feature has to be preselected in this way in order to realize one semantic choice.

Where there are alternatives, such that a given semantic option is realized **either** by this **or** by that set of features in the grammar, these are often determined by the environment. For instance, the grammar of personal medicine – the language used to describe one's ailments – is not the same in the doctor's consulting room as it is in a family or neighbourhood context: compare *I've got the most terrible tummy ache* with *my digestion's troubling me* as realization of some meaning such as "intensity and location of pain". The environment is generally the higher-level environment, either the immediate paradigmatic environment – that is, the other options that are being selected at the same time – or the social context as a whole.

Sometimes however the alternatives are not environmentally conditioned but appear initially as free variants, as simple alternative grammatical realizations of one and the same semantic choice. It may be that they are; it would be rash to pretend that there is no free variation in language. But in the grammatical realization of semantic options the alternatives usually turn out to represent more delicate semantic choices. In other words, there **is** a difference in meaning, although it is not so fundamental as the grammatical distinction would suggest (and therefore one begins by putting the two grammatical forms together as "having the same meaning"). This is a very general and important phenomenon and we have already seen it illustrated more than once. For instance, three forms of conditional threat:

> if you do that again I'll smack you
> do that again and I'll smack you
> don't do that again or I'll smack you

When one has made the point that all these are possible realizations of the semantic option of "threat", one tends to be satisfied and to stop there, saying merely "these all have the same meaning". But they have not the same meaning. They are all threats, and they represent the same semantic options **up to a point** – which means, here, up to a particular point in delicacy. But they are not free variants. There **is** a more subtle distinction between them, and this is shown by the fact that they realize more delicate sub-options in the semantic network.

One question that has been left out of consideration here is this. Is it necessary to recognize "semantic structures"? In explaining grammar, and in moving from grammar to phonology, we cannot account for everything simply by letting the grammatical networks wire into (preselect in) the phonological ones and delaying the formation of structures until the phonological stratum. We have to set up structures at the grammatical level. This is simply because, for most of the options in the grammar, it is not possible to specify their "output" directly in terms of phonological options. We can do this in the case of those realized by tone, cited above; these are realized directly by choices in the phonology. But we could not handle, for example, the grammatical system of mood in this way. For this, as for the majority of grammatical systems, we have to state the realization first in terms of configurations of functions – that is, of grammatical structures.

Similarly, in going from phonology to phonetics we set up phonological structures, such as syllable and foot, which are likewise configurations of functions.

By analogy, therefore, the question arises whether we need semantic (in Lamb's terms "semological") structures as well.

It is important to emphasize here that structure is defined as the "configuration of functions", since this is abstract enough to cover semantic structure if such a thing is to be formulated. The shape of a structure may vary; we may express it lineally or hierarchically or simultaneously. But all such shapes have in common the property of being configurations of functions.

The same would apply to semantic structures. Lamb suggested at one time (see Fleming 1969) that semantic structures were networks, grammatical (syntactic) structures were trees (hierarchical), morphological structures strings (linear) and phonological structures bundles (simultaneous). In the present account, grammatical and phonological structures are both trees composed of hierarchies of strings; but it remains the case that semantic structures need by no means have the same shape as structures at any other level. All that the term "structure" implies is that there will be some configurations of functions at that stratum, and that these will realize the meaning selections, the combinations of options in the meaning potential.

The combination of system and structure with rank leads to a fairly abstract grammar (fairly "deep", in the Chomskyan sense) and enables us to specify fairly accurately in theoretical terms – though not of course in rule-of-thumb terms – just how abstract it is. In principle, a grammatical system is as abstract (is as "semantic") as possible given only that it can generate integrated structures; that is, that its output can

346

be expressed in terms of functions which can be mapped directly onto other functions, the result being a single structural "shape" (though one which is of course multiply labelled). This is already fairly abstract, and it may be unnecessary therefore to interpose another layer of structure between the semantic systems and the grammatical systems given the limited purpose of the semantic systems, which is to account for the meaning potential associated with defined social contexts and settings.

On the other hand, it is possible that one might be able to handle more complex areas of behaviour by means of a concept of semantic structure. It may be, for instance, that the study of institutional communication networks, such as the chain of command or the patterns of consultation and negotiation in an industrial concern, might be extended to a linguistic analysis if the semantic options were first represented in semantic structures – since the options themselves could then be made more abstract. Various complex decision-making strategies in groups of different sizes might become accessible to linguistic observation in the same way. But for the moment this remains a matter of speculation. Sociological semantics is still at a rather elementary stage, and the contexts that have been investigated, which are some of those most likely to be significant in relation to socialization and social learning, are fairly closely circumscribed and seem to be describable by direct preselection between semantic and grammatical systems.

7 Uses of language, and *macro-functions*

These networks are what we understand by "semantics". They constitute a stratum that is intermediate between the social system and the grammatical system. The former is wholly outside language, the latter is wholly within language; the semantic networks, which describe the range of alternative meanings available to the speaker in given social contexts and settings, form a bridge between the two.

Like any other level of representation in a stratal pattern, they face both ways. Here, the downward relation is with the grammar; but the upward relation is with the extralinguistic context.

If we have tended to stress the instrumentality of linguistics, rather than its autonomy, this reflects our concern with language as meaning potential in behavioural settings. In investigating grammar and phonology, linguists have tended to insist on the autonomy of their subject; this is natural and useful, since these are the "inner" strata of the linguistic system, the core of language so to speak, and in their immediate context they are "autonomous" – they do not relate directly outside language. But they are in turn contingent on other systems which do relate outside language. Moreover we take the view that we can understand the nature of the inner stratal systems of language only if we do attempt to relate language to extra-linguistic phenomena.

Let us turn for a moment to the language of the young child. At an early stage it is possible to postulate very small protolinguistic systems in which the "grammar" relates directly to the function for which language is being used. For example, in an item such as *byebye mummy* the structure is a direct reflection of the meaning of the utterance: the structure is a configuration of Valediction and Person, and it represents just such options in the child's potential for verbal interaction with his parents. Here grammar and semantics are one.

At this stage the child has acquired a small set of functions or uses of language within each of which he has certain options, a range of meanings open to him. These meanings are expressed through rather simple structures whose elements derive directly from the functions themselves (Figure 13). Here there is no need to distinguish between functions and uses of language or between grammar and semantics.

This situation might represent an early stage in the evolution of human language, we do not know.

In the individual, as time goes on, the situations and settings in which language is used become more varied and complex, and the meaning potential associated with them becomes richer. We can no longer write a simple description in which the structure relates directly to the function and "function" equals "use".

Instead, the picture is something like this. We could list indefinitely many "uses of language". There are innumerable types of situation in which language plays a part, and innumerable purposes which the speaker makes language serve. It is a useful exercise just to think about these and attempt to categorize them from one's own experience; but this will not by itself provide a systematic basis for understanding grammar. Some of these uses can be systematized into social contexts and settings with at least partially specifiable behaviour potential associated with them. There are uses of language, such as those we have been exemplifying, in which some definable range of alternatives is open to the speaker and these are realized through language. Here we can specify, up to a point, the set of possible meanings that can be expressed.

Form of representation	Functions	Options (with their realizations)	Structures	Items
		a ⟶ ⎡b ('if *a*, then ⎣c either *b* or *c*')	n ⎡q ('*n* consists of *p* ⎣p followed by *q*')	(text)
Example	interactional	vale- diction ⟶ ⎡general (1) + V ⎣ V: *byebye* ⎣bedtime (2) V: *nightnight* address ⟶ ⎡non-personalized ⎣(3) ⎣personalized (4) + P: *mummy*	(i) Valediction (ii) Valediction + Person	byebye (1, 3) nightnight (2, 3) byebye mummy (1, 4) nightnight mummy (2, 4)

Figure 13 Structure and function in a child's interactional utterance

Note: This example is invented. For a genuine example drawn from the description of a child's linguistic system, see Halliday (1973).

In a few instances these are like the meanings of the child's protolanguage, in that they can be related directly to grammatical structures, as is often the case in the language used in games. Sometimes we would not even need to postulate a structure – we could go straight to the actual words and phrases used. Normally, however, we have to relate the meanings first to systematic selection within the grammar, from which the grammatical structures are then in turn derived.

That is to say, we relate the semantic systems to grammatical systems, regarding them as a form of "pre-selection", as illustrated in the last section. A choice in the semantics "pre-selects" an option in the grammar, or a set of such options.

But what is the nature and origin of the grammatical system? Grammar is the level of formal organization in language; it is a purely internal level of organization, and is in fact the main defining characteristic of language. But it is not arbitrary. Grammar evolved as "content form": as a representation of the meaning potential through which language serves its various social functions. The grammar itself has a functional basis.

What has happened in the course of the evolution of language – and this is no more than a reasonable assumption, corresponding to what happens in the development of language in the individual – is that the demands made on language have constantly expanded, and the language system has been shaped accordingly. There has been an increase in the complexity of linguistic function, and the complexity of language has increased with it. Most significantly, this has meant the emergence of the stratal form of organization, with a purely formal level of coding at its core. This performs the function of integrating the very complex meaning selections into single integrated structures. The way it does this is by sorting out the many very specific uses of language into a small number of highly general functions which underlie them all (cf. Chapter 14 of this volume).

We thus need to make a distinction, in the adult language system, between "function" and "use", a distinction which was unnecessary in the case of the child's proto-language. With the child, each use of language has its own grammar from which we can (in the idealized original state of the system) fully derive the structures and items employed in that use. Our example *byebye mummy!* could be described entirely in terms of the grammar of the "interactional" use of language.

With the adult this is not so. He may use language in a vast number of different ways, in different types of situation and for different purposes; but we cannot identify a finite set of uses and write a grammar for each of them. What we can identify, however, is a finite set of functions – let us call them "macro-functions" to make the distinction clearer – which are general to all these uses, and through which the meaning potential associated with them is encoded into grammatical structures.

These "macro-functions" have been recognized for a long time in "functional" theories of language (for this reason we retain the name "function" for them). But by using the notion of a grammatical *system*, we can show more clearly how they are embodied in the grammar, where they appear as relatively discrete areas of formalized meaning potential, or in other words relatively independent sets of options. We refer to these as "functional components" of the grammar.

Three principal components may be recognized, under the headings *ideational*, *interpersonal* and *textual*. The ideational component is that part of the grammar concerned with the expression of experience, including both the processes within and beyond the self – the phenomena of the external world and those of consciousness – and the logical relations deducible from them. The ideational component thus has two sub-components, the *experiential* and the *logical*. The interpersonal component is the grammar of personal participation; it expresses the speaker's role in the speech situation, his personal commitment and his interaction with others. The textual component is concerned with the creation of text; it expresses the structure of information, and the relation of each part of the discourse to the whole and to the setting.

We now need to relate these "macro-functions" to what the adult does with language. (By "adult" we mean someone who has developed the mature language system, as distinct from the child's proto-language referred to earlier.) The adult engages in a great variety of uses of language, which in themselves are unsystematized and vague. We attempt to impose some order on them, by identifying social contexts and settings for which we can state the meaning potential in a systematic way. But he does not have a different grammar for each of them. He has just one and the same grammar, which is called on in different ways and of which now one part is emphasized and now another.

The macro-functions are the most general categories of meaning potential, common to all uses of language. With only minor exceptions, whatever the speaker is doing with language he will draw on all these components of the grammar. He will need to make some reference to the categories of his own experience – in other words, the language will be **about** something. He will need to take up some position in the speech situation; at the very least he will specify his own communication role and set up expectations for that of the hearer − in terms of statement, question, response and the like. And what he says will be structured as "text" − that is to say, it will be operational in the given context. These are properties of nearly all acts of communication; by and large, every text unit is the product of options of these three kinds. It is not surprising, therefore, that these form the fundamental components of the grammar, since it is grammar that turns meanings into text.

This is just another way of saying that it is through its organization into functional components that the formal system of languages is linked to language use. When we say that realization of meaning potential − of options in semantics − is through the preselection of options in the grammar, this means in fact preselection within these functional components. The options in semantics depend on social context and setting, which are extra-linguistic factors. The options in the grammar are organized into general components which are internal to language. But these components are based on "macro-functions" that are extra-linguistic in origin and orientation. In the evolution of language as a whole, the form of language has been determined by the functions it has to serve.

We said earlier that input to semantics was social and specific, whereas its output was linguistic and general. We can now try and clarify this a little. It was not meant to imply that the social contexts and settings themselves are highly specific categories; in fact they are very general. But the range of alternatives which each one offers, the meaning potential available to the speaker in a given situation type, tends to be specific to the situation type in question; whereas the grammatical options through which the meaning selections are realized are general to the language as whole. In other words, the move from **general** social categories to **general** linguistic categories involves an intermediate level of **specific** categorization where the one is related to the other. An 'interface' of more specific features is needed to bridge the gap from the generalizations of sociology to those of linguistics. Let us attempt a pictorial representation of the general scheme (Figure 14).

An amorphous and indeterminate set of "uses of language" is partly reducible to generalized situation types, the social contexts and behavioural settings in which language functions. For any one of these situation types, we seek to identify a meaning potential, the range of

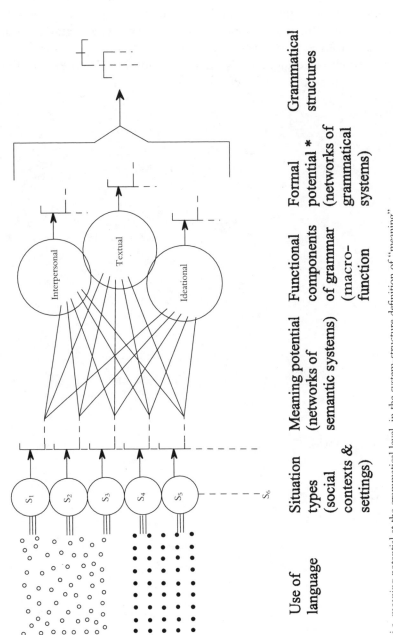

| Use of language | Situation types (social contexts & settings) | Meaning potential (networks of semantic systems) | Functional components of grammar (macro-function) | Formal potential * (networks of grammatical systems) | Grammatical structures |

* i.e. meaning potential at the grammatical level, in the system–structure definition of "meaning"

Figure 14 Situation types, functions and macro-functions

alternatives open to the speaker in the context of that situation type; these are expressed as semantic networks within which meaning selections are made. The options in the semantic network determine the choice of linguistic forms by "preselection" of particular options within the functional components of grammar. These grammatical options are realized in integrated structures formed by the mapping on to one another of configurations of elements derived from each of the "macro-functions".

Chapter Sixteen

THE HISTORY OF A SENTENCE
(1992)

We are here to celebrate history: the history of a great institution, since its foundation so many years ago. When we say the University of Bologna has a history, we are speaking from the standpoint of today, looking back over the events that led up to this present stage of its existence. Our own celebration is itself, of course, an event in the University's history. It is an event of a particular kind: a semiotic event, as is appropriate to an institution devoted to semiosis. And as an event in history, it also has a history of its own. Semiotic events are no different, in this respect: they have their own history, of other events that have preceded them in time and in some way contributed to their happening and to their significance.

I am concerned, in this paper, with the history of a semiotic event. But not a large event, like an international symposium; a small event, like a sentence, that is accessible to micro-analysis. So I shall think of it rather as a semiotic act, or **act of meaning** as I have generally called it. And this needs two brief comments, by way of explanation. First, it is obvious that the distinction between semiotic acts and other, by implication non-semiotic, acts is a problematic one. I would start from Vygotsky's view, of semiotically mediated activity, as distinct from tool-mediated activity (Vygotsky 1978: ch. 4); but I shall not engage with this here, and shall assume that we can treat certain phenomena as semiotic acts. Secondly, I take it that not all semiotic acts are realized in language, either directly, or indirectly via other levels of semiosis (denotatively or connotatively, in Hjelmslev's terms); but I shall take account only of those that are. So by "act of meaning" I am referring to just that subclass of semiotic acts that are semantic – that is, made of specifically linguistic meanings; and this entails that all such acts are realized in the form of wordings.

First published in *Bologna: la Cultura Italiana e le Letterature Straniere Moderne*, Vol. 30, edited by Vita Fortunati. A. Longo Editore, 1992, pp. 29–45.

Why should we be interested in the history of a semiotic act? Perhaps I could suggest a number of motivating factors – although they are all ultimately related, because they have to do with the changed and changing significance of semiotic processes in our late twentieth century post-humanistic society. The first is the familiar point that this is an information society, in which we spend much of our time and energy exchanging, not goods-&-services as in earlier times, but information. Any exchange of information is constituted of acts of meaning; that is what information is. Already control of the means of information is as vital as control of the means of production; and those who are planning our future lives for us say that the heart of a twenty-first century city will be its teleport, where no trains or aircraft come and go, but only messages. Semiotic events have assumed an importance far greater than they ever had before.

Any event, however small, has a history. An event that is manifested in the goods-&-services mode, like milking a cow, or building a house, is presaged by sequences of both micro and macro events that have made it possible and determined its significance; and we can adopt the same perspective towards an event in the semiotic mode, where the act performed was an act of saying rather than an act of doing. Of course, we have not usually troubled ourselves with the history of relatively trivial events such as these. To become part of history (to "get into the history books", as we put it), an event has to be in some sense catastrophic: winning a battle, for example. But – and this will lead in to the second reason for inquiring into the history of an act of meaning – in the meantime the concept of history itself has changed. On the one hand, marxist and populist historians replaced the single, catastrophic historical event with quantitatively massive classes of events that constituted major economic, political and sociocultural divides: whole groups of people starting to milk cows (*husbandry*) or build houses (*settlement*). And then the media took over. Whereas in the past it had been the historians who constructed history, by transforming doings into meanings (histori-ography) and thus providing each recorded event with a **history** of prior conditions relevant to its interpretation, in our time it has been the media who construct history, by the simple process of deciding what is news. When the University of Bologna comes to celebrate its second nine hundred years, historians of the twenty-ninth century will have a different task: the question of what is a historical event will have been decided for them, and their task will be that of interpretation, or reinterpretation, of what they find in their libraries of print or tape or film.

But what will they find there, from our present age? What is it that the media construe as "news" and so turn into the so-called "facts of history"? There are the familiar reports of catastrophes in the other, popular sense of the term: plagues, riots, floods, explosions and the like – semiotic transformations of non-semiotic events. But alongside these, and probably outnumbering them if we could find a sensible way of counting, are those items of news where the event itself is a semiotic one, and the report is thus a second order semiotic act: not a saying about a doing but a saying about a saying. A fiction about a fiction – both English and Italian used to refer to reporting and romancing by the same term (English *novel*, Italian *novella*). Here is part of a recent newspaper report, headlined "Free heroin may not cut drug crime":

A NSW Government body has warned that the supply of heroin to registered addicts may not lead to less drug-related crime.

The Bureau of Crime Statistics and Research surveyed 225 property offenders in NSW prisons and, of those who were also heroin users, nearly 90 per cent said the main reason for committing the offence was money to support their drug habit.

Last week the Premier, Mr Wran, suggested that the forthcoming national drug summit should discuss giving heroin to addicts to combat drug trafficking and the crimes addicts commit to support drug habits.

The bureau's report implies that a decrease in the price of heroin if it was offered free to addicts may result in a decrease in property crime. However, in Great Britain and other countries where such attempts had been made to control the heroin market, this had not occurred because the price of the drug had not dropped.

Among the survey's findings another is that heroin was the most popular drug consumed by the users questioned, with nearly 90 per cent saying they used it heavily or regularly.

On average, the heroin addicts used seven grams of the drug per week but some reported using as much as 35 grams.

Cash purchase was the main way of obtaining heroin and those among the user group spent between $100 and $10,000 a week on the drug, which has a street price of about $350 per gram. The average weekly heroin habit costs $2,000 and in annual terms about $100,000.

A large number of heroin users were found to have already committed property offences before they used heroin. This is in spite of the commonly held view that heroin addiction is the cause of criminal behaviour.

It was found, however, that as a heroin user's consumption increased, so did the likelihood that they would be involved in armed robbery and break, enter and steal offences.

About 78 per cent of heroin users cited property crime as their main source of income.

Break, enter and steal was the most prevalent crime among the heroin users and only 9 per cent of users had never committed a burglary.

The average number of armed robberies committed annually by each heroin user surveyed was eight, while the average number of burglaries was 143.

Although nearly 70 per cent of the heroin users had abstained at least once from regular drug use, nearly half had never sought or received any drug treatment.

The authors of the bureau's report, Mr Ian Dobinson and Ms Pat Ward, expressed concern over the lack of treatment available for the 'substantial number' of drug-dependent people in NSW jails. Apart from in-house psychiatrists the Department of Corrective Services provides no drug treatment.

While the report's major finding that there is a strong economic link between heroin use and property crime has been well known for some time, this is the first detailed study in Australia to examine the link between crime and addiction.

By Paul Bailey, *Sydney Morning Herald*

The reported event is itself a report, introduced by "A New South Wales Government body has warned that . . ."; and most of the text is a historicization of its content (e.g. "The bureau's report implies that . . .", "While the report's major finding that . . . has been well known for some time"). But much of that content is itself already a transformation of other semiotic acts; e.g. "nearly 90 percent [of heroin-using property offenders] said . . .", "About 78 per cent of heroin users cited . . ."; and the one paragraph that is not about the report begins "Last week the Premier, Mr Wran, suggested that the forthcoming national drug summit should discuss . . .". It is not really surprising that, in an age when so much of the socio-economic process takes a semiotic form, the events out of which history is constructed should be largely semiotic events, meanings rather than doings. But in order to be history, such events must also have a history: not only a **context of situation** – a higher level environment of social processes and relations – but also a history of prior semiotic events, of the same order of existence as the events themselves. There is, so to speak, a history of meaning, and the interpretation of any act of meaning must rest on other such acts that have preceded it and created the conditions for its occurrence.

So the third reason for being concerned with this topic is one that is enshrined in the conception and the practice of semiotics itself, and has to do with ways of understanding. As part of the present ideological transition the structure of knowledge is itself undergoing significant change, from the discipline-based construction that has dominated in the twentieth century, with its taxonomy of academic compartments defined by their subject matter like psychology and economics and linguistics, towards a construction that is based rather on themes: common questions and motifs that ignore divisions of content and take in any subject matter that is relevant to their concerns. The model for these thematic constructs is mathematics, which evolved around the theme of measuring things and has always stood out as an anomaly in our subject-based institutional structures; while early in the present century **structuralism** emerged as a thematic concept of this kind. Again not unexpectedly, in our information era, perhaps the most powerful concept to have developed thematically in this way, in recent years, has been that of understanding phenomena as systems and processes of meaning: namely **semiotics**.

The phenomena themselves may be of various kinds. In the natural sciences the exchange of meanings serves as **model** and **metaphor** for processes in biology, chemistry and physics. Where the processes we are concerned with are social ones they are often **directly constituted of** acts of meaning, in the form of the discursive practices of those involved; so we gain access to these processes through the analysis of discourse. And this is where the history comes in. If – to take Lemke's (1985) work as an example – an act of meaning in the field of science education, a particular intervention by the teacher in a physics class, can be seen to play a part in constructing a **thematic system**, which in turn is carrying a particular ideological load, then this means it must have a history. No such thematic **framing** (Thibault 1986) would be possible unless the act in question was part of some historical process, and specifically of a semo-historical process in which any given semiotic event has been preceded by others that created the conditions for its occurrence and for its range of possible interpretations.

In one sense this is simply the notion of intertextuality: the thematic system is an intertextual construct, and once it is recognized that any discursive formation must depend on complex **multi-accented** intertextual relations, such as are implied by notions of register and genre, then the historical principle is established. There is always a context in which any act of meaning comes into being. But the intertextual thematic system, or the **genre** in Martin's work (Martin 1986a), is in principle timeless. It is a network of semiotic relationships within which a given text, or a given act of meaning, is positioned and displays its proportionalities – shared features, resonances, dissonances, polysemies and the like. At some point, however, we have to introduce the arrow of time, because the extremely complex dialectic of system and process (as well as Markovian effects within the process itself) ensures that the meaning potential is constantly changing. What can be meant, at any moment in the discourse, is very much a product of history: of what could be meant, and what has been meant, before.

Of course when a semiotic event, or an event of any kind, is transformed into history, it acquires a posterity as well as an antecedence. If we treat the foundation of the University of Bologna as an event of history, it becomes a fulcrum: we have thereby defined not one category of related events but two, those leading up to the foundation and those subsequent to it. Since this particular event left an output, a lasting trace in the form of an institution, the subsequent history concerns itself with that. Similarly, an act of meaning may leave a trace in the form of a written or otherwise recorded text; and this likewise acquires a history: it may be read once and put aside, or reread, or re-enacted in performance (e.g. a dramatic text), and thus accumulate a series of different micro and even macro contexts. Other acts do not leave any institutional trace – among acts of meaning, most spoken ones are of this kind; so that their subsequent history is more like the ripples on a pond after one stone has been thrown in.

Here I am not using "history" in the sense of what occurs subsequent to a given focal event. By the "history of a sentence" I mean its prior conditions, those which led up to its production in speech or writing. And this perhaps requires one further disclaimer, at least for linguists: in referring to the prior history of a sentence I am not talking about its formal derivation. Linguists sometimes refer to the operation of generating a sentence by using the apparatus of a particular model of grammar as the "history" of that sentence. Such a sequence of logical steps is part of the interpretation of the derived form (for example, in a systemic grammar the paths taken through the network explain its paradigmatic relationship to all other forms); but it is not history. It is an analytic sequence using the metaphor of time, but it has no time track of its own. To put it another way: I am concerned with conditions that lead up to instantiation, not with the phenomenon of instantiation as such.

I think we can identify four strands or dimensions of history that are forerunners of every sentence, by virtue of which it becomes an act of meaning. Let me refer to these as (1) the intertextual, (2) the developmental, (3) the systemic and (4) the intratextual. I will try to describe, and illustrate, each of these in turn.

1 Intertextual history

Intertextual history is the temporally prior set of acts of meaning to which the given act of meaning makes allusion. This is familiar in literature and philology as *allusion* and in semiotics as *intertextuality*, and as such needs no exemplification (for a richly contextualized discussion see Threadgold (1986: passim and esp. pp. 21–2, 24, 31, 33, 35 and 44–5). In Threadgold's words (21–2): "At the moment of textual encounter, besides the text in focus, other discourses – discourse from other discursive formations which depend on the subject's positioning in other practices – cultural, educational, institutional – are always in play". (Note that this subsumes both text and subject; cf. my second heading below). What I want to do is just to examine the historical aspect of being "in play" from the point of view of linguistics – a linguistics that is situated within a general social-semiotic framework.

It is a commonplace of the history of literature that specific literary genres arise which have their own history within a culture, a history of growth, maturation and decay. There are familiar metaphors such as "golden" and "silver" periods. For example in Chinese poetry the lyric form known as *shi* is seen as growing in pre-Tang times, reaching maturity (a golden age) in Tang, and subsequently decaying – becoming imitative, rigid and formulaic. Leaving open the question whether the growth-&-decay model is generally applicable, we can trace a history of some kind in many functional varieties of a language, at least those that come to be in some sense institutionalized.

Let me take the example of scientific English. We can write a history of it (Bazerman 1988); and we can situate a particular text in some time zone of that history with a significant probability of being right – the longer the text, of course, the greater the probability, but even a single sentence may carry a rather clear signature of the semantic style characteristic of a particular period. For example:

> Hence increase of temperature, at the same time as on one account it increases the absolute quantity of heat in an elastic fluid, diminishes the quantity on another account by an increase of pressure.

We note that the sense of 'how hot?' has been represented nominally as *quantity of heat*, and likewise the sense of 'become hotter' as *increase of temperature*; and that these are entities which act on each other, and on another entity *increase of pressure*. The way they act on each other is by 'causing to become greater' and 'causing to become less', realized verbally as *increases* and *diminishes*. Historically this falls somewhere between an earlier semantic style in which *temperature* would have been nominalized in this way but not *increase of temperature*, at least not as Actor in a clause of this kind; and a later style in which *increase* would more probably have been *causes an increase* (later still: *is the cause of an increase*), and likewise *causes a diminution*. This suggests the nineteenth century, and earlier in the century rather than later. It is in fact from John Dalton, *A New System of Chemical Philosophy*, which was published in 1827.

The sentence carries with it its history at all levels, up to as far as we can pursue it along the chain of realization – up to the level of ideology, if we follow Martin (1986a). A physicist could locate it at its place in the history of knowledge. But that is a level of interpretation that is specific to this variety; whereas every text creates meaning at the semantic and lexicogrammatical levels. Obviously, this sentence is significant only as part of its text; and any one sentence may be untypical; but being untypical can be defined by reference to being typical, and what is typical is itself defined for a moment in history.

Typical, of course, does not imply univocal; the typical text is a polyphony, and often a cacophony, of voices – but this too can be as much the property of a single sentence, once we use our understanding of grammar to reveal it.

For this we will need a rich **grammatics**, an interpretative model of wordings and meanings which is based on – and explicitly problematizes – the concept of **realization** (cf. Threadgold 1986: 33). This is the only means of animating all levels of semiosis both **within** and **outside** language (the distinction may disappear in the process) while encompassing the contextual parameters of the text: who are acting in the given semiotic encounter, what they are enacting, and how the enactment is **semioticized** (the **tenor**, **field** and **mode** of a systemic theory). These concepts in turn enable us to introduce and operate with the mediating category of "register" as the concrete manifestation of intertextuality, and therefore of this aspect of history. This is not a taxonomic category; *a register*, like *a dialect*, is a useful fiction to live by, but it is a fiction – a more or less stable, and sometimes institutionalized, concatenation of semantic motifs which may at any

362

time (and typically will, in society as we know it) embody tensions, contradictions, and conflicting voices (Kress 1985).

It is in this sense that we can talk productively about the register of scientific English, to refer to a complex set of semantic motifs, and their lexicogrammatical realizations, that emerge historically as a recognizable semantic style. We know it when we see it. But the same theoretical perspective forces us to recognize that these motifs do not constitute some mythical organic unity (though they may, through the power of language, create a world which then gives the appearance of organic unity) but represent – not in any direct way, but through that same chain of realizations – the heterogeneous components that make up the socioeconomic order within which the scientific ideology arose. By examining the grammatical history of the favourite scientific clause as it evolved from Newton onwards, we see emerging a form of discourse which is highly explicit in its construction of argument (experimentation, formulation of general principles, logical steps in reasoning, and so on) and by the very same grammatical tokens highly implicit in its construction of content – so privileging the expert and perpetuating an intellectual elite (Halliday 1988a; Lemke 1990b; see also M. A. K. Halliday, *Collected Works*, Volume 5, Part 3).

This aspect of history – the intertextual one – is to the fore when we are considering institutionalized registers such as the discourse of science, political rhetoric, pop lyrics and the like. Here the accumulating body of related texts, clearly set apart by their context, form strong intertextual bonds through the closely shared experience of those who produce and consume them. Hence the semiotic history of the individual interactant tends to be subordinated to, or incorporated into, the history of the whole *speech fellowship* (Firth 1957d: 186–7). Even here, of course, the creation and interpretation of text is constrained by the individual's linguistic ontogeny; and this leads me on to my second strand, that of ontogenetic or developmental history.

2 Developmental history

Each interactant in an act of meaning has his or her own individual history as a **meaner**; including at one end of the scale the experiences, semiotic and other, that are unique to that individual, and at the other end the universals of human semiosis development – protolanguage ("child tongue") before language (mother tongue), speech before writing, generalization before abstraction and so on. In between these extremes are the shared experiences of particular communities: different social groups or sub-cultures within which children learn the linguistic construction of received reality.

The history that is unique to an individual is of interest in so far as we can learn from it about general principles of semogenesis. So when Nigel, at age two years and one month, says

Catch that dragonfly on Pauline's green toothbrush!

we may be amused at it, because it is not usual to hunt dragonflies with toothbrushes, nor – if you are doing – does it seem particularly relevant what colour the toothbrush is or who it belongs to; but it scarcely seems to deserve serious attention. However, if placed in its developmental context (this one is part of a longitudinal study of one child), almost any sentence will illustrate some significant points. The present one reveals, in its grammar, something of the ontogeny of clause construction (transitivity and mood) and of nominal group construction (modification); and displays a semantic system in which the distinction between descriptive and defining, as functions of the modifying elements, is not clearcut. Features like these emerge as part of its history.

We can also learn from this example something of the ontogeny of reality construction if this is on our agenda. But when we move up to this level we are more likely to want to focus on history that is shared among the members of a social group. In her paper on the ontogenesis of ideology, Ruqaiya Hasan investigates the development of the concept of "work" in early childhood and shows how a child's semantic feature network for *work* as something that excludes what women do in the home is constructed out of exchanges such as this one (Hasan 1986: 132–3):

Alison:	Is Pop home?
Mother:	No. They're all out. They're all at work.
Alison:	Bob and Mark are working.
Mother:	Yes, Bob's at work. Mark's at work. Everybody's at work.
Alison:	I not at work.
Mother:	No, you're only little.
Alison:	You's at work?
Mother:	I don't work. I look after you. ... Who'd look after you if Mummy went to work, eh?

Alison is then three years and five months, and this little exchange becomes part of the history of any subsequent discourse in which she engages, as speaker or listener, that is concerned with work. Now since Hasan finds comparable passages with many of the other mother–child dyads in her sample, in which the mother is building up a negative image of housework and child minding (not **real** work, boring, tiring etc.), she concludes that this is an aspect of the development history of all children growing up in this particular sociocultural context – a modern Australian city – and that the mother who says *I don't work. I just look after you.* has herself been through such a history in the course of her own childhood.

This is to look at the history of a sentence from the standpoint of its place in the transmission of ideology. This is indeed how ideologies are transmitted; not just as discrete components, such as the concepts of work, but rather as complex constructions – constructions that are typically discordant and rich in internal conflicts but function for the members of the group as coherent systems of beliefs and values. Such constructions are semantic ones: they are constituted out of the meaning potential of language, as instantiated in informal spontaneous discourse, and they depend on certain universal features of human development, and specifically language development. By these I do not mean concrete universals like the order of acquisition of grammatical elements, but the abstract principles underlying the development of every human being as one who can mean. These are principles such as: from protolanguage to language – children first construct a sign system like that of other species (as far as we know), without a grammar, and then transform it by introducing a distinct level of semiosis, a lexicogrammar; from micro-functions via macro- to meta-functions – meaning becomes simultaneously a mode of action, of reflection and of information, and thus every clause has a threefold grammatical structure; from generalization through abstraction to metaphor – these forming the foundation, respectively, of spoken language (embodying commonsense knowledge), written language (educational knowledge) and technical language (specialized knowledge).

So the developmental history of a sentence is the prior semiotic experience of those who enact it, as performers or receivers; and this ranges from experience that is unique to the individual, through that shared by a group, to that which is common to the human species as a whole. But in interpreting this experience we have had to refer, throughout, to features which pertain to language considered as a system: categories of transitivity and mood, for example, or lexico-semantic networks, metafunctional categories and so on. And these also have a history, which I will turn to next.

3 Systemic history

Individuals grow, mature and die; developmental history is a history of growth. Systems evolve; systemic history is of an evolutionary kind. Behind any sentence lies the evolution of the semantic systems and the lexicogrammatical systems (syntax, morphology, vocabulary) that have gone into making it up.

Let me take another example from scientific English – but this time from a school science textbook (year 6, age 11–12):

> This experiment will let you make some more observations about the
> direction in which water moves through a thin plant wall.
> The Process Way to Science, TPS book C, p. 55

All the grammatical properties of this sentence have evolved as part of the history of the English language. For example, in the structure of the nominal group: the sequence of nouns, as in *plant wall*; the embedding of prepositional phrases and clauses with defining function in postmodifier position, as in *some more observations [about [the direction [in which ...]]]*; the morphology, both Anglo-Saxon and Græco-Romance; the technical vocabulary, e.g. *observation, experiment, plant wall*; the grammatical metaphor, as in *make observations, the experiment will let you ...*; the verbal group complex *let ... make*; the tense *will let*; and so on. All these are instances of systemic categories within the overall system network of English grammar.

Each can be approached historically. To take the example of tense: here the writer has used the simple future, realized analytically as *will + let*. In Modern English this forms part of an iterative system which can generate tenses of considerable semantic complexity (I shall give an example in the next section). These forms evolve in speech, not in writing, so our access to their history is limited; but on the basis of the written evidence it is possible to construct some picture of how the system has been evolving since the earliest known pattern from some 1200 years ago (Strang 1970). This suggests an expansion, along particular lines, of the meaning potential associated with the location of processes in time one relative to another.

Why do such evolutionary changes take place? This raises, obviously, the question of the nature of historical explanations; and historians of language have been discouraged from asking such questions since cultural explanations went out of favour. There is good reason why they did: it is futile to focus on particular changes in the system of a language and try to relate them piecemeal to the history of society. But it is not futile – indeed it is highly effective – to relate changes in one part of the grammatical system to changes in other parts of the system over the same period of time, because such an overall view helps us to trace and to understand the history of prevailing semantic styles. This in turn can give us considerable insight into the fashioning of semiotic framing structures and into the development of ideologies (compare the example of scientific English given earlier).

It should be made very clear, in the light of current debate in semiotics, language and ideology, that to talk of the grammatical system is not to imply that meanings are somehow "fixed" or "given out there", or that the thematic and ideological constructions are manifested item by item in the outward forms of the grammar. To refuse to attend to the wording of language on the grounds that some linguistic theories are reductionist or "totalizing" is simply irresponsible – yet another pretext for refusing to engage seriously with language. On the contrary, there is no possibility of understanding these higher-level semiotic processes except by attending to the lexicogrammatical processes of which they are constituted. What is now urgent is that we should properly problematize the fundamental relationship (recognized in post-Saussurean linguistics as "realization") that articulates these various levels of the semiotic act.

While stressing the systemic dimension of history, however, as a coda to this part of the discussion (and in transition to the next and final heading) we should be reminded that the part played by the system in the history of any particular act of meaning is variable. Many sentences are stored readymade; they are more or less formulaic for the speaker and for the listener, and any given instance of their occurrence harks back to previous instances of the same wording rather than being engendered afresh by choosing within the system. Examples from English are:

> Take it or leave it!
> I couldn't believe my ears.
> It's a contradiction in terms.
> He doesn't know what he's talking about.
> Not by any stretch of the imagination.
> You can't change human nature.
> You must keep your eye on the ball.
> etc.

Of course these items are still located within the system and derive their meaning ultimately by semantic proportionality in the usual way; but their immediate source is the trace of earlier occurrences. (This is sometimes seen as a form of intertextual effect; but it is actually rather different. Intertextual potential is strongest where the act of meaning exploits the full resources of the system; it tends precisely to be weakened where the act of meaning is locked into a formula, since this inhibits the **search** for other semiotic input.)

4 Intratextual history

The school science text from which I quoted above contains, at intervals across two pages of text and illustrations, the following three sentences:

In this topic you will experiment with solutions and a thin wall made from plant material . . .

This experiment will let you make some more observations about the direction in which water moves through a thin plant wall . . .

Then try to explain your observations by using your hypothesis about the movement of water through plant walls.

Note how the grammar of this text unfolds in time: *a thin wall made from plant material* becomes *a thin plant wall*; *water moves through* [*a wall*] becomes *the movement of water through* [*plant walls*]. These are not likely to occur in the reverse sequence. Compare the following chain of expressions taken from an article in *Scientific American*:

[the mechanism by which] glass cracks
[the stress needed] to crack glass
as a crack grows
the crack has advanced
will make slow cracks grow
speed up the rate at which cracks grow
the rate of crack growth
[we can decrease] the crack growth rate [1000 times]
(T. A. Michalske and B. C. Bunker, 'The fracturing of glass',
Scientific American, December 1987)

If we focus on the last of these we can see that it has an intratextual history: the wording (*decrease*) *the crack growth rate* has evolved step by step from the original *glass cracks*. *Crack growth rate* is a new semiotic entity that has been created by the flow of the discourse. Or rather: it has not been created by the flow of the discourse; it has been created by the grammatical system of English catalysed by the flow of the discourse. The systemic history of the English nominal group and the

368

instantial history of this particular text converge to produce a wording that functions to package the information as required by the argument at that particular point in the construction of the text.

This kind of text dynamic is not simply a feature of planned written discourse. Here is an edited version of a passage of spontaneous conversation I noted down years ago; the labels show the tense selected at the verbal group:

	TENSE
Can I use the synthesizer?	
Well I'm afraid we *use* it ourselves in the morning	present
What, every morning? *Are you using* it now?	present in present
Yes, 'fraid so.	
How about this afternoon? Are you *going to be using* it then?	present in future in present
No. But this afternoon's no good.	
Why not?	
It*'s going to be being tested*.	present in future in present
Come off it! It*'s been going to be being tested* for ages.	present in future in past in present
It*'ll've been going to've been being tested* every day for about a fortnight soon.	present in past in future in past in present

The first part shows a typical build-up of tenses from a simple one-term tense choice, here present, *we use it*, to tenses of two and three terms: *are you using it, are you going to be using it* – a sequential pattern that is very characteristic of dialogue. Although in this particular instance the temporal sequence was from simple to complex, tenses of up to three terms are all very frequent and do not need a textual precursor; it would be perfectly normal to begin a conversation with *are you going to be using this machine this afternoon?* But tenses of four and five terms are much rarer, and usually need a text history of this kind to lead up to them – especially a dialogue, which is often a kind of semiotic *folie à deux* leading to all sorts of grammatical extravagances.

Of course, the relevance of intratextual history is not confined to instances such as these; they merely serve to underline its potential significance. Any act of meaning has a history along this dimension. The exception, of course, would be one that initiates a text. Clearly the concept of **intratextual** history implies that there is a point where a text begins, whereas in many registers at least we would find it hard to identify text boundaries. There are two relevant considerations here, however. One is that a text boundary is established semantically and in the lexicogrammar by cohesion: if a sentence is accessible from another, later sentence by some cohesive relation then it can be concluded that the two fall within the same text, and such cohesive patterns in fact constitute an important aspect of this dimension of history (Hasan 1984c). The other is that of transitional probabilities: if the grammar of a language is represented as a probabilistic system, as I would consider it to be, then the intratextual history of any sentence is the perturbation of its inherent probabilities by the selections made earlier in the text (as in the tense example above). The boundary of a text is then the frontier across which such effects do not obtain.

Text A

September 11, 1986

Dear tenant

IF YOU JUST WANNA HAVE FUN …

Come to *your* MOONCAKE NITE THEME PARTY next Saturday. That's September 20 – from 7.30p.m. until the wee hours!!

A sneak preview of the exciting line-up of activities includes:
    * Mr/Ms Tenant Contest
    * Find *Your* Mooncake Partner
    * Pass the Lantern Game
    * Bottoms Up Contest
    * Blow the Lantern Game
    * Moonwalking Contest
    * DANCING
    * PLUS MORE! MORE! MORE!

For even greater fun, design and wear your original Mooncake creation, and bring your self-made lantern passport!

But don't despair if you can't because this party is *FOR* you! Lantern passports can be bought at the door.

Just c'mon and grab this opportunity to chat up your neighbour. Call yours truly on *ext. 137* NOW! Confirm you really wanna have fun!! Why – September 20's next Saturday.

See you!

Public Relations Officer

P.S. Bring your camera to "capture" the fun!

Perhaps then we can think of the history of an act of meaning in terms of these four dimensions. It is unlikely, of course, that all these strands of history will be significant in any one instance; hence they are difficult to exemplify in relation to each other. Nevertheless let me try. In principle we could choose a sentence from any realm of experience, in any interpersonal setting and with any rhetorical force; I take one from a text (see Text A) that illustrates a well-known contemporary political phenomenon, the "disneyfication" of western man. (The targeted victim is typically male.) I shall focus on the last three lines actually consisting of four written sentences:

> Just c'mon and grab this opportunity to chat up your neighbour. Call yours truly on *ext. 137* NOW! Confirm you really wanna have fun!! Why – September 20's next Saturday.

Let me try to offer a brief sketch of its history, taking these four dimensions in the reverse order to that in which I introduced them.

Intratextually: there must be a **history** for the cohesive *this* in *this opportunity*, namely *the party* referred to throughout. But there are also a number of other antecedents: the repetition of *you wanna have fun*, the repetition of the date, the expression *yours truly* (the text has begun as a letter, so this functions as a coy variant of 'the writer'), and the way in which the mood and transitivity choices chime with those of the first paragraph: imperative + material: action in the first clause, declarative + relational: time in the last. The focal passage is obviously climactic (cf. the NOW!); if read aloud as a commercial, it would have the prosodic and paralinguistic features of the final sell.

Systemically: the passage derives from the **core** grammar of late-twentieth-century English in the Disneyland dialect. It combines a very simple grammar (no clause or clause complex structures that would not be found in the speech of a two-year-old) with bureaucratic vocabulary (*opportunity*, *confirm*), mixed with colloquialisms (*grab*, *chat up*) and garnished with comics-style orthography (*c'mon*, *wanna*). The interpersonal flavouring is that of condescension (*just*, *really*, *why* ...!).

Developmentally: this dialect has no native speakers (as far as I know!), so it has been learnt as a second dialect; both writer and readers must be presumed to be at least adolescent, because of the grammatical metaphor in *grab this opportunity to* .... Since the dialect functions as a trade jargon the writer has learnt it, perhaps under instruction, in the course of professional training. It allows no **play** for individual variation, so there is no trace of the writer's own developmental history up to that point.

371

Text B

30.8.86

Dear tenant

Celebrate Mooncake Nite With Us On September 20!

Buy your lanterns now! Because come September 20, they will be your "passport" to our Mooncake Nite at the Silks Lounge/Poolside on level 5. From 7.30 pm onwards!

Mooncakes, Chinese tea and pomelos will be served. So, do have an early dinner. There will be a Mr and Ms Tenant Contest where points will be awarded for *originality, presentation, appearance and talent*. All Mr and Ms Tenant hopefuls, please complete and return the attached form to the Concierge by *September 12*.

Prizes will also be given to the best "moonwalker" (as in dancing), the winners of the Bottoms Up Contest (with Chinese tea, naturally) and other fun games. Remember to bring your camera, lah!

Make sure *you* come. Call me at *ext. 137* to confirm your coming and please do so by *September 12*. You can count on our Mooncake Nite to be lots of fun! Just don't forget to bring your "passports!"

Yours sincerely

Public Relations Officer

Intertextually, there is an immediate intertextual reference to another text enacted two weeks earlier (Text B), both specifically in the wording (e.g. to *call me at ext. 137 to confirm your coming*) and in the general reference to the same future event; note, however, that the earlier text is in a mixed dialect, only partly disneyfied. Beyond this, there is intertextual resonance with countless other preceding texts in this dialect having comparable contexts of situation and culture; with particular items like *happy hour* (recalled by the present *have fun*). Behind these again lay texts in other, related registers: primarily perhaps television commercials, Disney story books and cartoons, and office routine such as appointments diaries.

What this brief historical sketch brings out – and a great deal more could be said about this example – is a semiotic act that looks at first sight like an impossible farrago of unrelated and partially conflicting features: some childhood ones, some "childist", some adult commercial and some adult professional. But that reveals the text for precisely what it is: an act of meaning addressed to adults endowed with minds like children, the assumption being that the off-duty executive (and the *tenant* that is being addressed is tenant of an *executive residence*) relaxes by regressing to childhood. Presumably the regression is only temporary; although in view of the well-known observation that people tend to behave the way they are treated (and that includes the way they are treated semiotically), perhaps what we are seeing is the regression of a whole culture into early adolescence, where it can then destroy itself with its arsenal of dangerous toys.

Clearly much of what I have been saying, and illustrating, would form part of any critical approach to text from a social-semiotic standpoint. But it does require one condition: that our interpretative resources should be solidly grounded in what I call ***grammatics***: a theory of grammar within a realizational framework – grammar being the systemic powerhouse where meanings are ultimately made.

But in choosing this particular perspective, of the "history of a sentence", I had two further considerations in mind. One was that it seems to me important, when we are dealing with discourse, to be aware of its temporality; and this not only in the familiar sense, that a text unfolds itself in time (the linearity of the text process), but more deeply, also, in the sense that meaning is itself a historical process. Meanings are made by people who have meant before; they relate to prior acts of meaning; and their source is a meaning potential that has been transmitted, as a metastable system (one that persists by constantly changing, in interaction with its environment), over a very long time. The impact of a text is dependent on its location in this complex semo-history, at the intersection of the various dimensions of that history where we ourselves are located when we enact it or hold it up for investigation.

The second consideration was a more practical one. It has often been observed (I have laboured the point myself) that one of the shortcomings of semiotic debate, much of which purports to be about discourse, is that very little of it actually engages with the text. This is partly because of a continued reluctance to base the study firmly in grammatics – on the pretext that this can lead to a sterile formalism, whereas meaning is "not just words", the meanings are "located in the reader" and so on. No doubt it is easy to point to examples of excessive concern with linguistic forms; but it is perverse to throw away the most powerful tool just because you have found someone else misusing it. It must also be recognized, however, that it takes a great deal of time to analyse a text – and still more time to present one's analysis. One could write a book about almost any text that is of interest and still not exhaust what is worth saying about it. So most of the time we find ourselves citing single sentences; and this narrowing of focus has serious limitations and dangers. One way to lessen and overcome these is to locate the sentence in its semiotic context of system and process; and that means construing for it a history. Only if we know what went before an act of meaning can we reasonably claim to judge its effect on what came after it.

And last of all, if I may end as I began: we are here to celebrate nine hundred years of continuous discourse, all of it building on that which has gone before. This is a quite remarkable piece of semohistory, and we can hardly avoid adopting a historical perspective on a time-enriched occasion such as the present one.

Chapter Seventeen

THE ACT OF MEANING
(1992)

If I had been choosing a title after finishing this paper, instead of before writing it as one always has to do, I should probably have sought a wording that was more suggestive of the power of language, because this was the motif that tended to emerge most strongly as I wrote. Ideally, perhaps, I should have needed to introduce this second motif alongside the original wording, so as to bring out the inevitable connection between the two. The power of language is vested in the act of meaning.

Many years ago, I wrote somewhere that the act of meaning is a social act; and so it is. It is also a biological act; and it is also a physical one. But these components are related, in a logical and also in a historical sequence. The history of western thinking, in the centuries following Galileo, often seems like a struggle to come to terms, one by one, with these differing and increasingly complex types of phenomena: first the physical, then the biological, then the social; and it seems to have taken three or four generations to crack each new code.

You may well object that nothing could be more complex than the phenomena of the physical universe. Certainly in understanding them physicists are involved in quite staggering efforts of integration and of abstraction; and we are no nearer "the end of physics" now than we ever were – or than the end of linguistics or the end of any other branch of knowledge. Or, if we are, this is, as Schaffer (1991) has convincingly shown, a cultural closure not a physical one: a limitation on our own ways of knowing, not on what there is to be known. But in another sense, physical systems-&-processes – that is, physical phenomena construed as the domain of systematic knowledge – are simpler to

First published in *Georgetown University Round Table on Languages and Linguistics: Language, Communication and Social Meaning*, edited by James E. Alatis. Washington, DC: Georgetown University Press, 1992, pp. 7–21.

apprehend, because we are able to interpret them purely as physical; whereas biological systems-&-processes are not just biological – they are also physical. And when we turn to social phenomena, these are not just social; they are social, and biological, and physical. The consequence is that, by this time, we no longer know an **instance** when we meet one. When one is confronted with social processes, what is a fact any more?

And this problem of instantiation – of the relation between observable phenomena and the system that, in some sense, "lies behind" them – becomes still more formidable when we reach phenomena of the fourth type, namely those of meaning, or semiotic ones, which are (the pattern is familiar!) at once also social, and also biological, and also physical. While we may criticize Saussure for having failed to solve this problem (that of the nature of *parole* and its relation to *langue*), we should rather give him credit for having problematized it in the first place, as Culler did (1977). This failure to construe the link, in semiotic systems-&-processes, between the *instance* – the act of meaning, in other words – and the *system* (prototypically, a language) has haunted our late twentieth-century linguistics, which has oscillated wildly between system and instance, creating a massive disjunction between the two. In the 1960s, if you dared to mention the text, you were dismissed as "data-oriented"; while in the 1980s if you ventured to refer to the system, you were attacked for "totalizing". But combining being data-oriented with totalizing is a useful recipe for understanding things; we sometimes call it scientific method.

So there is a gradient here, a cline of difficulty, as we move from physical to biological to social to semiotic systems; as we move along this cline we get further away from anything we can recognize as effects following from causes, causes leading to effects. But there is another cline, that of ever-increasing risk, as we move towards the more distinctively human processes. Already in the eighteenth century people felt threatened when scientists applied the methods of the physical sciences to biological systems, systems with life in them; and they – or their descendants – became more uncomfortable some three or four generations later when these same methods began to be applied to social systems, which have not only life but also value. Small wonder, then, that many react with dismay when the domain of science starts encroaching on those which are the most human systems of all, namely semiotic systems – which have not only life, and not only value, but also meaning.

It is threatening, no doubt, to discover that there are processes beyond our conscious control in those very acts of consciousness by which our own selves are most clearly defined. Linguists often start their papers with the formula "You're not going to like what I say"; no doubt this is partly because they are hoping to establish a claim for originality, as one has to do in order to gain tenure in these difficult times, but we don't hear this, as far as I can tell, from scientists or mathematicians – because it is also a spell, a call for protection against the dangers of apprehending the forces of meaning. The danger lies in **relating** the instance to the system, because that is the source of the power. You are safe in studying the system (as linguists traditionally did), because you do not reveal it at work in the form of text. You are safe in studying the text, as a philologist or student of style or of discourse, because you do not let it display the power of the system. But if you put the two together the text is revealed for what it is, an act that has meaning because it is not *sui generis*; it is the actualizing of a potential, by means of processes that are patterned – and therefore, in an important sense, predictable. So there is an emotional gradient here as well as an intellectual one. We resist being told how much of what we "choose" to say is programmed, either as readymade pieces of wording, as Pawley (1985) made clear, or in the probability profiles revealed by large-scale quantitative studies (Nesbitt and Plum 1988; Halliday and James 1993). Yet no child could learn a mother tongue if it was not characterized by massive regularities of these two complementary kinds.

Now a physical system is a physical system. But a physical **theory** is a semiotic system: a "system of related meanings", as Lemke (1990) describes it. We gain our understanding of physical phenomena – of phenomena of any kind, in fact – by using the special powers of a semiotic system to transform them (cf. Matthiessen 1991b). The seventeenth-century "founders of modern science" were aware of this power that language had, and were inclined to be somewhat suspicious of it, believing that phenomena were often distorted in the process of being transformed into meanings. Hence they took seriously Francis Bacon's cautions against what he called the "idols of the marketplace" (*idola fori*), one of the four kinds of idol that he felt impeded scientific thinking. The *idola fori* were the misconceptions that arose, in the words of Dijksterhuis (1961, 1986: Vol. 4, 184, p. 398; see also Vol. 5, Part 3),

> ... from the thoughtless use of language, from the delusion that to all names there must correspond actually existing things, and from the confusion of the literal and the figurative meaning of a word; ...

The physical scientists' defence against this semiotic idolatry turned out to be one of the ironies of modern semohistory. While they were committed to producing a "language of science" that would be free of ambiguity and metaphor (cf. Coetzee 1981), Newton and his successors developed a form of discourse that was almost certainly the most highly metaphorical the world had yet encountered, with all the ambiguity that connotes. But the metaphor they were aware of was metaphor in its canonical sense, the metaphoric use of the lexis; whereas the metaphor they created in their own discourse is a metaphor that lies in the grammar (Halliday 1988a; Martin 1990a; Halliday and Martin 1993a).

Meanwhile in the centuries that followed the notion of the power of language tended to recede into the background. The scientists got on with the business of doing science; and the linguists got on with the business of describing language, within their own definition of the task – for example, in England, the study of phonetics and spelling reform. For Saussure the only significance of an act of meaning – or "act of speaking", *acte de parole* – was as a piece of evidence for the system, not as a constitutive act. It is striking, therefore, to find that this motif, that of the power of semiotic processes, has re-emerged as a major theme in the late twentieth century. It has re-emerged, in fact, from a number of different directions, so that it is not easy to present a brief yet coherent account. But let me try and enumerate some of the work that I am familiar with (which is, obviously, only a small portion of the whole). We may perhaps identify five general headings: (1), language as means of access; (2), language as ideology; (3), language and social inequality; (4), language as metadiscourse (in the construction of reality); (5), language as model (for understanding systems of other kinds).

1 Language as means of access

The notion that language provides a means of access to particular domains, or spheres of social action, has been familiar since the 1960s: from the work of Gumperz and Hymes, in relation to functional varieties or "registers", and from Bernstein's work in relation to codes. I shall come back to Bernstein under another heading; the common factor here is that the mode of access is some variety of a language. Opening up access, in this semiotic sense, is now seen as a central task of language education. Jay Lemke's important book on science education is called *Talking Science*, and subtitled '*language, learning, and values*'. Britain now has a National Curriculum, and the teacher education materials on *Language in the National Curriculum* by Ronald Carter and his colleagues put in the foreground the learner's access to knowledge through language. Most "linguistic" of all are Australian genre-based curricula, especially those produced for the New South Wales Disadvantaged Schools Program under the leadership of J. R. Martin. These last are based explicitly on the view that in order to access knowledge of any kind you have to control the semiotic resources which construe that knowledge; and furthermore, that only by redesigning the curriculum around those resources – the generic construction, the discourse semantics and the lexicogrammar of the registers involved – can educators hope to open up to the learners the various discourses that make it possible to participate in the democratic political process (Lemke 1990a; Carter *et al.* 1990; Christie *et al.* 1991–92; New South Wales Disadvantaged Schools Program 1990; Matthiessen 1993b).

Work of this kind would not easily derive from, or reconcile with, a correspondence notion of language, the view that language is doing no more than reproducing a cognitive model of experience. Rather, it assumes a constructivist interpretation, whereby language actively construes human experience, from the "commonsense" constructions of the everyday mother tongue to the highly elaborate edifices of the disciplines as they are taught and researched in schools and universities. In this perspective, the grammar of every natural language is (among other things) a theory of human experience; it is through our acts of meaning that we transform experience into the coherent – though far from consistent – patchwork that we learn to project as "reality".

2 Language as ideology

In other words, activities such as these presuppose a Whorfian view of language, at least in terms of my perceptions of what Whorf was saying, which have always been different from the received interpretation of Whorf's views in the United States. Let me quote from a recent paper by Alan Rumsey, entitled 'Wording, meaning, and linguistic ideology' (1990):

> In common with Whorf, I believe that the best way to study the relationship between language structure and other aspects of social life is by looking for what he called "fashions of speaking": global complexes of features that "cut across the typical grammatical classifications, so that

such a 'fashion' may include lexical, morphological, syntactic and otherwise systemically diverse means coordinated in a certain frame of consistency" (Whorf 1956: 158).

To what did Whorf seek to relate such "fashions"? Most of the research that has been done on the so-called Sapir–Whorf hypothesis has been about language and *perception* or "cognitive processing" (cf. Lucy 1985). For present purposes, a better reading of Whorf is the revisionist one in Silverstein (1979), which takes him to be addressing himself to the Boasian problem of the relation between language as "primary ethnological phenomenon" and the "secondary rationalization" in terms of which speakers of the language understand it to operate (Boas 1974: 23 ff.).

(Rumsey 1990: 346)

Rumsey finds 'a certain kind of ideology developing "in conjunction with" certain kinds of language structures', a relationship which he characterizes as a dialectical one. The "frame of consistency" treated in his paper is one which relates certain cohesive devices to the grammar of reported speech, in English and in Ungarinyin; so here the dialectic is between language structures and "commonsense notions about the nature of **language** in the world" [my bold]; but for Whorf they could be commonsense notions about any aspect of the world. Other examples of such "frames of consistency" will be found in the work of Martin on Tagalog (Martin calls them "grammatical conspiracies"), and of Hasan on Urdu; the syndrome of features of transitivity and theme that developed in Early Modern English, first identified by Mathesius, would also constitute such a frame of consistency (Martin 1988; Hasan 1984a; Halliday 1990).

Language neither drives culture nor is driven by it; the old questions about which determines which can be set aside as irrelevant, because the relation is not one of cause and effect but rather (as Firth saw it, though not in these words) one of realization: that is, culture and language co-evolve in the same relationship as that in which, within language, meaning and expression co-evolve. Thus above and beyond the random, local variation between languages that was the subject matter of earlier typological studies, we may expect to find non-random variation realizing different construals of reality across major alterations in the human condition. But given that language and culture evolve together in this kind of relationship, it is inevitable that language will take on an ideological role. It has been accepted for some time that race and gender are constructed in language; and the "critical linguistics" developed by Roger Fowler and his colleagues in the late 1970s sought to ground this recognition in a deeper awareness of the role of **grammar** in such constructions – for example by examining the grammar of politically divergent texts which were reporting on one and the same racially charged event (Fowler *et al.* 1979). Within the same period, feminist studies of language moved on from gender pronouns and expressions of uncertainty to take account of the divergent roles in the grammar of transitivity taken up by female and male characters in popular romantic fiction (Thwaite 1983). Interestingly, this level of interpretation has now become generally accessible; see for example the article 'Romance in Cartlandia' by Peter Thomas in the *Guardian Weekly* of 29 March 1992. One can now cite numerous studies of the construction of ideology through acts of meaning (as examples, Kress and Hodge 1979, 1988; Threadgold *et al.* 1986; Threadgold and Cranny-Francis 1990; van Leeuwen 1989; Lemke 1990b; Thibault 1988); and it is a central concern of the Australian journal *Social Semiotics*.

3 Language and social inequality

And it is what Bernstein was telling us about 25 years ago. In a hierarchically ordered society there are likely to be major semiotic disjunctions between different levels in the hierarchy. Social classes are construed in language; hence they are validated (naturalized), re-inforced, and transmitted in language; thus, language is functioning as an agency of social inequality. Berstein's ideas got distorted even more than those of Whorf – partly because they are very threatening: if acted upon, they could disrupt the social order. But they are also difficult to grasp; and I think that this is because the phenomena he was observing, that he referred to as codes (or more fully as "sociolinguistic coding orientations"), fall squarely in the problematic middle ground between the system and the instance – between the **meaning potential** of language and the instantiated **act of meaning**. Such codes, in other words, do not form distinct linguistic systems (they are not different languages); but nor are they particularities of performance (either in the Chomskyan or in the Hymesian sense). Bernstein did once try to locate them with reference to a competence/performance dichotomy, but he soon abandoned this as a mistake; rather, such phenomena neutralize these distinctions, and force us to realize that the "system" and the "instance", by whatever names we choose to call them, are not in fact different phenomena – they are one and the same phenomenon seen by different observers. Let me use my favourite analogy here, that of the climate and the weather. Certain changes seem to be taking place around us today, quite serious ones, like global warming; but are these changes perturbations in the climate, or are they variations in the weather pattern? If you ask that question, it makes it seem as if there are two possible classes of event; but there are not. What the question means is, will I understand these changes better if I view them from the standpoint of a climate observer, or from the standpoint of a weather observer? We shall probably need both perspectives; but in any case, climate and weather are not different phenomena; they are different observational time depths. So it is with language; the language system, and the language instance or act of meaning, are one phenomenon not two; and codes, like Whorf's fashions of speaking, have to be observed in both perspectives.

Hasan has interpreted Bernstein's codes, in semiotic terms, using the concept of semantic variation. This is different from functional, or register, variation in one critical respect: in semantic variation there is a higher level constant – we can talk of semantic "variants"; whereas in register variation there is not. Registers are ways of doing different things; there is no level of interpretation at which, say, technocratic discourse and casual conversation become signifiers of a common signified. With codes there is; and in this respect, codes resemble social dialects; but whereas social dialects (like dialects in general) realize their higher level constant in the semantic system (that is, within language itself), codes come together only **outside** of language, in the culture. It is only at an abstract level in the context of culture that different codes can be seen to realize a common "signified".

Following up Bernstein's work two decades later, Hasan and her colleagues analysed semantically over 20,000 messages of spontaneous conversation between mothers and their pre-school children in the home, and subjected the results to a detailed cluster analysis. The analysis showed significant differences in the patterns of meaning that were adopted, respectively, by mothers of boys and mothers of girls. Their discourse did not constitute two different language systems (two climates); they were just random fluctuations in the semiotic weather. They were different codes – that is, consistent orientations to different ways of meaning, which construed boys and girls as different social beings. And the same study – same analysis, same data, same program – showed up other differences, equally significant both ideologically and statistically, between mothers from the working class and mothers from the middle class. And the children's own part in the dialogues revealed very clearly – not by direct imitation of the mothers, which would make no sense, but by a deeper semiotic resonance in their grammar – that they were, at three and a half years old, fully paid-up members of the social bond (Hasan 1990; Hasan and Cloran 1990).

4 Language as metadiscourse

There are three parts to this: construing experience, enacting interpersonal relations, creating a semiotic level of reality. In the 1960s, in what I called the "metafunction" hypothesis, I suggested that the content plane of language – the lexicogrammar and its higher level ordering as semantics – could be best understood as simultaneously constructing meanings of three different kinds: meaning as reflection – construing human experience; meaning as action – enacting interpersonal relationships; and meaning as texture, which I saw as having an enabling function with regard to the other two (Halliday 1967/68).

The centrepiece in the grammar of experience is the transitivity system. Davidse has shown, in her comprehensive *Categories of Experiential Grammar* (1991), how the transitivity system of English construes experience for those for whom it serves as mother tongue. For most recent generations, until the very recent ones, this has meant the Anglo-Celtic peoples; and I include "-Celtic" here, not just to recognize that the Celts now largely have to make do with English, or with French, but to make the substantive point that, from the more cryptotypic aspects of the grammar, it seems clear that Celtic semogenic resources have contributed significantly to the semantic potential of these two languages. The transitivity system has also figured prominently in French work in functional grammar and semantics, notably that of Bernard Pottier; and its role in reality construction is central to the thinking of Claude Hagège (e.g. Hagège 1985). And perhaps I might pay respect here to another distinguished Francophone colleague, the late Algirdas Greimas. Greimas was convinced, though from a different point of departure, of the essential unity of language and experience. Fabbri wrote of him (1992):

> On sait que, pour Greimas, langues (naturelles) et monde (naturel) ne sont pas séparés mais au contraire entrelacés comme dans un monogramme. Il s'agit pour lui de macrosémiotiques dans lesquelles les catégories du signifiant mondain sont les mêmes que celles qui constituent le plan du contenu du langage ...
>
> (Fabbri 1992: 21)

A very natural framework for modelling transitivity structures is one based on processes and participant roles, along with some third category of circumstantial elements. Martin has proposed, for Tagalog, an alternative interpretation of transitivity, one based on orientation. There can be more than one way of construing experience in grammar, and we may need a different grammatics to bring out the complementarities involved (Halliday 1967/68; Martin 1996a).

But the full creative power of an act of meaning arises from the fact that language **both** construes **and** enacts. It is not only a way of thinking about the world; it is also, at one and the same time, a way of acting on the world – which means, of course, acting on the other people in it. There has always been a place in studies of grammar for a few very general interpersonal systems such as mood; recently, however, not only have these systems come to be interpreted more theoretically, but also other kinds of interpersonal meaning have been brought under attention (e.g. Martin 1990b; Butler 1988). Martin talks of "interpersonal grammatization", and it has always seemed to me that interpersonal systems such as those realized by intonation (in many languages, such as English) should be understood as the enactment of social meaning through the systemic power of the grammar. The role of interpersonal grammar in learning is foregrounded in Lemke's work (e.g. 1988). In my view one of the significant facts about children's language development, in the context of language education, is that so many grammatical resources – including those which will eventually function overwhelmingly in experiential contexts – are developed first in the interpersonal domain. For example, at the time of transition from protolanguage to mother tongue (roughly, one and a half to two years old), a child may learn to give information that is not known to the listener (as distinct from rehearsing experience that has been shared) when he has hurt himself and needs to gain sympathy (Painter 1984); children typically first learn the logical semantics of conditionals in the context of threats and warnings (Phillips 1986), and they first master grammatical metaphor in the form of interpersonal metaphors of mood and modality (Halliday 1991).

But this conjunction of the experiential and the interpersonal depends in turn, for its efficacy as discourse, on meaning of a third kind, the creation of texture. Matthiessen (1992; cf. also 1991b) interprets and explains this as the grammaticizing of the semiotic process itself. The grammar creates its own "world three" – not quite in Popper's sense – which is a world that is made of meaning, the semiotic counterpart of our worlds of reflection and of action.

5 Language as model

Some time ago I started using the term "grammatics" to refer distinctively to grammar as a theoretical pursuit: grammatics as the study of grammar, parallel to linguistics as the study of language – but more especially applying the term to grammatical theory used as a source of explanation. Like all theories, a theory of grammatics is a semiotic system; but with the special characteristic that the phenomena it is designed to explain are themselves also semiotic systems – languages. Traditionally, linguists have usually tried to model their theories on theories that were designed to explain systems of other kinds; but in semiotics (which is not a discipline, but a thematic organization of knowledge like mathematics) all phenomena are being investigated and interpreted as systems of meaning, and this makes it possible to use grammatics as a way of explaining them. The most immediately accessible are other, non-linguistic, semiotics such as forms of art: not just literature, which can naturally be apprehended through the grammar (by means of a grammatics) because it is made of language (cf. Butt 1984, 1988a; Gregory 1985; Threadgold 1988), but also performance (dance and drama), music, and forms of visual art. Michael O'Toole (1989, 1995) uses grammatics for his investigations of painting, architecture and sculpture; Steiner (1988) and van Leeuwen (1988) for music; and Paul Thibault (1991a), starting from narrative theory, exploits grammatics as a resource for integrating the text into a broader framework of "social semiotics as praxis".

But it is now being suggested that some **physical** systems might be better understood if they could be modelled "as if" they were semiotic ones. This motif began to appear some time ago in the writings of post-quantum physicists, perhaps in conjunction with their renewed interest in the language of their own science; and as far as I call tell it seems to have an interpretation on two different levels: (1) that some physical systems **incorporate** semiotic ones (e.g. Prigogine and Stengers' example of the communication among molecules that is necessary for them to operate as a "chemical clock" – and compare, in biology, communication among the eggs in a clutch getting ready to be hatched); and (2) that some physical systems **are** semiotic (e.g. Bohm's interpretation of the speed of light as the maximum speed of propagation of a signal) (Prigogine and Stengers 1982: 147–8; Bohm 1980: 123). In either case, the critical event is an act of meaning. A physical system is no longer "just" a physical system. But, by the same token, a grammatics is no longer just a theory of grammar.

385

★★★

So in the past generation we seem to have rediscovered something of the power of language, recognizing that an act of meaning is not the coding and transmitting of some pre-existing information or state of mind, but a critical component in a complex process of reality construction – critical in that on the one hand it is itself part of reality, and on the other hand it is a metaphor for some other part. Semiotic systems, while they are components of human experience, along with physical, biological and social ones, are also theories about that experience (including about themselves, there being no constraint on their reflexivity (Lemke 1984d)). That is their metaphorical aspect; and it is the success of that metaphor, in one's semiotic acts, I think, that determines how effective one's discourse is going to be. This power of the act of meaning would not have been news to the sophists in ancient Athens, who constructed their grammatics in order to find out how language could persuade people of something even when it wasn't true. Or to the founders of modern science, who tried to design their language so that it would open up for them the gateway to new knowledge. And of course it is no news to my co-presenter tonight, Dell Hymes, who has proclaimed not only the power of language but also the need for a grammatics with which to apprehend it – as he said, writing about attaining the "joy and understanding" of Native American verbal art, "If we do not deal with the means, we cannot possess the meanings" (Hymes 1981: 5).

Nevertheless we cannot help noticing a contradiction here. In fact, relatively few of those concerned, however much they may be aware of, and may even celebrate, the power of the act of meaning, have actively tried to 'deal with the means' of its achievement. Unlike the works I have been citing in this paper (which do), most studies in semiotics – including what we might call "applied semiotics" – do not engage seriously with language; and many explicitly deny that it is relevant to do so. When physical scientists comment on language, they often seem content to treat it at the level of the eighth grade.

To be fair to those scientists, this is partly, I think, because they are aware that we – the linguists – have still not cracked the code of systems of this fourth order of complexity, semiotic systems. We do not yet fully understand the nature of our own fundamental abstractions, those of realization and instantiation, nor the complex multiple relationship that holds between them. And for our other colleagues there is probably

386

a further reason: that much of what we are able to tell them tends to be rather discouraging – like Bacon with his *idola fori*, we are obsessed with language doing its worst. We even hold conferences on lying.

I should plead guilty here too: in my paper at AILA in 1990 I particularly emphasized how the power of language functions to create and maintain all kinds of inequalities and hegemonies – not only citing the familiar examples of social class and sex (or "gender" as we now call it, in a ritual bow to these same idols), but also suggesting how our language locks us in to the twin myths of endless growth and of our own status as the lords of creation (myths of growthism and lordism, if you like these -istic terms). I stressed these inequalities, these antidemocratic fashions of meaning; and I did this so as to show that we need to learn to think grammatically, to become aware of such cryptotypic effects in our everyday "commonsense" language, if we want to continue to prosper as a species, or even if we want to survive.

So let me conclude by turning over the coin, and proclaiming instead the democratic potential of our familar semogenic resources. Our transitivity systems, for example, seem at first sight to be dominated by this apparently immutable hierarchic scale of animacy, privileging humanity over the rest of creation and, within humanity, the generalized human male. But the semantic space construed by transitivity is an elastic space; these are tendencies – they are not categorical, which means they can be reversed, or subverted. This is possible because when you override them, it does not force a reinterpretation; compare my example of *what the forest is doing*, which can be interpreted as an effective material process with *the forest* as Actor (and, potentially, as Agent, depending on what follows). (A categorical system is one you cannot subvert. Here, if you produce an "illicit" combination, it simply gets co-opted – that is, reinterpreted according to the category, or one of the categories, in question. Thus in English, in mental processes (only), the distinction of "+/– consciousness" is categorical; hence if I ask what the forest is thinking, or what the forest knows, the forest is thereby co-opted into the class of conscious beings – or else the process itself is metaphorized into something else, as in *what the forests are now seeing is total destruction*.) Interestingly, it is in symbolic processes that humans lose any such privileged status: any entity is equally acceptable as a signal source, e.g. *that rock formation tells you that the whole region was uplifted*.

We can also subvert the process by which the code barrier limits access to educational knowledge. (I do not think, by the way, that there is any significant difference, in this respect, among the various English-speaking countries. The British are always cited as uniquely class-ridden, but this is because they wear their classes on their sleeves, whereas in the United States the pattern is more covert – I think Paul Fussell is one who has made this point. But the same barriers are in place.) Since the disjunction between educational knowledge and commonsense knowledge is construed in the grammar, it can also be deconstrued in the grammar. Simply by spreading knowledge about language ("KAL", as it is called in the British work) one can do much to demystify educational discourse; but one can also use the grammar as a resource in order to bridge – or even to close – the gap. Two strategies suggest themselves. One, to provide stepping stones from "common sense" to technicality and grammatical metaphor within the experiential component of the grammar – agnate forms of discourse that form a gradation from the one to the other. The other strategy is to map more learner-friendly interpersonal meanings into the educational discourse. You have to be careful, in that second case, to avoid what Martin calls "childism" (1985); but I think it can be done.

In any case the disjunction is partly a matter of our own failure to understand the nature of commonsense knowledge, knowledge as construed – and learnt by children – in the language of daily life. Of course, children have to relearn a great deal once they come into school – they have to systematize and technicalize their own construction of experience; but that is no reason why we should not recognize how much they knew before they came. Ruqaiya Hasan's study of 'Rationality in everyday talk between mothers and children' shows the many forms of reasoning that are deployed in everyday discourse in the home; the three-year-old's grammar has plenty of varied resources for constructing sequences of argument (Hasan 1992b). What Hasan has shown is that different kinds of rationality are functional in different social contexts. Moving into the discourse of education is not a matter of transcending some opposition between non-rational and rational; it means recognizing the contexts in which different forms of rationality are deployed.

If we compare the discourses of today with those of a century ago, we become aware of the potential that the system has for change. This is a potential, of course, that has to be actively taken up, if we want it to change in a particular direction: taken up not by legislation or decree, but by changing our own habits of meaning, towards different frames of consistency. The semantic space can always be expanded; as I said before, it is an elastic space, indefinitely malleable – and semiotic growth, growth in meaning potential, is one kind of growth which does not use up natural resources or engender polluting side-effects! The system of language is always in transition – because every act of meaning transforms it, however microscopically, from what it was into something else. You cannot redesign it; but you can nudge it along by the innumerable small momenta (a phrase of Whorf's I never tire of repeating) of thoughtful acts of meaning. You can even reverse the marking, up to a point, as protagonists of the cause of women have done with English personal pronouns. This is because there is no insulation between the system and the text; the system is the text, only (as I put it earlier) it is being observed from a different time depth. Hence it is in the act of meaning that the power of language resides; and that is what makes linguistic systems, in the last resort, subject to the democratic process.

Chapter Eighteen

ON LANGUAGE IN RELATION TO THE EVOLUTION OF HUMAN CONSCIOUSNESS (1995)

1 Language and the human brain

In this paper I have tried to identify, and to illustrate, certain aspects of language which seem to me critical to a consideration of language and the human brain. In doing so I have assumed that language is what **defines** the brain of homo sapiens: what constitutes it as specifically human. I have tried to keep in view the three different time scales that must be considered: evolutionary (how the language-brain evolved in the species), developmental (how the language-brain develops in each child) and instantial (how the language-brain is activated in each act of meaning). The paper is in five sections. In Section 1, I discuss Gerald Edelman's theory of "neural Darwinism", as an account of brain evolution which takes language as the critical manifestation of consciousness in its human form. Sections 2 to 4 take up different perspectives on language itself, its development and its quantitative and qualitative character, while in Section 5 I refer to the work of particular scholars in other disciplines who, it seems to me, have contributed significantly to the rich interpretation of language that is needed here.

Darwin considered that consciousness evolved, and that it evolved by the same processes of natural selection as other biological attributes of species; furthermore that human consciousness, or "mind", was no exception – it had a history just like other forms of life. Edelman shows clearly that Darwin was right. His theory of neuronal group selection explains why consciousness is part of the physical world: why we can no

First published in *Of Thoughts and Words (Proceedings of Nobel Symposium 92: The Relation between Language and Mind)*, edited by S. Allén. London: Imperial College Press and the Nobel Foundation, 1995.

longer pretend that there is some mysterious entity (or non-entity), "mind" or whatever, that is *sui generis* beyond the reach of scientific enquiry. I am not suggesting that Edelman's theory is the complete or undisputed word. Like every other major advance in knowledge it is bound to be incomplete in certain respects, and is no doubt wrong in others – in any case, I am not competent to judge. But I am taking it as point of departure here[1] because it offers a coherent account of the evolution of **linguistic** consciousness, and one which is entirely compatible with what many linguists – particularly perhaps those working outside the Chomskyan paradigm – would say about the nature and functioning of language.

Again like other major advances, Edelman's theory has not appeared out of nowhere. Edelman is explicit in making reference to his own precursors: not merely in acknowledging specific contributions from other individual scholars but also, and more tellingly for readers who are not neurobiologists, in relating his work to the thinking in other disciplines. Aside from neuroscience itself, and other biological fields such as embryology and genetics, the disciplines he relates to most substantively are philosophy, psychology and linguistics. Edelman interprets their contributions, however, not as individual fragments serving as separate ingredients for an intellectual conglomerate, but rather as different complementary aspects of a concerted human endeavour to understand – a criterial manifestation of that very phenomenon of consciousness that he is setting out to investigate. In other words his viewpoint is not interdisciplinary so much as transdisciplinary.

Language, as the term is understood in everyday discourse – namely, language in its adult human form – holds a central place in Edelman's account. But considered in its relationship to human consciousness, language enters the picture at two quite different levels. On the one hand, language comes in as *phenomenon*: as the primary realization of consciousness, and hence a major source of insight into its nature. On the other hand language comes in as *metaphenomenon*: as the powerhouse of human intellectual endeavour – which involves constructing theories, including theories about the evolution of consciousness (and hence about the evolution of language itself). Let me make a brief comment from within the second of these two perspectives, just in contextualization of Edelman's own work. Theorizing, as a form of human intellectual endeavour, is part of the history of consciousness; it has its own evolutionary path, following some sort of dynamic such as that of successive refinements of categorization, from generalization through abstractness to metaphor, and characterized by particular "moments" in the history of human cultures (some more rapid, some more long-drawn-out) as cosmologies – theories of the human condition – are steadily built up. These cosmologies vary, naturally, with major changes in conditions of living: settled peoples tend to have different theories of the world from those of non-settled, hunting-gathering cultures; and within settlement, theories change as techno-logy changes. Mythic, religious and scientific cosmologies represent the theory-building aspect of consciousness associated with homo sapiens. (That this is not in fact an essentially different kind of activity from the commonsense use of language in everyday discourse becomes clear once we recognize that the grammar of every natural language is itself a theory of experience, albeit one that is typically lodged "below the level of" conscious awareness; I come back to this point below.)

Within these moments in the history of consciousness there are smaller cycles, irregularities and blips. The marriage of aristotelian and Christian theories in medieval Christendom is one such blip. The notable feature of the extended Eurasian culture band has been the constant interplay between orthodox and hermetic learning, in Judaeo-Christian, Hindu-Buddhist and Confucian-Taoist theorizing. In our "scientific" age since Galileo and Newton, a recurrent motif has been the oscillation between discipline-based and theme-based models of institutionalized knowledge; the twentieth century began with a strongly disciplinary base constructed by scholars of the century before – and immediately set about remodelling it, with "themes" such as structuralism, positivism, formalism, and then semiotics, cybernetics, cladistics. Edelman's class of "recognition theories", based on the principles of recognition and including evolution, immunology and neurology, is an example of an advance brought about by building on and then transcending the discipline-based structure of knowledge.

Language, in Edelman's account, is an essential condition of higher order human consciousness. I cannot hope to do justice to the richness and breadth of his theory; but I would like to show, as much as I can, how closely it resonates with what we could observe in investigating language from the social-semiotic standpoint. In the next few paragraphs I have tried to set out the features of Edelman's model that are salient in regard to language and linguistic theory (references are to pages in his *Bright Air, Brilliant Fire* (1992)).

"Mind", as William James observed, is not substance, it is process. It is process of a special kind, depending on special arrangements of matter: arrangements of brain systems, at molecular, cellular, organismic and transorganismic levels, and of systems of interaction between the brain and the rest of the body. The human cerebral cortex is "the most complicated material object in the known universe" (p. 17); not just in the number and density of neuronal networks (the cortical sheet accommodates around 10^9 neurons, with some 10^{15} connections, or "synapses") but even more in its morphology, the way the brain cells are arranged in functioning patterns. The complexities involved are much greater than the complexities found in any physical systems (p. 66). But the brain is far from being "precise and 'hardwired' like a computer" (p. 27); on the contrary, it is a self-organizing system, characterized by variation, non-unique specification, overlap, and constant change. A more accurate analogy would be with a self-organizing ecological system such as a jungle.

Consciousness is the outcome of the dynamically evolving morphology of the brain, taking place through natural selection operating on the phenotype (on variation in the structural and functional capabilities of individuals). Darwin was convinced of the evolutionary origin of species behaviour – including the human mind; "neural Darwinism" is the realization of Darwin's program, now enriched from genetics on the one hand and embryology on the other. This makes it possible to explain both the amazing speed of evolution of the human brain and the relation between evolution and developmental morphogenesis. One key factor here is epigenesis: the development of the individual follows the evolutionary trajectory of the species, and when this extends to behaviour it depends on modelling ("epigenetic events") (p. 47; cf. Lemke, in Section 5 below).

The view from biology is based on "population thinking": the phenomenon under investigation is not some idealized entity or abstract form but a population of individual members of a species. There is no room here for Cartesian dualism, either of substance or of property, still less for Cartesian conceptions of science (cf. Ellis in Section 5 below); nor for explanations in terms of teleology or purpose. "Population thinking considers variation not to be an error but ... to be real. Individual variance in a population is the source of diversity on which natural selection acts to produce different kind of organisms" (p. 73). This same process engenders other biological effects, of which the critical one here is that of "selective recognition". "Evolution, acting by selection on populations of individuals over long periods of time, gives rise to selective systems **within** individuals" (p. 74); these "somatic selection systems" work by recognition, selection (not instruction) and inheritability (or "memory"). The prototypical example of a selective recognition system is the immune system, which responds to the invasion of the body by foreign molecules "**without** requiring that information about the shape that needs to be recognized should be transferred to the recognizing system *at the time when it makes the recognizer molecules or antibodies*. Instead, the recognizing system **first** generates a diverse population of antibody molecules and then selects *ex post facto* those that fit or match" (p. 78). Such recognition systems are biological-historical systems: they are not found among physical systems (though they are subject to the laws of physics). Brains are selective recognition systems of this kind.

Such systems feature a "unit of selection", the locus where selection takes place. With the immune system this is the individual lymphocyte; with the evolutionary system (and evolution itself is also a selective recognition system) it is the individual specimen, the phenotype. With the brain, it is the "neuronal group", containing both excitatory and inhibitory neurons. Selection by neuronal groups takes place in two phases: "developmental selection" ("how the anatomy of the brain is first set up during development"), and "experiential selection" ("how patterns of responses are then selected from this anatomy during experience") (p. 83); from these processes arise two repertoires of neural networks, primary and secondary, which produce multiple brain maps. These brain maps interact with each other through a process of re-entry, or "re-entrant signalling"; and this "recursive synthesis" results in a "higher-order structure called a *global mapping*". The categorization process is thus not that of classical perception theory; it takes place by "disjunctive sampling of properties" (p. 87), depending on internal criteria of "value" laid down by evolutionary selection and further embodied in experience – the system is thus homeostatic, tending always to maintain the conditions that are necessary to continue life. This is the foundation of behaviour (only "occasional" species-specific behaviour patterns are selected for directly by evolution (p. 94)), and makes it possible to bridge the gap from what we think of as physiological to what we think of as psychological phenomena.

In Edelman's theory, it is neuronal group selection that leads to the emergence of consciousness, which comprises the three "higher brain functions" of perceptual categorization, memory and learning. Memory is "the specific enhancement of a previously established ability to categorize" (p. 102); its properties are generalization, association, and inexactness (due to the probabilistic nature of perceptual categorization). Learning depends on the interplay of perceptual categorization and memory, in conjunction with a value system that is separate from either. Thus the brain has evolved in coping with ever more complex environments; what is significant is not just the complexity of the organism but the complexity of its relationship with its environment.[2] And the brain evolved specialized areas which permitted it to construct purely internal relations having no immediate input; this enables it to form concepts by constructing maps of its own activities, a "mapping of types of maps" (p. 109). Such a conceptual centre is the frontal cortex.

Such is the nature of "primary consciousness" – which, unless there are other evolutionary paths to it, would be restricted to animals having a cortex; and possibly, for biochemical reasons, to those that are warmblooded (or, if not, are located in a warm enough ambience!). "So snakes are in (dubiously, depending on the temperature), but lobsters are out. If further study bears out this surmise, consciousness is about 300 million years old" (p. 123). What then of the "higher-order consciousness" of humans? This is almost certainly unique to homo sapiens: "While we may not be the only conscious animals, we are, with the possible exception of the chimpanzee, the only self-conscious animals. We are the only animals capable of language, able to model the world free of the present, able to report on, study, and correlate our phenomenal states with the findings of physics and biology" (p. 115). Thus higher-order consciousness includes consciousness of self and of past and future; and also reportable subjective experience, or "qualia". It is still the outcome of evolutionary processes operating in the physical universe: "minds do not exist disembodied" (p. 162); but it differs significantly from primary consciousness in that it is critically dependent on language. "Higher-order consciousness is based on the occurrence of direct awareness in a human being who has language and a reportable subjective life" (p. 115).

Primary consciousness is efficacious in that it enables the individual to "abstract and organize complex changes in an environment involving multiple parallel signals" (p. 121); it is limiting in that it lacks a concept of self and cannot model past and future as part of a correlated scene. This limitation – the "tyranny of the remembered present" (p. 125) – can be transcended only by the evolution of social symbols; that is, language. Language is necessary for distinguishing self from non-self and for remembering beyond the small memorial interval that illuminates the present. In our terms, these faculties require a stratified semiotic: language in its prototypical adult form, as distinct from the human infant's protolanguage (see further Section 2 below).

Language depends genetically on certain morphological changes: the evolution of the supralaryngeal tract (itself dependent on adopting a bipedal posture), and of certain specialized areas in the brain, Broca's and Wernicke's areas. But this is only one side of the story. Edelman asks: "Can we account for its (sc. language's) evolutionary emergence without creating a gulf between linguistic theory and biology? Yes," he continues, "provided that we account for speech in epigenetic as well as genetic terms. This means abandoning any notion of a genetically programmed language-acquisition device" (p. 126). Language emerges epigenetically in a definable developmental sequence (as a phonological-semantic complex before the appearance of syntax), and in dependence on interaction with other individuals in the environment. "This theory of speech is a nativist theory insofar as it requires the prior evolution of special brain structures. But it invokes no new principles beyond those of the TNGS (theory of neuronal group selection). It is not a computational theory, nor one that insists on a language acquisition device containing innate genetically specified rules for a universal grammar. Syntax is built epigenetically under genetic constraints, just as human faces (which are about as universal as grammar) are similarly built by different developmental constraints. The principles of topobiology apply to both cases" (p. 131). What is clear from Edelman's discussion is that the process has been part of human history since the evolution of humankind (p. 135); that it is a social process, including a "socially-constructed selfhood" (p. 133), and that the system must be a stratal one, with grammar evolving as the latest phase of all.

It seems to me that Edelman's theory, far from "creating a gulf between linguistic theory and biology", resonates sweetly and powerfully with much that linguistic theory has to offer. This is obscured if we see only the dominant paradigm, the model of language first formulated by Chomsky on a Bloomfieldian base and subsequently held in place by two generations of his followers; but this is far from universally accepted, and is regarded by Ellis, in the work referred to at the end of this paper, as fundamentally flawed. There have been significant departures (Edelman himself refers to Joan Bresnan's work (p. 129)), as well as ongoing work that has continued to build on other intellectual traditions within the field. In the next three sections I shall present certain findings, and associated theoretical constructs, which derived from a different tradition, functional and semantic in orientation; and specifically from work carried out within the systemic functional framework, relating to child language development (from the "proto-language" shared with other species to language in its uniquely human form) and to systemic features of mature, adult languages. It seems to me that these findings and interpretations accord well with the neural Darwinist conception of language as higher-order consciousness.

2 The developmental perspective

When in the early 1970s, through working with teachers engaged in initial literacy, I began investigating the earliest phases of language development in children, I was struck by a number of features of the child's "emergence into meaning", and of early semiotic encounters which seemed highly significant for the way language had evolved. I will refer here to six of these features: (1) "Meaning and moving": the correlations between linguistic and physical development; (2) "Proto-language": the emergence of a "child tongue" before the mother tongue begins to take over; (3) "Microfunctions": the functional contexts of the protolanguage; (4) "Macrofunctions": the strategy guiding the transition from protolanguage to mother tongue; (5) "Grammar last": the way the protolanguage (which has no level of grammar in it) is deconstrued and then reconstrued as a three-level system of "semantics/ grammar/phonology"; (6) "Telling": the development of the concept of imparting information, as the latest phase of all. The next few paragraphs deal with each of these in turn.[3]

1   Learning language is not learning sounds and words; nor is it learning to name and to refer. Rather it is, as I put it in the title of an earlier book, "learning how to mean". Meaning (acting semiotically) develops along with doing (acting materially) as interdependent modes of human behaviour; and both depend on interaction with the physical and social environment. We find various stages in a child's semiotic development, associated with the development of bodily postures and movement. (i) Premeaning: exchanging *attention*. This takes place from birth: it goes with moving the head and body, flexing the limbs, "pre-reaching". The two activities, material and pre-semiotic, are combined when the baby activates the whole body, including the organs of speech, accompanied by smiling and gurgling, in phase with the directed attention of its mother or other member of its "meaning group".[4] (ii) First steps in meaning: exchanging *signs* (see below, (2) for definition). This takes place from around four months;

it goes with lifting the head, aligning the body, rolling over, reaching and grasping an object. The sign (which may be realized, say, as a high-pitched squeak) is gaining attention and/or showing curiosity, "I want to be together with you", "I want to know what's going on" (meaning as interpersonal or experiential intentionality). (iii) Proto-language: exchanging *sign systems*. This takes place typically in the second half of the first year; it goes with crawling, mobility from one place to another. (The systems are described in (3) below.) (iv) Language: exchanging *words-in-structures* (lexicogrammar). This takes place typically early in the second year; it goes with walking, bipedal movement. It is only at this fourth stage that grammar begins to develop.

2   The protolanguage, or child tongue, is a semiotic of a type that has evolved in many species, perhaps all those with a certain level of primary consciousness (that exemplified by dogs in Edelman's discussion). Its elements are signs in the classical sense: that is, *meaning/expression pairs*, such that there is a redundancy between the two (the expression "realizes" the meaning, e.g. a particular miaow "means" 'I want milk'). (Note that the meaning here is non-referential; there is no "naming" involved.) Looking back at the protolanguage from the vantagepoint of (adult-like) language we can say that it has a semantics and a phonology (or kinology: the expression may be any combination of vocal and gestural) but no (lexico-)grammar.[5] The meanings develop around a small number of motifs: "I (don't) want, (don't) give me" (instrumental); "do this for/ with me" (regulatory); "let's be together, you-&-me" (interactional); "I'm curious about/(don't) like that" (personal), and may extend also to "let's pretend" (imaginative) and perhaps "what's that?" (heuristic – this is already transitional into language). The mode of expression children use in their protolinguistic signs is highly variable. Some prefer the gestural mode, others the vocal, others some mixture of the two. The origin of vocal expressions may be imitation of the child's own natural sounds (sighing, crying), imitation of adult sounds, or pure invention; they seem to adults to range over a wide phonetic space, but they appear quite stable once one describes them in terms of vocal postures rather than of articulatory categories. The critical feature of the protolanguage is that it is a system of social signs; the impetus – the semiotic energy – comes from the child, but the signs, and sign systems, can only be construed in interaction with the child's "others", the meaning group, who are (unselfconsciously, of course)

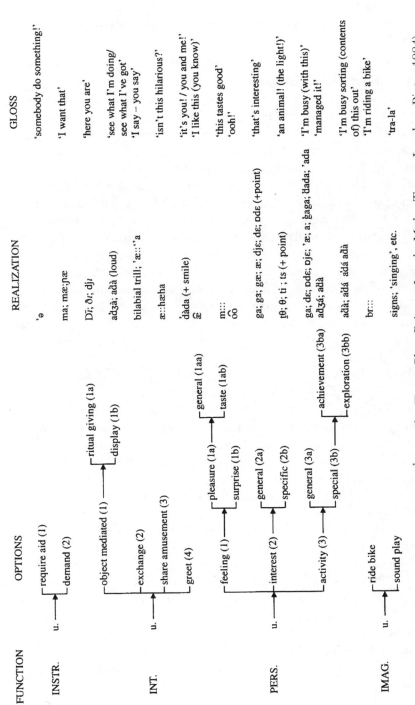

Figure 1 Hal's protolanguage at 12 to 13½ months (From Clare Painter, *Into the Mother Tongue*, London: Pinter 1984)

tracking the child's development by exchanging meanings with him throughout his waking hours.

3 The glosses used in the previous paragraph (instrumental, regulatory, interactional, personal, imaginative, heuristic) are semiotic contexts in which meaning first develops in the form of **contrast**: that is, as a network of systems, in the technical sense of this term in systemic theory – sets of options within a given material–semiotic situation, like 'I want'/'I don't want', or 'that's an interesting object'/ 'that's my favourite toy' (again, all adult language glosses are misleading because they imply referential meanings). A typical synchronic cross-section of a protolinguistic system is that of Hal at twelve to thirteen and a half months (Figure 1).[6] The overall system, of course, is in constant flux – typically expanding, although individual signs may drop out or change into something different; the optimum interval for such cross-sectional overviews seems to be about six weeks. As a developing system of this kind the protolanguage may continue to function for the child for six to eight or nine months or even more; but it then gets transformed, more or less rapidly, into a system of the adult kind, the "mother tongue". There is no clear evidence that any other species take this step.

Meanwhile the protolanguage provides the conditions for the emerging consciousness of self. Let us represent the microfunctions schematically as in Figure 2. This theorizes that meaning – semiotic activity – develops out of the child's sense of contradiction between the two primary modes of experience, the material (what goes on "out there") and the conscious (what goes on "in here"). In construing a sign, the child is projecting one mode through the intermediary of the other – construing conceptual order out of perceptual chaos (as Edelman says, "the world ... is an unlabelled place" (p. 99)). The projection of the material by the conscious transforms this impact between inner and outer experience into meaning. There are thus two variables involved. The projection may take the form either of 'this is how I want things to be' ("active") or of 'this is how things are' ("reflective"); the domain that is being projected may be either 'you and me' ("first/second person") or 'the rest of reality' ("third person"). The intersection of these two variables defines the "self" simultaneously (1) as source of projection and (2) as distinct (a) from the "other" (me from you) and (b) from the perceived environment. The transition from child tongue to mother tongue depends epigenetically on this social-semiotic construction of selfhood.

400

form of projection / domain of experience	active (what should be)	reflective (what is)
1st/2nd person (you & me)	regulatory 'do for me!'	interactional 'you + me together'
"3rd person" (all else)	instrumental 'give me!'	personal 'I like/wonder'

Figure 2 Microfunctions of protolanguage: semiotic origins

4 When children begin to move from protolanguage into language, typically when they are some way into the second year of life, the same underlying principles are extended to serve as the guiding strategy for the transition. It has been known for a long time that some form of opposition between demanding and describing is characteristic of the first phase of language (mother tongue) development;[7] we have been able to show (i) that this is systematically realized (construed) in the form of the expression, perhaps typically by intonation, voice quality or some combination of the two, and (ii) that it does not emerge "out of the blue" but is derived by generalizing from the microfunctional profile of the protolanguage. I labelled the opposition "pragmatic/ mathetic", to suggest 'language to act with' as against 'language to learn with'. Initially, in this phase, each utterance of the child is **either** one **or** the other: either 'this is the way I think things are' (objects, properties, processes like *moon, big ladder, green light, bird gone*), or 'this is the way I want things to be' (demands for goods or services, like *down!* ('I want to get down'), *mummy come!, more drink!*). The latter always demand a response; their pragmatic function is made entirely clear. The former do not; they may be self-addressed or other-addressed, but if addressed to another then that person must be someone who is sharing or has shared the experience. The child is describing, or annotating, but not yet telling – the meaning is mathetic (construing experience), not informative, and the child has still no concept of language as information.

5 Now for the first time the child has developed a "grammar": that is, a purely abstract level of semiosis "in between" the meaning and the expression. The sign-based system of the protolanguage has been deconstrued and reconstrued as a tristratal semiotic comprising

401

semantics, lexicogrammar and phonology. It should be emphasized that "lexicogrammar" is a single stratum, with a continuum from grammar (small closed systems with very general domains) to lexis (open-ended sets with very specific domains); it makes no sense to say that lexis develops before grammar. Children may take variable lengths of time to construe complex syntagms; but as soon as their utterance is being construed as a word, by the same token it is also functioning grammatically.

How does this grammaticization of the system of meaning come about? The strategy seems to be the fundamental principle of semogenesis, namely that of decoupling – the dissociation of associated variables. This can take place in many different contexts; here is the instance I myself first observed, a few days after the child in question had taken his first steps in walking. He had at the time, as part of his protolanguage, three signs that had become specialized to the three people in his meaning group, 'mummy', 'daddy', 'anna'; these were not yet referring, but were person-specific interactional, and were said always on a high level tone (not used in other expressions), as in Figure 3(a). Within a period of two or three days he deconstrued this system and reconstrued it as in Figure 18.3(b). The person-specific signs have now become names, while the interactional component has been grammaticized as a modal opposition of greeting (acknowledging presence) or seeking (overcoming absence). In other words, the child now has a proto-grammar consisting of two systems, one realized lexically, the other phonologically; the two systems are dissociated, hence freely combinable, and each utterance must select in both. In the event, it was another three months before the child followed up this development; but in this one move he had underpinned a semiotic of a fundamentally different kind.[8] This is the semiotic that embodies Edelman's "higher-order consciousness"; it has a new and distinctive kind of network, a lexicogrammar, at the core. (If the form of a grammar was genetically programmed, why would children first construe a semiotic of another kind, in which there is no trace of grammar at all?)

6   The final step to be taken in developing language in this specifically human sense is that of reconstruing the strategic opposition of "pragmatic/mathetic" into a new "metafunctional" form of organization. I shall return to this in the section of the paper that follows; but a brief account needs to be given from the developmental perspective. We can summarize under four headings. (i) The **opposition between**

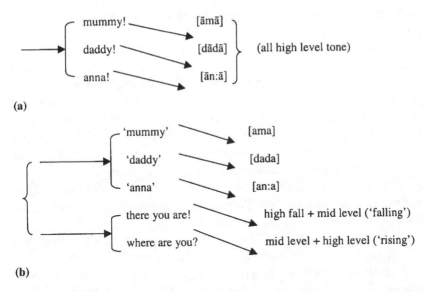

Figure 3 (a) System of person-specific interactional signs, with complex realization (articulation + intonation); **(b)** system **(a)** reconstructed as two simultaneous systems: one referring (now as "proper names"), realized by articulation; the other addressing (greeting or seeking), realized by intonation

pragmatic and mathetic develops into the grammar of mood and modality: grammar in its guise of *enacting interpersonal relationships* of all kinds, from rapidly alternating dialogic roles to ongoing patterns of familial, institutional and socio-economic hierarchy. (ii) The **experiential content** of both mathetic and pragmatic develops into the grammar of processes, things and properties (transitivity, systems of nominal categorization): grammar in its guise of *construing experience*, both that of the collective, embodied in the grammatical system, and that of the individual, embodied in the ongoing instantial selections. (iii) The child now develops the grammar of **relations between** processes (and other phenomena): grammar in its role of *building up commonsense logic*, construed as 'and', 'or', 'is', 'so', 'then', 'says', 'thinks' and so on (formal logic and mathematics are designed descendants of these). (iv) At the same time the child develops the grammar for construing itself: that is, for *engendering text*, as a parallel "virtual" universe that is made of meaning, and that has its own structure as metaphor for the structures it is imposing on the material world.

Once these two principles, the stratal and the metafunctional, have been established as semiotic foundations, the child has the potential for expanding his resources of meaning to an indefinite extent – of which, at present at least, we are not aware of any limitations. (This is not to say there cannot be any limitations). As part of this process, completing the transition into the mother tongue, the child has developed the power of "information": using language to tell people things that they do not already know. In other words, meaning has become a **way of sharing experience**, instead of just a way construing experience that has been or is being shared. This is a rather late development, which typically is not consolidated until the grammatical framework is in place: information does not exist until it is created by language, so "telling" involves both the interpersonal resources for exchanging (declarative and interrogative mood) and the experiential resources for creating the "commodity" that is being exchanged.

Thus it seems to me that what we have learnt about the ontogenesis of language – how the individual child develops the semiotic potential of the human species, in tandem with the development of the biological potential – is not only compatible with, but mutually supportive of, the theory of neuronal group selection as the neurobiological basis of consciousness, specifically higher-level consciousness or "mind". The epigenetic trajectory, in which the child follows the evolutionary path in dependence on and interaction with the (sociosemiotic and material) environment; the progression through primary symbolization and protolanguage; the late "slotting in" of lexicogrammar, turning a simple semiotic (sign system) into a stratified one; the simultaneous emergence of the metafunctions of construing experience and enacting inter-personal relations; and the progression from annotating shared experience to telling experience that was not shared (information) – all these resonate very positively with Edelman's evolutionary theory. Let me turn now to some considerations of language as higher-order consciousness with particular reference to its metafunctional character as action and reflection: as the semiotic resource with which human beings simultaneously enact their social processes and construe the experience of themselves and their environment.

3 How big is a language? Some quantitative features of human meaning potential

Language may be defined as a "meaning potential": a system-&-process of **choice**, choice which typically goes on below the threshold of attention, but can be attended to and reflected on under certain circumstances – most typically, though not exclusively, associated with the evolution of writing. We model this as a system network, showing (a) the sets or options, (b) their interconnections, and (c) their realizations. Text, spoken or written, is the effect (process/ product) of repeated passes through the network, manifested as a (typically continuous) flow of activity – pulmonic, glottalic and articulatory, in the case of spoken text. The system network models the potential, the process of selection, and the "output"; like all such theoretical models in linguistics, it is an abstract representation, not an attempt to model neural processes. In protolanguage, such selection takes place in a single pass. But in language the networks are layered, or **stratified**, in the way this concept was developed by mid-century linguists following Saussure, for example scholars such as Trubetzkoy, Martinet, Hjelmslev and Firth:[9] there is a **content** network, which generates words-in-structures, and an **expression** network, which generates speech sounds. The content network is further stratified into the **semantic** (we often refer to this as **discourse-semantic**) and the **lexicogrammatical**; this step, referred to above in the developmental context, turns language into a dynamic open system with an indefinitely large semantic potential (cf. the discussion in the final section of the paper below). An example of a partial lexicogrammatical network of English is given in Figure 4.

How big is a language? We can conceptualize the content plane as a kind of semantic space, multidimensional and elastic, which is capable of expanding to some indefinite extent. But if we think of it in digital terms, it can be quantified as the number of options that might be represented in a network of grammatical systems. Such networks are partially ordered: some systems are mutually independent (not associated), for example the primary systems of transitivity and mood: others are taxonomically associated, access to one being dependent on selection within another (e.g. if indicative, then either declarative or interrogative). If we pretend for the moment that all systems are binary, then given any set of n systems forming a network, if they form a simple taxonomy the number of possible options is just n + 1 (one system, two options; six systems, seven options; fifteen systems, sixteen options and so on); if they are all independent, then the number of possible options is 2^n (one system, two options; six systems, 64 options; fifteen systems, $2^{15} = 32,768$ options, and so on). Systems in a grammatical network fall, obviously, somewhere in between the two extremes: the most general at each rank (clause, phrase, group) tend to be independent, but as one moves in delicacy

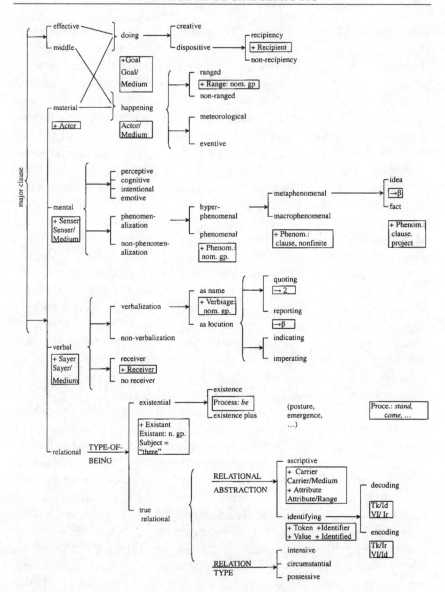

Figure 4

406

towards the ones that are more localized the degree of ordering naturally increases.

Let us take as an example the English verb, or rather verbal group. This may be finite or non-finite; let us first select "finite". We then have three primary or deictic tenses, past, present, and future; two voices, active and passive; two polarities, positive and negative, each with an unmarked and a marked variant; and two degrees of contrast, or focal stress, neutral (non-contrastive) and contrastive; thus:

$3 \times 2 \times 4 \times 2 = 48$ possibilities

But instead of temporal deixis (primary tense), we could have selected modal deixis; and here there are 24 possible options (three values, high, median and low; two angles, neutral and oblique; and four types, probable, usual, ready, and obliged), so instead of three choices of deixis we now have 27. There are also two forms of the passive, so not two voices but three; and with all these options there are twelve possible secondary tenses. If we calculate again:

$27 \times 3 \times 4 \times 2 \times 12 = 7,776$ possiblilities

However, if we choose contrastive focus, there are (1) various keys, or tonal options – let us recognize the principal set of eight; and (2) various possible loci – the exact number depends on other choices, but we can average it at two; so in the system of contrast instead of two options we recognize $1 + (8 \times 2) = 17$: non-contrastive, or contrastive in any of eight ways at either of two locations. Furthermore we could have chosen non-finite (no verbal deixis) as an alternative initial state, and that would give the further option of two aspects, perfective and imperfective, so the 27 becomes 29. We now have:

$29 \times 12 \times 3 \times 4 \times 17 = 70,992$ possibilities

Here, then, without double negatives, special third person forms, ellipses, more subtle modalities and tense variants – let alone the causative, inceptive, durative and other phases construed as verbal group complexes – we are getting towards 100,000 forms: all of these with one and the same lexical verb. But the network which specifies all these options is relatively simple (see Figure 5); this huge set of possibilities arises from the intersection of a fairly small set of fairly simple choices. That is what the grammar of a language is like.

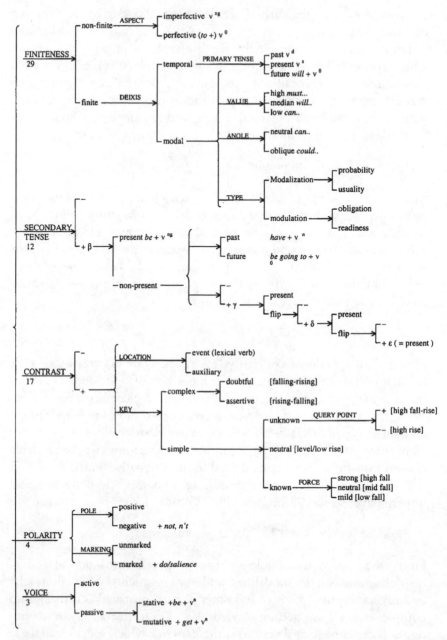

Figure 5

When I wrote the initial English clause grammar for the Penman artificial intelligence (text generation) project, at the Information Sciences Institute of the University of Southern California in 1980, it was a network consisting of 81 systems. When it had been installed into the program, I asked the project director, Professor William Mann, how many different selection expressions (clause types) he thought the network would specify. His estimate was somewhere in the order of 10^9 – say between half a billion and a billion. I am not claiming that my grammar got it right – far from it! My point is that this figure is entirely reasonable as an output for the clause grammar of a natural language. 10^9 is less than 2^{30}; it needs only 29 independent binary choices to yield that number of possibilities. The grammar was then extended by Christian Matthiessen, who worked with the Penman project for a number of years; the existing network has around 1,000 systems. Likewise the systemic grammar being developed by Robin Fawcett at the University of Wales: this differs descriptively in various aspects, but there are also about one thousand systems in the network.

Needless to say these networks do not contain any single point of entry into 29 independent binary systems. The actual organization is much richer: more complex, and also more indeterminate. The relations among the systems within the grammar – the patterns of grammatical *agnation* – involve not only simultaneity and dependence but also disjunct and conjunct entry conditions, such as "if both term x in system a and term y in system b are selected, then there is selection among terms within p, q, r in system c". Since it represents the grammar in paradigmatic form, the network construes these complex patterns of agnation. What the network does not display, however, are degrees of partial association between systems, because this depends on the probabilistic nature of the systems themselves.

When the grammarian says, for example, that every clause in English is (selects for) either positive or negative polarity, this means "with a certain measure of probability": a global, system-internal probability but one that is susceptible to local, environmental conditioning. The global probability might be "positive, 0.9; negative, 0.1"; but in certain contexts, such as sets of regulations, these probabilities might become equal, or even get reversed. Each instance – every clause that is actually spoken, or written, in English – modifies the probabilities of the system; these can therefore change in the course of time. Under typical conditions they change very gradually; but there may be more or less catastrophic moments, as in creolization and decreolization, or language death. Sometimes a probability profile will become increasingly skew, with one option tending towards zero and then perhaps disappearing altogether, like *thou* in the English second person system *thou/you*. But by and large the quantitative structure of a grammar seems to remain relatively stable from one generation to the next.

We seek to build such probabilities into the grammatics; they can be readily embodied in the representation of a system network. In the 1980 Penman grammar I attached to each system the values of either 0.5: 0.5 or 0.9: 0.1, interpreting it as either equiprobable or significantly skew; these values derived from some small-scale frequency studies I had carried out many years earlier, which suggested that at least the most general ("least delicate") systems in the grammar tended towards one or other of these two profiles (considering just those systems that could be represented as binary). Now that we have access to very large corpuses it becomes possible to test such a hypothesis; thus, using a sample of 18 million words (about 1.5 million clauses) of written English, Zoe James and I found that the relative frequency of simple past:present (primary tense) was 51:49 per cent; that of positive:negative (polarity) was 88:12 per cent. We interpret these figures as the manifestation of inherent probability within the system.[10]

These are global probabilities; they are of course subject to conditioning of various kinds. (1) Probabilities vary **locally** with the register (functional variety of a language; cf. further below): so, for example, while our provisional figures for the system of English verbal deixis were as in Figure 6, showing future having a very low probability (less than 0.6 per cent of primary tenses overall), when we examine the register of weather forecasting we find – no surprise! – that future leaps to the front as the favoured tense. (2) Probabilities vary **transitionally** throughout the unfolding of a text ("logogeneti-cally"): thus, Fawcett's GENESYS grammar referred to above presents the probabilities as shifting when one re-enters the system network. (3) Thirdly, probabilities vary **conditionally** according to selection in other systems: Fawcett's "preference re-setting rules" in fact operate

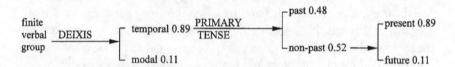

Figure 6   Probability profile of English "verbal deixis" system

410

not only on subsequent passes but also in the course of a single pass. All these may be seen as systematic aspects of the grammar of a natural language.[11]

It is important to stress that these quantitative properties of systems are part of the grammar of an individual, similarly to the options themselves and their realizations. I am not talking here about predicting particular sayings, which are the outcome of a complex mixture of system-internal, contextual (i.e. environmental) and random factors falling within the individual's subjective experience. It is of no great theoretical interest to try to predict what you or I are going to say next (even though in practice we are doing this with each other all the time). But it is part of our semiotic make-up, our higher-level consciousness, that our discourse as a whole will pattern quantitatively according to the probability profile of the grammar. This feature of discourse is one of the principal factors enabling children to learn their mother tongue. (It is of course a feature of the lexicogrammatical system as a whole; grammar and vocabulary are simply the two complementary aspects of a single stratum.)

By the same token, the quantitative changes referred to earlier take place in the grammar of the individual, as the "unit of selection", the locus of the evolution of the language. It may be that major categorical shifts in the system of a language take place primarily in the course of intergenerational transmission; we see the developmental cycle biologically as one of growth, maturity, senescence and eventual death, with growth (meaning "getting bigger") coming to an end in late adolescence, and we tend to assume that semiotically also maturity means stability – the adult's meaning potential stays the same, until it begins to decay. But the mature system is not impervious to change. I myself am aware of various changes that have taken place in my own grammar of English during my adult lifetime – including three or four within the verbal group, starting (and perhaps remaining) as changes in relative frequency but still restructuring the system in subtle and significant ways. This is the "instantiation" effect referred to earlier, whereby each instance (which means, in this context, each utterance received by and produced by the individual) perturbs the probabilities of the system: rather as each day's weather perturbs the probabilities of the climatic system, except that in a semiotic system, as opposed to a physical one, this effect takes place in three time dimensions – three "histories" at once, the *social-semiotic process* ("the language" as observed from a distance), the *individual brain* (the neuronal group networks), and the *text* ("the language" as observed from close at hand).

411

A language is a semogenic system: it is a system which creates meaning. This is a system of fourth-order complexity: it is physical; also biological (with added *life*); also social (with added *value*);[12] and also semiotic (with added *meaning*). All other human semiotic systems derive their specific potential for meaning from the general potential opened up by language. Such a system has three distinct histories: evolutionary (the phylogenetic evolution of human language, as particular languages), developmental (the ontogenetic growth of the individual's neurosemiotic potential) and individuating (the logogenetic unfolding of discourse, as particular texts). Let me briefly contextualize the preceding discussion, the probabilistic nature of the system, in terms of these three histories; then in the section that follows I will note some qualitative feature of language that will put this part in perspective. The examples, as elsewhere, relate to English.

Any piece of discourse unfolds as a flow of meaning, a complex interplay of the predictable and the unpredictable. From the standpoint of the *instance*, this means a construction of "given" and "new" in relation to the text itself and its environment ("context of situation"). From the standpoint of the *system*, it means its overall pattern of information and redundancy. If the bimodal hypothesis of the quantitative typology of systems turns out to be valid (it may not be), this would mean that the well-recognized marking principle in grammar has a quantitative basis, in that systems (again taking the binary as prototypical) are of two types: either both terms are equally (un)marked, with probabilities roughly equal at 0.5:0.5, or else one of the two is marked, with the probabilities skew at roughly 0.9:0.1. By reference to the mathematical theory of information these values define two critical cusps: (1) at 0.5:0.5, H (information) = 1, R (redundancy) = 0; (2) at 0.9:0.1, H = R = 0.5. Type (1), with zero redundancy, is maximally efficient mathematically – but not socially; one needs redundancy to allow for noise. With type (2), redundancy and information balance out. It seems that discourse unfolds as the interplay of grammatical systems of these two logogenetic profiles: the equiprobable, like past/present tense (and probably singular/plural [number], material/mental/relational [process type], intransitive/trans-itive), and the skew, like positive/negative polarity (and probably active/passive [voice], declarative/interrogative [mood], final/non-final focus [information]). It would also seem, ontogenetically, that a system having these properties would be maximally accessible to a learner; whereas one with no redundancy, or the same level of redundancy throughout, or with the degree of redundancy scattered randomly across all possible values, would be much more difficult for a learner to model progressively. In phylogenetic time, a probabilistic system of this kind achieves metastability: it is constantly being modulated, in dynamic interaction with the (material and semiotic) environment.

In all three dimensions of its history, the general tendency of a system of this kind is towards growth; the meaning potential is constantly tending to expand. (1) The system tends to **evolve** towards increasing semantic complexity: this clearly happened in the evolution of language itself, with the accumulating experience that constituted the human condition; we cannot observe this, but we can observe it happening with particular languages when that condition changes, which means that new semiotic resources (new registers) evolve in tandem with new material practices. (2) The **development** of each individual's language is another history of expansion, as successive areas of semantic space are colonized and existing ones filled out with greater delicacy; but this is in turn rests on a critical epigenetic progression, from (i) generalization, around age one to two [non-referring → "proper" (individual) reference → "common" (class) reference → taxonomic (class of classes) reference], through (ii) abstractness, around age four to six [concrete (perceptual) reference → abstract reference], to (iii) metaphor, around age nine to thirteen [primary construal → secondary construal of experience] (cf. Section 4 below). (3) The **unfolding** of a particular text, dialogic or monologic, is itself a form of growth as new instantial meanings are being created; we are most easily aware of this in technical discourse because this is the process whereby meanings come to be technicalized, but it happens all the time in the spontaneous exchanges of everyday encounter, as interactants engage in semiotic challenge and display. In all these histories, meanwhile, the past is always present; the system continues to accommodate the foundations of the construction of experience; the individual's grammar continues to embody the elements that first appeared (including even some protolinguistic ones); and the instances of discourse continue to incorporate a significant repertory of ready-worded "snatches", semiotic fragments from earlier instances of text. The old is then ongoingly recontextualized within the ambience of the new, and this too is a part of the fundamental semogenic process.

4 Re-coupling, variation, and metaphor: some qualitative features

In order to understand the nature of these processes we need to think both of the mechanisms of semiotic expansion and of the demands which provide the selective context in which this expansion takes place. Let us look at the latter first, returning to the earlier category of "metafunction" as the conceptual framework used to theorize these demands. We remarked above that the grammar (= lexicogrammar) of every natural language is a theory of human experience. This does not mean that the words and structures "correspond to" or "reflect" some pre-existing order of things. The categorization of reality is not something that is given to us "out there"; on the contrary, the grammar has to construct it, setting up the categories in terms of which we experience the world. And, as Ellis points out, when we semanticize experience in this way, by turning it into meaning, we do so not by recognizing phenomena that are inherently alike, but by treating as alike phenomena that are inherently disparate.[13] The order is one that we impose, through the "global mapping" in our higher-order consciousness.

We refer to this by saying that the grammar "construes experience" – or, if preferred, human beings construe experience in the forms of grammar. Again, we interpret this both in the systemic and in the instantial sense.[14] The grammatical *system*, as meaning potential, construes the accumulated experience of the species, together with features which may be specific to this or that particular culture band. The grammar of individual *instances* – the unfolding pattern of selections made within the system – construes the relevant individuated fragment of experience (real, putative or imaginary) **within and by reference to this ideational semantic space**. From this point of view, the hypothesis that the evolution of the brain into ever more complex morphology has been selected for by the increasingly complex relationship that exists between a "higher" organism and its environment, the need to construe richer and more "dimensioned" neuronal mappings of experience, fits well with what we find in the organization of grammar. At the same time, however, it is not the complete story. The grammar not only *construes*; it also *enacts* – or, again, human beings enact, in the forms of grammar, their "interpersonal" (intra-species, inter-organism) relationships. Systemically, in this interpersonal metafunction, the grammar constitutes both society and, through society, the individual self; instantially, the grammar enacts dialogic

414

roles and the ongoing "personification" of 'I' and 'you'. In the mainstream of western linguistics these enactive, interpersonal resources of language have been relatively neglected, treated as an appendage to the grammar rather than as an essential part of it.[15] Yet it is impossible to construe experience as a semiotic act on its own; it can only be done in mutual contextualization with an interactive event – no transitivity without mood! And orchestrating the two we find a third metafunctional network in the grammar, that we refer to as the "textual" because it *creates* the texture, which I described above (when approaching it ontogenetically) as a kind of "virtual reality", a parallel universe that is made of meaning and thus makes it possible at one and the same time both to construe experience and to enact social processes in the form of a semiotic act.[16] Systemically, the "textual" grammar creates the "flow of information", the semiotic mode of activity which, in human beings, is inseparably linked with the material; instantially, it gives structure to the individuated act of meaning.

So when we talk of the demands that are made on the semogenic resources of a grammar, we refer not only to its ideational (experiential and logical) resources but also to the interpersonal and the textual. In its interaction with the physical and social environment, grammar is a force for action as well as for reflection; and, in addition, it creates a semiotic environment all of its own. What then can we say about the mechanisms by which these resources are continually being expanded? I will say a few words about these resources, under three headings: de- and re-coupling, variation, and grammatical metaphor. And these have one thing in common: they depend on the unique nature of language as a stratified system.

Stratification was the most important single step in the evolution of human language: deconstruing the protolinguistic, "content/expression sign", and introducing a purely abstract, lexicogrammatical level of semiosis in between. By "purely abstract" here I mean one that does not interface directly with either of the two material frontiers of language: whereas the phonological system interfaces with auditory processes and the processes of speech production, and the semantic system interfaces with our perception of the outside world, and our own inner world of consciousness, grammar interfaces only with those two interfaces. This is also the most important step in the child's development of language. I mentioned above how Nigel first achieved it: by "splitting" a (non-referring) protolinguistic system of three signs, *ama dada anna* each on high level tone, into two simultaneous systems: one proto-ideational,

415

consisting of three referring "proper names", realized as variant articulation; one proto-interpersonal, consisting of two enacting moods, realized as falling vs. rising intonation. Once the stratal principle is well established, this kind of *decoupling and recoupling* becomes a major semogenic force. As an example, much later as the child's mood system develops we meet with a related phenomenon, when what starts as a single opposition between 'statement', realized as Subject before Finite operator **and** falling tone (e.g. *that's mìne*), and 'yes/no question' realized as Finite before Subject **and** rising tone (*is that mìne?*), is deconstrued and reconstrued as two simultaneous options, (1) mood: declarative/interrogative, realized as Subject ^ Finite versus Finite ^ Subject, and (2) key: certain/uncertain, realized as falling tone versus rising tone – giving a four-term set *that's mìne* ('I'm telling you'), *that's mìne* ('is that what you're telling me?'), *is that mìne* ('I'm asking you'), *is that mìne* ('you tell me'). The grammar now has two systems where there was just one before. We know that these processes take place ontogenetically because we can observe them; we may sometimes be able to observe them in the history of the system, in the case of languages with a known and recorded past; and we can find quantitative evidence for recognizing that a change of this kind is in progress.[17]

Secondly, a stratified semiotic is able to accommodate *variation*. Variation in language is essentially of three kinds: dialect, register, and code. (i) Dialectal variation does not in itself increase the meaning potential; it is the effect of drift in the realization of the semantic system, while the semantic system itself remains stable (or rather, evolves without such variation). (ii) Diatypic, or register, variation, on the other hand, does increase it: this is variation in the meaning potential that is associated with different forms of collective activity (the "division of labour"). As new social practices evolve, further semantic space is opened up; and variation occurs in the setting of grammatical probabilities in resonance with features of the semiotic context. We could return to the example of tense in weather forecasting, mentioned earlier: where clauses such as *tomorrow will be cloudy, with rain at times* become the norm, an alternative universe of experience is construed in which future is the unmarked temporal state. (iii) "Code" is being used here in Bernstein's sense; it has nothing to do with the thoroughly misleading notion of language itself being a code. Code variation also increases the meaning potential, although in a significantly different way. Code variation is semantic: it is variation in the meanings that are typically associated with, or "realize", specific situation types in the culture – here, the stratal relationship is that of language itself as realization of a higher-level semiotic. Through this kind of variation the system organizes itself to favour just those meanings that are selected for by the relevant sub-culture (of class, caste, clan, generation, gender or whatever); hence it is the code selection that transmits the culture, and cultural variation, across the generations. This then turns out to be the semiotic mechanism whereby social hierarchies of all kinds are maintained and perpetuated (Hasan has shown how this works, in a large-scale study of the semantic variation in the spontaneous discourse of mothers with their pre-school children).[18] By the same token, the transmission process can be subverted: new meanings can arise at the disjunctions, and social orders can be transformed – either unconsciously, or by conscious linguistic engineering. The semogenic potential of code variation is located mainly at this higher level of the social semiotic.[19]

The third of the semogenic resources I referred to is that of **grammatical metaphor**: the process whereby experience may be largely reconstrued as the individual reaches maturity. I emphasized earlier the metafunctional principle whereby language simultaneously construes experience and enacts interpersonal, social relationships; the central locus of selection here is the clause, which maps these two strands of meaning into a single configuration. Ideationally, the clause construes a "figure" in which the flux of experience is typically channelled into three motifs: a process, the participants in that process, and the attendant circumstances. Prototypically, the process is action, event, mental or symbolic process, or logical relation; the participants are perceptual entities, and their properties; circumstances are time, place, manner and other entities that may be involved. Languages differ in how this organic structure is made manifest; in many languages, English among them, it appears as a patterned deployment of word classes: processes realized by verbs; participants by nouns; circumstances by adverbs, and also by prepositional phrases which then accommodate other entities as indirect or oblique participants. So, for example, *rain was falling steadily on the rooftops.*

This schema has enormous ideational power for construing experience. Once the semiotic system has become stratified, it is already able to categorize; even where a given domain of experience is left unanalysed, like much of the weather, we can set up a categorization *it's raining/it's hailing/it's snowing.* If we continued to use the same kind of synthetic representation for more complex phenomena, saying e.g. *it's winging* when we saw a commotion in the air overhead, the potential for creating such semantic categories would obviously be fairly restricted; but if we construe this analytically as *birds are flying in the sky*, not only can we commute *flying* to *swimming*, *feeding*, or to *swooping*, *darting* (alternatives to, or kinds of, flying), we can commute *birds* to *insects*, or recategorize *birds* as *geese*, *swifts*, *cockatoos* and so on. This greatly increases the overall semogenic potential. Now, things are more readily categorized than actions and events: things tend to stay around, remaining in existence for a perceptible amount of time; and they display various characteristics which can be used for construing them into classes. So when entities are pulled out of the flux, they can be listed: *rain*, *hail*, *thunder*, *lightning* . . .; such lists often appear ontogenetically before clauses, like Nigel's 'things seen on an outing' (*bus*, *train*, *stick*, *stone*, *dog* . . .) where they form an instantial category, like an adult's shopping list; but a (syntagmatic) list of this kind may become systemized (paradigmatic) as a classificatory schema, a taxonomy. All languages embody extensive folk taxonomies, for the speakers themselves (kinship), their condition (emotions, diseases) and their environment (plants, animals, natural features and phenomena). These then may become further elaborated as "expert" taxonomies (e.g. those used by plant breeders or bird watchers), technical taxonomies (e.g. those of parts of tools and machines, raw materials, processes of manufacture), and perhaps also scientific taxonomies (as in biology, chemistry and medicine).[20] This is where, in English, and many other languages, the nominal group is put to work.

The nominal group is able to form sub-categories, not only paradigmatically by renaming (one kind of *bird* is a *toucan*), but also syntagmatically by expanding (one kind of *toucan* is a *grey-breasted mountain toucan*; likewise one kind of *switch* is an *automatic polarized reversing switch*, and so on); the expansions may also embody clause-type semantic configurations, such as *grey-breasted* 'whose breast is grey', *reversing* 'which reverses (the motor)'. But all the entries in such a taxonomy have the same experiential standing: a *toucan* is more general than a *grey-breasted mountain toucan*, and a *bird* is more general still, but all are equally part of the sensible material world, and any grammatical configuration in which a *grey-breasted mountain toucan* could appear could equally accept a *mountain toucan*, a *toucan*, or a *bird*. There might be textual or interpersonal constraints; but the semiotic ordering of experience would not be perturbed.

418

But other nominal groups, such as those that we typically find in scientific discourse, are of a different order. Here we meet expressions like *localized gravitational attraction, the sequential rupturing of interatomic bonds, vertebrate brain evolution, the orbital motion of an electron, the mutual adaptation of species*. These follow the grammar of the everyday nominal group – with one important difference: the nouns functioning as head are not regular participants. They are more like (and are very often derived from) names of processes: *attract, rupture, evolve, move, adapt*. A typical sentence from this register of discourse would be: *The goal of evolution is to optimize the mutual adaptation of species*; or: *On an atomic scale the slow growth of cracks corresponds to the sequential rupturing of interatomic bonds at rates as low as one bond rupture per hour*. These exemplify the phenomenon of "grammatical metaphor".

In metaphor in its traditional sense, one **word** moves into the domain of another; looked at from the other end, a lexico-semantic construct that is typically realized by one word is instead realized by another, which typically realizes something else: e.g. *sowed suspicion*, where 'provided grounds for', more typically realized as *caused*, is realized instead by *sowed*, which typically realizes 'scattered for cultivation'. This kind of metaphor is lexical. In grammatical metaphor, on the other hand, a grammatical-semantic construct that is typically realized by (a member of) one **class** is instead realized by (a member of) another class, which typically realizes something else: e.g. *planetary motion*, where 'process: do, etc', more typically realized as a verb (e.g. *move*), is realized instead by a noun, a class which typically realizes 'participating entity'. As long as we say *planets move* we are still in the realm of the first grammar, the primary semiotic construal of experience, in which the phenomenon is construed as happening (grammatically, a clause), with a process/verb *move* and a participating entity/noun *planets*. When this is reworded as a nominal group *planetary motion*, it takes on the grammar that is characteristic of classes of **things**. And just as in lexical metaphor there is a semantic **junction**, such that *sowed* (in *sowed suspicion*) carries over features of its typical sense as scattering seeds (and the metaphor is readily extended to *seeds of suspicion*), so also there is semantic junction in grammatical metaphor, such that the noun *motion* carries over features of the typical sense of a noun as the name of a participating entity. There now exists a thing called *motion*, and *planetary motion* is one kind, a sub-class of this thing. The sense of 'change location', as in *move*, has become objectified (in Whorf's sense; i.e. 'made into an object'; not 'made objective').

Grammar has always had this potential for "cross-coupling". But it came well to the fore in the classical languages of the iron age, such as Chinese, Sanskrit and Greek, where it became the resource for creating abstract, technical objects: in Greek, on the model of *praxis, poiēsis* 'doing, making' and *pragma, poiēma* 'thing done, thing made', hundreds of verbs were nominalized as technical terms, and these nouns, together with their associated nominal group constructions, formed the core of a new, typically written, mode of discourse. Such "junctional" meanings provide the cornerstones of a ***theory***, which is a designed semantic sub-system for reorganizing experience in a technological environment. But then in the "modern" period, with the emergence of experimental science, another major semiotic shift took place, further exploiting the stratal potential of language. In Newton's *Opticks*, for example, we regularly find patterns such as (pp. 156–7): *For in all whites produced by Nature, there uses to be a mixture of all sorts of Rays, and by consequence a composition of all Colours*, where *mixture* and *composition* are not functioning as technical terms; they are instantial nominalizations in which kinds of 'doing' have been construed as temporary 'things' to meet the requirements of the argument – as we find if we track them back in the text: this is preceded by *I could never yet by mixing only two primary Colours produce a perfect white. Whether it may be compounded of a mixture of three ... I do not know*, where both 'mixing' and 'compounding' start off as verbs. We do not find this kind of discoursal grammatical metaphor in Chaucer's technical writings. But the theorizing discourse of physical science involved sustained reasoning from observation and experiment, and this was achieved by extending the metaphoric potential still further. A typical sequence from modern scientific writing would be the following (*New Scientist* no. 1916, 21 March 1994, p. 37): ... *rapid changes in the rate of evolution are caused by external events*. Let us look at the textual environment in which this clause occurs.

The previous paragraph contained the clause *life does not evolve gradually but intermittently*; followed by various pieces of observational evidence (e.g. *from the study of fossil records*) and ending with *found ... that extinctions occur in waves*. The writers now turn all this into a 'thing', *rapid changes in the rate of evolution*, so that they can then take the next step of postulating what brings this phenomenon about (... *are caused by* ...). It happens to be someone else's postulate, but that does not affect the grammatical structure of the argument; the same pattern recurs later in the sentence when they give an example: *(evolutionary biologists have sought) an explanation of the demise of the dinosaurs in a meteorite impact.* We now have not only *change, evolution, extinction* but also *demise, impact* construed metaphorically as nouns. This is what enables the argument to proceed; it would be difficult to construct the logical-semantic progression and flow of information from one thesis to another if each had to be construed clausally every time. Thus each step gets "packaged" so that it can become a participant in a further process; and this "process" is itself the outcome of another grammatical metaphor whereby the logical-semantic relation '*x* happens, so *y* happens' is reconstrued in the form of a verb, *caused* – which may then be further metaphorized into a noun *cause* (*is the cause of;* cf. *sought an explanation of* above).

Thus the metaphoric reconstruction of the grammar is adapted to the evolution of forms of discourse embodying technical taxonomies and sequential argument (of which the present sentence is a typical example); it is useful for building theories. By the same token, it brings about a secondary semanticization, a semiotic reconstrual of human experience in which the flux (the "primitive ooze" as Firth used to call it, punning on Greek *protousia*) is not only analysed and "parsed out", as in the clausal grammar of our mother tongues, but made stable, bounded and determinate by the nominalizing grammar of systematic knowledge. Where the grammar of daily life presents the world as a mix of things and going-on, of order and disorder, stability and flux, the elaborated grammar of science reconstrues it as a world of things: it holds the world still, symbolically, while it is observed and measured – and also experimented with and theorized about. If this was the only grammar we had, of course, there would be nothing metaphorical about it; it would be the unmarked mode of categorizing experience. But it is not. **In all three dimensions of semohistory** – the evolution of the language system, the development of each child's meaning potential and the individuated unfolding of the text – **there is the same ordering**: the mixed, more compromising clausal grammar comes first, and the other is built up as an elaboration upon it.[21]

Ontogenetically, the metaphorical grammar comes fairly late: children can master the abstract (meanings without a perceptual correlate) at around age four to five (so this is when we put them into school); but they cannot cope with the metaphorical, in this sense of the semiotic reconstrual of experience, until puberty, the threshold of the adult condition. There seems to be a developmental semiotic progression along the following lines:

classifying:	specific to general	from age 1–2 (into mother tongue)
technicalizing:	concrete to abstract	from age 4–5 (into primary school)
theorizing:	congruent to metaphorical	from age 9–13 (into secondary school)

This is obviously highly schematic; but it draws attention to what I think is an important point. By the time the secondary grammar is developed, the everyday grammar has been in place for some time; it is already deeply installed as a theory of experience. Hence it does not get **replaced** by the metaphorical model; rather, the two co-exist and interpenetrate, and (in most cases at least!) the individual continues to move freely between more and less elaborated modes of discourse. There is no insulation between the two. But there is **conflict** – they cannot both be "true"; and so a complementarity is set up, such that experience has to be modelled from both standpoints in order to get a rounded picture of "reality", one which will enable us to go on interacting in increasingly complex ways with our environment. But the **principle** of semiotic complementarity is nothing new; it is there from the start in the grammar of the mother tongue, where many systems already embody competing and contradictory interpretations of experience: e.g. transitive and ergative as modellings of process, tense and aspect as modellings of time, count and mass as modellings of substance and so on.[22] The coexistence of competing representations is in fact built in to the semiotic mode of activity; that is how it is able to remain in cohort with activities in the material mode.

So it happens that when we come to construct our scientific models, the daily grammar's view of things is very much in the picture, even if typically below the level of conscious attention. This is perhaps especially true when we try to model **ourselves**, as we do when we come to elaborate the concept of "mind". Matthiessen has shown how the object of study of "cognitive science" is constructed out of the grammar of daily life: from the transitivity system of our Standard Average European languages, and in particular from the grammar of mental and symbolic processes (the "grammar of semiosis", as he puts it). It is quite natural that fundamental domains of human experience, even when theorized at the highest scientific level, should still be grounded in the inherited wisdom of the species, the categorization that lies at the heart of its grammar. But Matthiessen's contention is that this particular development has been one-sided: on the one hand privileging the "mental" over the "symbolic" in the grammar's construal of consciousness, and on the other hand, more broadly, privileging the

422

experiential aspect of the grammar over the interpersonal. We might get a richer, more rounded conception, one less tuned to computational and information-processing notions, if we complemented the folk grammar of 'thinking' with that of 'meaning' (saying, symbolizing); and still more – though much harder to achieve – if we complemented the wisdom deriving from the folk construal of experience with that which could be derived from the enactment of interpersonal relationships (harder because the latter is non-referential: it is "meaning-as-doing" rather than "meaning-as-knowing"). In other words, we can use our grammatics – our metatheory of grammar as theory – as a tool for thinking with, deconstruing the everyday grammar of experience to reveal the assumptions that lie beneath some of our fundamental organizing concepts.[23]

The metaphoric power of grammar is inherent in the stratal organization of language, which enables us to de-couple the lexicogrammatical/semantic interface and to re-couple it with a different ordering. All human adults can do this; and all human languages, however variable their primary construction of reality, have the same potential for reconstruing in another form. With current advances in biology and physics – not to mention changes in the social order, leading to less elitist and more democratic formations of knowledge – probably in the next period of history we will again be engaging in such a reconstrual. But perhaps the next one will be more of a synthesis, a new semantic arising out of the contradictions between the primary and secondary construals that some of us are living with today.

5 Sociological, philosophical, system-theoretic and cybernetic perspectives

In this final section, I should like to suggest the context for what I have been saying – to try to show where it fits in. Since language is a fourth-order system, at once physical and biological and social, as well as having its own special character as semiotic, the total context must be in terms of theories about systems of all these types. It will be clear that the ideological antecedents of my discourse lie not in the formal grammars and truth-conditional semantics of the latter part of the century, but in a more functionally-oriented linguistics: that of Sapir and Whorf, Malinowski and Firth, Bühler, Mathesius and Trubetzkoy, Hjelmslev, Benveniste and Martinet, among many others. It is beyond my present scope – and certainly beyond my ability – to characterize the present state of knowledge in other disciplines. But I should like to refer, even though inevitably in very simple and sketchy terms, to each of four scholars whose work seems to me to corroborate the relevance of the approach to language and mind that I have taken here: these are Basil Bernstein, John Ellis, Jay Lemke and Michio Sugeno. What follows is a brief encounter with some of their important ideas.

I referred earlier to Bernstein in acknowledging the concept of "code". This is a peculiarly difficult concept because it lies squarely at the fulcrum between language as *system* and language as *instance* – rather like today's "global warming", which people are uncertain whether to treat instantially as a long-term weather pattern or systemically as a deviation in the climate. But code as Bernstein theorizes it, and has continued to explore it in his more recent work, is an essential link in the chain of reasoning about language; furthermore, the kind of metaphoric reconstrual I have been discussing is itself a special case of code-type variation. More generally, however, it is Bernstein's overall theoretical principles I have in mind. Bernstein theorizes the social system-&-process in terms which not only accommodate language but offer a principled explanation of it as the critical social semiotic: the social foundations of meaning are, by the same token, the semiotic foundations of society. He shows how the forms of the social relationship are construed in discourse; and, through his investigations first of familial and latterly of pedagogic discourse practices, how these forms are transmitted through the class (or other) specialization of the culture of families and schools. Thus code variation, while instantial in its manifestations, is systemic in its effects: it gives differential access to the semiotic and material potential of the society. The distribution of power is closely bound up with forms of symbolic control (itself a highly condensed and complex theoretical concept). Bernstein's ideas about language have consistently been misrepresented by populist liberals, particularly in the United States; but they bring to linguistic theory a dimension that is otherwise lacking.[24]

John Ellis' book *Language, Thought, and Logic* sets out very clearly the critical features of mainstream twentieth-century linguistic philosophy which have made it so unfriendly an environment for those working on language in a social semiotic perspective. He contends that its weaknesses can be located in the three "classical theoretical traps" which have led to what he calls "initial missteps in theory of language".

One is the notion that language is primarily a means of communication and that it evolved essentially for that purpose; the idea of language as a code, with pre-coded meanings existing somewhere "in the mind", is a natural corollary of this particular fallacy. The second is that the primitive categories of language are (to express it in my own terms) ideational rather than interpersonal: that evaluative meanings arose later than descriptive ones, and are to be explained as derivative from them. (I disagree with Ellis, however, when he actually reverses the priorities, putting the evaluative before the descriptive; it seems to me that semogenic evidence of any kind suggests that they co-evolve, each being essential to the other.) The third misstep is the idea that when language sets up categories it does so on the basis of some pre-existing features of inherent likeness; whereas in fact linguistic categorization is precisely a process of treating as alike phenomena that are perceived to be different. Not only is the world an unlabelled place – it is an uncategorized place; there are no natural classes – or, what comes to the same thing, there are indefinitely many of them. Ellis goes on to expound his own view of lexicogrammar as imposing categories on experience: "construing experience", in the terms that I have used. The perspective adopted here is I think fully compatible with Ellis' theoretical stance.[25]

I have been drawing heavily on different aspects of Jay Lemke's work for some considerable time; there are two aspects which are particularly relevant here. One is his concept of *metaredundancy*, with which he is able to theorize the stratal relationship in language. This "realizing" relationship has proved problematic and elusive, resisting modelling either in terms of physical cause-&-effect (which involves real time) or of logical transformation (which involves replacement). Lemke shows that a stratified system is one in which there is a relationship of complex redundancies, which can be expressed summarily as follows: given a tri-stratal system S/LG/Ph, then a sound pattern Ph (a, b, c) is redundant with a wording pattern LG (l, m, n), and this entire complex (l, m, n / a, b, c) is redundant with a meaning pattern S(p, q, r). This relationship is reversible (and hence cannot, like cause-&-effect, be reduced to sequential binary relations); we can write either (1) p, q, r / (l, m, n / a, b, c) or (2) (p, q, r / l, m, n) / a, b, c. Expressed in terms of "realization": (1) "p, q, r is realized as the realization of l, m, n, in a, b, c", (2) "a, b, c realizes the realization of p, q, r in l, m, n". Since the system as a whole is metastable (cf. also the second point below), such that it persists by constantly changing in interaction with its own

425

environment, the relationship of language to its sociocultural context is also one of redundancy: the entire stratal complex S/LG/Ph realizes a higher-level semiotic construct (this is what makes possible the semantic variation shown by Hasan to be the mechanism for Bernstein's codes). This "redundancy of redundancies" is what Lemke characterizes as the "metaredundancy" of the system.

The second critical aspect of Lemke's work on language is his locating of it in the context of a general theory and typology of systems. Language is to be understood as an *eco-system* of a special kind. An eco-system is a self-organizing open system which evolves its own epigenetic pattern of development; and which is autocatalytic, subject to the law of self-organizing criticality – to moments of individual catastrophic change which in turn alters the environment so as to favour such change in others. Such systems persist through "ecological succession", as mosaics of microsystems of mixed age and mixed character. Human societies are eco-social systems, constituted out of the dialectic of the material and the semiotic, and having strong material semiotic couplings (as formulated in terms of metaredundancy above); the prototypical semiotic resource system is language. Language is thus an essential part of the human condition and of human history; moreover it has the special property that it is able to model not only the physical, biological and social systems that engender it, but also itself. The dialectic of system and instance that operates at all strata creates the necessary conditions for the system's ongoing change.[26]

The scholars I have referred to in these paragraphs engage with language from varied disciplinary and thematic standpoints; but one message to be gathered from their work is that it is unproductive and indeed distorting to reduce language to a communication code – or the brain to a digital computing mechanism. As far as the brain is concerned, the wave of reaction against behaviourist ways of thinking (which as a matter of fact were never very prevalent outside the United States) seems to have led some researchers in cognition into what looks rather like a new version of behaviourism, in which (with due apology to Milton) new "cognitive" is but old "con" writ large:[27] the mind is being modelled as a device for processing information. Bruner, one of the founders of cognitive science, has expressed his disquiet at this tendency that has arisen in the field.[28] It must have been tempting, at first, to think of the brain as a computer – although it might have seemed strange to expect that, because the human brain can design a machine capable of performing (some) operations which are (apparently) similar to its own, the brain itself would be of the same design. I have already quoted Edelman's observation that the human brain is more like a jungle than a computer; it evolves, in Lemke's typology, as a kind of eco-system – and also, of course, as a part of a bigger one, namely a human being.

Michio Sugeno takes the view that the way to improve computers is to make them function more like human beings; in other words, computing should be based on natural language. Sugeno began by taking up fuzzy logic, as first expounded by Lotfi Zadeh; he extended it to "fuzzy computing", with results already apparent in Japanese houses, where it is used to control appliances in the kitchen and in the laundry. The next step, he envisions (and his visions have a habit of turning into reality, as happened when he was able to teach his car to park itself), will have to be "intelligent computing": that is, controlling the computer directly by means of "wording", using the lexicogrammatical practices of everyday discourse – not constrained by the rules of formal logic, nor idealized so as to be rid of indeterminacy. Let me comment in conclusion on these two features, taking them however in the opposite order.

Scientists have sometimes raised the problem, as their twentieth-century world view, grounded in relativity and quantum physics, has swung steadily round towards uncertainty, flux, and the unbounded nature of the cosmos, that language is too fixed and too determinate to cope with the spirit of the age. I have pointed out elsewhere that this criticism should rather be levelled against their own designed metalanguages; it is not a noticeable feature of language itself. Recently I heard that, since it now appears that the primordial inflation of the universe and the big bang can have taken place only in "imaginary time", physicists would now like to have a tense system that will construe imaginary time for them (I think we could probably oblige!). I have stressed all along that language in its everyday, mother tongue guise is inherently indeterminate, abounding in ambiguities, blends, overlaps and "borderline cases", as well as in the kinds of complementarity referred to earlier. Rather than idealizing the indeterminacy out of the picture, discarding it as a marginal or pathological effect, our grammatics attempts to celebrate it as an essential and positive feature. We are not very good at this yet; it is not easy to model. But for Sugeno such indeterminacy is a critical element in natural grammars, one that is fundamental to his concept of intelligent computing.[29]

But perhaps even more critical, in Sugeno's view, is the way the linguistic potential is instantiated: how people explore, exploit and extend this elastic semantic space, not by following any rules of logic but by exchanging meanings with each other in particular social situations, situations which in turn instantiate the higher-level semiotic potential of the culture. The focus of attention is language-in-context: how people reason within these situations and argue about them; how they assign Bayesian-type probabilities through modality in the grammar; how they identify and value information; how they construe social relations and social processes; and how they make forecasts as the history of the discourse unfolds. To investigate this choreography of meaning, not just as a phenomenon but in such a way that it becomes the basis for intelligent computing, will need an intelligent grammatics; we might also add that it will need a very large corpus, since it is impossible to simulate these processes (to dream them up, or elicit them from others). At the same time, whatever its application to the future development of computing, the kind of linguistic research Sugeno is asking for, combining context-oriented functional semantics with a data-base of natural spontaneous discourse, is exactly what linguistics itself requires for a deeper understanding of language.

There is now a considerable and growing body of linguistic research in systemic-functional terms, developing the picture of language that I have tried to present here. I have referred to particular examples of this, from the work of Fawcett, Hasan, Martin, Matthiessen, and Painter, in very varying fields: computational linguistics, language and social process, grammatical semantics, discourse organization, and children's language development; and this also brings out something that I think is an essential feature of research in language, namely that it must be kaleidoscopic, constantly turning language round and around, as it were, and examining it in different contextual alignments. What I have not alluded to, as not directly germane to the topic of our discussions, is its significance for education. Learning, and more especially educational learning, is essentially a process of creating meaning; and it is meaning of more than one kind. There has proved to be some value in educational materials, and educational practices, that derive from the notion of grammar as the construal of experience; particularly where it is recognized to be, at one and the same time, the means whereby the learner enacts his or her personal relationships, both with the experiences being construed (for example, in the history class!) and with the "others" involved as interactants in the processes of learning.[30] Such "applied linguistic" activities supply a necessary component in the evolution of an effective and powerful grammatics.

Let me return at the very end to the neural-Darwinist perspective. Recent work in America has shown how evolutionary processes can be modelled in terms of a "law of self-organized criticality", whereby there will always be certain species which tend to increase in complexity, towards further-from-equilibrium ecological conditions, leading to periodical changes of a catastrophic kind like the intermittent avalanches in an accumulating heap of dry sand.[31] This kind of "punctuated equilibrium", they say, is just what is predicted by the Darwinian principles of natural selection. Biological processes are harder to model than physical ones, because they are more complex: they are physical (hence governed by the laws of physics), but they have other properties besides – they are dynamic open systems, having life, and therefore history, and the tendency towards increasingly complex patterns of exchange with their environment. Semiotic processes are of still higher orders of complexity. Even when we have an idea of how life evolved from matter, there is still a mystery about how meaning evolved from life: how semiotic processes grow (via the social) out of biological ones. Edelman has shown how higher-order consciousness results in identical manner from evolutionary processes in the brain; and higher-order consciousness is language. Language is not the outward and imperfect manifestation of some idealized entity called mind. It is an evolving eco-semiotic system-&-process, constituting the most recent phase of evolution of the mammalian brain. Higher-order consciousness is symbolic consciousness – or better (since "symbolic" might still imply the re-presentation of something that lies beyond), semiotic consciousness; and semiotic consciousness is another name for meaning.

Notes

1. The source that I have used here is Edelman (1992), which presents an account of the theory in lay terms. The technical presentation will be found in Edelman (1987) and in other works referred to in the notes to the later book.
2. See Lewin (1992) for a summary account of the relevant work in evolutionary neurobiology, by Harry Jerison, by John Allman, and by Robin Dunbar, among others.
3. These features emerge in the course of the study reported in Halliday (1975a). Subsequent research by Clare Painter (1984, 1989) and by Jane Oldenburg (1986) has added considerable further insights into children's protolanguage and the transition to mother tongue.

4. Margaret Bullowa used to say that when she was a medical student in Boston in the 1930s they were taught that babies were born unable to see or hear effectively and that they did not begin to "communicate" until about eighteen months old (i.e. with the onset of the mother tongue). This so obviously contradicts the experience of daily life that it seems hard to believe. It was from work beginning in the 1960s that a picture of the ontogenesis of meaning began to emerge; see Bullowa (1979) for a collection including respresentative samples of her own work and that of Trevarthen, Junker and others.

5. The emergence of grammar (as always, in the sense of 'lexicogrammar' – what we call "grammar" and "lexis" (lexicon, vocabulary) are simply the two poles of the continuous stratum of "wording") is the critical factor in the development of higher-order consciousness; homo sapiens = homo grammaticus. See Halliday (1978a, 1979b); Painter (1984, 1989); Oldenburg (1986).

6. This figure (cf. others in the studies referred to here) brings out the fact that the protolanguage is not dependent on the mother tongue; indeed one cannot tell from the protolanguage what the child's mother tongue is going to be. Cf. Qiu (1985) on protolanguage in (later to be) Chinese-speaking children.

7. See Lewis (1951) for an earlier account.

8. See Halliday (1975a, 1992, 1993b) for further discussion of this point.

9. Sydney Lamb did a great deal to clarify the nature and significance of stratification in language. An early paper (1964a) relates stratification to other theoretical concepts in linguistics. Lamb's recent thinking on the question may be found in Lamb 1999. Cf. also Martin's discussion in chapter 2 of Halliday and Martin (1993a).

10. See Halliday and James (1993) for a detailed account of this investigation. Halliday (1993b) gives further general background.

11. See Fawcett (1994), Fawcett and Tucker (1990), Fawcett, Tucker and Lin (1993).

12. Edelman uses "value" in a different – though related – sense: it is a feature of primary consciousness that it categorizes by value that accrues on the basis of experience (as distinct from genetic programming); see Edelman (1992: pp. 90 ff).

13. See Ellis (1993), chapter 3 (and final paragraphs of chapter 2).

14. For grammar as the construal of experience, and the significance of "instantiation" (relation of system to instance) in that context, see Halliday and Matthiessen (1999).

15. On the interpersonal metafunction see especially the discussion in Martin (1992), chapter 2; and also Lemke (1992).

16. On the textual metafunction see especially Matthiessen (1992).

17. Nesbitt and Plum (1988) investigate the intersection of interdependency (parataxis/hypotaxis) with type of projection (verbal /mental) in a corpus of

spoken English, and propose that the quantitative profile suggests an instance of ongoing semogenic decoupling.

18. Hasan developed the concept of "semantic variation" in the course of her research into the conversational interaction of mothers with pre-school children in a sample of English-speaking families in Sydney: see Hasan (1989, 1992b), Hasan and Cloran (1990).

19. It is important to distinguish the general theoretical concept of "code", as Bernstein developed it, from the massive distortions that surrounded his own application of the concept in the original "restricted/elaborated" opposition. See Bernstein (1971) for the original conceptualization; Hasan (1973) for a contemporary discussion of code in relation to other kinds of variation; chapter 3 "Elaborated and restricted codes: overview and some criticisms" in Bernstein (1990) for his own updating of the concept; and Sadovnik (ed., 1995) for recent discussions of Bernstein's work.

20. These different types of taxonomy are discussed in Halliday and Martin (1993a), especially chapters 2, 8 and 10.

21. This metaphoric shift from the clausal to the nominal construal of experience seems to be a characteristic of scientific discourse in every language; for a brief discussion of scientific Chinese in this respect see chapter 7 of Halliday and Martin (1993a). We do not know, of course, how much this is the effect of linguistic "borrowing", through translation and other processes of contact. It should be clearly stated that every natural language has the same potential for being extended metaphorically in this way (and also of course in other ways; language is itself an inherently metaphoric process, in its relationship to processes of the material world); the most plausible view would be that the particular form of grammatical metaphor that evolved in English and other "standard" languages of Europe selects for the same (or analogous) patterns from the total potential of other languages as they extend into the registers of science – especially, perhaps, because of the eco-social pressures which require this to happen very fast.

22. On transitive and ergative, see Davidse (1991, 1992); on tense and aspect, see e.g. Dahl (1985); on count and mass, Whorf (1956/1964, esp. pp. 140ff.). Cf. also chapter 6 of Halliday and Martin (1993a); Halliday (1967/68).

23. See discussion in Matthiessen (1993a); also Matthiessen (1991b) on the "grammar of semiosis".

24. See Bernstein (1971, 1990); Sadovnik (ed., 1995).

25. See Ellis (1993), passim but esp. chapters 1–3.

26. For "metaredundancy" see Lemke (1984d, esp. chapter 3); cf. Halliday (1992). For language, and semiotic systems in general, in relation to a general typology of systems see Lemke (1993).

27. From Milton's "On the New Forcers of Conscience under the Long Parliament" (1646). The original has "New presbyter is but old priest writ large".

28. See Bruner (1986, 1990). For a different view of mind, one that is in harmony with the present account of language, see James Gee (1992).
29. A lively account of Sugeno's work will be found in McNeill and Freiberger (1993). It is to be hoped that Sugeno (1993) will be forthcoming in print.
30. See Martin (1993) and the numerous references cited therein; also Halliday and Martin (1993a), Part 2 passim.
31. See Bak, Flyvberg and Sneppen (1994) for a summary account in non-technical terms.

APPENDIX: SYSTEMIC THEORY
(1994)

1 Origins of systemic theory

Systemic, or systemic-functional, theory has its origin in the main intellectual tradition of European linguistics that developed following the work of Saussure (see "Saussure, Ferdinand (-Mongin) de; Saussurean Tradition in Twentieth-Century Linguistics" in Asher 1994). Like other such theories, both those from the mid-twentieth century (e.g., the Prague school (see "Prague School Syntax and Semantics" in Asher 1994); French functionalism) and more recent work in the same tradition (e.g., that of Hagège), it is functional and semantic rather that formal and syntactic in orientation, takes the text rather than the sentence as its object, and defines its scope by reference to usage rather than grammaticality. Its primary source was the work of J. R. Firth and his colleagues in London (see "Firth and the London School" in Asher 1994). As well as other schools of thought in Europe such as glossematics it also draws on American anthropological linguistics, and on traditional and modern linguistics as developed in China.

Its immediate source is as a development of scale and category grammar (see "Scale and Category Grammar" in Asher 1994). The name 'systemic' derives from the term 'system', in its technical sense as defined by Firth (1957c); system is the theoretical representation of paradigmatic relations, contrasted with 'structure' for syntagmatic relations (see "Structure, Deep and Surface" in Asher 1994). In Firth's system-structure theory, neither of these is given priority; and in scale and category grammar this perspective was maintained. In systemic theory the system takes priority; the most abstract representation at any level is in paradigmatic terms. Syntagmatic organization is interpreted as the "realization" of paradigmatic features.

First published in *Encyclopedia of Language and Linguistics*, Vol. 8, edited by R. E. Asher. Pergamon Press, 1994, pp. 4505–8.

433

This step was taken by Halliday in the early 1960s so that grammatical and phonological representations could be freed from constraints of structure. Once such representations were no longer localized, they could function prosodically wherever appropriate (see "Phonology: Prosodic" in Asher 1994). The shift to a paradigmatic orientation added a dimension of depth in time, so making it easier to relate language 'in use' to language being learnt; and it enabled the theory to develop both in reflection and in action – as a resource both for understanding and for intervening in linguistic processes. This potential was exploited in the work done during the 1960s on children's language development from birth through their various stages of schooling (see "Systemic Grammar in Applied Language Studies" in Asher 1994).

2 Systems and their realization

The organizing concept of a systemic grammar is that of choice (that is, options in 'meaning potential'; it does not imply intention). A system is a set of options together with a condition of entry, such that if the entry condition is satisfied one option, and one only, must be chosen; for example, in English grammar, [system] 'mood', [entry condition] finite clause, [options] indicative/imperative. The option selected in one system then serves as the entry condition to another; e.g. [entry condition] indicative, [options] declarative/interrogative; hence all systems deriving from a common point of origin (e.g. [clause]) are agnate and together form a 'system network'. At the present stage of development, system networks for English grammar in computational form contain about 1,000 systems. An entry condition may involve the conjunction of different options; hence a system network is not a taxonomic structure but has the form of a lattice.

The system has one further component, namely the 'realization statement' that accompanies each option. This specifies the contribution made by that option to the structural configuration; it may be read as a proposition about the structural constraints associated with the option in question. Realization statements are of seven types:

(a) 'insert' an element (e.g. insert subject);
(b) 'conflate' one element with another (e.g. conflate subject with theme);
(c) 'order' an element with respect to another, or to some defined location (e.g. order finite auxiliary before subject);

(d) 'classify' an element (e.g. classify process as mental: cognition);
(e) 'split' an element into a further configuration (e.g. split mood into subject + finite);
(f) 'preselect' some feature at a lower rank (e.g. preselect nominal group: human collective); and
(g) 'lexify' an element (e.g. lexify subject: *it*).

When paths are traced through a system network, a 'selection expression' is formed consisting of all the options taken up in the various functional components. As the network is traversed, options are inherited, together with their realizations; at the same time, new realization statements continue to figure throughout. The selection expression constitutes the grammar's description of the item (e.g. the particular clause so specified); it is also, by reference to the network, the representation of its systemic relationship to other items in the language – since the grammar is paradigmatic, describing something consists in locating it with respect to the rest (showing its total lineage of agnate forms).

3 Other basic concepts

Systemic theory retains the concepts of 'rank', 'realization', and 'delicacy' from scale and category grammar. 'Rank' is constituency based on function, and hence 'flat', with minimal layering; 'delicacy' is variable paradigmatic focus, with ordering from more general to more delicate; 'realization' (formerly 'exponence') is the relation between the 'strata', or levels, of a multistratal semiotic system – and, by analogy, between the paradigmatic and syntagmatic phases of representation within one stratum. But in systemic theory, realization is held distinct from 'instantiation', which is the relation between the semiotic system (the 'meaning potential') and the observable events, or 'acts of meaning', by which the system is constituted.

The shift to a paradigmatic orientation led to the finding that the content plane of a language is organized in a small number of functionally defined components which Halliday labelled 'metafunctions'. According to this theory the grammar of natural languages evolved in simultaneously (a) 'construing' human experience (the 'experiential' metafunction) and (b) 'enacting' interpersonal relationships (the 'interpersonal' metafunction), both these being underpinned by (c) the resources of (common-sense) logic (the 'logical' metafunction; (a) and (c) are grouped together as 'ideational'). The stratal role of the lexicogrammar lies in mapping these

435

semantic components into a unitary construct, one that is capable of being linearized; in doing this, the grammar (d) 'creates' its own parallel universe in the form of discourse (the 'textual' metafunction; see also "Discourse" in Asher 1994). These metafunctions define the dimensions of semantic space; and since they tend to be realized by different structural resources – experiential meanings segmentally, interpersonal meanings prosodically, logical meanings in iterative structures, and textual meanings in wave-like patterns – they also determine the topological formations that are characteristic of human speech.

A systemic grammar is therefore 'functional' in three distinct though related senses:

(a) its 'explanations' are functional: both the existence of grammar (why grammar evolved as a distinct stratum), and the particular forms that grammars take, are explained in terms of the functions that language evolved to serve;
(b) its 'representations' are functional: a structure is an organic configuration of functions, rather than a tree with nodes labelled as classes;
(c) its 'applications' are functional: it developed as an adjunct to practices associated with language use, requiring sensitivity to functional variation in language ('register' variation). These considerations both relate it to, and at the same time distinguish it from, other functional theories.

4   Other features of the theory

Like the Firthian linguistics from which it evolved, systemic theory is oriented towards language as social process; the individual is construed intersubjectively, through engagement in social acts of meaning. This is not incompatible with a cognitive perspective, which has been adopted in some systemic work (notably Fawcett 1980); but it does rule out any claim for 'psychological reality'. Halliday formulated this general stance as 'language as social semiotic', thereby also locating systemic theory in the thematic context of semiotics, defined as the study of systems and processes of meaning. The relation between language and other sociocultural phenomena is then modelled on that of realization (the perspective here is Firthian rather than Hjelmslevian: see "Hjelmslev, Louis Trolle" in Asher 1994): language 'realizes' culture in the way that, within language, sound realizes wording, and the realization of wording in sound, in its turn, realizes meaning.

It follows from this that systemic theory gives prominence to discourse, or 'text'; not – or not only – as evidence for the system, but valued, rather, as constitutive of the culture. The mechanism proposed for this constitutive power of discourse has been referred to as the 'metafunctional hookup': the hypothesis that (a) social contexts are organic – dynamic configurations of three components, called 'field', 'tenor', and 'mode': respectively, the nature of the social activity, the relations among the interactants, and the status accorded to the language (what is going on, who are taking part, and what they are doing with their discourse); and (b) there is a relationship between these and the metafunctions such that these components are construed, respectively, as experiential, as interpersonal, and as textual meanings. Register, or functional variation in language, is then interpreted as systemic variation in the relative prominence (the probability of being taken up) of different options within these semantic components.

In fact such register variation (spoken/written, commonsense/ technical, transactional/expository, . . . and so on) lies on the continuum between system and text; the characteristic of systemic work is that it brings all parts of this continuum under focus of attention. Analogously, it encompasses both speaker and listener perspectives (in computational terms, text generation and parsing – there are, for example, no nonrecoverable operations such as deletion), and both synoptic and dynamic orientations; and uniquely among current theories, it assigns as much value to interpersonal and textual meaning as to ideational. On the other hand, in other respects systemic work is notably ill-balanced; there has been little study of morphology and phonology, and a disproportionate amount of research relates to English. These reflect on the one hand the contexts of its own development, especially the kinds of application for which it has been sought out; and on the other hand its requirement of comprehensiveness, demanding a coverage which is at once both broad and deep.

5 Development of systemic theory

The outlines of systemic theory were formulated in London in the 1960s by Halliday together with Huddleston, Hudson, and others, and in application to Bernstein's work by Hasan, Mohan, and Turner; other significant input came from the application of systemic concepts in curriculum development work, in the analysis of scientific writings and of natural conversation, and in descriptions of a number of Asian and

African languages. The theory was further developed in the 1970s: by Fawcett, Berry, and Butler in the UK; by Halliday and Hasan; and by Gregory and his colleagues in Toronto. Since 1980 systemic work has expanded considerably in various directions (for reference to work in artificial intelligence, child language development, discourse analysis and stylistics, and language education see "Systemic Grammar in Applied Language Studies" in Asher 1994). It is typical of systemic practice that major extensions both to description and to theory have taken place in these 'applied' contexts; for example, the very large systemic grammars of English that now exist in computational form (PENMAN 'Nigel'; COMMUNAL), and the extensive studies of children's writing and of the language of educational texts in science, history, and other subjects that have been carried out by Martin and his colleagues in contexts such as the New South Wales Disadvantaged Schools Program.

Since 1980, further studies have been devoted to languages other than English, notably Chinese (Fang; Hu; Long; McDonald; Ouyang; Zhang; Zhao; Zhu), French (Caffarel), Indonesian (Sutjaja; Wirnani), and Tagalog (Martin; see also "Tagalog" in Asher 1994); and work in text generation has begun to take in Chinese and Japanese (Matthiessen *et al.*) and German, French, Dutch (Bateman; Steiner). In English, Halliday's *Introduction to Functional Grammar* brought together some of his studies begun in the late 1960s (1967/68); and advances were made in all areas of the grammar: experiential (Davidse; Martin), interpersonal (Butler; Thibault), and textual (Fries; Hasan; Matthiessen). Matthiessen (1995b) presented a system-based account of English grammar, deriving from materials he had written to accompany the 'exporting' of the Nigel grammar.

Many general theoretical discussions have appeared (Fawcett; Halliday; Lemke, etc.), as well as new theoretical underpinning of key areas, especially lexicogrammar, discourse semantics (see "Discourse Semantics" in Asher 1994), and text structure (Matthiessen; Martin; Berry; Hasan, etc.) Matthiessen's (1993b) account of register theory emphasizes the integrative character of systemic work: while there are often alternative interpretations, especially where new problems are being addressed, these are not detached from their overall context in language and in linguistics. Thus there is no disjunction between grammar and discourse, or between the system and the text.

With the strengthening of what Halliday calls the 'grammatics' (that is, theory of grammar as metatheoretic resource), systemic writings have

438

increasingly foregrounded the constructive power of grammar; this is reflected in numerous studies which began with the 'critical linguistics' of the late 1970s (Fowler *et al.*; Kress and Hodge; subsequently Butt; Hasan; Kress; Lemke; Martin; McGregor; O'Toole; Thibault; Thread-gold; cf. Threadgold *et al.* 1986, and the journal *Social Semiotics*). In a large-scale investigation of natural conversation between mothers and their preschool children, Hasan and Cloran (1990) have developed semantic networks to explore the effects of social factors on children's learning styles, and their consequences for education. Martin's work on register and genre (1992) extends the constructivist model of language to include strata of genre and ideology. It is in this overall perspective that language becomes central to the educational initiatives of Martin, Rothery, Christie, and others in Australia; compare also the work of Carter *et al.* in the LINC ('Language in the National Curriculum') program in the UK.

In 1974 Fawcett organized the first systemic workshop, at the West Midlands College of Education, with 16 participants from four centres in the UK. Since then the workshop has been an annual event; the first international workshop was the ninth, held in Toronto (York University) in 1982. In the 1990s, now as 'International Systemic Functional Congress', meetings have been held in Scotland (Stirling 1990), Japan (International Christian University 1991), Australia (Macquarie 1992), Canada (British Columbia 1993), Belgium (Gent 1994) and China (Peking 1995); and regular national or international seminars/workshops are held in China, in Australia, and in different countries in Europe. The publication *Network* provides information on these activities, along with short articles, reviews, bibliographies, and conference reports. The regularly updated bibliographical data base now contains more than 1000 books and articles. Selected conference papers from 1983, 1985, 1986, and the years from 1988 onwards have appeared, or are appearing in published form.

6 Influences and trends

In the period from its inception in the early 1960s the main influences on systemic theory (other than those coming in via specific applications such as computational linguistics) have come from Lamb's work in stratificational grammar (1966) and from Sinclair's in discourse and in lexical studies. Lamb and Halliday collaborated regularly over a number of years. Sinclair had been an originator of scale and category grammar and his subsequent work exploited this, though in a complementary direction to Halliday's: Sinclair builds the grammar out of the lexis, whereas Halliday builds the lexis out of the grammar. Other input has come from Labov's quantitative methodology (though not his general perspective on language and society; see "Labov, William" in Asher 1994); from the theory and practice of corpus linguistics (Quirk (see "Quirk, Professor Sir Charles Randolph" in Asher 1994), Svartvik *et al.*; more recently Sinclair); from other work in functional linguistics (especially Thompson); and from poststructuralist semiotics in general.

A feature of systemic work is that it has tended to expand by moving into new spheres of activity, rather than by reworking earlier positions. This reflects an ideological perspective in which language is seen not as unique or *sui generis* but as one aspect of evolution of humans as sociocultural beings. Thus input often comes from outside the discipline of linguistics: from current theories in fields such as anthropology, literature, and neurology, and from developments in more distant sciences. Much systemic linguistics reflects transdisciplinary rather than disciplinary thinking in its approach to problems of language.

This orientation appears in some present trends and likely future directions. For example:

(a) systemic grammatics as model for other semiotic systems, especially forms of art: not only literature (Butt; O'Toole; Thibault; Threadgold) but also music (van Leeuwen; Steiner), visual imagery (Kress and van Leeuwen), and painting, architecture, and sculpture (O'Toole);

(b) further developments of register theory to investigate the linguistic construction of knowledge and structures of power;

(c) using available corpus data and programs to test hypotheses about the probabilistic properties of systems (Nesbitt and Plum; Halliday and James);

(d) further development of language-based educational programs, in initial literacy, secondary 'subjects', teacher education, language in the workplace, etc.;

(e) natural language processing, modelling systems of meaning (knowledge systems); developing integrated generation and parsing programs, including multilingual ones; and processing language in 'intelligent fuzzy computing' (Sugeno);

(f) further work in deaf sign (Johnston) and development of systemic research in neurolinguistics and the discourse of aphasia, dementia, etc.;

(g) greater emphasis on studies of the expression plane in a general systemic context.

Just as systemic theory is itself a variant of a broader class of theories (functional theories, perhaps with 'system-structure theories' as an intermediate term), so it itself accommodates considerable variation. Gregory's 'communication linguistics' foregrounds structures of knowledge and presents a dynamic 'phase and transition' model of discourse; Fawcett's computational modelling contrasts in various ways with that of Mattiessen and Bateman; Martin's register theory, with genre as a distinct stratum, contrasts with Hasan's view of register as functional variation realizing different values of contextual variables. This kind of variation in 'metaregister' is one of many ways in which systemic theory appears as a metaphor for language itself.

The standard introduction to systemic linguistics has been Berry (1975/77). Other introductory or summary works are Monaghan (1979), Halliday and Martin (1981), Butler (1985), Morley (1985), and, an original work in Chinese, Hu et al. (1989). The extensive series of publications emanating from the New South Wales Disadvantaged Schools Program is an excellent source for the systemic grammar of English in an educational context (see bibliography at end of Martin's paper in Halliday 1993d). Further introductory books from the mid 1990s include Eggins (1994), Butt et al. (1995), Matthiessen (1995b), Martin et al. (1997), Bloor and Bloor (1995), Thompson (1996).

BIBLIOGRAPHY

(1972) *Five to Nine: Aspects of Function and Structure in the Spoken Language of Elementary School Children*. Toronto: York University and the Board of Education for the Borough of North York.

Abercrombie, D. (1965) *Studies in Phonetics and Linguistics*. London: Oxford University Press (Language and Language Learning 10).

Abercrombie, D. (1967) *Elements of General Phonetics*. Edinburgh: Edinburgh University Press.

Albrow, K. H. (1962) 'The phonology of the personal forms of the verb in Russian', *Archivum Linguisticum* 14.

Albrow, K. H. (1968) *The Rhythm and Intonation of Spoken English*. London: Longmans (Schools Council Programme in Linguistics and English Teaching, Paper 9).

Allen, W. S. (1953) 'Relationship in comparative linguistics', *Transactions of the Philological Society*.

Allen, W. S. (1956) 'Structure and system in the Abaza verbal complex', *Transactions of the Philological Society*.

Allen, W. S. (1964) 'Transitivity and possession', *Language* 40.

Asher, R. E. (ed.) (1994) *The Encyclopedia of Language and Linguistics*, Vol. 8. Oxford: Pergamon.

Bailey, C.-J. N. (1974) *Variation and Linguistic Theory*. Washington, DC: Center for Applied Linguistics.

Bak, P., Flyvberg, H. and Sneppen, K. (1994) 'Can we model Darwin?' *New Scientist* 1916, 12 March 1994.

Bauman, R. and Sherzer, J. (eds) (1975) *Explorations in the Ethnography of Speaking*. Cambridge: Cambridge University Press.

Bazell, C. E., Catford, J. C., Halliday, M. A. K. and Robins, R. H. (eds) (1966) *In Memory of J. R. Firth*. London: Longmans (Longmans' Linguistics Library).

Bazerman, C. (1988) *Shaping Written Knowledge*. Madison: University of Wisconsin Press.

Benson, J. D. (1980) 'News, views and reviews in systemic linguistics and related areas', *Network*.

Benson, J. D. and Greaves, W. S. (1973) *The Language People Really Use*. Agincourt, Ontario: The Book Society of Canada.

Benson, J. D. and Greaves, W. S. (1984) *You and Your Language: The Kinds of English You Use*. Oxford: Pergamon Press.

Benson, J. D. and Greaves, W. S. (eds) (1985) *Systemic Perspectives on Discourse*, Vols. 1 & 2. Norwood, NJ: Ablex (Advances in Discourse Processes 16).

Benson, J. D. and Greaves, W. S. (eds) (1988) *Systemic Functional Approaches to Discourse*. Norwood, NJ: Ablex.

Benson, J. D., Cummings, M. J. and Greaves, W. S. (eds) (1988) *Linguistics in a Systemic Perspective*. Amsterdam and New York: Benjamins.

Benson, J. D. *et al.* (eds) (1989) 'Systems, structures and discourse', *Word* 40.

Berger, P. L. and Luckmann, T. (1966) *The Social Construction of Reality: A Treatise in the Sociology of Knowledge*. London: Allen Lane (Penguin Press).

Bernstein, B. (1962a) 'Social class, linguistic codes and grammatical elements', *Language and Speech* 5: 221–40.

Bernstein, B. (1962b) 'Linguistic codes, hesitation phenomena and intelligence', *Language and Speech* 5: 31–46.

Bernstein, B. (1964) 'Elaborated and restricted codes: their social origins and some consequences', in J. J. Gumperz and D. H. Hymes (eds) 1964.

Bernstein, B. (ed.) (1971) *Class, Codes and Control. Vol. 1, Theoretical Studies towards a Sociology of Language*. London: Routledge & Kegan Paul (Primary Socialization, Language and Education).

Bernstein, B. (ed.) (1973) *Class, Codes and Control. Vol. 2, Applied Studies towards a Sociology of Language*, London: Routledge & Kegan Paul (Primary Socialization, Language and Education).

Bernstein, B. (ed.) (1975) *Class, Codes and Control. Vol. 3, Towards a Theory of Educational Transmissions*, London: Routledge & Kegan Paul (Primary Socialization, Language and Education) (2nd edn 1977).

Bernstein, B. (ed.) (1990) *Class, Codes and Control. Vol. 4, The Structuring of Pedagogic Discourse*. London and New York: Routledge.

Bernstein, B. (1996) 'Codes and research', in *Pedagogy, Symbolic Control and Identity: Theory, Research, Critique*. London: Taylor and Francis.

Bernstein, B. (1997) 'Pedagogic discourse: a sociological analysis', in Emilia Ribeiro Pedro (ed.), *Discourse Analysis: Proceedings of the First International Conference on Discourse Analysis*. Lisbon: Edicoes Colibri & Associacao Portugesa de Linguistica.

Berry, M. (1975/77) *Structures and Systems* and *Levels and Links. Vols 1 and 2, Introduction to Systemic Linguistics*. London: Batsford.

Berry, M. (ed.) (1984) *Nottingham Linguistic Circular 13* (*Special Issue in Systemic Linguistics*). Nottingham: University of Nottingham.

Biagi, M. L. A. (1989). Paper presented to the Evolution of Scientific English workshop, University of Bologna, Centro di Studi sui Linguaggi Specifici and Centro Interfacoltà di Linguistica Teorica e Applicata.

Bickerton, D. (1972) 'The structure of polylectal grammars', in R. W. Shuy (ed.), *Sociolinguistics: Current Trends and Prospects*. Washington, DC: Georgetown University Press (Monograph Series on Languages and Linguistics 25).

Birch, D. and O'Toole, M. (eds) (1988) *Functions of Style*. London: Pinter.

Bloomfield, L. (1962) *The Menomini Language*. New Haven and London: Yale University Press.

Bloor, T. and Bloor, M. (1995) *The Functional Analysis of English: A Hallidayan Approach*. London: Arnold.

Bohm, D. (1980) *Wholeness and the Implicate Order*. London: Routledge & Kegan Paul (Ark Paperbacks, 1983).

Bolinger, D. (1961) *Syntactic Blends and Other Matters*. The Hague: Mouton (Janua Linguarum 14).

Briggs, J. P. and Peat, F. D. (1985) *Looking Glass Universe: The Emerging Science of Wholeness*. Glasgow: Simon & Schuster.

Brockman, J. (1995) *The Third Culture*. New York: Simon & Schuster.

Bruner, J. (1986) *Actual Minds, Possible Worlds*. Cambridge, MA: Harvard University Press.

Bruner, J. (1990) *Acts of Meaning*. Cambridge, MA: Harvard University Press.

Bullowa, M. (ed.) (1979) *Before Speech: The Beginning of Interpersonal Communication*. Cambridge: Cambridge University Press.

Butler, C. S. (1979) 'Recent developments in systemic linguistics', *Linguistics and Language Teaching Abstracts* 12.

Butler, C. S. (1985) *Systemic Linguistics: Theory and Applications*. London: Batsford.

Butler, C. S. (1988) 'Politeness and the semantics of modalized directives in English', in J. D. Benson *et al.*, 1989.

Butt, D. G. (1984) 'The Relationship between Theme and Lexicogrammar in the Poetry of Wallace Stevens.' Unpublished PhD dissertation, Macquarie University.

Butt, D. G. (1988a) 'Ideational meaning and the existential fabric of a poem', in R. P. Fawcett and D. J. Young (eds), *New Developments in Systemic Linguistics. Vol. 2, Theory and Application*. London and New York: Pinter.

Butt, D. G. (1988b) 'Randomness, order, and the latent patterning of text', in D. Birch and M. O'Toole (eds), 1988.

Butt, D. G. and Matthiessen, C. M. I. M. (2000) 'The meaning potential of language: mapping meaning systemically' (mimeo.). Macquarie University.

Butt, D. G. *et al.* (1990) *Living with English*. Sydney: Macquarie University.

Butt, D. G., Fahey, R., Spinks, S. and Yallop, C. (1995) *Using Functional Grammar: An Explorer's Guide*. Sydney: NCELTR, Macquarie University.

Carroll, J. B. (ed.) (1956) *Language, Thought and Reality: Selected Writings of Benjamin Lee Whorf*. Cambridge, MA: MIT Press.

Carter, R. (1987) *Vocabulary: Applied Linguistic Perspectives*. London: Allen & Unwin.

Carter, R. (ed.) (1990) *Knowledge about Language, and the Curriculum*. London: Hodder & Stoughton.

Carter, R. *et al.* (1990) *Language in the National Curriculum*. Nottingham: Department of English Studies, University of Nottingham.

Catford, J. C. (1965) *A Linguistic Theory of Translation*. London: Oxford University Press (Language and Language Learning 8).

Catford, J. C. (1977) *Fundamental Problems in Phonetics*. Bloomington: Indiana University Press.

Cedergren, H. and Sankoff, D. (1974) 'Variable rules: performance as a statistical reflection of competence', *Language* 50.

Chomsky, N. (1961) 'On the notion "rule of grammar"', *Structure of Language and Its Mathematical Aspects*. Providence, RI: American Mathematical Society.

Chomsky, N. (1962) 'Explanatory models in linguistics', *Logic, Methodology and Philosophy of Science*. Stanford: Stanford University Press.

Chomsky, N. (1966) *Topics in the Theory of Generative Grammar*. The Hague: Mouton (Janua Linguarum Series Minor).

Chomsky, N. (1975) *The Logical Structure of Linguistic Theory*. New York: Plenum Press.

Christie, F. *et al.* (1991/92) *Language as a Resource for Meaning*, Series 1–4. Sydney: Harcourt Brace Jovanovich.

Christie, F. (ed.) (1991) *Teaching English Literacy: A Project of National Significance on the Preservice Preparation of Teachers for Teaching English Literacy*, Vol. 2. Darwin, NT: Centre for Studies of Language in Education.

Christie, F. and Martin, J. R. (eds) (1997) *Genre and Institutions: Social Process in the Workplace and School*. London and New York: Cassell.

Coetzee, J. M. (1981) 'Newton and the ideal of a transparent scientific language', *Journal of Literary Semantics*.

Colby, B. N. and Colby, L. M. (1981) *The Daykeeper: The Life and Discourse of an Ixil Diviner*. Cambridge, MA, and London: Harvard University Press.

Cranny-Francis, A. (1990) *Social Semiotics: A Transdisciplinary Journal in Functional Linguistics, Semiotics and Critical Theory*. Wollongong: University of Wollongong.

Culler, J. (1977) *Saussure*. London: Fontana (2nd edn).

Cummings, M. and Simmons, R. (1983) *The Language of Literature: A Stylistic Introduction to the Study of Literature*. Oxford: Pergamon.

Dahl, Ö. (1985) *Tense and Aspect Systems*. Oxford and New York: Basil Blackwell.

Davey, A. (1979) *Discourse Production*. Edinburgh: Edinburgh University Press.

Davidse, K. (1991) 'Categories of Experiential Grammar.' Unpublished PhD dissertation, Catholic University of Leuven.

Davidse, K. (1992) 'Transitivity/ergativity: the Janus-headed grammar of actions and events', in M. Davies and L. Ravelli (eds), 1992.

Davidse, K. (1996) 'Ditransitivity and possession', in R. Hasan *et al.* (eds), 1996.

Davies, M. and Ravelli, L. (eds) (1992) *Advances in Systemic Linguistics: Recent Theory and Practice*. London and New York: Pinter.

de Beaugrande, R. (1994) 'Function and form in language theory and research', *Functions of Language*, 1.2.

de Beaugrande, R. (1996) *New Foundations for a Science of Text and Discourse*. Norwood, NJ: Ablex.

de Beaugrande, R. (1997) 'Linguistics – systemic and functional: renewing the "warrant"', in A.-M. Simon-Vandenbergen, K. Davidse and D. Noël (eds), *Reconnecting Language: Morphology and Syntax in Functional Perspectives*. Amsterdam: Benjamins.

de Matos, F. G. (1984) '20 years of applied linguistics: AILA Congresses 1964–1984', in J. Nivette, D. Goyvaerts and P. van de Craen (eds), *AILA Brussels 84: Proceedings*, Vol. 5.

Dennett, D. C. (1993) *Consciousness Explained*. Harmondsworth: Penguin Books (originally published Little, Brown & Co., 1991).

Dijksterhuis, E. J. (1961) *The Mechanization of the World Picture*. London: Oxford University Press (Princeton, NJ: Princeton University Press, 1986).

Dirr, A. (1928) *Einführung in das Studium der kaukasischen Sprachen*. Leipzig.

Dixon, R. M. W. (1965) *What Is Language? A New Approach to Linguistic Description*. London: Longman (Longmans Linguistics Library).

Dixon, R. M. W. (1966) 'Linguistic analysis of Dyirbal, an Australian language'. Paper presented to the Philological Society.

Dixon, R. M. W. (1970) *The Dyirbal Language of North Queensland*. Cambridge: Cambridge University Press.

Doughty, P. (1976) *Language, 'English' and the Curriculum*. London: Edward Arnold (Schools Council Programme in Linguistics and English Teaching).

Doughty, P., Pearce, J. and Thornton, G. (1972) *Exploring Language*. London: Edward Arnold (Schools Council Programme in Linguistics and English Teaching).

Douglas, M. (ed.) (1973) *Rules and Meanings: The Anthropology of Everyday Knowledge*. Harmondsworth: Penguin Books (Penguin Modern Sociology Readings).

Dunbar, R. (1992) 'Why gossip is good for you', *New Scientist* 1848, 21 November 1992.

du Ponceau, P. S. (1838) *A Dissertation on the Nature and Character of the Chinese System of Writing*. Philadelphia: American Philosophical Society.

Eco, U. (1973) *La Structtura Assente: introduzione alla ricerca semiologica*. Milan: Bompiani (Nuovi Saggi Italiani).

Edelman, G. (1987) *Neural Darwinism: The Theory of Neuronal Group Selection*. New York: Basic Books.

Edelman, G. (1992) *Bright Air, Brilliant Fire: On the Matter of the Mind*. New York: Basic Books; London: Allen Lane.

Edelman, G. and Tononi, G. (2000) *Consciousness: How Matter Becomes Imagination*. London: Allen Lane.

Eggins, S. (1994) *An Introduction to Systemic Functional Linguistics*. London: Pinter.

Ellis, J. M. (1993) *Language, Thought, and Logic*. Evanston, IL: Northwestern University Press (Rethinking Theory).

Ellis, J. O. (1958) 'General linguistics and comparative philology', *Lingua* 7. Reprinted in J. O. Ellis (1966b).

Ellis, J. O. (1966a) 'On contextual meaning', in C. E. Bazell *et al.* (eds), *In Memory of J. R. Firth*. London: Longmans (Longmans' Linguistics Library).

Ellis, J. O. (1966b) *Towards a General Comparative Linguistics*. The Hague: Mouton (Janua Linguarum Series Minor 52).

Ellis, J. O. and Davies, R. W. (1951) 'The Soviet linguistics controversy', *Soviet Studies* 3.

Ellis, J. O. and Halliday, M. A. K. (1951) 'Temporal categories in the modern Chinese verb' (unpublished). This series Vol. 8.

Elvin, M. (1973) *The Pattern of the Chinese Past*. London: Eyre Methuen.

Fabbri, P. (1992) *Pertinence et adéquation*. Limoges: PULIM, Université de Limoges (Nouveaux Actes Sémiotiques 19).

Fairclough, N. (1992) *Discourse and Social Change*. Cambridge: Polity Press.

Fawcett, R. P. (1980) *Cognitive Linguistics and Social Interaction: Towards an Integrated Model of a Systemic Functional Grammar and Other Components of a Communicating Mind*. Heidelberg and University of Exeter: Julius Groos.

Fawcett, R. P. (1983) 'Language as a semiological system: a reinterpretation of Saussure', in J. Morreall (ed.), *The Ninth LACUS Forum*. Columbia, South Carolina: Hornbeam Press.

Fawcett, R. P. (1992) 'The COMMUNAL project: how to get from semantics to syntax', *Proceedings of COLING 92, Fourteenth International Conference on Computational Linguistics, Nantes*.

Fawcett, R. P. (1994) 'Some recent developments in Systemic Functional Grammar'. Paper presented to Linguistics Association of Great Britain, April 1994.

Fawcett, R. P. and Tucker, G. H. (1990) 'Demonstration of GENESYS: a very large, semantically based systemic functional grammar', *Proceedings of the Thirteenth International Conference on Computational Linguistics*, Vol. 1, Helsinki.

Fawcett, R. P., Tucker, G. H. and Lin, Y. Q. (1993) 'How a systemic functional grammar works: the role of realization', in H. Horacek and M. Zock (eds), *New Concepts in Natural Language Generation*. London and New York: Pinter.

Ferguson, C. A. (1973) 'Some forms of religious discourse' (mimeo.).

Firth, J. R. (1935) 'The technique of semantics', *Transactions of the Philological Society 1935*. Reprinted in J. R. Firth, 1957d.

Firth, J. R. (1937) *The Tongues of Men*. London: Watts. Reprinted in J. R. Firth, *The Tongues of Men: and Speech*. London: Oxford University Press (Language and Language Learning 2), 1964.

Firth, J. R. (1945) 'Wartime experiences in linguistic training', *Modern Languages* 26.

Firth, J. R. (1946) 'The English school of phonetics', *Transactions of the Philological Society*.

Firth, J. R. (1949) 'Altantic linguistics', *Archivum Linguisticum* 1.2. Reprinted in J. R. Firth, 1957d.

Firth, J. R. (1950) 'Personality and language in society', *The Sociological Review* (Journal of the Institute of Sociology 42). Reprinted in J. R. Firth, 1957d.

Firth, J. R. (1956) 'Linguistic analysis and translation', in *For Roman Jakobson*. The Hague: Mouton. Reprinted in F. R. Palmer (ed.), 1968.

Firth, J. R. (1957a) 'Ethnographic analysis and language with reference to Malinowski's views', in R. W. Firth (ed.), *Man and Culture: An Evaluation of the Work of Bronislaw Malinowski*. London: Routledge & Kegan Paul. Reprinted in F. R. Palmer (ed.), 1968.

Firth, J. R. (1948) 'Sounds and prosodies' *Transactions of the Philological Society*. Reprinted in J. R. Firth, 1957d.

Firth, J. R. (1957c) 'A synopsis of linguistic theory 1930–55', in J. R. Firth (ed.), *Studies in Linguistic Analysis* (Special Volume of the Philological Society). Oxford: Blackwell. Reprinted in F. R. Palmer (ed.), 1968.

Firth, J. R. (1957d) *Papers in Linguistics 1934–1951*. London: Oxford University Press.

Firth, J. R. (1968) 'Linguistic analysis as a study of meaning', in F. R. Palmer (ed.).

Fishman, J. (1967) 'The sociology of language', in J. Fishman (ed.), *Readings in the Sociology of Language*. The Hague: Mouton.

Fleming, I. (1969) 'Stratificational theory: an annotated bibliography', *Journal of English Linguistics* 3.

Fowler, R. (1970) 'The structure of criticism and the languages of poetry: an approach through language', in M. Bradbury and D. Palmer (eds), *Contemporary Criticism*. London: Edward Arnold.

Fowler, R., Hodge, B., Kress, G. and Trew, T. (1979) *Language and Control*. London: Routledge & Kegan Paul.

Fries, C. C. (1940) *American English Grammar*. New York: Appleton-Century-Crofts (National Council of Teachers of English, English Monograph 10).

Fries, P. H. and Gregory, M. (eds) (1995) *Discourse in Society: Systemic Functional Perspectives* (Meaning and Choice in Language (Studies for Michael Halliday)). Norwood, NJ: Ablex (Advances in Discourse Processes 50).

Gee, J. P. (1992) *The Social Mind: Language, Ideology, and Social Practice*. New York and London: Bergin & Garvey (Series in Language and Ideology).

Gleason, H. A., Jr. (1965) *Linguistics and English Grammar*. New York: Holt, Rinehart & Winston.

Gleason, H. A., Jr. (1966) 'The organization of language: a stratificational view', Georgetown University Press: Washington, DC. Monograph Series on Languages and Linguistics 17.

Gleason, H. A., Jr. (1968) 'Contrastive analysis in discourse structure', Georgetown University Press: Washington, DC. Monograph Series on Language and Linguistics 21. Reprinted in A. Makkai and D. G. Lockwood (eds), 1973.

Goffman, E. (1963) *Stigma: Notes on the Management of Spoiled Identity*. Englewood Cliffs, NJ: Prentice-Hall.

Goffman, E. (1964) 'The neglected situation', *American Anthropologist* 66.

Goffman, E. (1967) *Interaction Ritual: Essays on Face-to-Face Behaviour*. Garden City, NY: Doubleday (Anchor Books).

Goodman, K. and Goodman, Y. (1979) 'Learning to read is natural', in L. B. Resnik and P. B. Weaver (eds), *Theory and Practice of Early Reading*, Vol. 1. Hillsdale, NJ: Erlbaum.

Gowers, E. (Sir) (1951) *ABC of Plain Words*. London: HMSO.

Gray, B. (1974) 'Towards a semi-revolution in grammar', *Language Sciences* 29.

Gregory, M. J. (1967) 'Aspects of varieties differentiation', *Journal of Linguistics* 3.2.

Gregory, M. J. (1980) 'Language as social semiotic: the recent work of M. A. K. Halliday', *Applied Linguistics* 1.1.

Gregory, M. J. (1985) 'Linguistics and theatre – Hamlet's voice: aspects of text formation and cohesion in a soliloquy', *Forum Linguisticum* 7.

Gregory, M. J. (1987) 'Meta-functions: aspects of their development, status and use in systemic linguistics', in M. A. K Halliday and R. P. Fawcett (eds), *Theory and Description*, Vol. 1.

Gregory, M. J. (1988) 'Generic situation and register: a functional view of communication', in J. D. Benson *et al.*, 1989.

Gregory, M. J. (1995) 'Generic expectancies and discourse surprises: John Donne's the Good Morrow', in P. H. Fries and M. Gregory (eds), 1995.

Gribbin, J. R. (1985) *In Search of Schrödinger's Cat: The Startling World of Quantum Physics Explained*. London: Wildwood House.

Gumperz, J. J. (1964) 'Linguistic and social interaction in two communities', in J. J. Gumperz and D. Hymes, 1964.

Gumperz, J. J. (1971) *Language in Social Groups: Essays Selected and Introduced by Anwar S. Dil*. Stanford, CA: Stanford University Press.

Gumperz, J. J. and Hymes, D. H. (eds) (1964) *The Ethnography of Communication* (American Anthropologist 66, Special Publication).

Gumperz, J. J. and Hymes, D. H. (eds) (1972) *Directions in Sociolinguistics*. New York: Holt, Rinehart & Winston.

Hagège, C. (1981) *Critical Reflections on Generative Grammar*, trans. by R. A. Hall, Jr. Lake Bluff, IL: Jupiter Press.

Hagège, C. (1985) *L'Homme de paroles: contribution linguistique aux sciences humaines*. Paris: Fayard.

Hagège, C. (1988) *Leçon inaugurale*. Paris: College de France.

Hagège, C. (1993) *The Language Builder: An Essay on the Human Signature in Linguistic Morphogenesis*. Amsterdam: Benjamins.

Hagège, C. (1997) 'Language as a faculty, languages as "contingent" manifestations and humans as function builders', in A.-M. Simon-Vandenbergen, K. Davidse and D. Noel (eds), *Reconnecting Language* Amsterdam/Philadelphia: Benjamins.

Hagège, C. (2000) *Halte à la mort des langues*. Paris: Odile Jacob.

Halliday, M. A. K. (1959a) Review of Joshua Whatmough: *Language: A Modern Synthesis*, *Archivum Linguisticum* (New series) 9.

Halliday, M. A. K. (1959b), *The Language of the Chinese 'Secret History of the Mongols'*. Oxford: Blackwell (Publications of the Philological Society 17).

Halliday, M. A. K. (1961) 'Categories of the theory of grammar', *Word* 17.

Halliday, M. A. K. (1963) 'The tones of English', *Archivum Linguisticum* 15.

Halliday, M. A. K. (1967a) *Intonation and Grammar in British English*. The Hague: Mouton (Janua Linguarum Series Practica 48).

Halliday, M. A. K. (1967b) *Grammar, Society and the Noun*. This volume, Chapter 2.

Halliday, M. A. K. (1967/68) 'Notes on transitivity and theme in English, Parts 1–3', *Journal of Linguistics* 3.1, 3.2, 4.2.

Halliday, M. A. K. (1969) 'Relevant models of language', *The State of Language* (*Educational Review* 22.1: 26–37).

Halliday, M. A. K. (1971) 'Language in a social perspective', *The Context of Language* (*Educational Review*, University of Birmingham 23.3). Reprinted in M. A. K. Halliday, *Explorations in the Functions of Language*. London: Edward Arnold (Explorations in Language Study), 1973.

Halliday, M. A. K. (1973) 'The functional basis of language'. This volume, Chapter 14.

Halliday, M. A. K. (1975a) *Learning How to Mean: Explorations in the Development of Language*. London: Edward Arnold (Explorations in Language Study) (New York: American Elsevier, 1977).

Halliday, M. A. K. (1975b) 'Learning how to mean', in E. H. Lenneberg and E. Lenneberg (eds), *Foundations of Language Development: A Multidisciplinary Approach*. New York: Academic Press.

Halliday, M. A. K. (1976) 'Anti-languages', *American Anthropologist* 78.

Halliday, M. A. K. (1978a) 'Meaning and the construction of reality in early childhood', in H. L. Pick, Jr and E. Saltzman (eds), *Modes of Receiving and Processing of Information*. Hillsdale, NJ: Lawrence Erlbaum Associates.

Halliday, M. A. K. (1978b) *Language as Social Semiotic: The Social Interpretation of Language and Meaning*. London: Edward Arnold.

Halliday, M. A. K. (1979a) 'Modes of meaning and modes of expression: types of grammatical structure, and their determination by different semantic functions', in D. J. Allerton, E. Carney and D. Holdcroft (eds), *Function and Context in Linguistic Analysis: Essays Offered to William Haas*. Cambridge: Cambridge University Press.

Halliday, M. A. K. (1979b) 'One child's protolanguage', in M. Bullowa (ed.), 1979.

Halliday, M. A. K. (1983) 'On the transition from child tongue to mother tongue', *Australian Journal of Linguistics* 3 (2), 201–16.

Halliday, M. A. K. (1984a) *Listening to Nigel: Conversations of a Very Small Child*. Sydney: University of Sydney Linguistics Department.

Halliday, M. A. K. (1984b) 'Language as code and language as behaviour: a systemic functional interpretation of the nature and ontogenesis of dialogue', in R. P. Fawcett *et al.* (eds), *The Semiotics of Culture and Language,* Vol. 1. London: Pinter.

Halliday, M. A. K (1985) *An Introduction to Functional Grammar.* London: Edward Arnold (2nd revised edn, 1994).

Halliday, M. A. K. (1986) 'Spoken and written modes of meaning', in R. Horowitz and S. J. Samuels (eds), *Comprehending Oral and Written Language.* New York: Academic Press.

Halliday, M. A. K. (1987) 'Language and the order of nature'. This volume, Chapter 5.

Halliday, M. A. K. (1988) 'On the language of physical science', in M. Ghadessy (ed.), *Registers of Written English: Situational Factors and Linguistic Features.* London and New York: Pinter.

Halliday, M. A. K. (1990) 'New ways of meaning: the challenge to applied linguistics'. This volume, Chapter 6.

Halliday, M. A. K. (1992) 'How do you mean?' in M. Davies and L. Ravelli (eds), 1992.

Halliday, M. A. K. (1993a) 'Language in a changing world'. This volume, Chapter 10.

Halliday, M. A. K. (1993b) 'Towards a language-based theory of learning', *Linguistics and Education* 5.2.

Halliday, M. A. K. (ed.) (1993c) *Language as Cultural Dynamic (Cultural Dynamics* 6, 1–2), 1–10.

Halliday, M. A. K. (1994) 'Systemic theory', in R. E. Asher (ed.), 1994.

Halliday, M. A. K. (1995) 'On language in relation to the evolution of human consciousness'. This volume, Chapter 18.

Halliday, M. A. K. (1996) 'On grammar and grammatics', in R. Hasan, C. Cloran and D. Butt (eds), *Functional Descriptions: Theory in Practice.* Amsterdam/Philadelphia: Benjamins, pp. 1–38.

Halliday, M. A. K. (1998a) 'On the grammar of pain', *Functions of Language* 7.1.

Halliday, M. A. K. (1998b) 'Things and relations: regrammaticizing experience as technical knowledge', in J. R. Martin and R. Veel (eds), 1998.

Halliday, M. A. K. (1998c) *Computing Meanings: Some Reflections on Past Experience and Present Prospects*, trilingual text, ed. C. Matthiessen, with Chinese trans. by Wu Canzhong and Japanese trans. by Kazuhiro Teruya. English trans. in G. Huang and Z. Wang (eds), *Discourse and Language Functions.* Beijing: Foreign Language Teaching and Research Press.

Halliday, M. A. K. and Fawcett, R. P. (eds) (1987) *New Developments in Systemic Linguistics. Vol. 1, Theory and Description.* London and New York: Pinter.

Halliday, M. A. K. and Hasan, R. (1976) *Cohesion in English.* London: Longman.

Halliday, M. A. K. and James, Z. L. (1993) 'A quantitative study of polarity and primary tense in the English finite clause', in J. M. Sinclair, M. Hoey and G. Fox (eds), *Techniques of Description: Spoken and Written Discourse (A Festschrift for Malcolm Coulthard)*. London and New York: Routledge.

Halliday, M. A. K. and Martin, J. R. (eds) (1981) *Readings in Systemic Linguistics*. London: Batsford.

Halliday, M. A. K. and Martin, J. R. (1993) *Writing Science: Literacy and Discursive Power*. London and Washington, DC: Falmer Press (Critical Perspectives on Literacy and Education).

Halliday, M. A. K. and Matthiessen, C. (1999) *Construing Experience through Meaning: A Language-based Approach to Cognition*. London: Cassell (Continuum).

Halliday, M. A. K. and Peng, F. C. C. (eds) (1992) *Current Research in Functional Grammar (Language Sciences* 14.4). Oxford: Pergamon.

Halliday, M. A. K., Gibbons, J. and Nicholas, H. (1990) *Learning, Keeping and Using Language: Selected Papers from the Eighth World Congress of Applied Linguistics, Sydney, 1987*. Amsterdam: Benjamins.

Halliday, M. A. K., McIntosh, A. and Strevens, P. (1964) *The Linguistic Sciences and Language Teaching*. London: Longman.

Handscombe, R. J. (1966) *The First Thousand Clauses: A Preliminary Analysis*. Leeds: Nuffield Foreign Languages Teaching Materials Project.

Harris, S. (1980) *Culture and Learning: Tradition and Education in Northeast Arnhem Land*. Darwin: Northern Territory Department of Education.

Harris, Z. S. (1951) *Methods in Structural Linguistics*. Chicago: University of Chicago Press.

Harris, Z. S. (1955) 'From phoneme to morpheme', *Language* 31.

Harste, J. C. and Burke, C. L. (1977) 'A new hypothesis for reading research', in P. D. Pearson (ed.), *Reading: Theory, Research and Practice*. Clemson, SC: National Reading Conference.

Hart, N. W. M., Walker, R. F. and Gray, B. (1977) *The Language of Children: A Key to Literacy*. Reading, MA: Addison-Wesley.

Hasan, R. (1964) 'A Linguistic Study of Contrasting Features in the Style of Two Contemporary English Prose Writers.' Unpublished PhD dissertation, University of Edinburgh.

Hasan, R. (1965) *Grammatical Analysis Code*. Leeds: Nuffield Foreign Languages Teaching Materials Project.

Hasan, R. (1973) 'Code, register and social dialect', in B. Bernstein (ed.), 1973.

Hasan, R. (1984a) 'The nursery tale as a genre', *Nottingham Linguistics Circular* 13.

Hasan, R. (1984b) 'Ways of saying: ways of meaning', in R. P. Fawcett *et al.* (eds), *The Semiotics of Culture and Language*, Vol. 1. London and Dover, NH: Frances Pinter.

Hasan, R. (1984c) 'What kind of resource is language?', *Australian Review of Applied Linguistics* 7.1.

453

Hasan, R. (1985a) 'Meaning, context and text: fifty years after Malinowski', in J. D. Benson and W. S. Greaves (eds).

Hasan, R. (1985b) 'Lending and borrowing: from grammar to lexis', in J. E. Clark (ed.), *The Cultivated Australian: Festschrift in Honour of Arthur Delbridge (Beiträge zur Phonetik und Linguistik 48)*.

Hasan, R. (1986) 'The ontogenesis of ideology: an interpretation of mother-child talk', in T. Threadgold *et al.* (eds), 1986.

Hasan, R. (1987a) 'Offers in the making: a systemic-functional approach' (MS).

Hasan, R. (1987b) 'Directions from structuralism', in N. Fabb *et al.* (eds), *The Linguistics of Writing: Arguments between Language and Literature*. Manchester: Manchester University Press.

Hasan, R. (1987c) 'The grammarian's dream: lexis as most delicate grammar', in M. A. K. Halliday and R. P. Fawcett (eds), 1987.

Hasan, R. (1989) 'Semantic variation and sociolinguistics', *Australian Journal of Linguistics* 9.2.

Hasan, R. (1991) 'Questions as a mode of learning in everyday talk', in Thao Lê and M. McCausland (eds), *Language Education: Interaction and Development*. Launceston: University of Tasmania.

Hasan, R. (1992a) 'Meaning in sociolinguistic theory', in K. Bolton and H. Kwok (eds), *Sociolinguistics Today: International Perspectives*. London: Routledge.

Hasan, R. (1992b) 'Rationality in everyday talk: from process to system', in J. Svartvik (ed.), *Directions in Corpus Linguistics: Proceedings of Nobel Symposium 82, Stockholm, 4–8 August 1991*. Berlin and New York: Mouton de Gruyter.

Hasan, R. (1992c) 'Speech genre, semiotic mediation and the development of higher mental functions', *Language Sciences* 14.4.

Hasan, R. (1994) 'On some goals of linguistic description: reflections on certain binary perspectives'. Paper presented at the twenty-first International Systemic Functional Congress, University of Gent, 1–5 August 1994.

Hasan, R. (1995a) 'On social conditions for semiotic mediation: the genesis of mind in society', in A. R. Sadovnik (ed.), *Knowledge and Pedagogy: The Sociology of Basil Bernstein*. Norwood, NJ: Ablex.

Hasan, R. (1995b) 'The conception of context in text', in P. H. Fries and M. Gregory (eds), 1995.

Hasan, R. (1996) *Ways of Saying: Ways of Meaning. Selected Papers of Ruqaiya Hasan*, ed. C. Cloran, D. Butt and G. Williams. London: Cassell.

Hasan, R. (1999) 'Speaking with reference to context', in M. Ghadessy (ed.), *Text and Context in Functional Linguistics*. Amsterdam and Philadelphia: Benjamins.

Hasan, R. and Cloran, C. (1990) 'A sociolinguistic interpretation of everyday talk between mothers and children', in M. A. K. Halliday, J. Gibbons and H. Nicholas (eds), 1990.

Hasan, R. and Fries, P. H. (eds) (1995) *On Subject and Theme: A Discourse Functional Perspective*. Amsterdam and Philadelphia: Benjamins.

Hasan, R. and Martin, J. R. (eds) (1989) *Language Development: Learning Language, Learning Culture (Meaning and Choice in Language, Vol. 1)*. Norwood, NJ: Ablex (Advances in Discourse Processes 27).

Hasan, R. and Williams, G. (eds) (1996) *Literacy in Society*. London: Longman.

Hasan, R., Cloran, C. and Butt, D. (eds) (1996) *Functional Descriptions: Theory in Practice*. Amsterdam: Benjamins.

Heath, T. (Sir) (1981) *Aristarchus of Samos: The Ancient Copernicus*. New York: Dover Books (Original Greek published with English translation. Oxford: Clarendon Press, 1913).

Heisenberg, W. (1990) *Physics and Philosophy: The Revolution in Modern Science*. London: Penguin Books (first published 1958).

Henderson, Eugénie, J. A. (1951) 'The phonology of loanwords in some Southeast Asian languages', *Transactions of the Philological Society* 1951. Reprinted in F. R. Palmer (ed.), 1970.

Henderson, Eugénie, J. A. (1966) 'Towards a prosodic statement of Vietnamese syllable structure', in C. E. Bazell *et al.* (eds), 1966.

Hill, T. (1958) 'Institutional linguistics', *Orbis* 7.

Hill, T. (1966) 'The technique of prosodic analysis', in C. E. Bazell *et al.* (eds), 1966.

Hillier, H. (1992) *The Language of Spontaneous Interaction between Children Aged 7–12: Instigating Action*. Occasional Papers in Systemic Linguistics. Nottingham: University of Nottingham Department of English Studies (Monographs in Systemic Linguistics 4).

Hjelmslev, L. (1961) *Prolegomena to a Theory of Language*, trans. by J. Whitfield. Madison: University of Wisconsin Press (Danish original: Copenhagen, 1943).

Hockett, C. F. (1954) 'Two models of grammatical description', *Word* 10.

Hockett, C. F. (1961) 'Linguistics elements and their relations', *Language* 37.

Hockett, C. F. (1968) *The State of the Art*. The Hague: Mouton.

Horvath, B. M. (1985) *Variation in Australian English: The Sociolects of Sydney*. Cambridge Studies in Linguistics 45. Cambridge: Cambridge University Press.

Hu, Z. L., Zhu, Y. S. and Zhang, D. L. (1989) *A Survey of Systemic Functional Grammar* (in Chinese). Changsha: Hunan Educational Publishing House.

Huddleston, R. D., Hudson, R. A., Winter, E. and Henrici, A. (1968) *Sentence and Clause in Scientific English* (Final report of OSTI Research Project 'The Linguistic Properties of Scientific English'). London: Communication Research Centre, University College London.

Hudson, R. A. (1971) *English Complex Sentences: An Introduction to Systemic Grammar*. Amsterdam: North Holland.

Hunston, S. (1993) 'Evaluation and ideology in scientific writing', in M. Ghadessy (ed.) *Register Analysis: Theory and Practice*. London: Pinter.

Hymes, D. H. (1962) 'The ethnography of speaking', in T. Gladwin and W. C. Sturtevant (eds), *Anthropology and Human Behavior*. Washington, DC: Anthropological Society of Washington.

Hymes, D. H. (1964) 'Directions in (ethno-) linguistic theory', in A. K. Romney and R. G. D'Andrade (eds), *Transcultural Studies in Cognition* (*American Anthropologist* 66, Special Publication).

Hymes, D. H. (1981) '*In Vain I Tried to Tell You': Essays in Native American Ethnopoetics*. Philadelphia: University of Pennsylvania Press.

Jakobson, R. (1963) 'Efforts towards a means-ends model of language in inter-war continental linguistics', in C. Mohrmann *et al.* (eds), 1963.

Jerison, H. J. (1973) *Evolution of the Brain and Intelligence*. New York: Academic Press.

Junker, K. S. (1979) 'Communication starts with selective attention', in M. Bullowa (ed.), 1979.

Katz, J. J. and Fodor, J. A. (1963) 'The structure of a semantic theory', *Language* 39.2.

Kidd, S. (1838) *Lecture on the Nature and Structure of the Chinese Language*. London: University College.

Kidd, S. (1841) *China, or Illustrations of the Symbols, Philosophy, Antiquities, Customs, Superstitions, Laws, Government, Education and Literature of the Chinese*. London.

King, M. and Rentel, V. (1979) 'Towards a theory of early writing development', *Research in the Teaching of English* 13.

Klemperer, V. (2000) *The Language of the Third Reich: LTI – Lingua Tertii Imperii*, trans. by M. Brady. London: The Athlone Press (German original: *LTI: Notizbuch eines Philologen*. Leipzig: Philipp Reclam, 1968).

Kress, G. R. (1976a) 'Introduction', in M. A. K. Halliday, *System and Function in Language: Selected Papers Edited by Gunther Kress*. London: Oxford University Press.

Kress, G. R. (ed.) (1976b) *Halliday: System and Function in Language: Selected Papers*. Oxford: Oxford University Press.

Kress, G. R. (1985) *Linguistic Processes in Sociocultural Practice*. Geelong, Vic.: Deakin University Press.

Kress, G. and Hodge, R. (1979) *Language as Ideology*. London: Routledge & Kegan Paul.

Kress, G. and Hodge, R. (1988) *Social Semiotics*. London: Polity Press.

Labov, W. (1964) *The Aims of Sociolinguistic Research*. Bloomington, IN: Linguistic Society of America Linguistic Institute Sociolinguistics Seminar.

Labov, W. (1972) *Language in the Inner City: Studies in the Black English Vernacular*. Philadelphia: University of Pennsylvania Press (Conduct and Communication 3).

Labov, W. (1974) 'On the use of the present to explain the past', in L. Heilmann (ed.), *Proceedings of the Eleventh International Congress of Linguists*, Vol. 2. Bologna: Mulino.

Lamb, S. M. (1964a) 'On alternation, transformation, realization and stratification', in C. I. J. M. Stuart (ed.), *Report of the Fifteenth Annual (First International) Round Table Meeting on Linguistics and Language Study.* Washington, DC: Georgetown University Press (Monograph Series on Languages and Linguistics 17).

Lamb, S. M. (1964b), 'Stratificational linguistics as a basis for machine translation'. Paper presented to seminar on Mechanical Translation, Tokyo. Reprinted in A. Makkai and D. G. Lockwood (eds), 1973.

Lamb, S. M. (1965) 'Kinship terminology and linguistic structure', *American Anthropologist* 67.

Lamb, S. M. (1966a) 'On the mechanization of syntactic analysis', in D. G. Hays (ed.), *Readings in Automatic Language Processing*. New York: Elsevier.

Lamb, S. M. (1966b) *Outline of Stratificational Grammar.* Washington, DC: Georgetown University Press.

Lamb, S. M. (1970) 'Linguistic and cognitive networks', in P. L. Garvin (ed.), *Cognition: A Multiple View.* New York: Spartan Books.

Lamb, S. M. (1974) 'Dialogue' in H. Parret (ed.), *Discussing Language.* The Hague: Mouton (Janua Linguarum Series Maior 93).

Lamb, S. M. (1999) *Pathways of the Brain: The Neurocognitive Basis of Language.* Amsterdam and Philadelphia: Benjamins.

Langendoen, T. D. (1968) *The London School of Linguistics: A Study of the Linguistic Theories of B. Malinowski and J. R. Firth.* Cambridge, MA: MIT Press (Research Monograph 46).

Leech, G. N. (1966) *English in Advertising: A Linguistic Study of Advertising in Great Britain.* London: Longman (English Language Series 3).

Lemke, J. L. (1982) 'Analysing science classroom discourse' in S. Brice Heath (ed.), *Language in Professional Contexts.*

Lemke, J. L. (1984a) 'Action, context and meaning', in J. L. Lemke (ed.), 1984d.

Lemke, J. L. (1984b) 'The formal analysis of instruction', in J. L. Lemke (ed.), 1984d.

Lemke, J. L. (1984c) 'Towards a model of the instructional process', in J. L. Lemke (ed.), 1984d.

Lemke, J. L. (1984d) *Semiotics and Education.* Toronto: Victoria University (Toronto Semiotic Circle Monographs, Working Papers and Prepublications 1984. 2).

Lemke, J. L. (1985) *Using Language in the Classroom.* Geelong, Vic.: Deakin University Press.

Lemke, J. L. (1988) 'Genres, semantics and classroom education', *Linguistics and Education* 1.1.

Lemke, J. L. (1990a) *Talking Science: Language, Learning, and Values.* Norwood, NJ: Ablex (Language and Educational Processes).

Lemke, J. L. (1990b) 'Technical discourse and technocratic ideology', in M. A. K. Halliday, J. Gibbons and H. Nicholas (eds.), 1990.

Lemke, J. L. (1992) 'Interpersonal meaning in discourse: value orientations', in M. Davies and L. Ravelli (eds), 1992.

Lemke, J. L. (1993) 'Discourse, dynamics, and social change', in M. A. K. Halliday (ed.), 1993d.

Lewin, R. (1992) 'Secret life of the brain', *New Scientist*, 5 December 1992 (Supplement 4).

Lewis, M. M. (1951) *Infant Speech: A Study of the Beginnings of Language.* 2nd edn, enlarged. London: Routledge & Kegan Paul.

Lovelock, J. (1989) *The Ages of Gaia: A Biography of Our Living Earth.* Oxford: Oxford University Press.

Lyons, J. (1966) 'Towards a "notional" theory of the "parts of speech"', *Journal of Linguistics* 2.

Lyons, J. (1968) *Introduction to Theoretical Linguistics.* Cambridge: Cambridge University Press.

Lyons, J. (1970) *Chomsky.* London: Collins.

Lyons, J. (1973) 'Linguistics'. *Times Higher Education Supplement,* 7 December 1973.

Mackay, D. and Simo, J. (1976) *Teach Your Child to Read and Write, and More.* Harmondsworth: Penguin Books.

Mackay, D., Thompson, B. and Schaub, P. (1970) *Breakthrough to Literacy: Teacher's Manual.* London: Longman (Schools Council Programme in Linguistics and English Teaching) (2nd illustrated edn. 1978).

Maclean, W. (1972) 'Pragmatical Aspects of Plastic and Graphic Modalities of Semioses: Multiple System Processes of Communication Viewed in Context'. Introductory remarks at the symposium of the American Association for the Advancement of Science, 139th Annual Meeting, Section 4: Health, Behavior and Social Processes (mimeo.).

Maina, S. J. (1987) 'Principles adopted for the enrichment of Kiswahili language', *New Language Planning Newsletter* 2.2.

Makkai, A. (1977) 'The nature of the present crossroads in linguistics', in A. Makkai, V. B. Makkai and L. Heilmann (eds), *Linguistics at the Crossroads.* The Hague: Jupiter Press.

Makkai, A. and Lockwood, D. G. (eds) (1973) *Readings in Stratificational Linguistics.* University, AL: University of Alabama Press.

Malcolm, K. (1985) 'Communication linguistics: a sample analysis', in J. D. Benson and W. S. Greaves (eds), 1985, Vol. 2.

Malinowski, B. (1923) 'The problem of meaning in primitive languages', in C. K. Ogden and I. A. Richards, 1923, Supplement 1.

Malinowski, B. (1935) *Coral Gardens and Their Magic,* Vol. 2. London: Allen & Unwin; New York: American Book Co.

Mann, W. C. (1983) *An Overview of the Nigel Text Generation Grammar* and *An Overview of the Penman Text Generation System.* Marina del Rey: Information Sciences Institute, University of Southern California (ISI/RR-83-113,114).

Mann, W. C. and Matthiessen, C. M. I. M. (1983) *Nigel: A Systemic Grammar for Text Generation*. Marina del Rey: Information Sciences Institute, University of Southern California (ISI/RR-83–105).

Mann, W. C. and Matthiessen, C. (1985) 'Demonstration of the Nigel text generation computer program', in J. D. Benson and W. S. Greaves (eds), 1985, Vol. 1.

Martin, J. R. (1985) *Factual Writing: Exploring and Challenging Social Reality*. Geelong, Vic: Deakin University Press; Oxford: Oxford University Press (1989).

Martin, J. R. (1986a) 'Grammaticalizing ecology: the politics of baby seals and kangaroos', in E. A. Grosz *et al.* (eds), *Language, Semiotics, Ideology*. Sydney: Sydney Association for Studies in Society and Culture.

Martin, J. R. (1986b) 'Intervening in the process of writing development', in C. Painter and J. R. Martin (eds), *Writing to Mean: Teaching Genres Across the Curriculum*. Applied Linguistics Association of Australia, Occasional Paper 9.

Martin, J. R. (1988) 'Grammatical conspiracies in Tagalog: family, face and fate – with regard to Benjamin Lee Whorf', in J. D. Benson *et al.* (eds), *Linguistics in a Systemic Perspective*. Amsterdam: Benjamins (Current Issues in Linguistic Theory 39).

Martin, J. R. (1990a) 'Literacy in science: learning to handle text as technology', in F. Christie (ed.), *Literacy for a Changing World*. Hawthorn, Vic: Australian Council for Educational Research.

Martin, J. R. (1990b) 'Interpersonal grammatization: mood and modality in Tagalog', *Philippine Journal of Linguistics* 21.1.

Martin, J. R. (1991) 'Intrinsic functionality: implications for contextual theory', *Social Semiotics* 1.1.

Martin, J. R. (1992) *English Text: System and Structure*. Amsterdam and Philadelphia: Benjamins.

Martin, J. R. (1993) 'Technology, bureaucracy and schooling: discursive resources and control', in M. A. K. Halliday (ed.), 1993c.

Martin, J. R. (1996a) 'Transitivity in Tagalog: a functional interpretation of case', in M. Berry *et al.* (eds), *Grammatical Structure: A Systemic Functional Perspective*. Norwood, NJ: Ablex.

Martin, J. R. (1996b) 'Metalinguistic diversity: the case from case', in R. Hasan, C. Cloran and D. Butt (eds), 1996.

Martin, J. R. (2000) 'Beyond exchange: appraisal systems in English', in S. Hunston and G. Thompson (eds), *Evaluation in Text: Authorial Stance and the Construction of Discourse*. Oxford: Oxford University Press.

Martin, J. R. and Matthiessen, C. (1991) 'Systemic typology and topology', in F. Christie (ed.), *Literacy in Social Processes: Papers from the Inaugural Australian Systemic Linguistics Conference, Deakin University, January 1990*. Darwin: Northern Territory University.

Martin, J. R. and Rothery, J. (1980–1) *Writing Project: Report 1980, 1981*. Sydney: Linguistics Department, University of Sydney.

459

Martin, J. R. and Veel, R. (eds) (1998) *Reading Science: Critical and Functional Perspectives on Discourses of Science*. London and New York: Routledge.

Martin, J. R., Matthiessen, C. and Painter, C. (1997) *Working with Functional Grammar: A Workbook for Halliday's Introduction to Functional Grammar*. London: Arnold.

Mathesius, V. (1928) 'On linguistic characterology with illustrations from Modern English', in J. Vachek (ed.), *A Prague School Reader in Linguistics*. Bloomington, IN: Indiana University Press.

Matthews, W. K. (1953) 'The ergative construction in modern Indo-Aryan', *Lingua* 3.

Matthiessen, C. (1985) *Select Bibliography of Systemic Linguistics*. Sydney: University of Sydney.

Matthiessen, C. (1989) 'Review of M. A. K. Halliday's "Introduction to Functional Grammar"', *Language* 65.

Matthiessen, C. (1991a) 'Lexico(grammatical) choice in text generation', in C. L. Paris, W. R. Swartout and W. C. Mann (eds), *Natural Language Generation in Artificial Intelligence and Computational Linguistics*. Boston: Kluwer.

Matthiessen, C. (1991b) 'Language on language: the grammar of semiosis', *Social Semiotics* 1.2.

Matthiessen, C. (1992) 'Interpreting the textual metafunction', in M. Davies and L. Ravelli (eds), 1992.

Matthiessen, C. (1993a) 'The object of study in cognitive science in relation to its construal and enactment in language', in M. A. K. Halliday (ed.), 1993c.

Matthiessen, C. (1993b) 'Register in the round: diversity in a unified theory of register analysis', in M. Ghadessy (ed.), *Register Analysis: Theory and Practice*. London: Pinter.

Matthiessen, C. (1994) 'Paradigmatic organization: 30 years of system networks – today's potential'. Paper presented at the twenty-first International Systemic Functional Congress, University of Gent, 1–5 August 1994.

Matthiessen, C. (1995a) 'Theme as an enabling resource in ideational knowledge construction', in M. Ghadessy (ed.), *Thematic Development in English Texts*. London: Pinter.

Matthiessen, C. (1995b) *Lexicogrammatical Cartography: English Systems*. Tokyo: International Language Sciences Publishers.

Matthiessen, C. and Bateman, J. (1992) *Systemic Linguistics and Text Generation: Experiences from Japanese and English*. London and New York: Pinter.

Matthiessen, C. and Halliday, M. A. K. (forthcoming), *Outline of Systemic Functional Linguistics*.

Matthiessen, C. and Nesbitt, C. (1996) 'On the idea of theory-neutral descriptions', in R. Hasan, C. Cloran and D. Butt (eds), 1996.

Maw, J. (1963) 'Some Interesting Features in Written Instructions to Workmen'. Unpublished MA dissertation, Edinburgh University.

McCusker, B. (1983) 'Fundamental particles', in R. Williams (ed.), *The Best of the Science Show*. Melbourne: Nelson.

460

McDonald, K. (1991) 'Cultural innovation and economic modernization: the context of language education today', in F. Christie (ed.).

McGregor, W. (1990) 'Language and ideology of a police tracker story in Gooniyandi', in M. A. K. Halliday, J. Gibbons and H. Nicholas (eds), 1990.

McIntosh, A. (1961) 'Patterns and ranges', *Language* 37. Reprinted in McIntosh and Halliday, 1966.

McIntosh, A. (1966) 'Linguistics and English studies', in McIntosh and Halliday, 1966.

McIntosh, A. and Halliday, M. A. K. (1966) *Patterns of Language: Papers in General, Descriptive and Applied Linguistics*. London: Longmans (Longmans' Linguistics Library).

McKellar, G. B. (1990) 'The language of neurolinguistics: principles and perspectives in the application of linguistic theory to the neuropsychology of language', in M. A. K. Halliday, J. Gibbons and H. Nicholas (eds), 1990.

McNeill, D. and Freiberger, P. (1993) *Fuzzy Logic: The Discovery of a Revolutionary Computer Technology – and How It Is Changing Our World*. Melbourne: Bookman.

Mead, G. H. (1934) *Mind, Self and Society from the Standpoint of a Social Behaviorist*. C. W. Morris (ed.), Chicago and London: University of Chicago Press.

Meščaninov, I. I. (1949) *Glagol (The Verb)*. Moscow and Leningrad: USSR Academy of Sciences.

Mitchell, T. F. (1951) 'The language of buying and selling in Cyrenaica', *Hesperis*.

Mohan, B. A. (1968), 'An Investigation of the Relationship between Language and Situational Factors in a Card Game, with Specific Attention to the Language of Instructions'. Unpublished PhD dissertation, University of London.

Mohan, B. A. (1974) 'Do sequencing rules exist?' *Semiotica*.

Mohan, B. A. (1986) *Language and Content*. Reading, MA: Addison Wesley.

Mohrmann, C., Norman, F. W. and Sommerfelt, A. (eds) (1963) *Trends in Modern Linguistics*. Utrecht: Spectrum.

Monaghan, J. (1979) *The Neo-Firthian Tradition and Its Contribution to General Linguistics*. Tübingen: Niemeyer (Linguistische Arbeiten 73).

Morley, G. (1985) *An Introduction to Systemic Grammar*. London: Macmillan.

Needham, J. (1958) 'The translation of old Chinese scientific and technical texts', in A. H. Smith (ed.), *Aspects of Translation*. London: Secker & Warburg (Studies in Communication 2).

Nesbitt, C. and Plum, G. (1988) 'Probabilities in a systemic grammar: the clause complex in English', in R. P. Fawcett and D. J. Young (eds), *New Developments in Systemic Linguistics. Vol. 2: Theory and Application*. London and New York: Pinter.

New South Wales Disadvantaged Schools Program (1990) *Write It Right*. Erskineville, NSW: Department of Education and NSW Education and Training Foundation.

Newton, I. (Sir) (1952) *Opticks, or a Treatise of the Reflections, Refractions, Inflections and Colours of Light*. New York: Dover Publications (based on the fourth edition, London 1730; originally published 1704).

Ogden, C. K. and Richards, I. A. (1923) *The Meaning of Meaning*. London: Kegan Paul (International Library of Psychology, Philosophy and Scientific Method).

Oldenburg, J. (1986) 'The transitional stage of a second child – 18 months to 2 years', *Australian Review of Applied Linguistics* 9.

Ong, W. J. (1958) *Ramus: Method, and the Decay of Dialogue, from the Art of Discourse to the Art of Reason*. Cambridge, MA: Harvard University Press.

Ornstein, R. and Ehrlich, P. (1989) *New World, New Mind: Changing the Way We Think to Save Our Future*. London: Methuen.

O'Toole, M. (1989) 'Semiotic systems in painting and poetry', in M. Falchikov, C. Poke and R. Russell (eds), *A Festschrift for Dennis Ward*. Nottingham: Astra Press.

O'Toole, M. (1994) *The Language of Displayed Art*. London: Leicester University Press (Pinter).

O'Toole, M. (1995) 'A systemic-functional semiotics of art', in P. H. Fries and M. J. Gregory (eds), *Discourse in Society. Vol. 3, Meaning and Choice in Language*. Norwood, NJ: Ablex.

Painter, C. (1984) *Into the Mother Tongue: A Case Study in Early Language Development*. London and Dover, NH: Pinter.

Painter, C. (1989) 'Learning language: a functional view of language development', in R. Hasan and J. R. Martin (eds), 1989.

Palmer, F. R. (ed.) (1968) *Selected Papers of J. R. Firth 1952–1959*. London: Longmans (Longmans' Linguistics Library).

Palmer, F. R. (ed.) (1970) *Prosodic Analysis*. London: Oxford Unversity Press (Languge and Language Learning 23).

Pawley, A. (1985) 'On speech formulas and linguistic competence', *Lenguas Modernas* (Universidad de Chile) 12.

Pearce, J., Thornton, G. and Mackay, D. (1989), 'The programme in linguistics and English teaching, University College London, 1964–1971', in R. Hasan and J. R. Martin (eds), 1989.

Peng, F. C. C. (1985) 'What is neurolinguistics?', *Journal of Neurolinguistics* 1.1.

Phillips, J. (1986) 'The development of modality and hypothetical meaning', *Working Papers 3*. Sydney: University of Sydney Linguistics Department.

Pike, K. L. (1943a) 'Taxemes and immediate constituents', *Language* 19.

Pike, K. L. (1943b) *Phonetics: A Critical Analysis of Phonetic Theory, and a Technic for the Practical Description of Sounds*. Ann Arbor: University of Michigan Press.

Pike, K. L. (1954–1960) *Language in Relation to a Unified Theory of the Structure of Human Behavior*. Glendale, CA: Summer Institute of Linguistics. 2nd edn: The Hague: Mouton, 1967.

Pike, K. L. (1959) 'Language as particle, wave and field', *Texas Quarterly* 2.

Pike, K. L. (1962) 'Dimensions of grammatical constructions', *Language* 38.

Podgórecki, A. (1973) ' "Second life" and its implications' (mimeo).

Postal, P. M. (1964) *Constituent Structure: A Study of Contemporary Models of Syntactic Description*. Bloomington, IN: Indiana University Publications in Anthropology, Folklore and Linguistics, Publication 30.

Postal, P. M. (1968) 'The Epilogue', in R. A. Jacobs and P. S. Rosenbaum, *English Transformational Grammar*. Waltham, MA: Xerox College Publishing.

Pottier, B. and Bourquin, G. (1966) Preface to *Actes du Premier Colloque International de Linguistique Appliquée*. Nancy: Faculté des Lettres et des Sciences humaines de l'Université de Nancy (Annales de l'Est, Mémoire no. 31).

Poynton, C. (1987) *Language and Gender: Making the Difference*. Oxford: Oxford University Press.

Pribram, K. H. (1971) 'The realization of mind', *Synthèse* 22.

Pribram, K. H. (1973) 'Problems concerning the structure of consciousness' (mimeo.).

Prigogine, I. and Stengers, I. (1982) *Order Out of Chaos: Man's New Dialogue with Nature*. London: Heinemann (Fontana Paperbacks, 1985).

Putnam, H. (1961) 'Some issues in the theory of grammar', *Proceedings of Symposium in Applied Mathematics* 12: 25–42.

Qiu, S. J. (1985) 'Transition period in Chinese language development', *Australian Review of Applied Linguistics* 8.

Quine, W. V. (1948) 'On what there is', in *Review of Metaphysics*. Reprinted in W. V. Quine, 1953.

Quine, W. V. (1953) 'The problem of meaning in linguistics', in *From a Logical Point of View*. Cambridge, MA: MIT Press.

Quirk, R. (1959) *Charles Dickens and Appropriate Language*. Durham: University of Durham Press.

Quirk, R. (1960) 'Towards a description of English usage', *Transactions of the Philological Society*.

Reed, T. B. W. (1956) 'Linguistics, structuralism, philology', *Archivum Linguisticum* 8.

Ricci, M. (1953) *China in the Sixteenth Century: The Journals of Matteo Ricci 1583–1610*, trans. from Latin by Louis J. Gallagher, New York: Random House.

Riegel, K. F. (1972) 'Language as labor: semantic activities as the basis for language development', in K. F. Riegel (ed.), *Structure, Transformation, Interaction: Developmental and Historical Aspects. Vol. 1, Topics in Human Development*. Basel: Karger.

Riegel, K. F. (1973) 'Some theoretical considerations of subcultural differences in language development'. Paper presented at the second biennial meeting of International Society for the Study of Behavioral Development. Ann Arbor, Michigan.

Robins, R. H. (1952) 'Noun and verb in universal grammar', *Language* 28.

Robins, R. H. (1957) 'Aspects of prosodic analysis', *Proceedings of the University of Durham Philosophical Society* I, Series B (Arts), I. Reprinted in F. R. Palmer (ed.), 1970.

Robins, R. H. (1961) 'John Rupert Firth' (obituary), *Language* 37.

Robins, R. H. (1963) 'General Linguistics in Great Britain 1930–1960', in C. Mohrmann, F. W. Norman and A. Sommerfelt (eds), 1963.

Robins, R. H. (1967) *A Short History of Linguistics*. London: Longman (Longmans Linguistics Library).

Romney, A. K. and D'Andrade, R. G. (eds) (1964) *Transcultural Studies in Cognition* (*American Anthropologist* 66, Special Publication).

Rose, D. (1993) 'On becoming: the grammar of causality in Pitjantjatjara and English', in M. A. K. Halliday (ed.), 1993c.

Rumsey, A. (1990) 'Wording, meaning, and linguistic ideology', *American Anthropologist* 92.2.

Sacks, H., Schlegloff, E. A. and Jefferson, G. (1974) 'Simplest systematics for the organization of turn-taking in conversation', *Language* 50: 696–735.

Sadovnik, A. R. (ed.) (1995) *Knowledge and Pedagogy: The Sociology of Basil Bernstein*. Norwood, NJ: Ablex.

Salmon, V. (1966) 'Language planning in seventeenth-century England: its context and aims', in C. E. Bazell *et al.* (eds), 1966.

Salmon, V. (1979) *The Study of Language in 17th Century England*. Amsterdam: Benjamins (Studies in the History of Linguistics 17).

Sankoff, D. and Laberge, S. (1978) 'The linguistic marketplace and the statistical explanation of variability', in D. Sankoff (ed.), *Linguistic Variation: Models and Methods*. New York: Academic Press.

Schaffer, S. (1991) 'Utopia limited: on the end of science', *Strategies* 4/5.

Schegloff, E. A. (1968) 'Sequencing in conversational openings', *American Anthropologist* 70. Reprinted in J. J. Gumperz and D. Hymes (eds), 1964.

Searle, J. (1965) 'What is a speech act?' in M. Black (ed.), *Philosophy in America*. London: Allen & Unwin; Ithaca, NY: Cornell University Press.

Simon, H. A. (1969) *The Sciences of the Artificial*. Cambridge, MA (2nd edition 1981).

Sinclair, J. McH. (1987) *Looking Up: An Account of the COBUILD Project in Lexical Computing*. London and Glasgow: Collins.

Sinclair, J. McH., and Coulthard, M. (1975) *Towards an Analysis of Discourse*. London: Oxford University Press.

Sinclair, J. McH., Jones, S. and Daley, R. (1970) *English Lexical Studies*. Department of English, University of Birmingham (OSTI Project C/LP/08 Final Report).

Sinclair, J. McH. *et al.* (1990) *Collins COBUILD English Grammar*. London: Collins.

Spencer, J. and Gregory, M. (1964) 'An approach to the study of style', in N. E. Enkvist, J. Spencer and M. Gregory, *Linguistics and Style*. London: Oxford University Press (Language and Language Learning 6).

Stalin, J. V. (1950) 'Concerning Marxism in linguistics', English version in *New Times* No. 26, 28 June 1950. Original in *Pravda*, 20 June 1950.

Steiner, E. (1988) 'The interaction of language and music as semiotic systems:

the example of a folk ballad', in J. D. Benson, M. J. Cummings and W. S. Greaves (eds), 1988.

Steiner, E. and Veltman, R. (eds) (1988) *Pragmatics, Discourse and Text: Explorations in Systemic Semantics*. London: Pinter; Norwood, NJ: Ablex.

Strang, B. M. H. (1970) *A History of English*. London: Methuen.

Strevens, P. (1965) *Papers in Language and Language Teaching*. London: Oxford University Press (Language and Language Learning 9).

Strevens, P. (1977) *New Orientations in the Teaching of English*. London: Oxford University Press.

Sugeno, M. (1993) 'Toward intelligent computing'. Plenary paper presented to the Fifth International Fuzzy Systems Association World Congress, Seoul.

Sugeno, M. (1995) 'Intelligent Computing'. Paper presented to the second conference of the Pacific Association of Computational Linguistics (PACLING II), University of Queensland, Brisbane.

Suzuki, D. (1990) *Inventing the Future: Reflections on Science, Technology and Nature*. London and Sydney: Allen & Unwin.

Svartvik, J. (1966) *On Voice in the English Verb*. The Hague: Mouton (Janua Linguarum Series Practica 63).

Tambiah, S. J. (1969) 'Animals are good to think and good to prohibit', *Ethnology* 8.

Tench, P. (ed.) (1992) *Studies in Systemic Phonology*. London and New York: Pinter.

Tench, P. (1996) *The Intonation Systems of English*. London: Cassell.

Thibault, P. J. (1986) *Text, Discourse and Context: A Social Semiotic Perspective*. Toronto: Victoria University (Toronto Semiotic Circle 3).

Thibault, P. J. (1988) 'Knowing what you're told by the agony aunts: language function, gender difference and the structure of knowledge and belief in the personal columns', in D. Birch and M. O'Toole (eds), 1988.

Thibault, P. J. (1991a) *Social Semiotics as Praxis: Text, Social Meaning Making and Nabokov's 'Ada'*. Minneapolis: University of Minnesota Press.

Thibault, P. J. (1991b) 'Grammar technocracy and the noun: technocratic values and cognitive linguistics', in E. Ventola (ed.), *Functional and Systemic Linguistics: Approaches and Uses*. Berlin: Mouton de Gruyter.

Thompson, G. (1996) *Introducing Functional Grammar*. London: Edward Arnold.

Threadgold, T. (1986) 'Semiotics-ideology-language', in T. Threadgold *et al.* (eds), 1986.

Threadgold, T. (1988) 'Stories of race and gender: an unbounded discourse', in D. Birch and M. O'Toole (eds), 1988.

Threadgold, T. and Cranny-Francis, A. (eds) (1990) *Feminine/Masculine and Representation*. London and Sydney: Allen & Unwin.

Threadgold, T. *et al.* (eds) (1986) *Semiotics, Ideology, Language*. Sydney: Sydney Association for Studies in Society and Culture.

Thwaite, A. (1983) 'Sexism in Three Mills and Boon Romances.' Unpublished BA dissertation, University of Sydney, Department of Linguistics.

Torr, J. (1997) *From child tongue to mother tongue: a case study of language development during the first two and a half years*, Monographs in Systemic Linguistics 9. Nottingham: University of Nottingham.

Trevarthen, C. (1979) 'Communication and cooperation in early infancy: a description of primary intersubjectivity', in M. Bullowa (ed.), 1979.

Trevarthen, C. (1987) 'Sharing makes sense: intersubjectivity and the making of an infant's meaning', in R. Steele and T. Threadgold (eds), *Language Topics*, Vol. 1. Amsterdam and Philadelphia: Benjamins.

Trew, T. (1979) ' "What the papers say": linguistic variation and ideological difference', in R. Fowler *et al.* (eds), 1979.

Turner, G. J. (1970) 'A linguistic approach to children's speech', in G. J. Turner and B. A. Mohan, *A Linguistic Description and Computer Programme for Children's Speech*. London: Routledge & Kegan Paul (Primary Socialization, Language and Education).

Turner, G. J. (1973) 'Social class and children's language of control at age five and age seven', in Bernstein (ed.), 1973.

UNESCO (1975) *Interactions between Linguistics and Mathematical Education*. Report of a symposium sponsored by UNESCO-CEDO-ICMI, Nairobi. Paris: UNESCO (ED-74/CONF. 808), 1975.

Ure, J. (1982) 'Introduction: approaches to the study of register range', in J. Ellis and J. Ure (eds), *Register Range and Change*. Berlin: Mouton; *International Journal of the Sociology of Language* 35.

Ure, J. and Ellis, J. (1974) 'Register in descriptive linguistics and linguistic sociology', in O. Uribe-Villegas (ed.), *Issues in Sociolinguistics*. The Hague: Mouton.

van Dijk, T. A. (1972) 'Text grammar and text logic', in J. S. Petöfi and H. Rieser (eds), *Studies in Text Grammar*. Dordrecht: Reidel.

van Leeuwen, T. (1988) 'Music and ideology: towards a sociosemantics of mass media music', *Working Papers 2*. Sydney: Sydney Association for Studies in Society and Culture.

van Leeuwen, T. (1989) 'Changed times, changed tunes: music and ideology of the news', in J. Tulloch and G. Turner (eds), *Australian Television: Programmes, Pleasures and Politics*. Sydney: Allen & Unwin.

Ventola, E. (ed) (1991) *Functional and Systemic Linguistics: Approaches and Uses*. Berlin and New York: Mouton de Gruyter.

Vygotsky, L. S. (1978) *Mind and Society*. Cambridge, MA: Harvard University Press.

Ward, D. (ed.) (1972) *Report of the Contemporary Russian Language Analysis Project*. Language Centre, University of Essex.

Watts, A. F. (1944) *The Language and Mental Development of Children*. London: Heath.

Wells, C. G. (1986) *The Meaning Makers: Children Learning Language and Using Language to Learn*. Portsmouth, NH: Heinemann Educational.

Wells, R. S. (1960) 'Nominal and verbal style', in T. A. Sebeok (ed.), *Style in Language*. New York: MIT Technology Press and Wiley.

Whatmough, J. (1956) *Language: A Modern Synthesis*. London: Secker & Warburg.

Whitley, E. M. (1966) 'Contextual analysis and Swift's "little language" of the *Journal to Stella*', in C. E. Bazell *et al.* (eds), 1966.

Whorf, B. L. (1941) 'The relation of habitual thought and behavior to language', in L. Spier (ed.), *Language, Culture and Personality: Essays in Memory of Edward Sapir*. Menasha, WI: University of Wisconsin Press. Reprinted in J. B. Carroll (ed.), 1956.

Whorf, B. L. (1945) 'Grammatical categories', *Language* 21. Reprinted in J. B. Carroll (ed.), 1956.

Whorf, B. L. (1956) 'A linguistic consideration of thinking in primitive communities', in J. B. Carroll (ed.), 1956.

Wignell, P., Martin, J. R. and Eggins, S. (1987) 'The discourse of geography: ordering and explaining the experiential world', in J. R. Martin, P. Wignell and S. Eggins (eds), *Writing Project Report 1987*. Sydney: University of Sydney Linguistics Department.

Wimsatt, W. C. (1986) 'Developmental constraints, generative entrenchment, and the innate – acquired distinction', in P. Bechtel (ed.), *Integrating Scientific Disciplines*. Dordrecht: Martinus-Nijhoff, pp. 185–208.

Winograd, T. (1972) *Understanding Natural Language*. Edinburgh: Edinburgh University Press.

Yates, F. (1964) *Giordano Bruno and the Hermetic Tradition*. London: Routledge & Kegan Paul.

Yates, F. (1966) *The Art of Memory*. London: Routledge & Kegan Paul. (Harmondsworth: Penguin Books, 1969).

Yngve, V. (1986) 'To be a scientist', *The Thirteenth LACUS Forum*. Lake Bluff, IL: Linguistic Association of Canada and the United States.

Zanarini, G. (1982) 'Rileggendo Galileo: riflessioni sul linguaggio della formazione scientifica', *Giornale di Fisica* 23.2: 109–25.

INDEX

mode, *continued*
  synoptic   130–1
Mohan, B.   82, 229, 245, 331, 437
mood   9, 15, 53, 180, 183, 198, 202–10,
    240–1, 316, 324, 331, 343–6,
    364–5, 371, 384, 403–5, 415–16,
    435
morpheme(s)   19–20, 47, 103–5, 167, 194
morphology   120, 123, 126, 158, 170,
    172, 194, 202–4, 224, 317, 344,
    366, 393, 414, 437

narrative(s)   68, 82, 168, 187, 190–1, 385
network(s)   6–17, 23–5, 28–9, 68, 71,
    80, 85, 180–1, 184, 193–4,
    219–20, 248, 251–2, 264, 269,
    305, 308–10, 323–47, 352–4,
    359–60, 364–6, 393–4, 415,
    434–5, 439
  semantic   325–7, 330–6, 341–5, 354
  system   8–9, 12, 23, 29, 180–1, 248,
    310, 327, 335, 340, 366, 405, 410,
    434–5
neurolinguistics   140, 440
Newton, Sir Isaac   26–7, 65, 119, 153,
    156–8, 173, 363, 378, 392, 420
Nigel   12, 25, 93–4, 252, 291, 303–8,
    313, 322, 364, 415, 418, 438
nominal   19–21, 48, 54–8, 61, 66–8,
    72–3, 130–3, 147–8, 156–9,
    203–5, 210, 364–8, 403, 418–20,
    431, 435
noun(s)   22, 28, 45, 50, 53–9, 62–73,
    92–4, 97–8, 119, 123, 129, 147–8,
    156, 159, 182, 185, 192, 204, 240,
    244, 255, 261, 282, 305, 366,
    417–21

ontogenesis   172, 196, 239, 280, 364,
    404, 430
ontogenetic   197, 250, 363, 412
order
  natural   116–18, 125–8, 134
  social   84, 86, 116–18, 125, 135, 153,
    245, 259, 381, 423
  socioeconomic   146, 363

paradigmatic   7–9, 193–5, 209, 254,
    266, 327, 345, 360, 409, 418,
    433–5
parataxis/paratactic   17, 157, 252, 332,
    338, 342–3

participant roles   66–8, 207, 384
Penman text generation project   17, 25,
    407–10, 438
phonetics   15, 120, 187, 346, 378
phonology   13–15, 19, 95, 132, 187–9,
    196, 210, 256, 300, 323, 344–7,
    397–8, 402, 434, 437
  phonological   15, 27, 41, 57, 86–7,
    103, 113, 197, 201, 266, 336,
    344–6, 396, 415, 434
Plato   96–9, 108
polarity   6, 9, 15, 24, 44, 209, 409–12
predicate   98, 101, 181
pronoun(s)   58, 164–6, 343, 381, 389
prosodic   11, 14, 16, 187, 189, 371, 434
protolanguage/protolinguistic   7, 12–16,
    21, 172, 196, 240–1, 251, 263,
    321, 348–51, 363–5, 384,
    395–405, 413–15, 429–30

realization   18, 21, 113–14, 120, 181–4,
    193, 195, 201, 210, 238, 242, 254,
    265, 300, 308, 317, 323, 326, 330,
    334, 336, 341, 345–6, 352, 362,
    380, 386, 391, 393, 403, 416, 425,
    434–6
  statement   183–4, 341, 434–5
redundancy   3, 122, 253, 398, 412, 425
referential   118, 274, 400
register   27, 157–9, 168, 186, 189, 191,
    194–6, 250–1, 255–60, 268, 274,
    282, 298, 359, 362–3, 382, 410,
    416, 419, 437–41
  variation   191, 258–60, 382, 437
regulatory   80, 306–13, 336–8, 398–401
rheme   143, 155, 182, 202, 207, 210
rheomode/rheomodal   119, 125, 128–9,
    134
rhetoric   89, 95–9, 106, 113–14, 186,
    252, 363
rhetorical structure   195, 197
Roget, P. M.   54, 109, 173, 337–9,
    342–3

Sanskrit   92, 148, 419
Saussure, F.   76, 111, 113, 138, 186,
    195–6, 212, 233, 235, 242, 267,
    376, 378, 405, 433
scale-and-category grammar   40
semantic   16, 22, 40, 50, 62, 69, 77,
    83–6, 97, 100, 109, 114, 122, 126,
    129–30, 133, 143–6, 150–2, 156,